# HUMAN
# DIVERSITY
# IN EDUCATION

## AN INTEGRATIVE APPROACH

# HUMAN DIVERSITY IN EDUCATION

## AN INTEGRATIVE APPROACH

**Kenneth Cushner**
**Averil McClelland**
**Philip Safford**

Kent State University

**McGRAW-HILL, INC.**
New York   St. Louis   San Francisco   Auckland   Bogotá
Caracas   Lisbon   London   Madrid   Mexico   Milan   Montreal   New Delhi
Paris   San Juan   Singapore   Sydney   Tokyo   Toronto

This book was developed by Lane Akers, Inc.

This book was set in Times Roman by Arcata Graphics/Kingsport.
The editor was Lane Akers;
the production supervisor was Denise L. Puryear.
The cover was designed by Caliber/Phoenix Color Corp.
The photo editor was Anne Manning.
Project supervision was done by The Total Book.
R. R. Donnelley & Sons Company was printer and binder.

**HUMAN DIVERSITY IN EDUCATION**
**An Integrative Approach**

2 3 4 5 6 7 8 9 0 DOH DOH 9 0 9 8 7 6 5 4 3 2

ISBN 0-07-014998-4

Library of Congress Cataloging-in-Publication Data

Cushner, Kenneth.
    Human diversity in education: an integrative approach / Kenneth
Cushner, Averil McClelland, Philip Safford.
        p.      cm.
    Includes bibliographical references (p.   ) and index.
    ISBN 0-07-014998-4
    1. Intercultural education—United States.      2. Individual
differences in children—United States.      3. Sex differences in
education—United States.      I. McClelland, Averil.      II. Safford,
Philip L.      III. Title.
LC1099.3.C87        1992
370.19'341—dc20                                    91–32200

**Photo Credits**
p. 2, Steve Shapiro/Gamma Liaison; p. 14, Renee Lynn/Photo Researchers; p. 38, Elizabeth Crews; p. 72, Elizabeth Crews; p. 98, Thomas S. England/Photo Researchers; p. 128, Spencer Grant/Photo Researchers; p. 150, Elizabeth Crews; p. 168, Susie Fitzhugh/Stock, Boston; p. 192, Steve Takatsuno/The Picture Cube; p. 214, Jean-Claude LeJeune/Stock, Boston; p. 240, Rona Beame/Photo Researchers; p. 258, Elizabeth Crews; p. 288, Elizabeth Crews/Stock, Boston; p. 316, Hella Hammid/Photo Researchers.

# ABOUT THE AUTHORS

KENNETH CUSHNER is assistant professor of education and director of the Center for International and Intercultural Education at Kent State University. He received his doctoral degree in curriculum and instruction from the University of Hawaii while a degree participant with the Institute of Culture and Communication at the East-West Center in Honolulu. He has taught in schools and directed numerous international educational programs in the United States, Europe, Australia, West Africa, the Middle East, Central America, and the Soviet Union. He has authored numerous articles in the field of international and intercultural education, and is coauthor of the text *Intercultural Interactions: A Practical Guide.*

AVERIL McCLELLAND is assistant professor of cultural foundations of education and director of the Project on the Study of Gender and Education in the College of Education at Kent State University. She received her undergraduate degree in sociology with honors from Hiram College, and her M.Ed. and Ph.D. in cultural foundations from Kent State University. The author of several articles on gender issues in education, she is currently completing a sourcebook on the history of girls' education in the United States. Professor McClelland is currently a Member Center Director with the National Council for Research on Women.

PHILIP SAFFORD is professor of special education at Kent State University. His Ph.D. was earned through the combined program in education and psychology at the University of Michigan, with specialization in special education and developmental psychology. Previously he had been a teacher of emotionally disturbed children and also a coordinator and director of special education in residential treatment programs. He has authored three books, all concerning special education for infants, toddlers, and preschool age children with disabilities, as well as numerous journal articles. He has directed or codirected a number of training, research, and demonstration projects supported by federal and state grants in special education.

# CONTENTS

# PREFACE

This book is about human differences—physical, social, and psychological differences. More specifically, it is about the ways in which human differences are experienced in school, and about teaching practices that view those differences as resources, not deficits. It is a book that we hope will both inform and disturb you. We want to *move* you to think, to feel, to understand the concept of difference—what it means in the lives of students and teachers.

It is important to note that recent conceptions of diversity are expanding to include differences based on gender, ethnicity, race, class, culture, age, and handicapping condition. However, our knowledge of how these differences affect human interaction is relatively new and has not yet found its way into our visions of schooling or teacher education. Meanwhile our school-age population is rapidly becoming increasingly poor and increasingly nonwhite, while the majority of those entering teaching continue to be white, middle class, and female. Fewer than 12 percent of entering teachers represent what we have traditionally termed minority populations.

This book is an attempt to address this issue. It does not offer simple, easy-to-follow guidelines. Rather it attempts to capture the *experience* of diversity from a variety of perspectives and to offer general frameworks within which specific problem situations can be addressed. Many people ask us to provide them with cookbook approaches to working with difference. However, we cannot. We are convinced that such cookbook approaches are not only impossible, but also unethical given the realities of today's schools.

Throughout this book we have attempted to outline an approach to human diversity that differs from much of the contemporary literature. We do not equate diversity with a notion of the "other." Rather, we begin with the proposition that all Americans are, to some degree, multicultural because they live in a multicultural society. Although we describe and give many examples of differences between particular ethnic, racial, religious, class, gender, and exceptionality groups, ours is not a "group" approach. We are aware that there is as much diversity *within* groups as *among* them, and thus we are inclined to focus on the individual rather than the group.

The book is divided into three major parts. In Part One, we begin with a general exploration of the issues related to diversity and the individual. Our centerpiece is a culture-general framework for understanding intercultural interactions. Such a framework helps illuminate common aspects of intercultural interactions, including the strong emotional experiences one is likely to have when confronted with those who are very different from oneself. In Part Two, we explore how the various issues of multicultural education, gender-sensitive education, and special education have been addressed in the United States. Part Three provides a review of practical strategies which the professional can use to help reframe her or his interactions in the classroom. Again, we have avoided the temptation to be prescriptive, believing that the professional educator is the only one really able to survey particular classrooms and/or schools, explore possible strategies, and then make changes that fit local needs.

We want to stress our belief in the power of individual teachers and schools both to reconceptualize the nature of schooling in a diverse society and to make whatever specific modifications are needed in particular contexts. Changes will not occur overnight, and they will often be met with considerable resistance. Consequently, we must learn to measure our successes in inches rather than miles, realizing that the momentum gained through many small steps will eventually produce the larger changes so badly needed.

At this point we would like to thank the many individuals who have helped to make this book possible. Judy Charlick, Brian Grieves, David Grossman, Neal Grove, Will Hayes, Denise Stewart, Bob Vadas, and Linda Zimmer-Vadas all provided critical incidents. Elizabeth Safford was tireless in tracking down many of the literary excerpts that add spice to the book. Our editor, Lane Akers, helped clarify our vision of the book and helped to stimulate us and keep us on track. Valuable feedback was provided by our reviewers: Nicholas Appleton, Arizona State University; Kenneth Carlson, Rutgers University; Paul Markham, University of Maryland; Myra and David Sadker, American University; Kenneth Teitelbaum, SUNY Binghamton; Linda Tillman, Kent State University; and Nancy Winitzky, University of Utah. For their time, effort, and encouragement we are extremely grateful.

Finally, we invite all readers of this text, both instructors and students, to share with us your own experience in dealing with diversity, so that we might integrate it with our own and with others' scholarship in this fast-growing field.

*Kenneth Cushner*
*Averil McClelland*
*Philip Safford*

# HUMAN DIVERSITY IN EDUCATION

## AN INTEGRATIVE APPROACH

# PART ONE

# HUMAN DIVERSITY:
# A PROBLEM AND
# AN OPPORTUNITY

# CHAPTER 1

# HUMAN DIVERSITY AND EDUCATION: AN OVERVIEW

*Alice: "Would you tell me, please, which way I ought to go from here?"*
*The Cat: "That depends a good deal on where you want to get to."*

Lewis Carroll

## HUMAN DIVERSITY AS EXPERIENCE: THE IMPORTANCE OF STORIES

Lewis Carroll's *Alice in Wonderland*[1] is a classic story about a little girl who finds herself in a fantastic world quite unlike the world she is used to. All the rules of perception and behavior that she has come to believe are normal and right are turned inside out and upside down in the strange land at the bottom of the rabbit hole, and she must learn about other ways of thinking, other ways of knowing, and other ways of acting.

Like many novelists, Lewis Carroll told the story of Alice as a way of pointing out some of the peculiar aspects of the society in which he lived. He hoped, perhaps, that his readers might learn something about their own world by reading about Alice's odd and sometimes funny experiences.

Storytelling is a time-honored way of teaching because it creates scenes that we can imagine in our minds, that we can look at somewhat objectively, and that we can identify with and learn from. Carol Christ writes that "without stories there is no articulation of experience. . . . Stories give shape to lives. As people grow up, reach plateaus, or face crises, they often turn to stories to show them how to take the next step."[2] Stories often are meaningful to people on several levels. At one level they may be simply entertaining. At another, they may illustrate ideas or morals or values common to a group of people. And at still another level, they may create meaning in people's lives by identifying unnamed feelings and experiences for those who read or hear them. This capacity for "depth" is one of the most important attributes of stories, for it allows us to use them to describe very complex ideas. Christ notes that

> the importance of stories [is] something most people intuitively know. When meeting new friends or lovers people reenact the ritual of telling stories. Why? Because they sense that the meaning of their lives is revealed in the stories they tell, in their perception of the forces they contended with, in the choices they made, in their feelings about what they did or did not do.[3]

There are a great many stories in this book, partly because we believe that learning should be a meaningful experience in and of itself. Some stories are about people who really lived or are living and events that actually happened. Others are fables, folktales, or parables, often from other societies. Still others have been created to illustrate certain ideas and concepts, or to offer a set of possible solutions to problems. To a large extent, however, we use stories for their power to speak about complex human experiences—in this case, about the experiences people have with the fact of human diversity.

In some ways, then, this is a book of stories that, like the story of Alice, tell about different life worlds in which people participate. And because, in order to venture into different worlds, it is necessary to leave our own, we will begin with a story about just how hard it is to leave cherished beliefs and values behind.

\*     \*     \*

### A Parable

Once upon a time there was a group of people who lived in the mountains in an isolated region. One day a stranger passed through their area and dropped some wheat grains in their field. The wheat grew. After a number of years, people noticed the new plant and decided to collect its seeds and chew them. Someone noticed that when a cart had accidentally ridden over some of the seeds, a harder outer covering separated from the seed and what was inside was sweeter. Someone else noticed that when it rained, the grains that had been run over expanded a little, and the hot sun cooked them. So, people started making wheat cereal and cracked wheat and other wheat dishes. Wheat became the staple of their diet.

Years passed. Because these people did not know anything about crop rotation, fertilizers, and cross-pollination, the wheat crop eventually began to fail.

About this time, another stranger happened by. He was carrying two sacks of barley. He saw the people starving and planted some of his grain. The barley grew well. He presented it to the people and showed them how to make bread and soup and many other dishes from barley. But they called him a heretic.

"You are trying to undermine our way of life and force us into accepting you as our king." They saw his trick. "You can't fool us. You are trying to weaken us and make us accept your ways. Our wheat will not let us starve. Your barley is evil."

He stayed in the area, but the people avoided him. Years passed. The wheat crop failed again and again. The children suffered from malnutrition. One day the stranger came to the market and said, "Wheat is a grain. My barley has a similar quality. It is also a grain. Why don't we just call the barley grain?"

Now since they were suffering so much, the people took the grain, except for a few who staunchly refused. They loudly proclaimed that they were the only remaining followers of the True Way, the Religion of Wheat. A few new people joined the Wheat Religion from time to time, but most began to eat barley. They called themselves The Grainers.

For generations, the Wheat Religion people brought up their children to remember the true food called wheat. A few of them hoarded some wheat grains to keep it safe and sacred. Others sent their children off in search of wheat, because they felt that if one person could happen by with barley, wheat might be known somewhere else too.

And so it went for decades, until the barley crop began to fail. The last few Wheat Religion people planted their wheat again. It grew beautifully, and because it grew so well, they grew bold and began to proclaim that their wheat was the only true food. Most people resisted and called them heretics. A few people said, "Why don't you just admit that wheat is a grain?"

The wheat growers agreed, thinking that they could get many more wheat followers if they called it *grain.* But by this time, some of the children of the Wheat Religion children began to return from their adventures with new seed—not just wheat, but rye and buckwheat and millet. Now people began to enjoy the taste of many different grains. They took turns planting them and trading the seed to each other. In this way, everyone came to have enough sustenance and lived happily ever after.[4]

\*     \*     \*

## HUMAN DIVERSITY AND THE SCHOOLS: THE NEED FOR CHANGE

This parable speaks to us on both a literal and a metaphorical level. On the metaphorical level it carries many messages. It applauds diversity and recognizes that a society cannot function to its fullest when it ignores the ideas, contributions, efforts, and concerns of any of its people. It illustrates some of the consequences of unreasonable prejudice but also recognizes the powerful emotions that underlie a prejudiced attitude. It indicates the power of naming something in a way that is familiar and comfortable to those who are uncomfortable about accepting something new.

But perhaps more critical to the concerns of this book, the story recognizes the tendency people have to resist change. People are creatures of habit who find it difficult to change, whether at the individual level, the institutional level, or the societal level. People often work from one set of assumptions, one pattern of behavior. Because of the way in which they are socialized, these have become so much a part of them that they find it very difficult to think that things can be done in any other way. Some habits people develop are positive and constructive; others are negative and limiting. The story shows us that sometimes even a society's strengths can become weaknesses. And yet new circumstances and opportunities arise in each generation which demand that new perspectives, attitudes, and solutions be sought.[5] Such circumstances are evident today in the changing face of the American classroom. When we look at the characteristics of students and teachers in American schools, we see change that has occurred more rapidly, perhaps, than our ability to modify, not only our instructional strategies, classroom management, and curricular materials, but our attitudes as well.

### Changing Characteristics of School Populations

One important change in student populations is an increase in the number of children traditionally considered members of ethnic, national, or racial minority groups. In 1976, for example, 24 percent of the total school enrollment in U.S. schools was nonwhite. In 1984, this percentage had increased to 29 percent. By the year 2000, people of color will comprise one-third of all students enrolled in public schools,[6] and it is projected that, by 2020, they will comprise 46 percent. Startling changes are already occurring in a number of places in the country. For example, students from so-called minority cultural groups already comprise more than 50 percent of the school populations in California, Arizona, New Mexico, Texas, and Colorado.[7] In these states, minority children will find themselves in the uncomfortable position of being the majority in a world whose rules are set by a more powerful minority.

Along with ethnic and racial diversity often comes linguistic diversity. Increasing numbers of children are entering school from minority language backgrounds and have little or no competence in the English language. While Spanish is the predominant first language of many children in the United States, an increasing number of students are entering the schools speaking Arabic, Chinese, Hmong, Khmer, Lao, Thai, and Vietnamese.[8] Since a person's language structures many of the symbolic meanings that are important to understanding the world, children whose symbol systems differ from those of the group that is dominant in the society have much in common with Alice: they often find themselves in a ''fantastic'' world where little makes sense to them.

Another characteristic of student populations in public schools is the diversity of the children's family patterns. Recent research on the changing demographics of our families graphically portrays the changing lifestyle of our youth. For instance, in 1942, 60 percent of families matched the purported white, middle-class ideal of the nuclear family consisting of two parents and their children (and, if one believes the images often portrayed in basal readers until quite recently, a dog and a cat all living happily together in a white house surrounded by a neat picket fence!). In these families, the father's role was to leave home every day to earn the money to support the family and the mother's role was to stay at home and raise the children. In 1984, less than 10 percent of American families matched that ideal.

It is estimated today that approximately two-thirds of all marriages in the United States will be disrupted through divorce or separation. More than ten different family configurations can be found represented in today's classrooms—and a significant one of these is the single-parent family, often a mother and child or children living in poverty. Increasingly, this single parent is a teenage mother. Consider some of these facts: each day in the United States, 40 teenagers give birth to their third child; in Florida in 1985, 1,000 children were born to mothers under the age of 11; 12 million American youngsters live below the poverty level; a teenager in the United States is twice as likely to give birth out of wedlock than in any other country in the world. It is a mistake to think that this population is limited to the so-called urban ghettos of our country. In Illinois for instance, a survey of the counties having the largest percentage of unwed mothers revealed that Cook County, where the city of Chicago is located, came in fifth. The first four counties were downstate and rural.[9]

Poverty, however, is not limited to the "children of children," nor even to children of single parents. In the United States, 25 percent of students are from poor or lower socioeconomic backgrounds, 20 percent live in single-parent homes, 14 percent are at risk of dropping out, 14 percent are children of teenage mothers, 15 percent are physically or mentally handicapped, 14 percent are children of unmarried parents, 40 percent will live with divorced parents before the age of 18, and 25 to 33 percent will be latchkey children with no one to greet them when they come home from school.[10] Thus, a random sample of 100 children in the United States would reveal 12 born out of wedlock, 40 born to parents who will divorce, 15 born to parents who will separate in the next five years, 2 born to parents who will die in the next five years, and 41 who will reach age 16 "normally." Clearly, the family pattern that was once considered normal, that provided the image of the "right and proper" kind of family and guided policies that governed our institutions, is now in the very definite minority!

While it is true that diversity with respect to ethnicity, race, and social class is increasing as a characteristic of the nation's public school children, it is also the case that their total numbers are decreasing. The Commission on Work, Family, and Citizenship of the William T. Grant Foundation notes that

> the number of American youth is shrinking dramatically. Between 1980 and 1996, our youth population, ages 15–25, is expected to fall 21 percent, from 43 to 34 million. Young people as a percentage of the nation's population will also decline from 18.8 to 13 percent . . .[11]

Thus, the children who are sitting and will sit at the nation's school desks should be important to us not only because we value their ethnic and social diversity, but also because they are vital resources. Marian Wright Edelman, Director of the Children's Defense Fund, describes the change in striking terms:

> Children are not only a precious resource, then, but an increasingly scarce one. Until recently, America's youth has been relatively plentiful, allowing the society to survive and the economy to grow, despite the waste of many young lives through society's neglect. That margin for error no longer exists. The ratio of workers to retirees has shrunk and will continue to shrink in the coming decades. And one in three of the new potential workers is a member of a minority group.[12]

The list of children considered to be ''at risk''—at risk of poverty, at risk of emotional deprivation, at risk of substandard health, and, in sum, at risk of not receiving an effective education—has been modified in recent years. Edelman notes that

> twenty-five years ago, [such a list] would probably not have included abused and neglected children . . . [or] homeless children in the sense that they are defined now—those who are still with their parents but in family units that are consigned to a nomadic, often squalid existence on the streets and in shelters that can never be a substitute for a stable family home.[13]

Similarly, before the enactment of Public Law 94–142 in 1975, many children with handicapping conditions who are now in school would not have been included because the community (or state, or nation) had not yet taken any responsibility for their welfare or education. Listen to the comments of a student who met many obstacles to achieving an education:

> I'm in the tenth grade at school. I got straight A's the last five years. To get into the high school I'm going to, I really had to fight because they said they didn't allow anyone with wheelchairs. One counselor said, ''It's against our policy.'' Some of my classrooms are upstairs, all my Social Studies and English. I really had to fight them. Then I found out that another girl had gone there ten years ago. How she got upstairs was really neat. The football team—they made arrangements ahead of time—whenever she had classes upstairs they met and carried her up and down the stairs.
>
> In the fourth grade I had the same fight. Then, I was on crutches. They said, ''You can't go because somebody might knock you over and hurt you.'' They said, ''Use a wheelchair.'' So I bought a wheelchair just to make them happy and never used it. This year it was just the opposite. They said they didn't allow wheelchairs. Finally I just showed up at the beginning of the year and they had to let me go.[14]

Thus, to the increasing number of ethnically, linguistically, and economically diverse children in public school classrooms have been added children who have striking differences in family structure, lifestyle, health, and physical and mental ability.

Finally, there is a kind of difference among children that is perhaps most fundamental of all, one that is so basic as to have been overlooked as a matter of inquiry for nearly all of our history. That difference is gender. Because we have included both girls and boys—at least in elementary education—since the very beginning of the common school in the United States, and because our political and educational ideals assume that sex is a difference that makes no difference in schooling, the effect of gender on the actual education received by children in school has not been analyzed until quite recently. In the past twenty years, however, considerable research on differences in the social and educational lives of boys and girls in school has been done. Shakeshaft writes:

Two messages emerge repeatedly from the research on gender and schooling. First, what is good for males is not necessarily good for females. Second, if a choice must be made, the education establishment will base policy and instruction on that which is good for males.[15]

To some extent, the problem of gender in education is a problem related to the education of girls, because for the most part, girls have not been considered as *educationally* any different from boys. Yet the experiences of girls in school are in many ways quite different from the experiences of boys. It is also the case that educational outcomes for girls differ from those of boys. In short, girls who sit in the same classroom with boys, read the same materials as boys, do the same homework as boys, and take the same examinations as boys, often are not treated in the same ways as boys, and thus frequently do not achieve the same educational outcomes as boys. In another sense, however, gender is an important issue for both boys and girls, since gender structures a child's perceptions of self and sets up the emotional and cognitive landscape in which the child grows. How and why this is so will be the subject of a later chapter. The point here is that a consideration of gender is fundamental to a consideration of diversity because gender has been shown to *be* a difference that makes a difference in American schools.

## Students and Teachers: A Clash of Cultures?

A disturbing reality, given the increasing heterogeneity of students in public schools, is the relative homogeneity of the teaching force. In the United States, 88 percent of the teaching force is white and 67 to 68 percent is female.[16] And it is projected that well into the next century new teachers will be increasingly female and white. This statistic is not surprising. Teachers in the United States have always been mostly female, and mostly white, at least since the early part of the nineteenth century. However, this statistic raises interesting issues about the cultural knowledge and economic backgrounds of teachers in contrast to the cultural knowledge and economic backgrounds of students.

Both schools and the teachers who inhabit them are to a large extent "culture-bound." That is, they are somewhat like the Wheat Religion people and The Grainers in our story: unwilling or unable to look beyond their own view of the world. Indeed, one of the purposes of schooling has always been to transmit the dominant cultural beliefs, values, and knowledge represented by these teachers to the next generation. In addition, it is a strong characteristic of most people—teachers included—to believe that their own cultural tradition represents the "best" way. So, for middle-class, white teachers, the perception of both power and virtue often combine to lessen the chance that they will be very interested in trying to understand the cultural differences that lie at the heart of the lives of many of their students. At best, such teachers are predisposed to regard diversity as interesting; at worst, they are likely to regard it as a deficit. They will seldom come to their classes with the notion that diversity is an exciting and enriching phenomenon. Sara Lawrence Lightfoot, a professor of education at Harvard and someone who has committed her professional life to understanding and assisting with issues of diversity in schools, describes many *good* teachers as "wishing that the diversity they see in September will somehow fade away as the class becomes a group."[17]

The race and social class of the majority of the nation's teachers, however, is not the only important part of the statistical picture. A large proportion of our teachers are also female, and that raises another issue related to the importance of gender in education. While it is true that teachers have a good deal of authority in the classroom, it is not true that they have much authority in the schools—authority to set the rules and develop the curriculum. While reasons for this may vary, an important one has to do with the way in which large numbers of women entered the teaching profession in the 1830s and 1840s. Prior to that time, the person behind the schoolroom desk was a schoolmaster—a man. However, after about 1830, a growing national industrial base provided more and more jobs for men, leaving empty places in the classroom. At the same time, the American common school idea—elementary education for all children—was being promoted by educational leaders. Conveniently, it was determined that women, who were ''natural mothers'' and therefore somehow possessed of the knowledge, skills, and talents needed to deal with young children, must also be ''natural teachers.'' The elementary school was projected as an extension of the home and the teacher an extension of the mother. The fact that women would work for about one-third of the wages paid to male teachers was also a significant factor in their employment in American schools.[18]

In part because of the history of their entry into the profession, female teachers have never had the status that male teachers once had. Unfortunately for *all* teachers, the low status of women in the profession now is also associated with teachers more generally. Administrators, who have higher status, are almost all male. Thus, in our society, schools have become organized in such a way that leadership and policy are very often the province of men, and mostly of white men.[19]

Several consequences follow from these considerations. First, because the nation's teachers are primarily white, some children in the schools are missing important role models due to the relative paucity of people of color in the teaching force. Second, and equally critical, is that because teachers tend to be bound to the knowledge and values of the white middle class, many do not have significant knowledge or experience with people from other cultural backgrounds to bring to bear on classroom interaction. Less than 5 percent of education students in the United States claim fluency in a language other than English, fully three-fifths are completely monolingual, and most have not ventured more than 100 miles from their home![20] Finally, the traditional identification of teaching as ''women's work'' is not consistent with the power and authority to make change, even if teachers were convinced that change is necessary.

We believe that change is imperative. The children who are coming into our schools are unlike any previous generation of students seen in American public education. Today, more than ever before, we have the obligation and responsibility to address the needs of children and youths from a variety of backgrounds. At the same time, we must begin to prepare the young people in our charge with the perspectives, attitudes, knowledge, and skills that will enable them to interact effectively with others who are different from themselves, in the context of an increasingly interdependent global society.

The bottom line is that, like it or not, teachers will encounter people who increasingly are not like themselves. We must learn to work effectively in a world of transition, of change, and of difference.

Much of the responsibility for change must lie with teachers and teacher educators. Unfortunately, those who would be teachers typically learn *what* the problems are and *what* should be taught, but do not learn *how* to modify their own actions in order to reach the kinds of students in their charge. More important, the question of change itself—change in perception, change in belief, change in attitude, change in behavior, and change in values—seldom is addressed.

This book is about those changes, and more. It is about change in the act of teaching, change in the institution we know as the school, and ultimately, change in society. Ideally, the changes we will discuss in this book will result in increasing numbers of individuals who are able to enjoy the rewards society has to offer—including the educational opportunities available through the school. Equally important is that the changes we will propose enable individuals and groups, both in the United States and around the world, to interact in a more positive manner for the enrichment of all.

## HUMAN DIVERSITY AND CHANGE: ANOTHER VIEW

In many ways, our current position parallels that of the Wheat Religion people and the Grainers, each in their turn. We are reaping the sometimes bitter harvest of a struggling educational system that seemingly can rely only on old habits, customs, and beliefs in the face of changing circumstances. Consider this true story, reported by a fourth-grade teacher in an urban elementary school:

> This has not been a good week. A child in my class—a ten-year-old girl—was brought to school by the police, her hands in handcuffs, for being truant. Let me tell you how that happened. For some time now, months, in fact, she and her brother have had lice. Every Monday, the school nurse examines their heads to see if they can remain in school. Their mother treats the lice, but the place where they live must be infested with them, because they keep becoming reinfected. My student has missed, oh, maybe twenty days during this grading period alone. This week, when the nurse checked her, the lice were back. But we couldn't send her home, because we couldn't contact her mother because they don't have a telephone. So she stayed in the clinic all day. The next day, her brother was sick and stayed at home. But my student didn't tell her mother that she was supposed to stay home, too. Instead, she got on a bus and went to a shopping mall where the police, knowing she was probably supposed to be in school, picked her up and brought her back. But they brought her back in *handcuffs*! And not just with her wrists cuffed in front, but with them cuffed behind her back. I asked them if that was necessary. They said it was "standard procedure."[21]

It seems that we are like this little girl: as individuals, as an educational system, as a nation, we are handcuffed to a system based on certain beliefs, assumptions, and behaviors that do not serve us well today. The increased diversity in our society and schools demands that we change our habitual ways of interacting with and educating our children. Yet it requires considerable effort to overcome our own fears, habits, and conditioned ways.

It is possible to look at this from yet another perspective. Rather than being threatening, new ways can be liberating. People can dream of better ways of doing things and then act to build models and tools to achieve those dreams. The gap between the ability to dream and to build is relatively small. Human beings do have a tremendous capacity to design and build most of what we can dream about. The gap between our ability to build toward change and then to *accept that change,* however, is far greater. It is here that we confront people's habits, assumptions, and prejudices. These become barriers that stand in the way of our acceptance and implementation of new designs. It is here that we must focus much of our attention if we expect to integrate the innovations that we know must take place.

We also note that the link between instruction in new methods and subsequent behavior change is weak at best. What people are taught may not be what they learn; what they learn may not be put into practice. Yet given the right combination of circumstances change is possible. It is our contention that individuals can be powerful agents of change—once they understand the barriers they face and some of the underlying processes of learning and interaction that contribute to the creation and maintenance of those barriers. When people engage in critical thinking and reflection about themselves and their interactions with others, and when they are armed with the knowledge and skills that allow them to effectively plan and enter into desired changes, new ways of thinking, of acting, and of perceiving can emerge that may transform the old traditions into the new.

Consider the insightful comments of an experienced teacher as she reflects on her approach to teaching in a multicultural environment:

> Each year I greet thirty new children with a clear picture in mind of who shall be called ''bright'' and who shall be called ''well-behaved.'' Ask me where these ''facts'' come from and I will probably refer to my professional background. Yet I doubt that the image I carry of the intelligent, capable child has changed much since my own elementary school days. It has been intellectualized and rationalized, but I suspect it is much the same, and that image was never black (could insert any group here). The few adult blacks I knew were uneducated laborers and I never played with a black child. During my first ten years of teaching, in a southern city and an eastern suburb, I had a total of three black children.
>
> What, then, did I bring to this integrated school in which I had taught for the past five years? My luggage had ''liberal'' ostensibly plastered all over it, and I thought it unnecessary to see what was locked inside. . . .
>
> In the beginning it was more comfortable to pretend the black child was white. Having perceived this, I then saw it was my inclination to avoid talking about other differences as well. Stuttering, obesity, shyness, divorced parents—the list was long. My awkwardness with black children was not a singular phenomenon. It uncovered a serious flaw in my relationship with all children.
>
> As I watched and reacted to black children, I came to see a common need in every child. Anything a child feels is different about himself which cannot be referred to spontaneously, casually, naturally, and uncritically by the teacher can become a cause for anxiety and an obstacle to learning.
>
> The role of the teacher changes. From the often negative function of judge and jury, the teacher can rise to the far more useful and satisfying position of friend. Strangers hide feelings and pretend to be what they are not. Friends want to know and talk about everything. It is a good environment in which to learn.[22]

All change begins with self. From there, one can begin to effect change in others. The kinds of change we address in this book have to do with the way most people (not only teachers) interact with those who are very different from themselves. We begin in the first section by looking at the way people learn to be functioning members of the specific groups to which they belong. We pay particular attention to the interaction between individuals who have been socialized by different groups. The second section of the book looks at the various ways society has approached human diversity, with particular attention to the schools. The third section presents a framework within which a variety of ideas and strategies can be employed to reach out more effectively to the diverse cultural elements that are a part of the experience of all individuals in the school.

To address the need to practice a new way of thinking, we have included activities at the end of some of the chapters. These are an important element of this text, and we urge you to participate in these exercises as you read the text.

## ACTIVITIES

1 Stories can play an important role in transmitting knowledge about what is expected of the individual as she or he is growing up. What stories were you told as a child? Who told you these stories? What important lessons were you expected to learn? How have these stories influenced your life?

2 In most preliterate societies stories play a critical role in explaining and defining people's place within the world. Locate a story, myth, or legend from another part of the world. What society does it represent? Who are the main characters in the story? Do these characters appear in other stories from this part of the world? Whom is the story meant to address? What important information is being communicated? How is this communication similar to and different from the manner in which you were taught?

3 Personal stories, those stories told about the early lives of individuals often help people to learn important things about themselves. What stories were told about you by parents, other relatives, or family friends that helped you to gain insight into yourself? What did you learn? Compare the effectiveness of simply being told about that characteristic in yourself and having it told through some form of story.

## REFERENCES

1 Lewis Carroll, *Alice in Wonderland* (Mount Vernon, NY: Peter Pauper Press, 1951).
2 Carol P. Christ, *Diving Deep and Surfacing* (Boston: Beacon Press, 1980), p. 1.
3 Ibid., p. 2.
4 Told by J. E. Rash at the Mediterranean Youth Environment Conference, Cartagena, Spain, August 1985.
5 Ibid.
6 H. L. Hodgkinson, *All One System: Demographics of Education—Kindergarten through Graduate School* (Washington, DC: Institute for Educational Leadership, 1985).
7 From Minority to Majority Education and the Future of the Southwest. (Boulder, Colorado: WICHE, Western Interstate Compact of Higher Education, 1988).
8 R. Oxford-Carpenter, L. Pol, M. Gendell, and S. Peng, *Demographic Projections of Non-English-Background and Limited-English-Proficient Persons in the United States to the Year 2000 by State, Age, and Language Group* (Washington, DC: National Clearinghouse for Bilingual Education, InterAmerica Research Associates, 1984).
9 Illinois State Board of Education, Office of Management and Policy Planning, *A Study of Teacher Trends and Traits* (Springfield, IL: Illinois State Board of Education, 1987).
10 Statistics on these kinds of categories vary depending on the methods of counting (and often, the purposes) of those compiling them. These particular statistics can be found in the following publications: Center for Education Statistics, *Digest of Education Statistics* (Washington, DC: U.S. Government Printing Office, 1987); ''Here They Come, Ready or Not,'' *Education Week* (May 14, 1986); H. L. Hodgkinson, op. cit. ref. 5; M. M. Kennedy, R. K. Jung, and M. E. Orland, *Poverty, Achievement, and the Distribution of Compensatory Education Services* (Washington, DC: U.S. Government Printing Office, 1986).

**11** Commission on Work, Family, and Citizenship, "American Youth: A Statistical Snapshot," (The William T. Grant Foundation, 1987), cited in Marion Wright Edelman, "Children at Risk," in Frank J. Macchiarola and Alan Gartner (eds.), *Caring for America's Children* (New York: The Academy of Political Science, 1989), p. 21.

**12** Edelman, op. cit., ref. 10, p. 22.

**13** Ibid., p. 20.

**14** R. Goodwin and B. Krauss (eds.), *An Exceptional View of Life: The Easter Seal Story* (Washington, DC: Potomac Publishing, 1977), n/p.

**15** Carol Shakeshaft, "A Gender at Risk," *Phi Delta Kappan* vol. 67, no. 7, March 1986, p. 500.

**16** Center for Education Statistics, op. cit., ref. 9.

**17** Sara Lawrence Lightfoot, in an interview with Bill Moyers as part of the "World of Ideas" series, American Broadcasting Corporation, 1989.

**18** Nancy Hoffman, *Women's "True" Profession: Voices from the History of Teaching* (New York: The Feminist Press, 1981), p. xix.

**19** Myra H. Strober and David Tyack, "Why Do Women Teach and Men Manage? A Report on Research on Schools," *Signs: Journal of Women in Culture and Society* vol. 5, No. 3. Spring 1980, pp. 494–503.

**20** N. L. Zimpher, "The RATE Project: A Profile of Teacher Education Students," *Journal of Teacher Education* vol. 40, no. 6, November–December 1989, pp. 27–30.

**21** Story reported in a conversation with one of the authors by Robert E. McClelland, a fourth-grade teacher in the Cleveland, Ohio, schools, January 27, 1990.

**22** Vivian Gyssin Paley, *White Teacher* (Cambridge, MA: Harvard University Press, 1979), pp. xiv–xv.

# CHAPTER 2

# THE CULTURE LEARNING
# PROCESS

*It is often hard to learn from people who are just like you. Too much is taken for granted. Homogeneity is fine in a bottle of milk, but in the classroom it diminishes the curiosity that ignites discovery.*

Vivian Gyssin Paley

## WE SEE WHAT WE EXPECT TO SEE

By this time, you should understand that when we talk about human diversity in the modern world, we are talking about a very complex set of phenomena. Studying diversity is made even more difficult because, for the most part, we take differences for granted. That doesn't mean that we like them, or even that we know very much about them. It does mean that, in American society, diversity is part of the landscape of our minds. We see it all around us, and we *expect* to see it. The United States has been a pluralistic society almost since its inception, and to some extent we have always "made room" for people of different backgrounds, different beliefs, and different ways of doing things. By "making room," however, we mean that so long as "they" don't interfere too much with "us," we leave "them" alone.

We believe the time has come for all Americans to begin to consider seriously the implications of real interaction between diverse individuals and groups. At that point, of course, we very quickly come face to face with our own beliefs about who is acceptable, who is "better," and who can safely be ignored. When faced with new evidence, we often are like the Prince in the following story: baffled and sometimes depressed.

\*     \*     \*

### The Prince and the Magician\*

Once upon a time there was a young prince who believed in all things but three. He did not believe in princesses, he did not believe in islands, and he did not believe in God. His father, the king, told him that such things did not exist. As there were no princesses or islands in his father's domain, and no sign of God, the prince believed his father.

But then, one day, the prince ran away from his palace and came to the next land. There, to his amazement, from every coast he saw islands, and on these islands, strange creatures whom he dared not name. As he was searching for a boat, a man in full evening dress appeared along the shore.

"Are those real islands?" asked the young prince.

"Of course they are," said the man in full evening dress.

"And those strange creatures?"

"They are genuine and authentic princesses."

"Then God must also exist," cried the prince.

"I am God," said the man in evening dress with a bow.

\* From *The Magus, A Revised Version* by John Fowles. Revised edition and Foreword Copyright © 1977 by John Fowles Ltd. First edition copyright © 1965 by John Fowles Ltd. By permission of Little, Brown and Company.

The young prince returned home as quickly as he could.

"So, you are back," said his father, the king.

"I have seen islands, I have seen princesses, and I have seen God," said the young prince reproachfully.

The king was unmoved. "Neither real islands, nor real princesses, nor a real God exists."

"I have seen them," said the prince.

"Tell me how God was dressed."

"God was in full evening dress."

"Were the sleeves of his coat rolled back?"

The prince remembered that they had been. The king smiled.

"That is the uniform of a magician. You have been deceived."

At this, the prince returned to the next land and went to the same shore, where once again he came upon the man in full evening dress.

"My father, the king, has told me who you are," said the prince indignantly. "You deceived me last time, but not again. Now I know that those are not real islands and real princesses, because you are a magician."

The man on the shore smiled. "It is you who are deceived, my boy. In your father's kingdom there are many islands and many princesses. But you are under your father's spell so you cannot see them." The prince pensively returned home. When he saw his father, he looked him in the eye. "Father, is it true that you are not a real king, but only a magician?"

The king smiled and rolled back his sleeves. "Yes, my son, I am only a magician."

"Then the man on the other shore was God."

"The man on the other shore was another magician."

"I must know the truth—the truth beyond magic," said the prince.

"There is no truth beyond magic," said the king.

The prince was full of sadness. He said, "I will kill myself."

The king, by magic, caused death to appear. Death stood in the door and beckoned the prince. The prince shuddered. He remembered the beautiful but unreal islands and the unreal but beautiful princesses. "Very well," he said, "I can bear it."

"You see, my son," said the king, "You, too, now begin to be a magician."[1]

*      *      *

In many ways, educators must be magicians. They, too, must help students ''see'' what is not obvious, and learn things that are new and may be contrary to what they already ''know.'' In addition, they have the responsibility of predicting tomorrow's needs (both of individuals and those of societies) and then, using ideas and materials which come largely from the past, equipping students with the knowledge, skills, attitudes, and behaviors to meet those needs. In the simplest of times, this has not been an easy task. In times when the future was relatively predictable, however, educators could at least depend on the fact that they *knew* what kind of lives they were helping to prepare students to lead.

That is no longer the case today. Today, the educator needs all the knowledge and skills more often attributed to magicians—and perhaps some of the magician's tricks as well. The fact is that we do *not* know what the world will be like thirty, twenty, or even ten years from now. What we *do* know, however, is that the coming generations will have to deal with both the process and the outcomes of change.

As the United States and many other nations of the world experience further technological innovation; changing economies; altered political systems and—our particular interest here—increased diversity of ethnicity, religion, language, health, and lifestyle citizens must learn to interact in ways that are more inclusive and less discriminatory, and in ways that will encourage the full participation of all its members in a common social life. Even in areas of this country where human diversity seems limited—neighborhoods, suburbs, and small towns where people still pretty much share common beliefs, similar occupations, perhaps even similar religions—people in communities and schools confront issues of difference in terms of gender, family composition, and exceptionality. They also face the likelihood that young people today will have to interact and cooperate with people from other countries in order to carry out their work, whatever it may be. In fact, between now and the year 2000, people of color, white women, and immigrants will comprise more than 85 percent of the new workers entering the labor force.[2]

In addition, we must remember that there is a very large number of neighborhoods—and sometimes towns—where, although the people who live there have a great deal in common, what they have in common is different from the things "we" share. The tendency of all human beings is to assume that "normal" life is the life "we" lead. In the United States, the norm (that is, the standard against which we measure ourselves) is primarily white, Protestant, and middle class, because that is the group that has decision-making power in this society. Whether they like it or not, however, *all* people will increasingly come into contact with others whose hopes, dreams, attitudes, values, and ways of interaction are quite different from their own. No longer are we a segregated, insular people.

## Current Views: A Perception of Crisis

This growing contact and interaction increases the likelihood of conflict and confrontation and creates the perception that we face a crisis. The word *crisis* comes into our language from a Greek word which means *turning point*. However, Americans most often think of crisis as something negative—an upset, a problem that must be solved or eliminated, *now*. People in other parts of the world, however, may interpret the idea a little differently, and a different interpretation may help us view our situation from another perspective. The Chinese word for crisis, for example, is *wei-chi*. The first part of the word, *wei*, means *danger*. Crisis does imply a dangerous set of circumstances, a kind of threat to our comfort, perhaps even a threat to life. Certainly we will be in a dangerous situation if we do not act to change people's knowledge base, their attitudes, and their ways of interaction. The second part of the word, *chi*, means *opportunity*. A perceived crisis may not present only a threat. The situation may present an opportunity for us to learn and grow as we try to come to grips with changing circumstances. Change and growth demand risk taking and a bit of discomfort, as the parables of the Wheat Religion and the Magician suggest. The opportunity exists for us to grow with the challenge.

## Transitional Views: Finding a Common Ground

When people of diverse backgrounds meet, successful outcomes depend, to a great extent, on the degree to which positive and functional perspectives develop and common ground is sought and found. As professional educators, we must teach children of diverse backgrounds who come to us with a variety of learning styles, modes of behavior, and attitudes with which we are not familiar, and of which we may even disapprove. At the same time, we must prepare our students for the kinds of interactions they are certain to face in our interdependent, global society. This requires a knowledge of how people learn to be cultural beings, of how we can teach our students to negotiate cultural differences, and of the potential obstacles that face us due to the fact that we, ourselves, are cultural beings.

Fortunately, we already have some ideas to help us. In this chapter we will explore some dominant themes that recur as people attempt to define the word *culture;* we hope this discussion will contribute to our ability to reconceptualize bio-psycho-social differences in a positive way. We will also briefly discuss the process of socialization and the notion of ethnocentrism; consider the nature of culture learning and the intercultural adjustment process; and examine the psychological processes of perception, categorization, and attribution which have been associated with the process of cross-cultural or intercultural interaction.

## DOMINANT THEMES IN THE DEFINITIONS OF CULTURE

If you were to review the historical, anthropological, sociological, and psychological literature, you would find literally hundreds of definitions of the word *culture.*[3] Since we cannot depend on a single, universally accepted definition of this crucial term, it is helpful to look for common themes that run through the many definitions.

### Culture as a Social Construction

First, *culture* usually refers to something that is made by human beings rather than something that occurs in nature. When you look out over a body of water, for instance, neither the water itself, the beachfront (usually), nor the horizon is considered a part of your culture. These are naturally occurring components of the environment. How we *think about,* and what we *do with* the natural environment, however, is usually dependent upon our culture. A hallmark of the general attitude of western civilization for at least 500 years has been the belief that human beings were, in some sense, apart from nature, that, indeed, nature was something to be "conquered," something to be put into our service, something to be *used.* Traditional Native American societies, on the other hand, have an entirely different view of the natural environment. Rather than seeing themselves as opposed to nature, many Native Americans (and others, around the world) believe strongly in the place of human beings *within* the natural world. And, since in their view we are a part of nature, it behooves us not to interfere with it too much.

Clearly then, different sociocultural groups perceive the world in very different terms. It is also true that the cultural beliefs and attitudes of a particular group can and do change. Western peoples are now beginning to see the damage they have caused to the environment, and to consider not only ways to "clean it up," but ways of rethinking the relation of human beings to nature.

Thus, in our example of the beachfront, the waterfront condominiums and hotels; the piers and boardwalk; the boats; any litter, including medical waste that may wash ashore;

and even the thin layer of suntan lotion that might be left floating on the water's surface would all be considered part of (western) culture. Furthermore, the condos, the boats, and the litter are not only products of our culture, they also represent our attitudes toward the natural environment. Thus human culture and the natural environment are always connected, usually in a variety of ways.

Clearly, then, culture consists of interrelated components of material artifacts (the condos and boats), social and behavioral patterns (we have medical waste and we toss it in the water), and mental products (it's "all right" to toss litter in the water because somehow, the water will take care of it, and anyway, there's a *lot* of water).

## Culture as a Shared Phenomenon

Another common feature of definitions of culture is that culture is seen as a collective creation. Culture is *socially constructed* by human beings *in interaction with one another*. Cultural ideas and understandings are shared by a group of people who recognize the knowledge, attitudes, and values of one another, and who also agree on which cultural elements are better than others. That is, cultural elements are usually arranged in a hierarchy of *value*. Attitudes about children's place in the economy provide a good example. In the United States before the middle of the nineteenth century, children were regarded as economic assets to their families and to the community. That is, they worked, not only on the farm or in the shop, but often for money which went to help support the family. Zelizer makes a distinction between the "useful" and the "useless" child in talking about the change that occurred during the last half of the century:

> By 1900 middle-class reformers began indicting children's economic cooperation as unjustified parental exploitation, and child labor emerged for the first time as a major social problem in the United States. . . . By 1930, most children under fourteen were out of the labor market and into schools.[4]

This is another instance of the dynamic, or changing, nature of cultural ideas. The notion that children "do not belong" in the labor market, and that parents whose children do work may be exploiting them, has become a highly valued idea in our society, but it is one that is relatively new. In contrast to beliefs in colonial America, we "believe" that children should be in school when they are young. In families that need resources that can be brought in by children, there is a sense that somehow the family is doing something "wrong." Today, we place a greater value on the "useless" child than we do on the "useful" one, but that has not always been the case.

## Culture as Cultivation

A third theme that runs through the definitions of culture is the idea of nurturing and growth—as in *horticulture,* the nurturing of plants. When applied to human social groups, *culture* in this sense most often refers to knowledge of the arts—music, dance, literature, the visual arts—of fine foods and drink, and of a certain style of interaction reserved for a social elite. A "cultured" person is one who is nurtured—helped to grow—by appreciation of the arts and participation in artistic or literary life. Our experience, however, may tell us that it is frequently people of comfortable circumstances who have the time, energy, and inclination to devote to such pursuits. Thus the notion of an elite group enters into the picture.

The idea of culture as "belonging" to an elite also carries with it the notion that this kind of "culture" has more value than what we might call "folk" culture. It is well to be aware of the "spin" placed on this meaning of culture because, as educators, it is often assumed that we are responsible for inculcating all youngsters with a particular "brand" of "culture"—in our case, the traditional western, white, upper- and middle-class "culture" that is generally the focus of such phrases as "the best of western civilization." Certainly, it is true that great art, beautiful music, and meaningful literature have been given to the world by western peoples. But western contributions do not represent all that is great and beautiful in human culture.

More generally, the theme of culture as growth and development implies that systems of meaning are to be taught to the young as a means of nurturing them, or bringing them up. Thus, to *enculturate* a child is to help that child become a member of her or his social group. In the United States, however, that may mean helping a child negotiate the different cultural patterns of all the social groups in which he or she participates.

## Using Cultural Themes in Analyzing Human Diversity

In our consideration of commonalities in the definitions of culture, we have discussed three themes: culture as a socially constructed and dynamic phenomenon; culture as shared by a group that decides through a process of interaction what ideas, attitudes, meanings, and hierarchy of values belong to that group; and culture as a set of ideas that is passed on to the young as a means of nourishing the next generation. Viewed from a thematic perspective, then, culture is a universal phenomenon.

There are other universal aspects of culture as well. For example, Webb and Sherman note that

> Cultures solve the common problems of human beings, but they solve them in different ways. . . . Each provides its people with a means of communication (*language*). Each determines who wields power and under what circumstances power can be used (*status*). Each provides for the regulation of reproduction (*family*) and supplies a system of rules (*government*). These rules may be written (*laws*) or unwritten (*custom*), but they are always present. Cultures supply human beings with an explanation of their relationship to nature (*magic, myth, religion,* and *science*). They provide their people with some conception of time (*temporality*). They supply a system by which significant lessons of the culture (*history*) can be given a physical representation and stored and passed on to future generations. The representation usually comes in the form of dance, song, poetry, architecture, handicrafts, story, design, or painting (*art*). What makes cultures similar is the problems they solve, not the methods they devise to solve them.[5]

It is possible to think of overarching cultural ideas that are associated with certain modern nation-states—for example, the notion of justice in the United States. In most countries of the world today, however, it is more typical that political entities (cities, states, provinces, nations) are composed of a *variety* of groups of people who interact with one another to varying degrees. Each group shares a common heritage or set of beliefs or circumstances that provide the substance for cultural ideas with which they identify and to which they bear a degree of loyalty. Individual identification with and loyalty to this smaller group may conform to or conflict with their identification with and loyalty to the larger political society. This pattern of multiple identifications and loyalties in a single nation-state is often referred to as *cultural pluralism.*

In order to understand the implications of pluralistic patterns for education, we must be able not only to analyze different cultural and political communities, but also to understand the relations between them. In other words, we should be able to apply the themes we have discovered to an analysis of culture at work within an individual, a social group, a community, or a society.

## Subculture, Microculture, Minority, and Ethnic Group

In order to try to understand the complexities of cultural patterns, social scientists have gone to some pains to develop concepts and constructs that are useful in talking about and describing cultural pluralism. Some of these terms are used interchangeably and may cause confusion. Four of the terms most commonly used to describe social groups that share important cultural elements, but are smaller than a whole society, are *subculture, microculture, ethnic group,* and *minority group.*

*Subculture* is a term used frequently by sociologists to refer to a social group that shares characteristics that distinguish it in some way from the larger cultural group or society in which it is embedded. Generally, a subculture is distinguished by sharing either a major unifying set of ideas and/or practices (like the *corporate culture* or the *drug culture*), or a demographic characteristic (like the *adolescent culture* or the *culture of poverty*).[6]

*Microculture* is also a term that refers to a social group that shares important traits, values, and behaviors that set it apart to some extent from the larger political society (usually called the *macroculture*) of which it is a part. Although the terms *microculture* and *subculture* are often used interchangeably, the term *microculture* seems to imply a greater linkage with the larger culture, and emphasis is often put on the degree to which the microculture acts to interpret, express, and/or mediate the ideas, values, and institutions of the political community.[7] Thus, for example, the family, the workplace, or the classroom can be thought of as a microculture embedded in the larger culture of the neighborhood, the business, or the school. And all of these are thought to be embedded in the larger community and/or the nation.

*Minority group* as a sociological term refers to a social group that occupies a subordinate position in a society. Wagley and Harris define a minority group as one that experiences discrimination and subordination within a society, is separated by physical or cultural traits disapproved of by the dominant group, shares a sense of collective identity and common burdens, identifies membership according to a socially invented rule of descent, and is characterized by marriage within the group.[8] Note that these criteria do not fit all groups we might think of as minority groups. For example, women are often referred to as a "minority group" because they are thought to be oppressed, even though they constitute more than half the population and do not, as a rule, marry within their group. Similarly, students who are African-American or Native American or Hispanic—which are "minority groups" in terms of their numbers in the total population—often constitute a majority of the population in a school; the school is then often referred to as a "majority-minority school."

*Ethnic group* is a term often used when describing human groups who share a common historical heritage. When asked to complete the statement "I am _____" with as many descriptors as can be thought of, those statements that reflect identification with some collective or reference group are often indicative of one's ethnic identity. When one responds that she or he is Jewish or Polish or Italian, one is identifying with a group of people who share a common heritage, history, celebrations and traditions, who may enjoy similar foods or speak a common language other than English. A sense of peoplehood, or the feeling that one's own destiny is somehow linked with that of others who share this knowledge, reflects identification with an ethnic group.

## When "Cultures" Interact

While these terms are useful in allowing us to study and describe different cultural groups within a nation-state, they are *not* especially useful in understanding either exactly how the subcultural or microcultural group relates to the larger culture or how to account for the conflicts one individual experiences that seem to relate to a mixture of cultural elements. The situation in a modern, pluralistic society is that most, if not all, individuals, are *multicultural* in that they participate in several different cultural systems *simultaneously,* systems that may be large or small, dominant or subordinate, educative or miseducative. This fact makes predicting behavior and developing effective educational plans—which depend, in part, on being able to predict behavior—very difficult unless one can discover to what extent any particular cultural element is strong enough in the individual to govern that person's thinking, dreaming, and behavior.

Perhaps an example would be helpful. Gollnick and Chinn describe two hypothetical women who live in New York City, and are 30 years old, white, middle class, Italian-American, and Catholic. One of these women identifies very strongly with her Italian-American heritage and her church and not very strongly with her age group, her class status, her gender, or her urban life. The other woman defines herself as a feminist, enjoys her urban life, and is conscious of her age, but does not pay very much attention to her ethnic background, her religion, or her social class.[9] The significance of these patterns lies not only in each woman's self-definition, but in the attitudes, values, knowledge, and behavior that such definition entails. Thus, the first woman may well spend more time with family than with nonrelated friends, may be a member of a right to life group, might choose wine rather than Perrier, may be knowledgeable about and participate in Italian ethnic organizations, and is likely to understand, if not speak, Italian. The second woman may find her most intimate companions among women's groups, be prochoice in her stand on abortion, choose to live in the city despite the possibility of living in a small town or the country, and—if she does not have children—hear her biological clock ticking.

There is some danger of stereotyping here—we do not really *know* that these choices and attitudes are a part of each woman's life until we actually look. But they are at least somewhat predictable from what we do know about the salient cultural ideas associated with particular ethnic, religious, gender, class, and age groups. Another point worth mentioning here is that one element in the cultural mix of each woman's life may serve to mediate another—even a more powerful one. For example, the influence of feminism in the second woman's life might indicate a prochoice stance on abortion; however, her

Accompanying the use of a distinct language among the hearing impaired are patterns of behavior that are particular to the group, including early childhood socialization practices. Children of deaf parents may grow up in environments with much greater visual orientation; lights may accompany a ringing telephone or doorbell, or people may depend upon gestures in interpersonal communication. The deaf community is also very tightly knit, placing strong emphasis on social and family ties. Eighty to ninety percent of people who are hearing impaired marry others with hearing losses. A strong in-group orientation develops, making it difficult for outsiders to enter.

Interactions between hearing and hearing-impaired populations are often filled with feelings of anxiety, uncertainty, and a threat of loss. These feelings are all similar to those encountered in cross-cultural encounters. Using this as an example, it is easy to see the range of possible cross-cultural interactions that can occur between individuals and groups that have distinct subjective cultures. You might think about interactions you have had with those from other backgrounds and try to identify points of discomfort and possible conflict. A very simple exercise is to try to remember the first time you were allowed to sleep overnight at a friend's house, or the first time you went to a church, synagogue, or mosque with someone whose religion was different from yours. The tendency is always to feel a bit unsure, and in some cases, to wonder why "those" people don't do things the "right" way.

## Socialization and Ethnocentrism

The process by which we all come to believe that there is a "right" way to think, express ourselves, and act is called *socialization*. It is the process by which individuals learn what is required of them in order to be successful members of a given group.

Socialization is a unique process in that it simultaneously looks to the future and the past. It looks forward to where people are expected to be and backward to determine what behaviors, values, and beliefs are important to continue. It is like the dead speaking to the living. Socialization is such a potent process that people, once they have been socialized, are hardly aware that other realities can exist.

The word *ethnocentrism* refers to the tendency people have to view the world exclusively from their own perspective, resulting in the belief that one's own way of doing things is best and one's own group is markedly superior to another. The ancient Greeks were convinced of their superiority to others. The English word *barbarian* comes from the Greek word *barbaroi,* which means *foreigners.* Nineteenth- and early twentieth-century English citizens spoke of others as "lesser breeds." The name that many Native American peoples use to identify themselves, when translated into English, means something to the effect of "the real people." The names given to other groups by Native Americans, on the other hand, translate into such phrases as "the eaters of flesh." Ethnocentrism appears to be a feature of all cultures; in fact, it may be considered a cultural universal.

In the early days of the development of the discipline of anthropology, for example, the western anthropologists who developed the discipline largely studied so-called primitive peoples. Comparing these civilizations to their own more technological societies, they "saw" differences that were perceived ethnocentrically as deficits. Warren's 1873

textbook on physical geography introduced its readers to the "races of man" in the following manner:

> The Caucasian race is the truly cosmopolitan and historical race. The leading nations of the world, those who have reached the highest state of civilization and possess a history in the true sense of the word, belong to it. It has, therefore, not improperly been called the active race; while the others, embracing the uncivilized or half-civilized peoples, have been termed the passive races.[13]

The notion of a hierarchy of cultures was built into the early anthropologists' thinking about other societies. At the top of the hierarchy were the highly "civilized" peoples (like the Europeans who popularized the concept). At the bottom were the more primitive "savages" or "natives." Everyone else was placed somewhere in between and thought of as potentially "moving up," at least to some degree. This is merely one of many models that anthropologists used, including the familiar "stone age—bronze age—iron age," based on the assumption that the logical progression is either upward through the hierarchy or from left to right along a continuum toward progressively more "advanced" societies.

European anthropology developed in the context of an intellectual tradition that already was highly ethnocentric; in fact, the idea of a hierarchy or continuum of cultures was current well before anthropology existed as a scientific discipline. In 1824, half a century before Warren wrote his textbook, Thomas Jefferson wrote:

> Let a philosophic observer commence a journey from the *savages* of the Rocky Mountains, eastwardly towards the sea coast. These he would observe in the earliest stages of association, living under no law but that of nature, subsisting and covering themselves with the flesh and skins of wild beasts. He would next find those on the frontiers in the *pastoral stage,* raising domestic animals to supply the defects of hunting. Then succeed our own *semi-barbarous* citizens, the pioneers of the advance of *civilization,* and so in his progress he would meet the gradual shades of *improving man* until he would reach his, as yet, most improved state in our seaport towns. This, in fact, is equivalent to a survey, in time, of the progress of man from the infancy of creation to the present day.[14]

Jefferson's categories foreshadow those of the early anthropologists. And in many ways we have not moved very far beyond this framework in our thinking. Books with such titles as *Affable Savages,*[15] and commonly used terms as *developed* versus *underdeveloped nation,* or First World versus Third World, perpetuate adherence to the idea that there is movement toward some other "ideal" or "better" position, generally one that looks a great deal like our own.

While a certain degree of ethnocentrism serves to bind a people together, it can become a serious obstacle when those who adhere to particular ideas begin to interact with one another. One major expression of ethnocentrism is a strong resistance to change. People resist change under the best of circumstances. This was one of the messages of the story of the Wheat Religion presented at the beginning of Chapter 1. If people believe that their way of doing things is best, why should they change? Consider the case of the United States and the adoption of metrics. At this time, *all* other countries of the world have adopted the metric system as their means of measurement. The United States is the only country to hold on to something they feel is very dear to them. A goal of this text, and of your professional preparation as an educator, is to help people (your-

self and later your students) become less ethnocentric and more appreciative of difference so that the viewpoints of others are considered on their own terms.

## THE PROCESSES OF CULTURE LEARNING

### Culture Is a Secret

Learning about culture is made more difficult because most people know very little about themselves: their socialization, the assumptions they make, what has conditioned them, their ethnocentric behavior, and the various cultural patterns that have become so ingrained in their makeup as to become nearly invisible. Consider, for example, the way you learned to speak your first language. Do you remember how it happened? If you have taken another language in school, perhaps it was difficult for you—but your *own* language, now that was easy! Or so it seems. The way one learns one's culture, like the way one learns one's own language, is a secret.

Another way of looking at culture is to consider it as hidden recurring patterns of behavior and thought. We say *hidden* because people generally do not have easy access to vocabulary and concepts with which to talk about what these patterns are, how they learned these patterns or how to teach them to others. The learning of language again provides an example. Most readers of this book have spent a good portion of their life speaking and interacting in the English language. Suppose you met a non-English speaker who wished to learn the language. How would you teach them to correctly pronounce the sentence ''Can you tell me the time?'' when that person might more easily say ''Can you dell me the dime?'' What might a person be told that would enable her or him to make the appropriate sound? Go ahead. Try it. How would you teach someone to make the correct sounds?

If you have determined that a little puff of air passes out of the mouth when the ''t'' sound is made in such words as *tell* and *time* as opposed to the ''d'' sound, you are on the right track to discovering the secret. Correct speakers of English aspirate their stops; that is, some air passes out of the mouth when such letters as ''t,'' ''p,'' or ''k'' are spoken. We call this a secret because while most of us do this quite regularly and easily, you probably were not able to describe it to others. This practice has become so much a part of your behavior that you take it for granted and are often unable to communicate it to others. A further secret must also be learned. We aspirate our stops only in the beginning and in the middle of words, not at the end. We do not aspirate the ''t'' in *hit, bit,* or *cat.*

How were these rules learned? Probably not in formal sessions with your parents or by reading language texts. These rules are typically learned by trial and error in our early socialization, having proper models and being reinforced by those around us. This pattern is often hidden from us, as are the results. Culture, too, can be conceived of as patterns that are often hidden from our conscious behavior and thought.

Acquiring cultural knowledge is similar to learning a language. Few people receive formal education in how to be an appropriate member of any particular cultural group. Rather, people are culturally socialized by observing others, through trial and error, and by continuous reinforcement. In other words, culture and language are learned affectively and through experience, not cognitively. It is not until the process of schooling begins that the use of language gains a cognitive focus, generally through such activities as grammar, reading, and spelling lessons. But because we eventually gain knowledge of the structure and use of our language, we can begin to talk about it.

This same sequence of events does not usually occur, however, in the case of cultural knowledge. Few people ever take a formal course in "culture." Few ever learn why they behave the way they do, or why they think many of the things they do. Fewer still ever evaluate the assumptions they make. People, generally, lack the concepts and vocabulary with which to talk about these things. Cultural knowledge, like language, is often taken for granted. It is only when we confront someone with different cultural knowledge, who behaves or thinks differently, that we are reminded that our way of doing things may not be the only way.

A problem emerges, however, when people confront differences with which they are unfamiliar. Lacking both an outsider's perspective on the elements of their own culture and a vocabulary with which to discuss that culture, they are unable to speak with others about the situation. People typically respond first on an emotional level; they may become quite frustrated, may make negative judgments about others, and then may end an interaction at this point of frustration. This must be avoided if productive encounters are to result.

## The Adjustment Process

Whenever people make significant changes in their lives, they have a myriad of reactions, experiences, and new phenomena to which they must adjust. Most people have experienced a major transition of some sort in their lives: an extended period away from home for the first time; the transition from school to work, or from work back to school or retirement; the transition from single life to married life or vice versa; a move across country; a significant period living and working overseas or with another cultural group within one's own country. What major transitions have you made in your life?

Our society, too, is in a period of almost overwhelming transition. This is evident from the shift in populations in schools around the country and the demands placed upon teachers and students who must interact over an extended period of time. When thinking about making transitions and living and working in a culturally diverse setting, we can learn a significant amount from what cross-cultural trainers have to say about the adjustment process in an international setting. It is suggested that as people strive to integrate themselves into a new cultural setting, they must successfully accommodate a series of predictable phases. It has been hypothesized that people experience four marked phases during their adjustment to an international or intercultural setting.[16] If the experiences people have were placed on a graph with one's emotional experiences along the vertical axis and time across the horizontal axis, the resulting image would appear as a "U." Hence this description of the process of adjustment has been termed the *U-curve hypothesis*[17] (see Figure 2.1).

Initially, most people are intrigued and enraptured by the prospect of an international experience. They have some preconceptions or preconceived ideas of what to expect, of what the new culture will be like, and how they might integrate into the new setting. Overcome with excitement, new sensations, and perceived opportunity, individuals enter what has been appropriately termed the *honeymoon phase*. Early in a new experience, at

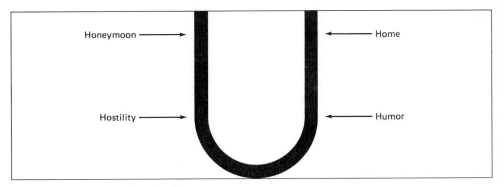

**FIGURE 2.1**    U-curve hypothesis.

the upper-left-hand segment of the "U," everything seems like heaven. The new sights, places, smells, food, dress, people, physical environment—the objective cultural differences—entirely envelop one. However, this places considerable demands upon one's physiological and psychological self. Adjusting to all that is new puts one's body in a state of constant stress and anxiety. This is exciting, but only to a point.

After some time, the constant demand to adjust to new stimuli and to function well within a new setting may become too difficult to accept. Most people react to the stress by entering a state of *hostility* and begin to move down the left side of the "U." In this phase, people generally attempt to cope with three problems: (1) Other people's behavior does not make sense to them. (2) One's own behavior does not produce the expected result. (3) There is so much that is new in the environment that the individual has no ready-made answers to the questions that may arise. In the school context, such responses can be experienced in countless ways. New teachers must integrate their ideals and hopes with the accepted methods and attitudes of a well-established teaching staff. New children must learn to understand the expectations and behaviors of others—peers, teachers, as well as other school staff. New families entering a community must also learn how things operate. You can probably imagine numerous other situations in the school where considerable adjustment must take place.

During the hostility phase, individuals may become so frustrated by their inability to make sense of their world that they begin to react in an aggressive, and perhaps hostile, manner. Many begin to take their frustrations out on others in their immediate surroundings: family tensions may rise, peer relationships may suffer, classroom or workplace frustration may increase, or one may begin to criticize people in the new setting for their inability to get things done the way one feels they should. Highly ethnocentric reactions may emerge during this phase, which, if not checked, can create severe interpersonal problems. This is perhaps the most critical phase of the adjustment to working across cultures, since it is here that the subjective cultures of the two parties become evident and potential conflicts emerge. One has a critical choice to make at this point: remain and learn how to function effectively within the new setting, or allow the frustrations to build and thereby force one to leave the unpleasant situation.

In this phase, those who will most probably succeed in their new setting begin to confront the new cultural environment. Individuals must cope with embarrassment, disappointment, frustration, anxiety, and identity problems. Once one begins to understand the subjective culture in which one finds oneself and is able to understand why people behave as they do, one can begin to emerge from this reactive, hostile phase and enter the third phase—just up the right-hand side of our "U." Reaching this third phase, often referred to as the *humor phase*, is a positive step. One is now beginning to understand more of the new culture and can begin to laugh at some of the mistakes and assumptions he or she made earlier in the experience.

Finally, people who become well adjusted climb the final leg of the "U" and enter the phase called *home*. In this phase, individuals are able to interpret the world and interact with others both from their own perspective and from the perspective of members of the other group. A major change occurs in the ability to process information and to understand the world in ways similar to those in the other group. The individual now shows indications of becoming more genuinely appreciative of differences, as the world now seems reasonable and acceptable from more than one point of view.

Most individuals require a significant amount of time before they begin to understand the more subtle, subjective aspects of another culture to the depth that is required for them to work effectively with others in that cultural group. Some suggest that this period may be as long as two years—a significant amount of time which you must fully keep in mind!

In the schools, the adjustment process we have been discussing is at least a two-sided one. Increasing numbers of students—immigrants, refugees, or temporary residents—will experience the various stages of the adjustment process as they make the transition to a new culture. Teachers should expect that students, and their families, will confront many changes and personal reactions during this process. This may make it difficult for students to fully understand their new environment and attend to their schooling. Teachers—especially those in highly pluralistic settings—may find that they, too, require a period of adjustment before they feel comfortable and are able to capably carry out their responsibilities. Teachers, students, families, and school administrators must be aware of this dynamic and expect that changes in all parties will take place given the necessary time.

The question to ask yourself becomes: Am I willing to accept some discomfort, ambiguity, and uncertainty for a significant period of time until things begin to make sense and fall into place for me? As an educator, you must be able to answer "yes." You must consider this a necessity if you are to achieve the goals you have set for yourself, as well as for your young students.

Many of the specific dimensions of subjective culture will be presented and expanded upon in the next chapter. Here, we are going to introduce some other major barriers to understanding—issues related to perception, cognition, and the processing of information—those dimensions that begin to come together in the last stage of the adjustment process.

## Perception and Categorization

People receive millions of bits of information every day through their sense organs. To think that people can respond to each and every individual piece of information is expecting too much; a person's physical and emotional systems would be overwhelmed.

Because of the need to simplify things, people organize their world into categories; into each category, they put items that share similar characteristics. People then generally respond to the category to which an individual item belongs.

*Perception* refers to the stimulation of the sense organs: that is, what people immediately report seeing, hearing, feeling, tasting, and smelling. While no two people have exactly the same physiological structure and therefore no two people perceive stimuli identically, those with healthy nervous systems tend to perceive similar things in the environment in similar ways. However, sense perception alone is not sufficient. We also need to make sense out of the busy world around us. This is the point at which people place what has been perceived into a category that gives it meaning. That meaning usually is given definition by cultural knowledge. *Categorization* refers to what is done with information once it is perceived by the various sense organs, how it is organized, and the meaning that is attached to it.

Some examples may enhance your understanding of the influence cultural knowledge has on one's cognitive processes. Physicists, for example, tell us that the human eye can distinguish more than 8 million colors. There is no practical reason nor is it humanly possible even to consider all these fine variations of shade and hue, let alone to react to each individual color. People, therefore, group colors according to some scheme. The most familiar to you is probably the one based on the spectrum in which red, orange, yellow, green, blue, indigo, and violet are the major categories. When asked about the color of the sky, an American's response typically is "blue." A sapphire is blue, oceans depicted on a map are blue, and robin's eggs are blue. Grass, however, is green, as are the leaves of most trees and the inside of a kiwi fruit.

In traditional Japanese language, however, the term *aoi* refers to colors that span blue and green wavelengths. When asked the color of the sky, the response would be "aoi." When asked the color of grass, the response would again be "aoi." How would you explain this? Certainly the entire Japanese population is not color-blind! Rather, whereas Euro-Americans have learned to place these particular stimuli into different categories (blue and green), traditional Japanese would group them together.

Here is a second example. While an American and an Indian Muslim might both "see" the animal identified as *dog* in a similar way, most westerners think of dogs as pets, companions, and in some cases as important members of their family. A Muslim, however, confronted by the same creature, would consider the dog filthy, a lowly animal, and something to be avoided at all costs—similar to the reaction a North American might have to a pig. Some Filipinos or Pacific Islanders, on the other hand, may place a dog in the category of food. It is not uncommon to find dog meat as part of the human diet in many parts of the world.

Although the same actual stimuli impinge on all people, one's cultural upbringing determines what meaning is given to things and how to make sense out of the world. This means that children from various backgrounds may come to school having different perspectives on such things as what constitutes valid knowledge, how knowledge or experience is verified, the meaning of an education, and the role of a teacher.

Think about your immediate reaction to hearing that some people would just as soon eat the very dog you might consider to be a lovable member of the family. This, perhaps, brings up the most critical element in intercultural interaction and the barrier most difficult to cross—the judgments or *attributions* people make.

## The Attribution Process

People make judgments about others based on the behavior they observe. They judge others to be competent or incompetent, educated or naïve, well intentioned or ill intentioned. Psychologists call these judgments *attributions*.[18] People are always making attributions—it is an unconscious process. Psychologists tell us that within about 7 seconds of meeting someone new, initial judgments are made that, if negative, are very difficult to change.

Unfortunately, human judgment is fallible, and certain errors repeatedly occur in human thought. One of these has been called the *fundamental attribution error,* a phrase that describes the tendency people have to make judgments about themselves in ways which are very different from the way they make judgments about others.

For instance, when people fail at a given task, they are likely to look for blame in the situation, not in themselves. It is not atypical for students who have failed a given exam, for example, to look for fault in the situation. They may say or think such things as the professor was unfair, the readings were too difficult, the material was not well explained in class, and so forth. When people see others fail, on the other hand, the tendency is to put a trait label on that individual. When another fails, the tendency is to say things like: "of course they failed, they hardly studied," "they were out late the night before," "they are generally lazy or stupid," and so forth. Such responses are generally referred to as making trait-state distinctions; that is, people tend to look for situational responses to explain their own shortcomings and trait explanations to explain the failings of others.

While the fundamental attribution error appears to be common among all people, the situation becomes a bit more complex when we consider the interaction of gender, especially in terms of the example used above. In schools in the United States, boys have a tendency to make more situational attributions than girls. As such, a boy might explain his failure on a given exam as due to an overextended schedule, a recent bout with the flu, a problem at home that had him preoccupied, or the teacher who "*gave* him the poor grade." American girls, on the other hand, are more likely to blame themselves, attributing failure to lack of intelligence or ability. When the boy does well, however, he will often attribute his success to a personal trait. It is not uncommon to hear boys make such statements as "I earned that A" or "I worked hard for that grade!" If the girl does well, success is often attributed to luck or to a "mistake."[19] Success in another may be attributed to luck, while failure is likely to be attributed to a negative personal trait. The person may be seen as lazy, uneducated, or not committed. It is the negative trait labels people make about others that often become generalized into negative stereotypes of that group.

Remember the story of the Wheat people and the Grainers that you read at the beginning of Chapter 1? The people of each group were so accustomed to their own ways that they each thought of the others as "heretics." Because people have a need to simplify their world, and because they cannot react to each unique aspect of their environment, they construct categories, label these categories, and place people with similar traits within them. The trait labels often given to those who are in some way "other," frequently become negative stereotypes of the group. *Stereotypes,* in fact, are nothing more than categories invented by people to describe other people. Here we find that the processes of perception, categorization, attribution, and development of ethnocentric attitudes combine to create a potentially harmful situation. Although any cultural group may teach its members to categorize other groups either positively or negatively, most stereotypes end up as negative labels placed on groups of people.

A relatively common and concrete example may illustrate this point. Children from some cultural groups (Mexican-American, African-American) are taught to demonstrate respect for elders or persons in authority by avoiding eye contact. Hence a child being reprimanded by a parent or teacher would avoid gazing in that person's eyes. Caucasian-American children, and most teachers (remember the demographics of the teaching profession!) are taught to look a person of authority in the eye. Imagine the outcome of an interaction involving an African-American or Mexican-American child being reprimanded by a caucasian teacher. The child, as she or he has been taught, looks away from the gaze of the teacher. In accordance with his or her own cultural knowledge, the child is demonstrating respect. The teacher, expecting to make eye contact, interprets the child's behavior as a message that conveys "I am not listening to you" or "I do not respect you." The teacher, then, may make the judgment that the child is being disrespectful or insolent. This incorrect judgment may jeopardize future interactions between this teacher and student.

Imagine you are reviewing the files of the following two students.[20] What kind of judgments would you make about these children? What kind of academic program would you recommend? Would you expect them to "fit in" with your regular class program? Would you suggest any special intervention such as special classes for gifted or handicapped students? Would you recommend any extra-curricular activities that would help develop special skills in these children?

*Sam Edder.*   Sam Edder did not begin speaking until he was 3 years old. He has always had trouble with school, often remaining withdrawn and unsociable. He was even removed from school at one time because of his emotional instability. Sam's test scores are well below average except for his performance on creativity measures. In this area he shows some potential. Other than reading intently and playing a musical instrument, Sam seems to have few interests and expresses little in the way of personal or vocational goals. Sam's parents are of European descent, with high school educations.

*Bill Ridell.*   Bill has never spent much time in school. He started late because of an illness and was withdrawn several times due to continued sickness. Bill has been labeled "backward" by school officials. He has suffered from a variety of ailments and is going deaf. Although his creative performance shows some promise, Bill's IQ score is low (81), as are his scores on other achievement indices. However, Bill enjoys building things and mechanical pursuits, has good manual dexterity, and would like someday to be a scientist or railroad mechanic. Although Bill's mother is well educated, his father has had no formal schooling and is unemployed.

What do you think? What judgments are you able to make about these two children? What other information would you like to have? As a teacher, how would you work with these children?

Now let's check your attributions for accuracy, as well as for the assumptions you were making. The descriptions of Sam Edder and Bill Ridell are actually case studies of real people. Sam Edder's file is that of Albert Einstein and Bill Ridell's is that of Thomas Edison. How quick were you to make faulty attributions about the potential for success of these students?

Effective intercultural communication occurs when both parties to an interaction suspend judgment, seek to understand the reasons behind the other's actions, and are then able to explain the other's behavior according to its intent. The goal of making *isomorphic attributions,* that is, judgments of the causes of another's behavior that are shared by both parties, is not unreasonable. When this occurs, misunderstanding and miscommunication can be reduced. In the examples above, the effective teacher would understand that there is more going on than meets the eye. This teacher would withhold judgment until all needed information is available. You can easily see how quick and faulty attributions are often inaccurate, as well as potentially dangerous. How many other Einsteins and Edisons have slipped through the cracks because of individuals who make quick judgments that may determine an individual's future prematurely? How will *you* prevent such actions from happening?

## NOT MAGIC, BUT KNOWLEDGE

At the beginning of this chapter, you read a story about a prince who met a magician. The magician gave the prince a different view of the world, one that appeared strange and somewhat unbelievable to him, but very exciting. The prince's father, the king, being disinclined to have his son's worldview changed, attributed dishonest motives to the magician. ''You have been deceived,'' he said. But the prince persevered, returning once more to the magician's island. And once again, the magician told him that ''reality'' was broader than he had imagined. And the prince was sad, for letting go of cherished beliefs often causes a sense of loss. Confronting his father, the prince demanded to know if he, too, were a magician. ''Yes,'' said the King. The prince was hostile. ''I want the truth,'' he said, clinging to the belief that there was indeed a final Truth. ''There is no truth beyond magic,'' said the King, and the prince felt sadder still.

But the prince, like those of us who have the courage and the will to open our eyes to the beautiful and rich diversity around us, found that he could learn to live in a world without absolute Truth. And he became a magician, himself—a magician whose stock in trade was knowledge.

## ACTIVITIES

1 Number a paper from 1 to 20. Next, rather quickly complete the statement ''I am _____'' twenty times with the first things that come to your mind. When you are finished, categorize your responses according to underlying commonalities. This strategy can help you to gain a picture of the image you have of yourself. How many entries do you have that represent individual affiliations? How many represent collective affiliations? How many are family affiliations? What do your responses indicate about you? Compare your responses with others'. How do you account for any major differences?[21]

2 Construct a ''cultural'' profile of yourself. What information completes the following profile?[22]
   a Your racial identity
   b Your ethnic identity
   c Languages spoken at home
   d Languages learned outside of home
   e Religion

**f** Socioeconomic class

**g** Age group

What experiences have you had that increased or decreased your sense of belonging to a certain group? Which of the above are most and least significant to you? Which groups place you at an advantage in American society? Which groups place you at a disadvantage in American society? What are the implications for you as you anticipate your role as a teacher? What experiences have you had with persons from groups different from your own? At work? In social settings? Through friendships? Travel?

**3** For each of the following reference group categories describe a specific group to which you belong or with which you identify. Then choose three that are important to you or that are representative of you. For these three, select three or four characteristics or ideals of that group that you especially value.

Example:

| Category | Group | Characteristic or Ideal |
|----------|-------|------------------------|
| State | Citizens of Washington state | Conservative, environmentally responsible, value life in sparsely populated state with rural and wilderness areas |

| Category | | Characteristic or Ideal |
|----------|---|------------------------|
| Nationality | | |
| State | | |
| City or town | | |
| Age | | |
| Sex | | |
| Family | | |
| Ethnicity | | |
| Religion | | |
| Occupation | | |
| Institution | | |
| Profession | | |
| Social status | | |
| Political affiliation | | |
| Race | | |
| Economic status | | |
| Marital status | | |
| Sport | | |
| School | | |

**4** *Family tree exercise:* Each of us can trace our roots to someplace. Trace your family's heritage as far back as possible. In what parts of the world did your family (or families) originate? What motivated them to leave their homeland for their new world? What hardships did they face when they first arrived? How did they overcome these? What did these individuals do when they first arrived? How did this influence what family members do today? What languages did they speak when they arrived? What family traditions or practices have been carried on over the years that are special or unique to you? How are the experiences of your family similar to those faced by various immigrants and refugees today?

**5** What major transitions have you made in your life? Identify one that extended over a rather lengthy period? On a graph, trace out your emotional experiences from the time when you first

36 PART ONE: HUMAN DIVERSITY: A PROBLEM AND AN OPPORTUNITY

began the experience until the time when you felt completely "at home." Can you identify distinct phases in your experience that are similar to those presented in the chapter?

6 The notion of stereotypes is introduced in this chapter. Explore the concept of stereotype in terms of yourself and the education profession. The generalized picture of education students is predominantly caucasian and middle class (88 to 94 percent), predominantly female (67 percent), predominantly monolingual (68 percent), and poorly traveled (few have traveled more than 100 miles from their home or have aspirations to international travel). How do you compare to this stereotypic image? What is useful about having stereotypes? What is potentially harmful about using stereotypes?

REFERENCES

1 John Fowles, *The Magus, A Revised Version* (Boston: Little, Brown, 1977).
2 *Workforce 2000* (Washington, DC: U.S. Department of Labor, Workforce 2000 Project Office, 1987).
3 See, for example, Alfred L. Kroeber and Clyde Kluckhohn, *Culture: A Critical Review of Concepts and Definitions* (New York: Vintage Books, 1963).
4 Viviana A. Zelizer, *Pricing the Priceless Child: The Changing Social Value of Children* (New York: Basic Books, 1985), pp. 61, 97.
5 Rodman B. Webb and Robert R. Sherman, *Schooling and Society,* 2d ed. (New York: Macmillan, 1989), pp. 49–50.
6 Brian M. Bullivant, "Culture: Its Nature and Meaning for Educators," in *Multicultural Education: Issues and Perspectives* (Boston: Allyn and Bacon, 1989), p. 28.
7 James A. Banks, "Multicultural Education: Characteristics and Goals," in *Multicultural Education: Issues and Perspectives* (Boston: Allyn and Bacon, 1989), p. 7.
8 Cited by Christine L. Bennett in *Comprehensive Multicultural Education: Theory and Practice* (Boston: Allyn and Bacon, 1990), p. 42, from a discussion in J. R. Feagin, *Racial and Ethnic Relations* (Englewood Cliffs, NJ: Prentice-Hall, 1978), p. 11.
9 Donna M. Gollnick and Philip C. Chinn, *Multicultural Education in a Pluralistic Society* (St. Louis, MO: Mosby, 1983), pp. 21–22.
10 Kenneth Cushner and Gregory Trifonovitch, "Understanding Misunderstanding: Barriers to Dealing with Diversity," *Social Education,* vol. 53, no. 5, (Sept. 1989, pp. 318–322.
11 Richard W. Brislin, *Cross-Cultural Encounters: Face-to-Face Interaction* (New York: Pergamon Press, 1981).
12 Harry Triandis, *The Analysis of Subjective Culture* (New York: Wiley-Interscience, 1972).
13 D. M. Warren, *An Elementary Treatise on Physical Geography* (Philadelphia: Cowperthwait and Co., 1873), p. 86.
14 Cited in Roy Harvey Pearce, *The Savages of America: A Study of the Indian and the Idea of Civilization* (Baltimore: Johns Hopkins University Press, 1965), p. 155.
15 Francis Huxley, *Affable Savages* (New York: Viking Press, 1957).
16 Gregory Trifonovitch, "Culture Learning—Culture Teaching," *Educational Perspectives,* vol. 16, No. 4, 1977, pp. 18–22.
17 S. Lysgaard, "Adjustment in a Foreign Society: Norwegian Fulbright Grantees Visiting the United States," *International Social Science Bulletin,* Vol. 7, 1955, pp. 45–51.
18 F. Heider, *The Psychology of Interpersonal Relations* (New York: John Wiley & Sons, 1958).
19 Myra Sadker and David Sadker, *Sex Equity Handbook for Schools,* 2d ed. (New York: Longman, 1990).
20 From a simulation developed by John Rader.

**21** Activity suggested by Richard Brislin in ''Increasing Awareness of Class, Ethnicity, Culture and Race by Expanding on Students' Own Experiences,'' in I. Cohen (ed.), *The G. Stanley Hall Lecture Series,* vol. 8 (Washington, DC: American Psychological Association, 1988), p. 153.

**22** *Approaches to Teaching Instructor's Manual of Learning Activities* (Kent, OH: College of Education, Kent State University, 1989).

# CHAPTER 3

# ANALYZING INTERCULTURAL INTERACTION

*When David Livingstone's work in Africa became known, a missionary society wrote to him and asked, "Have you found a good road to where you are?" If he had, the letter indicated the society was prepared to send some men to help with his work. Livingstone's answer was clear and to the point. "If you have men who will come only over a good road, I don't need your help. I want men who will come if there is no road."*

L. Smith

### Critical Incident: Alden High School—A Crisis Is Brewing!

Alden High School is an urban school of approximately 1,600 students in grades 9 through 12. Approximately 50 percent of the students are African-American, 30 percent are caucasian, 10 percent are Hispanic, and 10 percent are Native American, Asian, or Middle Eastern. A majority of students come from families at or below the poverty level. There is a large vocational program with more than half of the juniors and seniors enrolled. Approximately 25 percent of the faculty is African-American; the rest is caucasian. Alden has an aging faculty with an average age of 43. Last year, the principal, Mr. Henderson, was unable to hire any minority teachers. This year he was able to attract four new African-American faculty members.

In January of last year, Mr. Henderson met with the black teachers at their request. They had many concerns, ranging from not enough black head coaches and the need to hire more black teachers to the way white teachers were dealing with the black students. They felt that the white teachers did not appreciate the need for the proposed Martin Luther King recognition activities; they were disappointed at the lack of white response to a request for donations to the United Negro College Fund; and they felt a negative response to Black History Month activities.

As a result of this meeting, a Human Relations Committee was formed. This volunteer group planned and organized a 2-day race relations institute. The results of the workshop were disastrous. Instead of improving race relations in the school, a step was taken backward. The situation in the school became worse. A group of white teachers sent around a list of possible themes for the coming school year which were perceived as racist by the black teachers. A group of concerned black teachers and parents sent letters to community leaders and higher-level administrators voicing their concern. Once parents of the Hispanic students became aware of the situation, they started demanding equal attention to address the needs of their children. Not only the black students, but Native American, Hispanic, and Asian students became increasingly alienated from school-related activities.

In March, Mr. Henderson met with the equal opportunity officer in the district and with a group of white and black teachers. While concerns were aired, none of the problems were solved. A discussion was begun, but as Mr. Henderson puts it, "We have a long way to go. We definitely have some white teachers who are insensitive to the needs of others as well as some black teachers who perceive the white teachers as racist. I'm not quite sure how to begin addressing the students' needs, except to say that we will continue to bring the various parties together to address whatever needs arise. I only hope people will stay with me for the long haul."

## LESSONS FROM THE SOCIAL SCIENCES: APPLYING CROSS-CULTURAL PSYCHOLOGY

In the United States, increasing numbers of schools are becoming more and more diverse in terms of the background and expectations of their student populations. This situation gives rise to untold numbers of possible conflicting interactions. Increasingly, cross-cultural misunderstandings and disputes are an underlying cause of many serious problems in the schools. A disturbing factor is that many of these misunderstandings may go unrecognized by both teachers and administrators. Because they are unrecognized, they may become the root cause of lingering disputes which eventually present themselves as crisis situations.[1] How can people best prepare to recognize and deal with the problems that may arise under such conditions?

Over the past few decades, a variety of different programs for schools have been designed to address concerns voiced by ethnic, racial, religious, and other groups in the United States. While there are similarities between them, in practice many of these programs quickly became oriented to issues related to particular groups; which group often depended on regional demographics. In the northwest, for instance, programs have tended to emphasize Asian and Native American issues; in the southwest, Hispanic and Native Americans became the focus; in the south and east, African-American and Central American issues were emphasized.

A problem with the *culture-specific* approach is that the information and training are often presented before any foundation of *culture-general* concepts is developed. Hence, many of the facts learned about a particular group are soon forgotten, or cannot be applied outside a specific context. Underlying principles are rarely noted and therefore cannot be applied to interactions in other contexts.

In contrast to this kind of culture-by-culture approach is an approach to understanding diversity that is less specific but more inclusive. This culture-general approach derives in part from principles developed in the field of cross-cultural training and intercultural interaction. Cross-cultural psychologists have, for some time, been developing concepts and training strategies which can become rich resources for educators working in culturally diverse settings.

The distinction between culture-specific and culture-general is an important one to understand. A *culture-general* concept is one that applies to all cultural groups. Such a concept, for example, is that learning styles differ from culture to culture. A *culture-specific* variation of this suggests that children from a particular background may learn how to learn in a specific manner. Children of Hawaiian ancestry, for instance, learn best in in-context situations.[2] While most teachers may not ever have Hawaiian children in their classrooms, it is most helpful for them to recognize that cultural knowledge influences learning styles in many different ways and that specific understanding of these ways can be accumulated. When culture-specific concepts are introduced and studied, one is compelled to attend to detailed and unique information about one cultural group at a time. Culture-general concepts, on the other hand, can be applied to a wide variety of cross-cultural situations as they arise.

Culture-general concepts enable people to handle situations where more than two cultural groups are interacting. Such approaches attempt to help people understand the range of encounters one might experience when individuals from *any* two groups interact. A conceptual framework which enables the study and categorization of a wide range of possible interactions is most useful to us in our study of individual and group differences and the misunderstandings they can cause.

While the culture-specific programs referred to above were often conducted by dedicated people who had valuable firsthand knowledge of a particular cultural group, their content and training methodologies were, for the most part, neither grounded in concepts from cross-cultural interaction nor research-tested.[3] Further, in many of today's schools, understanding a single cultural group may or may not be helpful in enabling students to succeed. Not only are more cultural groups represented in schools today, but any member of a particular group may be influenced by a number of cultural elements in addition to her or his "folk culture."

## A CULTURE-GENERAL FRAMEWORK FOR UNDERSTANDING INTERCULTURAL INTERACTIONS

Brislin, Cushner, Cherrie, and Yong have developed a framework for understanding a range of experiences people are certain to encounter in their intercultural interactions.[4] This framework is research-based and provides a comprehensive eighteen-theme structure for analyzing, understanding, and studying intercultural interactions in a wide variety of situations, including those found in many schools and communities. This approach to studying intercultural interactions is grounded in the realization that people have similar types of experiences and similar reactions to their cross-cultural encounters regardless of whom they are interacting with, where they are, or their own role in a new setting.

The eighteen themes presented in the culture-general framework can be grouped into three broad categories: emotional experiences, knowledge areas, and the bases of cultural differences.

### Emotional Experiences Resulting from Encounters with Cultural Differences

**1** *Anxiety:* As people encounter many unfamiliar demands, they are likely to become anxious about whether or not their behavior is appropriate.

**2** *Disconfirmed Expectations:* People may become upset or uncomfortable, not because of the specific circumstances they encounter but because the situation differed from what they expected.

**3** *Belonging:* People have the need to fill a niche, to feel that they belong, and feel at home, but they often cannot because their status is that of "outsider."

**4** *Ambiguity:* When living and working across cultures, the messages one receives are often unclear; yet decisions must be made and appropriate action must be taken.

**5** *Confrontation with one's prejudices:* People may discover that previously held beliefs about a certain group of people may not be accurate or useful when interacting with another culture.

### Knowledge Areas That Incorporate Many Cross-Cultural Differences and That People Find Difficult to Understand

**6** *Work:* Numerous cultural differences are encountered in work-related settings. Difficulties can arise related to proper relationship between on-task behavior and social interaction, the onus of control, decision-making strategies, and attitudes toward creative effort, for example.

**7** *Time and Space:* Various attitudes exist regarding the importance of being "on time" to appointments, as well as the proper spatial orientation for people to adopt when interacting with each other.

**8** *Language:* Language differences are probably the most obvious problem which must be overcome when crossing cultural boundaries. Attitudes toward language use, the difficulties of learning another language, and its relation to education are addressed in this area.

**9** *Roles:* There is a generally accepted set of behaviors people perform in relation to the roles they adopt. Tremendous differences exist with respect to the occupants of these roles, and how these roles are enacted in different social groups.

**10** *Importance of the group versus the importance of the individual:* All people act at some times in their individual interest, and at other times according to their group allegiances. The relative emphasis on group versus individual orientation varies from culture to culture and may have a significant impact on the daily lives of individuals as well as on the way they learn.

**11** *Rituals versus superstition:* All cultures have rituals which help people meet their needs as they cope with life's everyday demands. People in all cultures also engage in behaviors that "outsiders" may label superstitious. One's rituals may be seen by others as based on superstitions.

**12** *Social hierarchies—Class and status:* People often make distinctions based on various markers of high and low status. These distinctions differ from culture to culture. They may have significant impact on the educational process.

**13** *Values:* People's experiences in broad areas such as religion, economics, politics, aesthetics, and interpersonal relationships become internalized. Understanding these internalized views, and the range of possible differences, is important to cross-cultural understanding.

### The Bases of Cultural Differences

Most of the themes in this third category are related to the ways in which people in different cultures think about and evaluate information.

**14** *Categorization:* Since people cannot attend to all the information they receive, people group similar bits of information into categories. Different cultures may put the identical piece of information in different categories. This causes confusion when people who use different sets of categories must interact.

**15** *Differentiation:* Information in areas which are important to people becomes more highly refined or differentiated. As a result, new categories may be formed. Outsiders may not differentiate information in the same way as insiders, thus causing confusion over seemingly small details.

**16** *Ingroup–outgroup distinctions:* People the world over divide people into ingroups—those with whom they are comfortable and can discuss their concerns—and outgroups—those who are kept at a distance. People entering other cultures must recognize that they will often be considered outgroup members, and that there will be behaviors associated with ingroup membership in which they will never participate.

**17** *Learning styles:* The style in which people learn best may differ from culture to culture. Teachers must be able to adapt their instruction to their students' preferred learning styles if they are to help them achieve to their fullest.

**18** *Attribution:* People observe the behavior of others and reflect upon their own behavior. Judgments about the causes of behavior are called *attributions*. Effective intercultural interaction is facilitated when people can make *isomorphic* (shared, or agreed-on) attributions.

These eighteen themes serve to describe and explain intercultural interactions and misunderstandings in highly diverse settings. As we have said, preparation for all the possible types of intercultural interactions one might encounter is impossible, even in a long-term education and training program concerned with one specific culture. But it is becoming clear that people can be prepared for the similarities in experience. People's emotions *will* be aroused to such an extent that at times they may be incapable of objectively dealing with the task at hand. What it is that causes these emotional upheavals can be identified, studied, and understood. That is the primary purpose of the eighteen-theme culture-general framework.

At least three controlled studies have looked at the impact of the culture-general framework in intercultural settings. Broaddus used the eighteen-theme framework with an undergraduate group of social psychology students.[5] Ilola employed culture-general training in the preparation of undergraduate education majors.[6] Cushner tested the effectiveness of the culture-general framework with a multinational group of adolescent exchange students about to live in New Zealand on a year-abroad high school exchange program.[7]

Results of these studies show the culture-general framework to be quite effective for teaching concepts of cross-cultural interaction and adjustment. However, such learning is but a small part of intercultural training: subsequent behavior change is critical. In these studies, those who had culture-general training were better able to apply the concepts learned to their own intercultural interactions than were members of the control groups. Those with training also experienced less culture shock as measured by responses on a culture shock adjustment inventory. In addition, increased levels of empathy toward others have been identified in those using the culture-general framework. But perhaps most promising is that students trained using the culture-general framework demonstrate more skill at solving interpersonal problems in an intercultural setting than do those who do not receive the training. Trained individuals perceive themselves to be in better control of their environment and are more confident and better equipped to take control when faced with problems. These results suggest that individuals who have worked with the culture-general themes develop a vocabulary and framework which they can apply to their own experiences. Within this framework, concepts related to cultural knowledge and cross-cultural interaction do not remain a "secret." Rather, one develops the intellectual tools needed to discuss and examine these intangibles.

In this chapter, we will begin to look closely at how some of the eighteen themes interact, paying particular attention to people's emotional responses to their intercultural encounters.

## PEOPLE'S EMOTIONAL EXPERIENCES

Most people expect that they will be faced with unfamiliar behavior and customs when interacting with people from other backgrounds. They are not as prepared, however, for the impact these interactions will have on their feelings—on their anxieties, emotions, prejudices, and sense of belonging—what psychologists call their *affective experiences.* Remember how we described the initial stages of the U-curve of adjustment in Chapter 2. Very early in any intercultural situation, people will experience intense feelings. These cannot be avoided—and we are not sure that they should be. People can, however, be prepared to better anticipate, understand, and accommodate typical as well as idiosyncratic reactions and thus to cope with potentially stressful situations in a more positive manner.

In the field of intercultural and international relations it is quite common to hear of people experiencing what has become known as *culture shock.* The words often conjure up images of failure to adjust to an overseas or intercultural environment; disorientation; anxiety; and a myriad of strategies chosen to cope with the stressful situation. Culture shock is seen by many as a disease, a failure to adjust to the demands of living in an unfamiliar environment.

Culture shock, however, is not a disease suffered by an unsuccessful few. It is experienced by nearly everyone who makes a successful intercultural adjustment. Culture shock implies a disorientation that occurs whenever someone moves from their known, comfortable surroundings to an environment which is significantly different and in which their needs are not easily met. A significant number of children in our schools may experience the equivalent of culture shock when they enter the classroom from a home environment where they have been socialized in a manner which is different from that expected of them in the school.

People adjusting to new cultures or environments call upon a wide range of strategies in their attempt to make sense out of their world and to work in the new setting. Characteristic of individuals and institutions able to change and to accommodate diversity is a certain degree of flexibility. When an individual or institution can modify its behavior as the circumstances demand, the chance of successful adaptation and task effectiveness is increased. Those people and institutions that cannot make the necessary adjustments become debilitated, stressed, and are generally unable to function effectively. Attaining goals becomes difficult at best. (Unfortunately for many children from minority backgrounds, the school, as an institution, tends to be highly resistant to change and relatively inflexible in its approach to differences.)

Common to all people are the strong emotions which accompany the experience of culture shock. These emotions can be extremely draining, and are often cited as the reason people begin to enter the hostility stage of the U-curve. The human being can only accommodate so much stress.

### Some Comments on Stress

It is common today to hear people speak of being highly stressed or living in a very "tense" society. The many demands placed on people as they try to manage their daily lives and cope in a rapidly changing society have their impact on the individual.

Selye defines *stress* as the "nonspecific response of the body to any demand made upon it."[8] For instance, a new teacher anticipating a first meeting with the parents of a child who has Down's syndrome and has been the object of ridicule by classmates may feel acute anxiety. This might manifest itself in a variety of ways, including a "cold sweat," a knot in the stomach, or a racing pulse. This is called a *nonspecific* response because it is similar to the feeling you would experience when confronted by any sort of threat—such as the feeling you have when preparing to give a speech in front of hundreds of people, or when a speeding car is bearing down on you. While the intensity of the reaction will depend on how competent the person feels to deal with the specific situation, in general, stress accompanies any pressure or demand when the individual perceives his or her adaptive capabilities as insufficient.

Selye's concept of a *general adaptation syndrome* is often used to explore the various stages of stress and its impact on the individual.[9] In the first stage of the general adaptation syndrome the body's defensive forces are readied for action. In this alarm reaction, certain signals are sent throughout the body via a variety of chemical or nervous pathways. Certain activating hormones, among them adrenalin which brings about the "fight or flight" reaction, are released. These first-stage reactions are aroused in most novel situations for which the individual does not feel adequately prepared—from the point of view of an "outsider" or newcomer, the cross-cultural encounter may be overloaded with novelty.

The second stage of the general adaptation syndrome is characterized by resistance. In this stage, the heart beats faster, breathing quickens, blood-clotting mechanisms prepare the system for a potential loss of blood, muscles are tensed, the actions of the digestive system are slowed, and sugar is pulled out of the liver into the bloodstream to provide extra energy to meet the emergency.[10] Simultaneously, another set of hormones are released, some of which can have such long-term debilitating effects as gastric and duodenal ulcers. The body is now ready to take vigorous action; it is in a state of physical readiness, mental alertness, and high emotion.

The problem with these types of general responses is that they are no longer adaptive in the kinds of situations in which they generally arise. These reactions originally evolved in response to the human animal's needs in the natural environment. Today, the "danger" to which most people usually respond to is not to their physical safety, but rather to their self-esteem or social self. As Barna has stated, we are "saving one's face instead of one's skin."[11]

Stressful interpersonal situations usually require understanding, empathy, and calm deliberation in order to better understand the miscommunications and misperceptions that may occur. General reactions which accompany stressful situations often get in the way of effective interaction. The length of time one remains in this readiness and resistance situation, and the speed with which one successfully "releases" after the perceived need to mobilize passes, will affect the long-term wear and tear on the body.

It takes a considerable period of time in a new setting before events become predictable and the individual feels competent to deal with whatever happens. Until this stage is reached people may be highly aroused. In this state they may not be able to rest or let down their guard. (Oddly, people are more likely to take on greater loads of stress than they are to search for ways to alleviate the problem.) A hazard of remaining in this state of arousal is that it may cause people to perceive a wide range of relatively non-dangerous circumstances as threatening.[12] People generally cannot be objective under such circumstances, and, having a tendency to perceive events as threatening, may respond in a defensive manner. Unless a person handles this stage well, the third stage, exhaustion, will occur.

The third stage of the general adaptation syndrome is *exhaustion*. This occurs whenever the resistance stage is so severe and long-lasting that a person's store of "adaptation energy" is depleted. This exhaustion phase is of great value to the body.[13] Selye says that depression is needed to "prevent us from carrying on too long at top speed."[14] If the individual does not let this stage occur as needed, and continues forcing additional stimuli and high levels of activity, recuperation will not occur.

Barna provides a nonmedical example which may help to paint a clearer picture.[15] Suppose the car in front of you makes a sudden stop and you are forced to brake quickly to avoid an accident. The braking response is the specific action that would help you appropriately cope with the impending threat and reduce the likelihood of danger. The nonspecific, systemic response that begins when danger is sensed is also present and should also be disengaged, just as you take your foot off the brake pedal when it is no longer needed. The problem, however, is that it takes a considerably longer time for the entire system to disengage than for you to remove your foot from the brake: time for the heart to stop pounding, the muscles to relax, and hormones to be metabolized. Continuing to drive in traffic will cause the body to remain in this highly stressed stage for some time, as if the threat were constantly there. The "wear and tear" on the body may be significant.

We have been speaking of stressors as stimuli which elicit the need for adaptation. Lazarus defines *stressors* as "any demands which tax the system, whatever it is, a physiological system, a social system, or a psychological system."[16] The social and psychological demands of living and working with diversity can elicit the stress response. For that reason, we must begin to address the emotional responses people experience in their daily interpersonal and intercultural interactions. We can look to specific causes of this stress response and begin to understand them and how to better cope with them. We must keep in mind, however, that in the diverse school setting, teachers, students, administrators, and parents will all have their emotions aroused for a variety of reasons at a variety of times.

## Anxiety

There are numerous circumstances in which people encounter behavior that occurs for unknown or unclear reasons: acceptance into and rejection from various groups often happens for unknown reasons; students exhibit behavior which is unexpected or assumed to be uncalled for at the moment; parents may respond to children in a manner which the teacher believes interferes with the education and best interests of the child; community members may voice concerns about a proposed curriculum change on the basis of an unknown agenda. These situations, and others like them, will cause individuals to reflect on their own behaviors and to decide what changes might be needed to meet their goals. All this thinking about necessary changes and ventures into the unknown almost invariably results in anxiety.

*Anxiety* is an uncomfortable feeling caused by some object or event, often resulting in a desire to avoid that object or event. Anxiety differs from *fear* in that fear is specific; one can have a fear of snakes, a fear of heights, or a fear of tunnels. Anxiety is less specific; one is aware of some uncomfortable feeling but is usually unable to identify the exact cause. People can be anxious about an upcoming test, for instance, but unable to pinpoint the exact reason.

*Anxiety* is a better term than *fear* to describe people's feelings about working with those who are different from themselves. Usually people are aware that they are upset, but they cannot explain why. Once they become anxious, people report a variety of psychological symptoms, including working under a great deal of tension, frequent worry, being afraid that people might hurt them, and occasional feelings of uselessness. When among those from one's own group, people are better able to verbalize reasons for their feelings, reasons such as fear of rejection by a friend or uncertainty as to how to go about making suggestions to those in authority. People's ability to verbalize their feelings when in their own social group lessens the unpleasant emotional reactions which accompany anxiety.

When working with unfamiliar people, neither the reasons for one's anxious feelings nor the positive behaviors to resolve those feelings are often available. In such circumstances, people may adopt ineffective methods to cope with their anxiety, such as focusing on somatic symptoms (for example, stomach aches) or avoiding the situation altogether.

Anxiety can occur in many different contexts in the school setting and may be expressed in a multitude of ways. Let's go back to Alden High School and take a glimpse into a classroom.

---

### Critical Incident: The Students Are Anxious, but Why?

Mary McConnell was exhausted! Normally she could cope with the challenges of being homeroom teacher for ninth-graders, but today had been extremely difficult. All morning her class had taken standardized tests and they had been "impossible." They had taken a long time to settle down in their seats; everyone had to sharpen their two required pencils, and halfway through the process, the pencil sharpener had mysteriously broken.

One boy just would not stop talking and cracking jokes from the back of the room. He was often encouraged by remarks and giggles from the girls around him. Two girls had flatly refused to take the tests, and Ms. McConnell had sent them to the principal's office. Three students had marked their answer sheets in patterns without even reading the questions. Ms. McConnell had tried to enlist the students' genuine participation, but they had refused. Two of them then put their heads down on their desks and would not respond to her at all.

Mary McConnell knew she was facing a high level of resistance in the room. However, she could not understand what was going on. Can you? Select the response which, to you, best explains the situation.

**1** The students were very anxious because they didn't like the strict time limits of standardized tests.

**2** These students had scored low on standardized tests in past years, and because they expected to do so again, felt quite anxious.

**3** When the pencil sharpener broke and the students couldn't sharpen their pencils, they became anxious about marking their answer sheets correctly.

**4** The students did not like having their daily classroom routine interrupted by such a long activity.

## Rationales

**1** You chose number 1. There is a grain of truth to this. For some students who work slowly, strict time limits can be unnerving. In addition, people from some cultures do not have the same orientation to time as others may. However, there is more going on in this case. Please choose again.

**2** You chose number 2. This is the best response for these circumstances. By the time these students from the inner city have reached high school, they may have had many negative experiences with standardized tests, which tend to reflect white, middle-class culture and suburban school settings. Their expectations of failure are strong. While most probably could not verbalize the reasons for their reactions, they probably felt that they wouldn't do well and therefore may have tried to avoid the situation and/or relieve their tensions. That is the behavior that Ms. McConnell was seeing. Teachers need to be sensitive to the anxieties of students who have regularly had the experience of receiving low grades and test scores.

**3** You chose number 3. While this may be of concern to a few students, it does not realistically explain the generalized resistance Mary McConnell felt. Please choose again.

**4** You chose number 4. On the contrary, students usually enjoy interruptions to the daily routine. They may not have enjoyed this particular type of interruption, however. There is more going on here. Please choose again.

If Ms. McConnell had been sensitive to the issue at hand, she would have directly addressed the students' anxiety about test taking. The fact that she did not, and that the students did not identify the cause of their uneasiness, was the direct cause of the students' undirected misbehavior. Billy Davis, who grew up in a family of migrant farm-workers, speaks of the irrelevance of tests, and of the practical experiences assumed in the classroom, to his own home life, and of the anxiety he suffered as a result.

> No expert in measurement knows better than I the wishful thinking inherent in the concept of culture-free testing. I have sat with cold, damp hands, holding my breath, hoping the teacher would not call on me. . . . We never had a private bathroom, or a kitchen sink, or an oven. I never owned a tricycle, bicycle, or pets (stray dogs are a separate category). We did not "go on vacations," "have company," "take lessons," or "pack luggage,". . . . For years I owned no hairbrush, toothbrush, nail file, or pajamas. I could go on. In short, the ordinary middle class world was strange to me and its terms frightened me.[17]

Uncertainty seems to be the greatest cause of anxiety and its accompanying reactions. The probability of uncertainty seems greatest when there is a significant degree of ambiguity in the external situation. Intercultural interactions are fraught with uncertainty and ambiguity.[18]

Sarason cites three situations which elicit responses of threat, challenge, or inability to cope;[19] they are: (1) ambiguous situations where individuals must structure their own task requirements and personal expectations, (2) well-defined situations where the individual feels unable to respond adequately, and (3) situations defined in idiosyncratic ways where the individual does not have readily accessible patterned behavior to call upon. Groen and Bastiaans find the common denominator of psychosocial stressors in western society to be the difficulty people have in anticipating future events and their limited ability to modify their behavior to meet such events.[20] Again, uncertainty occurs because individuals have no readily identifiable formula or script to guide their actions.

There are many causes of anxiety for students; test-taking is just one. The need to make friends and be accepted is a high stressor for some children, as is the constant threat of failure which hangs like a sword of Damocles over the heads of others. Anxiety-producing contexts in which children live are often unobservable to teachers and other adults and many arise from circumstances over which they have no control. The sense of duty and obligation to those left behind, similar to the survivor guilt identified by survivors of the Nazi holocaust,[21] has been documented to be a cause of great stress and anxiety among many immigrants from war-torn Central America.[22] Many of these immigrant youths, while among the most successful of all the subgroups of Hispanics in the United States, live with the knowledge that while they were sent out of Central America, their siblings and parents had to remain. Concern for the safety and future of those left behind, or grief for the dead, becomes a hardship which consumes those who had the good fortune to have been able to leave.

Clearly, students' anxiety affects classroom management and discipline. Kindsvatter, looking at discipline more as a process than as a ''product,'' presents a four-phase model for a comprehensive program of discipline.[23] The four phases are prevention, control maintenance, control intervention, and behavior adjustment. In the *prevention* phase, the most important, an effective teacher can reduce inappropriate behavior by creating the optimum classroom conditions. To do this requires knowledge of basic human needs or drives and of the consequences if they are not satisfactorily met. After physical needs are satisfied, people generally need confirmation of identity, stimulation, and security. The negative counterpart of these three needs is a sense of anonymity, boredom, and anxiety. In the classroom setting, if children do not feel secure, accepted, and comfortable, they will become anxious over how well they are doing, how they are perceived by others, and begin to question why they are in school.

However, anxiety should not be perceived only as a negative phenomenon; it does have a positive side. Consider this example: before an exam, if you experience too little anxiety you will probably not study enough. On the other hand, if you are experiencing too much anxiety, it may debilitate you; you may become so anxious that you cannot study. A moderate amount of anxiety encourages people to seek out the appropriate behaviors so they can achieve their goals. A moderate amount of anxiety may encourage new teachers to learn as much as they can about their new students and their parents, may encourage a principal to learn what he or she can about the staff, or may prompt students to study about and interact with those from other backgrounds.

## Ambiguity

Ambiguity, cited above as a major contributor to stress, is also presented in the culture-general framework.[24] *Ambiguity* here generally refers to the conditions which occur when two or more interpretations of a given situation are possible, or when there is a certain degree of uncertainty.

One of the major problems people face in ambiguous situations is that they lack sufficient information or experience to make an appropriate judgment. Sometimes they are aware of the choices available to them but are unable to choose. More often, people have no real clue as to what the various possibilities might be; however, they are aware that some choice must be made. When an important decision must be made and the relevant information is not available, stress and frustration may result. To overcome this, people must consciously choose to make guesses to ''fill in'' the context or to set up judgmental standards. People frequently fill in information without realizing they have done so. If the information they fill in is inappropriate, an entirely different set of problems may result.

Teachers and students are wise to be aware that in intercultural settings they will probably be operating with less information than usual, yet will still be required to make decisions of some significance. Students from different backgrounds may incorrectly interpret cues from their peers or teachers, leading to misunderstandings. Teachers may misinterpret students' behavior. Students, parents, and teachers may all be operating under different assumptions, a situation that can be especially confusing and frustrating. Developing an open mind so that one can accept divergent or unfamiliar meanings can alleviate a great deal of this stress. Patience and the ability to withhold judgment or check one's attributions will also help. Consider the following situation, which could easily occur in any school experiencing an influx of international students.

### Critical Incident: Face-Saving

Mrs. McMillen teaches an advanced-level course in Algebra–Trigonometry. Her class of twenty has some of the school's top students. For the first grading period, one of her students, a 16-year-old from India who is in his second year of U.S. education, received a B. The day after report cards were issued this student's father requested an immediate meeting with the principal. At the meeting the father was obviously quite upset with his son's grade because his son had always achieved A's and had led last year's honor roll with a perfect 4.0 grade-point average.

The principal explained that, according to Mrs. McMillen, the student had earned a C on one particularly difficult test, causing his average to drop to a B. He also stated that Mrs. McMillen had said that the boy was one of her best students and that he could still get an A in the course.

At the end of the meeting, the father announced that he wanted his son transferred from the advanced level of the course to the regular level of the course. The principal asked the father to postpone his request for one day while he considered the situation further.

What would you suggest the principal do to help resolve this problem?

1 Realizing the importance of this student's grades to the father, the principal should talk to Mrs. McMillen to see if there is some way to justify changing the grade to an A.

2 Refuse to discuss the issue any further and tell the father to stop interfering in his son's education.

**3** Collect all the student's homework and tests and point out all shortcomings to the father.

**4** Talk to the student privately and encourage him to try to reason with his father.

Here we have a typical case of an ambiguous situation. Teachers know (or think they know) the purpose of grades. Teachers also think they know what parents expect regarding the grading of students. Here, the teacher has assigned a grade which seems unacceptable to a parent. A decision is being forced on the principal. Neither party has complete knowledge or understanding of the system and assumptions under which the other lives.

Rationales for the four choices follow.

**Rationales**

**1** You chose number 1. Although this may seem like a challenge to Mrs. McMillen's judgment, this will probably be the best solution to the problem. The father's emphasis on having his son achieve perfect grades rests on his desire to maintain the high "image" his family has attained. Having his son get an A in this and other courses is thus a "face-saving" issue for this Indian family, a common concern in many Eastern cultures. The principal, aware of the importance of this grade for the family's private and public image, might, therefore, be justified in discussing with Mrs. McMillen some way to change it, at least for this grading period. Presuming her ultimate agreement, this would be the most sensitive way to deal with the situation.

**2** You chose number 2. This would probably not help the situation. In fact, to attack the father for his concern would be highly counterproductive. More attention should be given to the cause of the father's intense feelings about grades. Please choose again.

**3** You chose number 3. This seems logical, but it will only reinforce the real basis of this problem. The student's father places a high premium on his son's grades because they reflect the worth of the entire family. Pointing out his son's math weaknesses will make the situation worse. Look elsewhere for an explanation of the cause and solution of this problem and try again.

**4** You chose number 4. This could exacerbate an already touchy situation. The problem at this point is not with the student, but with the father. In addition, the cultural background of the family would probably not lend itself to this type of plan. The son is in no position to challenge his father or to persuade him to change his mind. Please choose again.

Ambiguity is a difficult problem to cope with, but there are ways to deal with it beyond passive acceptance and a fatalistic attitude. The trait *tolerance for ambiguity* has been identified as one of the key characteristics of a successful and well adjusted individual in an intercultural setting (see Chapter 2). Ambiguity can be very uncomfortable. It can also be a stretching and enriching experience.

## ORDERING ONE'S WORLD

Many of the emotional responses discussed above can be traced to our thought processing—how people interpret the world around them. While these processes are cultural universals, one's socialization does color the manner in which they unfold.

In a rapidly changing and fast-moving world people's thinking cannot remain rigid and unchanged. Rather, it is necessary to be able to acquire information and new skills relatively quickly in order to meet the demands that face us daily.

## Categorization

We have already discussed people's need to simplify their world, to sift through the vast array of stimuli that constantly present themselves, and to organize that information into categories that make sense. This process, called *categorization,* is a universal one. However, as we have seen, people from different cultural backgrounds do not order their worlds in the same manner.

For example, most American educators divide the school day into academic subjects, special subjects (physical education, music, art), and lunch and recess. European educators might divide the school day solely by academics; the various special activities have no place in the formal school day. If European children participate in sports it is usually outside the school context.

Ethnicity, gender, religion, or handicapping condition are examples of categories which help people adjust to their complex world. The boundaries which separate groups, however, are not always rigid, but can frequently be manipulated to attain one's goals and to serve one's needs. For instance, students may use the category caucasian most of the time when describing themselves, but may switch to Irish or Polish if scholarships for people of these ancestries suddenly become available. Similarly, a student who has a slight handicapping condition might, in most instances, place little emphasis on this condition. However, if scholarship monies become available, or special circumstances dictate, that student might bring this condition to the forefront.

The concept of the *prototype image* is a critical one in the analysis of categories. For most categories which people form, there is one set of attributes or criteria which best characterizes the members of the category. In other words, there is a clear example of what the category encompasses. This becomes a "summary" of the group and is what is most often thought of when the category is mentioned. For instance, when asked to think about a bird, a certain prototypic image comes to one's mind. For most readers of this book, the prototypic image of a bird might be a creature about 8 or 9 inches long (beak to tail feathers), brown or perhaps reddish in color, that has feathers, flies, and nests in trees. The image you conjured up probably was not of a turkey, penguin, ostrich, or even a chicken. Yet each of these has all the critical attributes which characterize members of the bird family; they all have feathers, hollow or lightweight bones, and beaks, and lay eggs.

Now consider your prototypic image of the students you will teach. Stop for a moment and conjure up in your mind what your typical student looks like. What are your students capable of doing? How do they behave? What are they most likely to study? In reality, very few of your students will have much in common with this typical, or prototype, image you have of a student. Consider the "average" American classroom. It may not be quite what you have in mind (recall the demographics presented in Chapter 1). Your task as you work through this book is to broaden your categories for students, their capabilities, and how you will interact with them as a teacher.

Once people have learned to unite certain critical elements to form categories, they tend to use that category in their thinking, while paying little, if any, attention to the elements that make it up. Similarities are emphasized; there is little awareness of the differences between members of the category. This is what often occurs in interactions with other people.

## Stereotypes

While usually thought of as negative, stereotypes are really nothing more than categories. In the most general sense, the word *stereotype* refers to any sort of summary generalization that obscures the differences within any group.[25] Stereotypes exist because they enable the acquisition of a significant amount of information in a relatively short period of time. Often, certain characteristics attributed to groups of people are so central to an individual's thinking about those groups that they will be resistant to change even when proved inaccurate. A strong adherence to the stereotypes then often leads to prejudicial behaviors which may be negative, often hostile, and usually are not based on firsthand experience.

In a stressful, quickly changing, ambiguous situation (like many that arise in school and community settings), it is tempting to grasp at any easily available information which helps one interpret the situation. Once a stereotyped label is attached to a group of people, any individual person associated with that group is likely to be defined by the stereotype. While it may be tempting to use stereotypic information at such times, teachers must be cautious about making decisions based on such information, and must be careful about the accuracy of their stereotypes. Like other learned behaviors, ways of categorizing and stereotyping can be changed, expanded, and adapted if one is aware of the processes at play. Stereotypes are disconcerting for both parties in any interaction. Consider the following incident.

### Critical Incident: The First Days

Andre is a 23-year-old student teacher assigned to work with Mrs. Lipton, a social studies teacher at Alden High. African-American and from a middle-class background, Andre always prided himself on knowing a lot about people at all socioeconomic levels and from many different ethnic groups. Andre would especially like to relate well to the black students, and he intends to show them that he is really one of them.

While walking down the hall on his first day in school, Andre sees a group of black males standing near a group of lockers. They are wearing their typical casual clothes—jeans, t-shirt, and so forth—Andre is in his teaching clothes—shirt, tie, and jacket. Andre greets the group with "What's happening, bro?" They look at him and continue with their own conversation. Andre tries to strike up a conversation by asking about any good "rap" groups in the school, saying that he has done some "bad rappin' " himself. The boys eye him up and down, then slowly move on down the hall. Andre is puzzled. He'd thought that they would respond to his approach and would see him as a "brother."

The next day, Andre sees the same group again and begins to approach them. Seeing him coming, one of the group steps forward and quite sarcastically says, "Hey Bro! You be down in Room 104 (the teacher's lounge), not in my face!" Then the group walks away. Andre does not understand the group's obvious hostility and rejection.

Why do you think the students rejected Andre's attempts to be friendly?

  1 The group feels that Andre's clothes are too "different." They just can't relate to this different looking adult.
  2 The group does not accept Andre because they see him as a teacher—an outsider, regardless of his color.
  3 Andre's use of Black English is obviously incorrect. This immediately labels him as a phoney—someone who cannot be trusted.
  4 Andre came on too hard. He was seen as pushy and was rejected for this.

Rationales

  1 You selected number 1. It is very true that adolescents are very conscious of "looking right" and "fitting in." It is possible that the students saw Andre's clothing as something foreign to them and he thus became the object of rejection. While this answer is partially correct, there is a more fundamental explanation. Please select another response.
  2 You selected number 2. Although Andre may have been saying all the right things, it seemed to make little, if any, difference. Andre was an adult; a teacher. In the school environment, students put him in the category of authority figure, outsider, someone who, at least at the outset, cannot be trusted. As a teacher, he should not expect to be included as one of the group at their level.
  Their remark telling him he should be in Room 104 indicates that he is a teacher and they expect him to act like one. New teachers, especially student teachers, are usually anxious to be accepted by students. This is normal, especially as they may not be far removed from the lives and concerns of high school students themselves. Given time, Andre can establish the rapport he wants within the course of his interactions in the classroom setting and in other school-related activities, but in the role of teacher—not peer.
  3 You selected number 3. Although Andre is trying very hard to present himself as one of the group, if he is not accurate in his use of language, he will be seen as a phoney and quickly rejected. While this may be a contributing factor in his rejection, there is a better explanation for the group's reaction. Please try again.
  4 You selected number 4. Coming on too hard can be a strong component in rejection from any group. Adolescents, like most other groups, do not want to feel pressured and may be suspicious of anyone who tries too hard to be friendly. A less aggressive approach would probably allow Andre to begin a more natural relationship with the group. While there may be some truth to this explanation, there is an alternative which better captures a more fundamental explanation. Please try again.

## PREJUDICE, ETHNOCENTRISM, AND DISCRIMINATION—THE EMOTIONAL RESPONSE

Discussions of categorization and stereotyping understandably lead to discussion of issues of prejudice and discrimination. It seems to be human nature to surround oneself with others who provide social acceptance and help in times of need.[26] As a result, people spend a considerable amount of time and energy learning the norms of behavior of the groups they want to belong to. One consequence of this is that individuals begin to think that the behaviors they exhibit are "good" and that those of "others" are either not as good, or in fact, are bad. Recall that *ethnocentrism* refers to the tendency people have to make judgments based on their own standards and to apply those standards to others. Allport suggests that underlying the concepts of ethnocentrism and prejudice is the tendency to evaluate others as good or bad based on closely held standards of what constitutes appropriate behavior.[27] When people make judgments about others that are harsh, discriminatory, or involve rejection, such that emotions of anger, disgust, or a desire to avoid contact are felt, then the judgments are called *prejudicial.* The word *prejudice* also implies a lack of much thought or care in making the judgment; people's responses are quick, narrow in scope, and not based on accurate information. Prejudice appears to be a cultural universal; that is, people around the world behave in similar ways toward certain other groups.

Prejudice at first seems like an entirely negative phenomenon. It is easy to judge others' prejudices (and even our own) harshly. But we need to understand that if prejudice did not have a psychological function it would quickly disappear.[28] Just as fear encourages people to prepare for danger or pain makes people aware of some problem that might cause permanent damage, prejudice must serve some adaptive purpose.

Katz suggests that prejudice serves at least four functions.[29] The first function of prejudice is an *adjustment function.* People need to adjust to the complex world in which they live, and if holding certain prejudicial attitudes aids that adjustment, then they will be maintained. For instance, the belief that members of certain minority or handicapped groups are not capable of achieving at a high level means that a teacher will not need to find alternative methods of reaching them. This obviously reduces the work-related responsibilities of the teacher, thus making life a bit easier, but it also often prevents individuals from achieving their full potential.

A second function served by prejudice is the *ego-defensive function.* Katz suggests that people hold certain prejudicial attitudes because they protect self-concepts. If individuals want to think of themselves as academically talented, or perhaps just as good students or teachers—even though they may not be very successful—they may be inclined to view another, more successful group as cheaters. Holding this attitude protects the self-image of these individuals, and they do not have to examine the reasons for their own lack of success. The ego-defensive function also protects a positive view of one's ingroup. Rejection of others then becomes a way of legitimizing one's own viewpoint as well as a way of avoiding the possibility that the others may have a legitimate point of view and standards.

The third function, the *value-expression function,* refers to attitudes people use to project or to demonstrate their own self-image to others. If people believe that they are custodians of the truth about the role of education, for instance, or that the god of their religion is the one true god, then other groups must be incorrect in their thinking. If one's group has attained success through the use of highly valued technology, then those who do not have this technology must be backward. The value-expressive function presents a certain image to the world. The ego-defensive function protects that image through attitudes and behaviors that tend to put blame on others.

Finally, the *knowledge function* has to do with the way information is organized. Some prejudicial attitudes provide knowledge about the world as viewed by people's ingroups. Some groups, for instance, might consider certain outgroup members undesirable peers or romantic partners. Holding these attitudes allows some people to make quick decisions when faced with choices in their daily lives.

There is often a close relationship between the knowledge and adjustment functions. The former has to do with the information that people in one's ingroup believe is important to know and understand, the latter with how people use that information in making decisions. Consider the issue of friendships and romantic relationships referred to above. There can be severe consequences if there are violations of the use of shared knowledge. People can be expelled from their ingroup for entering into relationships with the ''wrong'' partners.

Psychologists generally consider there to be three components of prejudice: cognitive, affective, and behavioral. The phrase *cognitive component* refers to the process of categorization. The affective component is the feelings which accompany one's thoughts about a particular group of people. The affect attached to any statement can, obviously, be positive or negative. It is the affective component which is most often thought of when we think of prejudice. The *behavioral component* is the discriminatory behavior which people who harbor prejudices are capable of directing toward others—especially when the prejudiced people are in positions of power.

Educators can work with each of these dimensions in different ways. We have seen that the categorization process is a cultural universal. As a species we seem to be stuck with it! As educators, about all we can do is be cognizant of this fact, make a point of informing others about it, and perhaps work to broaden one's categories. On the other hand, the affective and behavioral components seem to be within our control, and, therefore, can become a focus for your work in education. Strategies and programs which have demonstrated reduction in negative affect and behavior toward other groups will be presented in Part Three.

## The Ingroup–Outgroup Distinction

One dimension of human behavior common to every culture and group is the division into ingroups and outgroups.[30] *Ingroups* are defined as those people who are psychologically close, comfortable, and trusting of one another, and who prefer to spend considerable time together. Members of an ingroup provide support for each other, can be called upon in time of need, and provide close and warm relationships. *Outgroups* refer to those people who are generally kept at a distance and actively discouraged from becoming members of one's ingroup. In extreme cases, outgroup members are actively discriminated against—kept from jobs, citizenship, and educational opportunities.

One difficulty individuals coming into new situations face is that they are entering a situation in which people have already formed their ingroups. The newcomer has usually left his or her close friends behind and is thus often without an ingroup. Those in the new or hosting group already have their ingroups established, and, ordinarily, are not thinking of adding new members. Think of times when you were new to an area, to a job, or to any group of people. Others already had their groups formed. It was you who spent considerable time meeting new people, ''learning the ropes,'' and trying hard to find your place. A similar situation greets most teachers in new schools; they must find their ingroups among already existing groups of teachers, staff, and students. A good deal of time is often required to establish new ingroups.

At certain times, defining ingroup and outgroup relationships across cultures leads to unexpected feelings. Americans traveling to Greece, for instance, often complain that the locals are extremely ''nosey.'' They want to know everything about the visitors, including a considerable amount of personal information about such things as salary, family, religion, and personal political preferences. Surprised by what Americans consider invasion of their private lives, many inaccurate judgments are made.

Understanding this situation demands knowledge about who is considered a member of the ingroup. For most Americans, members of the ingroup include family and friends. Rarely included are foreigners newly arrived in the country. Among most Greeks, however, ingroup members include family, old friends, and visitors to their country. As a result, the Greeks are offering ingroup membership to newly arrived Americans. And ingroup membership permits mutual access to personal information. The Greeks assume that the Americans will want to participate in discussions that are typical of ingroup membership. What the Greeks consider a compliment (an offer of ingroup membership) is taken as an insult by the Americans (invasion of privacy). An understanding of ingroup–outgroup distinctions would help reduce the problem.

Consider the following experience related by a student attempting to improve her ability to use sign language.

Not long ago I wanted to improve my signing skills. The best way I could think of doing this was to interact with hearing-impaired adults whose primary language was ASL (American Sign Language). With this in mind I decided to join a hearing friend who had regularly attended meetings at the Southsiders Deaf Club, a local social club primarily for adults with hearing impairments.

At the first meeting we attended everyone was warm and welcoming. People eagerly introduced themselves to me, using their speech as much as possible, signing rather slowly to me, and using syntax in their communication which was more ''English-like'' as opposed to ASL syntax.

The next couple of meetings I attended were similar to the first except that the extra efforts made to communicate with me had decreased. I often felt as an outsider. This feeling was new for me. In new situations I usually start conversations. In this situation I became introverted; quiet; often alone. If no one initiated conversation with me I did not interact with them. I avoided eye contact at all costs. In retrospect I realized that because eye contact is extremely important when using a visual language that I was not only being introverted, I was being downright antisocial! Trapped with my own feelings of inadequacy I realized I was sending out a strong signal that I did not want to be engaged in conversation, even though this is not what was intended. Even when I did manage some conversation I asked for considerable clarification and engaged in a great deal of ''nodding and smiling.'' I wasn't fooling anyone. They knew I was struggling and they weren't trying to help me. In fact, they often went to my friend for clarification, using her as an interpreter for me. I really began feeling like my language skills were as a child. Boy, did I feel out of it!

It eventually became a chore to get myself to go to those meetings. I avoided club members when I saw them on the street or in the shops. I felt inadequate, anxious, rude, uncomfortable, and guilty all at the same time. Part of my feelings I now realize were due to my unwillingness to make sufficient effort. I wanted everything to be as smooth as at the first meeting, forgetting that it was I who was the outsider and would have to make the changes in order to fit in. I was also not accustomed to paying so much attention to visual stimuli. My exhaustion after the club meetings might have been due, in part, to the extra effort required to watch all the time. I guess I had to learn to listen with my eyes. This mental exhaustion must be very similar to someone trying to function in an environment where they do not speak the language.[31]

## Belonging—And the Emotional Response

People are inherently social beings. The need to belong is rooted deeply in our social and biological past. For many people, the fear of being excluded from the group—of being an outcast—is far greater than is the fear of dying. In fact, anthropologists have identified the practice of exclusion in some societies as the ultimate punishment. In effect, exclusion from the society *meant* death as the individual no longer existed in the minds of others.

People belong to a variety of social groups. Some memberships are involuntary, such as family, race, or social class; others are more likely to be voluntary, such as political party membership, religious affiliation, and neighborhood. As one progresses through life, the nature and number of the groups one affiliates oneself with changes. But all group affiliations do have certain similarities and provide us with certain benefits. Peplau and Perlman have proposed six needs that are fulfilled by social relationships, and have suggested that different needs are met by different social networks.[32] The six needs are those for

1 *Social integration* (a feeling of shared concerns and activities, commonly provided by family and/or friends;

2 *Attachment* (a sense of security and commitment), which most often comes from a romantic partner or from the family;

3 *Sense of reliable alliance* (assurance of continuing assistance), commonly met by the family or peer group;

4 *Reassurance of worth,* predominantly provided by coworkers, and, to students in school, by teachers and other students;

5 *Guidance,* which may be offered by mentors, teachers, or older kin;

6 *Opportunity to nurture,* provided by offspring or other dependents.

At the center of all affiliative behavior is the need for the self-confirmation, attention, emotional release, esteem, and security that help to provide structure, meaning, and stability in people's lives. Recall that any person belongs to a range of social groups and networks. Some may be characterized by a high degree of intimacy (for instance the family and close friends). These relationships are fundamental to the development of attitudes, values, and emotions. Other, secondary groupings may operate with less personal contact and more formal rules. These (work, community, etc.) may prove important in providing a role and an identity for the individual in the greater social fabric. The needs fulfilled by various groups may overlap to some extent depending on the situation and the personalities involved. Psychologists have shown, for instance, that when people are in situations which cause anxiety they tend to seek out others who might help them interpret their reactions and who will also validate those reactions.

Human beings, thus, find meaning and security by belonging to various networks. When people feel excluded from these networks or their contacts are reduced or altered in some way, they may begin to experience various negative responses, such as feelings of loneliness and alienation, loss of self-esteem, and a decreased sense of direction or purpose. Such deficiencies in social relationships can be both qualitative and quantitative. It is normally the quality of the relationship that most affects the individual, however. For instance, adolescents may have peer groups comprised of many individuals who would be considered "friends." If something happens to cause a separation from one's "best friend," feelings of loneliness, isolation, and perhaps depression may follow. What is considered a deficiency is also highly subjective and will differ for various individuals and groups. Adult caucasians from the United States, for instance, tend to accept separation from their parents and siblings more readily than Hispanics, who generally carry strong attachments to their whole family throughout their lives.

Isolation from a group due to social incompetence may be just as profound as that which arises from physical separation. In the cross-cultural context, isolation is extremely likely due to lack of language and social skills required to communicate effectively in another cultural context. Whatever the cause of the isolation, psychologists tell us that people tend to react in the same manner; they become more negative, rejecting, self-deprecating, self-absorbed, less responsive, and perhaps hostile. Consider the following incident.

---

### Critical Incident: Rosita Feels Like an Outcast

Rosita Gomez arrived in the United States 2 months ago from El Salvador. She is an orphan being sponsored by an American family. Before her arrival, her American parents went to Alden High School and provided the administrators and faculty with information about her situation. To make her adjustment easier, a number of teachers organized a group of students to act as sponsors for Rosita. The students were to teach her about the school and community and help her with transition problems, as well as offer friendship.

In the last 2 months, the students have helped Rosita in school and have been friendly to her. They have encouraged her to join various clubs, to become involved in student council, and to attend after school extra-help sessions whenever needed. Rosita, though, is often left out of students' social activities such as parties, group movie dates, and volleyball games and thinks she is being treated as an outcast. She feels lonely and afraid. This confuses the Alden High students and teachers very much as they have put out so much effort to make Rosita feel as much at home as possible.

How might you explain this situation?

1 Rosita, having had such a major transition in her life recently, is magnifying the situation. Once she gets over her initial culture shock she will feel better.

2 The students do not like Rosita and are trying to have as little contact with her as possible.

3 The students feel they have been put upon by their teachers, and are taking it out on Rosita.

4 The students' social activities usually involve only a small group of people who are very familiar with each other. Rosita would not "fit in" well with this group and is therefore not encouraged to attend.

### Rationales

1 You chose number 1. The circumstances of Rosita's life might make some people overly sensitive in a new situation. She could very well be experiencing the phenomenon often referred to as *culture shock*. However, culture shock is a very general term which refers to an overall reaction to a complex series of events, so to use the term by itself

is often not very useful. There is something more specific going on here. Please choose again.

2 You chose number 2. The students are having what appears to be extensive contact with Rosita in school. If they did not like her, they would probably forgo school contact as well. There is a better explanation. Please choose again.

3 You chose number 3. While it does take a considerable amount of time and effort to help anyone adjust to a new environment, if they felt put upon, the students would most likely not help Rosita at all, school included. There is another explanation. Please choose again.

4 You chose number 4. In every culture there exist ingroups, groups of people who are comfortable with each other, share similar values, and seek each other's company. Ingroups allow people to share their concerns, laugh and joke about problems as a way to reduce tensions, and generally just let their hair down. The students in this situation represent such an ingroup. Rosita has left her ingroup behind in El Salvador and wants—indeed, needs—to be part of a new ingroup. The students do not see Rosita as one of their ingroup, at least not yet. She would not understand most of their jokes, does not have the intimate and extensive knowledge of others that this group shares, and would not enter into conversation easily. The students, thus, do not invite Rosita to share in their social activities. Rosita's nonmembership in an ingroup makes her feel like an outcast. The formation of ingroups is a naturally occurring phenomenon, and they do provide support and intimacy for their members. Not belonging to an ingroup, Rosita is missing a substantial support system so needed during her difficult transition to a new culture. This is the best answer.

## The Attribution Process

As we have seen the attribution process can be a source of misunderstanding and conflict in intercultural settings. We looked at an example of a typical misunderstanding based on misattribution in Chapter 2 (page 33). In that case, a teacher made a wrong judgment of a student based on eye contact. The teacher judged the child to be disrespectful when in fact the child was merely acting as he had been socialized to act: that is, demonstrating respect by *avoiding* the eye contact.

Another situation, this one more typical in the university context, revolves around learning style and is not uncommon in the experience of foreign student advisors in the United States.[33] Say a graduate student from Nigeria has a research paper assigned to him. The professor, finding in the paper a collection of paragraphs copied verbatim from a variety of textbooks and other resources, grades the paper F and writes *plagiarized* across the top. In most American universities, plagiarism demands some form of disciplinary action. Since this case involves a student from overseas, the professor first calls in the foreign student advisor. The professor may ask, ''Is there something else going on here that I do not understand? I don't want to see this student expelled from school.'' The professor should be commended for showing some attributional ambiguity. She does not know for certain if the attribution should be the one that she would make with an American student, ''He got caught cheating,'' or if there is another explanation which might indicate a less severe problem. In fact, there is, and it is related to the way this student has learned to present information. This person comes from a culture which tells him that knowledge is not necessarily attached to the developer of that knowledge. While

Euro-American students are trained to associate knowledge with people (e.g., relativity theory with Einstein), students from many other cultures are not necessarily expected to constantly make this association. Knowledge may be considered "open" and usable by anyone without constant reference to those who developed that knowledge. When the foreign student writes a paper without citation, he or she is employing a strategy familiar in his own society, although writing without citation is considered plagiarism in Euro-American institutions.

The fundamental attribution error (see Chapter 2) is prevalent in such situations. Recall that people have a tendency to place a "situational" attribution on themselves and a "trait" attribution on others. This tendency is probably more prevalent in cross-cultural situations because there is so much behavior that is unfamiliar to both parties in any interaction. With so many new behaviors being observed, even people who are aware of the attribution process at play in intercultural situations cannot always make correct attributions. People need to respond quickly to situations as they arise. Many attributions will also be wrong simply because people do not have all the information they need about the other culture to make valid conclusions.

People are well advised to take situational factors into account when making attributions. These factors include the influence of other people on one's behavior, or time pressures which force one to hurry. Situational factors also include prior experiences, such as the cultural influences that have helped to shape an individual. People are able to make situational judgments about themselves because they have the needed information about the pressures of their environment and their personal histories. This information is usually not readily available when making attributions about others. Thus, trait attributions are made. In the example above, the student would be labeled a cheater.

In American culture, success and failure are typically attributed to four factors: native ability, effort, difficulty of task, and luck.[34] Native ability and effort seem to be the most dominant factors. People have a tendency to explain successes in terms of "I," while they explain failure in terms of "they."[35] That is, when a person succeeds, the success is explained by one's skill. When one loses, the failure is explained in terms of "their" luck or unfair actions. Parents tend to explain their children's successes by referring to their own good parenting skills and personal sacrifices, while they tend to explain their children's failures by referring to "bad schools" or "ineffective teachers." Similarly, teachers explain successes in terms of their own efforts and failures in terms of "that awful class."

Hunter and Barker provide some examples of how the invalid attribution of failure to native ability is dangerous.[36] They suggest that we are a "math phobic" nation, not due to lack of native ability, but because students are taught to mechanically manipulate numbers, not to understand mathematical concepts. Such sayings as "Yours is not to question why, just invert and multiply" express this attitude. Many people also believe, as a result of their school experiences, that they have little or no artistic ability. Lane and Walberg suggest that many of the problems children from families struggling with poverty encounter in school are not due to genetics or native ability, but to lack of language development.[37] It is clear that when faulty attributions are made regarding students' native ability, one's effectiveness as a teacher is reduced.

Of the four contributors to success and failure named above, the only one completely under our control is effort; people cannot control ability, task difficulty, or luck. People tend to put forth effort if they believe that their effort will influence the outcome. Research on high achievers in such diverse areas as athletics, the arts, mathematics, and business suggest that successful people put forth enormous effort.[38] If students or teachers perceive that their success will be determined by either ability, task difficulty, or luck, they may tend to limit the effort put forth. If they perceive that a considerable amount of their success will be determined by effort, and they believe they can control this, they stand a far better chance of meeting with success.

In order to improve our ability to make isomorphic attributions, we must understand how and why attributions are made. One important contributor to an attribution can be a vivid and colorful incident in which the individual is involved.[39] Vivid, personalized incidents tend to overwhelm one's information-processing capacity, and often carry more weight than they should in the formation of a final attribution. Consider this example.

> John is excited about teaching in a highly integrated urban school setting known for its high-achieving and involved student body. He feels well prepared in matters of multicultural education, is able to suspend judgment about others in most instances, and has extensive experience in cross-cultural settings. He is fully aware of the tendency teachers have to talk about students in the lounge between classes. He has just returned from reviewing student files and was especially impressed by the standardized test scores, personal statement of goals, and parental desires of one of the students, Bob Williams. He is looking forward to working with this student. On his mentioning this in the staff lounge, one of the teachers remarks on how much trouble this student is: his loud mouth, his wisecracks, and his general lack of interest in school events. What should John do? His initial judgments were favorable, although now they are colored by this intense verbal input from his peers.

Most people have a strong tendency to place a great deal of weight on personal experience. Our new teacher has now had a vivid experience, in which information about a student he didn't actually know was given to him orally, probably delivered in an emphatic tone and with some colorful gestures—all quite different from the dull reading in the files. But look at the situation more closely. The teacher is one person. The file was compiled over many years and includes valid, reliable data from standardized tests as well as personal statements from the student and parents about his hopes for his education. John now has information from many individuals, plus the one teacher in the lounge. The weight of the evidence is still in favor of the contents of the file. However, the vivid personal experience in the teachers' lounge is likely to have more weight than it should. The tendency to react to vivid events is especially strong in intercultural settings due to their ambiguity, to the need people have to make judgments, and to the anxiety one is often experiencing. People should ask whether they are overreacting to one colorful incident, or whether there is other information which might be used before coming to a conclusion.

## A MAP WHEN THERE IS NO ROAD

Chapter 3 has introduced a culture-general framework designed to provide a structure for understanding the range of experiences one might encounter in intercultural interactions. Such a framework is especially useful for teachers as it is impossible to predict with any certainty the exact cultural patterns of individuals with whom you will have extensive contacts. In fact, it is most probable that all of us will continue to have extensive interactions with a variety of people from many different backgrounds.

Regardless of the particular people involved in any interaction there will be certain emotional experiences to be faced, as well as a knowledge base that must be acquired. The culture-general framework introduced in this chapter can help sensitize people to the variety of experiences they are certain to encounter, whether they are teachers in a diverse classroom or community, students new to a particular school or region of the country, or new teachers entering the professional ranks.

Like David Livingstone in the quotation that opens this chapter, we want people who are willing to come into relatively uncharted territory, people who can live with sufficient ambiguity to be comfortable where there are no "roads." A culture-general framework, however, can provide the first set of tools we need to build those roads—links between people who have much to offer one another.

## ACTIVITIES

1 In the chapter you were introduced to eighteen culture-general themes. Apply these themes to your own life experiences. How have you experienced each of these? In what contexts are you familiar with them? How do they affect your social interactions? Your work? Your schooling? How might you expect to encounter them in your future role as a teacher?

2 One way to gain expertise in living and working with others is to broaden your base of experiences. Make a few visits to a "culturally different" place in which you are not known. You might choose a place of worship, a soup kitchen or homeless shelter, or a school in an area which differs from your own. Begin simply by observing those around you. Document your feelings, emotional reactions, the assumptions you make, and the questions you have. As much as possible, document your responses in terms of the eighteen-theme framework. After some time, check out your assumptions by interviewing some of the people and asking for clarification.

3 In this chapter you have been introduced to the *critical incident,* a short vignette which brings together people from two different cultures or backgrounds who have some task to fulfill which ends at a point of conflict. Recall a cross-cultural experience you have had, or have observed, which falls under one of the eighteen themes. Prepare a short vignette designed to teach about a culture-general issue.

4 This exercise will encourage you to analyze some cultural differences face to face while enabling you to apply some of the concepts introduced in the text. Find someone from a culture different from your own (preferably outside your immediate, known group) to interview. Try to choose someone you think will have different attitudes, opinions, and experiences from yourself. Choose some questions from the list that follows. Before you interview the person, answer these questions for yourself. For each of the questions, follow up with "Why?" in order to explore underlying values. Take notes on your answers. Discuss the questions and the "why" with the other person until you have found at least five major areas where there are clear differences between your answer and the other person's. Prepare a short paper which summarizes your findings.

   a Whom should you obey?
   b Who makes decisions (at home, school, community)?
   c How should you behave with others (elders, children, neighbors . . .)?
   d Whom should you respect? How do you show respect?

    e How should you act in public so you bring credit or honor to your family?

    f Whom should you seek advice from when you need it?

    g Whom should you trust?

    h What does it mean to be successful in life?

    i What are the signs of success?

    j What provides "security" in life?

    k Who should your friends be?

    l Where, and with whom, should you live?

    m Whom should you marry? At about what age? Who decides?

    n What is expected of children when they are young?

    o What should you depend on others for?

    p When should you be self-sufficient, if ever?

    q What should you expose to others and what should be kept private?

    r How should you plan for your future?

    s What should be remembered from your heritage?

    t What was better when you were young or during your parents' youth?

    u What do you wish for your children that you could not have?

5 The following exercise was developed by Robert Kohls. Individually or in groups, discuss in some detail what a society would be like if it were based on one of the following premises. What would society be like if people believed

    a In reincarnation?

    b That there was no God?

    c That everything that happened was fated to happen?

    d That a person's worth was determined by his or her social status at birth?

    e That certain ethnic or racial groups were intellectually inferior?

    f That a passive approach to life is preferable to an active approach?

    g That old people are to be honored, revered, and deferred to in all instances?

    h That aesthetic values are of supreme importance and should be used to determine every major issue in life?

    i That rights of the group are more important than rights of the individual?

    j That women are superior to men?

    k That what we consider "normal" or "average" is mundane and exceptionalities at all extremes are preferable?

6 Differences exist. Consider a child from a group different from yours whom you might one day teach. What differences exist between yourself and the child? Why do they exist? If you desire to maintain contact and interactions with this child what might you have to do to adjust to the situation?

## MORE CRITICAL INCIDENTS

### A Model Minority[40]

Wellington Chang was a sixth-grade student in a San Francisco neighborhood elementary school. Recently arrived from Hong Kong, he spoke very functional, though accented, English.

    His sixth-grade class was multiethnic, with students of African-American, Hispanic, and various Asian backgrounds, as well as a few caucasians. His teacher, Mr. Fenwick, was a competent teacher with over 25 years experience in the classroom. Caucasian himself, he had watched as the district's population was transformed into an incredibly heterogeneous mixture of ethnic and linguistic groups. He prided himself on his ability to adapt to the ever changing and complex environment.

Though Wellington seemed quiet enough at first, he increasingly exhibited what Mr. Fenwick described as disruptive behavior, including talking, laughing, and teasing other students. This perplexed Mr. Fenwick, since his experience with Chinese young people was that they were among the most hard-working and diligent students.

Far from being disruptive, Mr. Fenwick found most Chinese students to be relatively passive individuals whom he had to encourage to be more participatory. Thus Wellington's behavior seemed to him particularly disturbing and he punished him more severely than other non-Chinese offenders, even though his behavior was no worse than theirs.

On a routine visit, a school inspector noticed this discrepancy and discussed it with the school principal.

If you were the principal, what explanations for Mr. Fenwick's behavior might you give the inspector? Now, given the following alternatives, which provides the most insight into the situation?

**1** Mr. Fenwick believes that no matter where they come from, all Chinese will behave in the same manner.

**2** Mr. Fenwick is operating from very limited experience with ethnic minorities in the United States and does not realize that Wellington's behavior is well within the normal range for U.S. sixth-graders.

**3** Mr. Fenwick's expectations about Chinese being a model minority cause him to judge Wellington too harshly.

**4** For some reason, Mr. Fenwick has taken a personal dislike to Wellington.

## Rationales

**1** You chose number 1. Hong Kong, where Wellington comes from, is a highly urbanized environment. The majority of Chinese from the People's Republic come from a very different, often a rural, setting. In addition, socioeconomic and class differences between Chinese from Hong Kong and mainland China may also be at play. Mr. Fenwick has mistakenly put all Chinese in a single category, failing to make the finer distinctions necessary to more fully understand this group. This is the best response.

**2** You chose number 2. We know that Mr. Fenwick has had extensive interaction with ethnic minorities in the school setting. There is a more appropriate response. Please choose again.

**3** You chose number 3. Prior experience and expectations can often predispose one to expect certain behavior. In this case the text states that Mr. Fenwick did have certain prior experiences with Chinese that were quite different from those he is having with Wellington. It may very well be that Mr. Fenwick has unrealistic expectations of Wellington given his prior experience. This answer is partially correct.

**4** You chose number 4. There is no indication in the story that Mr. Fenwick has taken a personal dislike to Wellington. Please select an explanation that reflects possible intercultural interaction.

## The Proposal Process

The principal at Wilson High called a staff meeting for all social studies personnel to discuss upcoming curriculum changes. Stu Abrams, a social studies teacher for 11 years, reread some materials he wished to see incorporated into the program in which he taught. He was looking forward to integrating these multicultural materials into the program. For a long time he had felt the district was ignoring the influx of Filipino, Vietnamese, and Samoan immigrants into the community. It was about time for change.

Jose, a second generation Filipino teacher, was also asked to attend the meeting. Jose had developed a close relationship with Stu, and they were to work on this committee together. They had worked on many other projects together. The principal asked Stu to review his proposal, the substance of which was already known to the others at the meeting. The proposal went through with little modification and it was agreed to take the next step toward eventual implementation. Since this had taken less time than expected, the principal asked Jose to say a few words about the curriculum development project he had been working on. Again, most of the people at the meeting knew of this project. Jose gave an outline of his thinking, and Stu then asked some rather difficult questions that forced Jose to think on his feet and to defend some of his earlier assumptions. The principal ended the meeting. Jose then told the principal that he preferred not to work on the committee with Stu as originally planned. Jose seemed upset. The principal was puzzled.

What insights can you provide into the reason why Jose asked to be removed from Stu's committee? Which of the following alternatives provides the most insight?

1  Jose wanted to do some additional work on his own proposal and see it ultimately adopted by the group.

2  Jose was jealous that Stu's proposal had passed on to the next step with little modification.

3  Jose felt that Stu withdrew his friendship at the meeting.

4  Jose felt that he, being an ethnic minority himself, should have his suggestions adopted.

Rationales

1  You chose number 1. It is possible that Jose wanted to improve his proposal and get it adopted. However, he would have to leave the group he was working with to do this. Please choose another alternative.

2  You chose number 2. Jealousy is always a possible reaction when one person succeeds and another does not. However, among Filipinos this does not occur often; it is probably not the main reason for Jose's request. In addition, since Stu's idea had been known previously by others in the group, Jose probably knew that it would be approved. Please choose another alternative.

3  You chose number 3. This is the best answer. Stu knows that, in most American professional circles, a person can be both a friend and a critic who makes constructive suggestions. (This is true in most English-speaking countries.) In fact, if Stu did not make constructive suggestions that in the long run would improve a friend's proposal, that friend could criticize Stu for not helping him out. Among Filipinos, however, the roles of friend and critic are differentiated, or separated. The same person cannot easily fill both roles. Filipinos for the most part have set expectations about what a friend is, and Stu's behavior violated these expectations. It is possible that if Stu had made these suggestions in private Jose might not have felt so badly. Even then, however, Stu would want to be sure he was making suggestions in a style acceptable to Filipinos (and, in general, others from Southeast Asia). This preferred style would include saying a num-

ber of good things about a proposal, being much more indirect that he would with an American, and keeping the tone of the meeting light with jokes and anecdotes.

4 You chose number 4. While some might feel this, there is no indication that this is the case for Jose. Please select another alternative.

---

### "Typical American Practice"

"Class, I'd like you to welcome Keiko, an exchange student from Japan who will be attending Central High School for the second semester," said Mr. Cooper at the beginning of his American Government class. Keiko had experienced similar introductions and welcomes in all of her classes during her first day of school in the United States. The friendliness of the faculty and students impressed her and made her feel right at home.

As time went on, however, Keiko felt that the teachers and students were ignoring her more and more. Very few students talked to her, and only offered a brief hello in the hallway or cafeteria. Keiko got mostly A's, but her teachers never called on her in class. She began to wonder if she had somehow offended the people at her new school, and she gradually became withdrawn and isolated.

What do you think has happened here to cause this unfortunate situation? Now, given the following alternatives, which would you select as most appropriate?

1 The students resent Keiko's high grades and are showing their jealousy of her.

2 Americans have a tendency to offer foreigners a special welcome and then quickly treat them like everyone else.

3 Keiko demands too much attention and has unrealistic expectations that everyone will treat her in a special way.

4 The faculty members are obviously insincere in their initial welcomes. They are probably acting on a directive from the principal.

### Rationales

1 While jealousy and resentment over grades are always a possibility, there is no evidence this is happening here. Please choose again.

2 Cultures differ in the amount of attention given to sojourners. Visitors to the United States frequently comment that Americans are polite during initial interaction but then seem indifferent at meeting the visitor a second or third time. For instance, foreign students may be introduced and made to feel welcome, but those same students seem to be forgotten a few days later. Keiko seems to be receiving this "typical" American treatment. It would help if Americans and all hosts tried to put themselves in the place of the newly arrived person and then to make them feel really at home, especially by including them in social activities.

3 Most sojourners have some type of unrealistic expectation, and Keiko is probably no different. But she does not appear overly demanding of her hosts. Her puzzlement and withdrawal seem well founded and understandable. Look elsewhere for the real problem here.

4 This explanation has no basis in the narrative above. So far as we know, the faculty were sincere in their welcome and acted on their own initiative. Their behavior is the real problem, but their motives probably are not. Please choose again.

### From Providence to San Francisco[41]

Joao was a teenager from Providence, Rhode Island, who had been sent to live for 2 years in San Francisco with his aunt and uncle. This was the first time that Joao had been away from his own family in Providence, which was strongly united and felt a deep pride in its Portuguese heritage. Joao's family emigrated from Portugal when he was a child.

The high school in San Francisco that Joao began attending was one that included students from a variety of ethnic and cultural groups. Joao knew that the school had a good reputation as being a place where students from different backgrounds got along well together. So Joao did not worry about the fact that he would be the only Portuguese in the student body. He looked forward to attending the new school.

During Joao's first week in the school, he discovered that several members of the faculty viewed him as belonging to a group of students who spoke Spanish. A few teachers greeted him in Spanish; one said Joao might like to join a club mainly for Central American students.

Joao felt resentful at being thought of as from anywhere other than Portugal. During his second week, a teacher gave Joao a notice to take home to his uncle; it was in Spanish. Joao startled the teacher by loudly protesting, "Please try to remember; I'm Portuguese!"

If Joao asked for your advice, what would you say?

**1** "Joao, you probably don't realize this. But you must have felt resentment at being sent to San Francisco to live with your aunt and uncle. Your sense of unity with your family in Providence was very strong and, deep down, you probably hated to leave it."

**2** "Joao, you had been attending schools in Providence where many other students were native Portuguese, just like you. The idea of going to school with students from other ethnic and cultural groups—but no Portuguese—must have deeply disturbed you."

**3** "Joao, you probably were deeply upset about being identified as a member of an ethnic or culture group other than your own. You feel proud to be a native Portuguese, so you just couldn't adjust to being viewed as a Spanish speaker from Mexico or Central America."

**4** "Joao, you know that your parents in Providence kept you under tight discipline. You never had to learn any self-discipline. It was inevitable that on this first experience living away from your parents, you would do something to embarrass yourself."

### Rationales

**1** Number 1 may contain an element of truth. However, there is no information in the story to support this interpretation. The story actually says that Joao "looked forward to attending the new school." Another suggestion for Joao is much better than this one. Go back and choose again.

**2** Number 2 could be true to some extent. However, the schools in Providence include students from many ethnic and cultural groups. Joao would have been accustomed to going to school with students from different backgrounds. One of the other suggestions is better than this one. Go back and choose again.

**3** Number 3 is the best suggestion for Joao. The story says that Joao's family "felt a deep pride in its Portuguese heritage." While going to school in Providence, Joao had other native Portuguese students with whom to share his ethnic pride. It is very likely that the students in his high school in Providence included people from non-Portuguese backgrounds. But their presence might have helped Joao become even more strongly aware of his contrasting identity.

When Joao entered the school in San Francisco, he probably had no difficulty becoming accustomed to the presence of students from a variety of backgrounds. But it was difficult for him to be identified by some of the teachers as a member of a non-Portuguese group. Because he felt strongly Portuguese, their viewing him as a Central American confused Joao. His rude comment to the teacher probably resulted from his confusion.

The teachers meant to be helpful to Joao, of course. They probably thought of him as coming from one of the Spanish-speaking countries to the south because they needed to fit him into one of the ethnic and cultural categories already familiar in the school. Since the Portuguese language is quite similar to Spanish (so that Joao actually did understand when addressed in Spanish), they found it convenient to categorize him with the other Spanish-speaking students.

4 Number 4 might be true in some cases in which young people are away from home for the first time. But there is nothing in this story to support it. Go back and choose again.

## REFERENCES

1 Sheldon Varney and Kenneth Cushner, "Understanding Cultural Diversity Can Improve Intercultural Interaction," *NASSP Bulletin,* vol. 74, no. 528, October 1990, pp. 89–94.

2 Kenneth Cushner, "Cross-Cultural Psychology and the Formal Classroom," in Richard W. Brislin (ed.), *Applied Cross-Cultural Psychology* (Beverly Hills: Sage Publications, 1986), pp. 98–120.

3 Ibid.

4 Richard Brislin, Kenneth Cushner, Craig Cherrie, and Mahealani Yong, *Intercultural Interactions: A Practical Guide* (Newbury Park: Sage Publications, 1986).

5 Darrell Broaddus, "Use of a Culture-General Assimilator in Intercultural Training," Ph.D. thesis, Indiana State University, Terre Haute, 1986.

6 Lisa Ilola, "Intercultural Interaction Training for Preservice Teachers Using the Culture-General Assimilator and a Peer Interactive Approach," Ph.D. thesis, University of Hawaii, Honolulu, 1988.

7 Kenneth Cushner, "Assessing the Impact of a Culture-General Assimilator," *International Journal of Intercultural Relations,* vol. 13, no. 2, 1989, pp. 125–146.

8 H. Selye, *Stress Without Distress* (New York: J. B. Lippincott, 1974), p. 27.

9 LaRay M. Barna, "The Stress Factor in Intercultural Relations," in Dan Landis and Richard Brislin (eds.), *Handbook of Intercultural Training,* vol. 2, *Issues in Training Methodology* (New York: Pergamon Press, 1983), pp. 19–49; see also, H. Selye, *The Stress of Life* (New York: McGraw-Hill, 1956).

10 D. Oken, "Stress: Our Friend, Our Foe," in *Blueprint for Health* (Chicago: Blue Cross Association, 1974).

11 Barna, op. cit., p. 23.

12 I. L. Janus, "Vigilance and Decision Making in Personal Crisis," in G. V. Coelho, D. A. Hamburg, and J. E. Adams (eds.), *Coping and Adaptation* (New York: Basic Books, 1974).

13 Barna, op. cit., p. 23.

14 H. Selye, "On the Real Benefits of Eustiers," *Psychology Today,* vol. 11, no. 10, March 1978, pp. 60–70.

15  Barna, op. cit.

16  R. S. Lazarus, "The Concepts of Stress and Disease," in L. Levi (ed.), *Society, Stress, and Disease,* vol. 1, *The Psychosocial Environment and Psychosomatic Disease* (London: Oxford University Press, 1971), p. 54.

17  Billy Davis, *The Ripe Harvest: Educating Migrant Children* (Coral Gables, FL: University of Miami Press, 1972), p. 15.

18  A. S. Dibner, "Ambiguity and Anxiety," *Journal of Abnormal and Social Psychology,* vol. 56, 1958, pp. 165–174.

19  I. G. Sarason, "The Test Anxiety Scale: Concept and Research," in C. D. Spielberger and I. G. Sarason (eds.), *Stress and Anxiety,* vol. 5 (Washington, DC: Hemisphere Publishing, 1978).

20  J. J. Groen and J. Bastiaans, "Psychological Stress, Interhuman Communication, and Psychosomatic Disease," in C. D. Spielberger and I. G. Sarason (eds.), *Stress and Anxiety* (Washington, DC: Hemisphere Publishing, 1975).

21  Bruno Bettleheim, *Surviving and Other Essays* (New York: Vintage Books, 1980).

22  Marcelo M. Suarez-Orozco, "Becoming Somebody: Central American Immigrants in U.S. Inner-City Schools," *Anthropology and Education Quarterly,* vol. 18, 1987, pp. 287–299.

23  Richard Kindsvatter, "A New View of the Dynamics of Discipline," *Phi Delta Kappan,* vol. 59, no. 5, Jan. 1978, pp. 322–325.

24  Brislin et al., op. cit.

25  Brislin, *Cross-Cultural Encounters: Face to Face Interaction* (New York: Pergamon Press, 1981).

26  Ibid.

27  Gordon Allport, *The Nature of Prejudice* (Cambridge, MA: Addison-Wesley, 1979).

28  Brislin, op. cit.

29  D. Katz, "The Functional Approach to the Study of Attitudes," *Public Opinion Quarterly,* no. 2 (summer) 1968, pp. 164–204.

30  R. Levine and D. Campbell, *Ethnocentrism* (New York: John Wiley & Sons, 1972).

31  As told to one of the authors by Carolyn Strand, May 1990.

32  L. Peplau and D. Perlman (eds.), *Loneliness: A Sourcebook of Current Theory, Research and Therapy* (New York: John Wiley & Sons, 1982).

33  Brislin et al., op. cit.

34  I. H. Frieze, "Causal Attributions and Information Seeking to Explain Success and Failure," *Journal of Research in Personality,* Vol. 10, No. 3, Sept. 1976, pp. 293–305.

35  B. Weiner, "A Theory of Motivation for Some Classroom Experiences," *Journal of Educational Psychology,* vol. 71, no. 1, Feb. 1979, pp. 3–25.

36  Madeline Hunter and George Barker, "If At First . . .: Attribution Theory in the Classroom," *Educational Leadership,* vol. 45, no. 2, October 1987, pp. 50–53.

37  John Lane and Herbert Walberg, *Effective School Leadership* (Berkeley, CA: McCutchan, 1987).

38  Howard Gardner, *Frames of Mind: The Theory of Multiple Intelligence* (New York: Basic Books, 1983).

39  Brislin, op. cit.

40  Incident created by David Grossman of the East-West Center, Honolulu, Hawaii.

41  Extracted with permission from: K. Cushner, *"They Are Talking about Me!" and Other Stories for Exchange Students* (New York: American Field Service International Program, 1990).

# CHAPTER 4

# COMMUNICATING ACROSS CULTURE

*The most immutable barrier in nature is between one man's thoughts and another's.*

William James

\*     \*     \*

### A Story

Four men, a Persian, a Turk, an Arab, and a Greek were standing in a village street. They were traveling companions, making for some distant place. At this moment, however, they were arguing over the spending of a single piece of money which was all they had between them.

"I want to buy angur," said the Persian.

"I want uzum," said the Turk.

"I want inab," said the Arab.

"No!" said the Greek. "We shall buy stafil."

Another traveler passing by, who happened to be a linguist, said, "Give me the coin. I will satisfy all your desires."

At first they would not trust this man. Ultimately they let him have the coin. He went into the shop of a fruitseller and bought four small bunches of grapes.

"This is my angur," said the Persian.

"But this is what I call uzum," said the Turk.

"You have bought me inab," said the Arab.

"No," said the Greek, "this in my language is stafil."

The grapes were shared among all the men, and each realized that the disharmony had been due to his not understanding the languages of the others.

\*     \*     \*

## SIMILARITY OF NEEDS—DIFFERENCES OF EXPRESSION

This story at first seems to suggest that there is one simple way to solve everyone's communication problems. This is usually not so. Looked at from another perspective, however, the story suggests that while people may appear to be very different (in this case, in terms of language), when looked at more closely, they are actually quite similar. While the "packaging," in this case the specific words used, may vary, the underlying desire and need may be the same.

The linguist in this story may be likened to the teacher or counselor. The travelers are your students. Each may express her or his wants, needs, interests, intentions, and goals in different ways. It is the teacher's responsibility to interpret what the students say and do, and then to help guide them in a way that enables them to realize their goals.

In the culture-general framework introduced in Chapter 3, 18 themes or topic areas were presented which emerge time and time again as points of miscommunication and misunderstanding in human interactions. Of these, some are developed through the socialization process and are referred to as *knowledge areas*.[1] Included in the knowledge areas are the manner in which people learn to communicate—both how they learn and use verbal language and the way they learn and use nonverbal means of communication. Understanding these knowledge areas will assist in the interpretation of many everyday behaviors of people.

## THE COMMUNICATION PROCESS

In many ways, this book is *all* about communication; how to increase the likelihood that the message one intends to send is, in fact, communicated to others, as well as how to better understand the messages sent to you. As a professional educator, your responsibility is to communicate your intentions, knowledge, and skills to your students. But even lack of communication, or no communication at all, communicates something, whether intentionally or not. There is no such thing as noncommunication. Silence, as well as miscommunication, sends a message.

Singer states, and we want to say for this text that

it is a basic tenet of this work that communication is a process. As such it is continually operating, through feedback, with the environment and with everyone and everything in that environment. It is an ongoing process that never ceases, until we die. It is applicable regardless of the level of analysis. The same process operates whether one considers intra- or interpersonal communication, intra- or intergroup communication, or intra- or international communication. Of course, the specifics of how that process operates change as one changes the actors and settings, but the process remains constant.[2]

People communicate for a variety of reasons. They communicate to express their intentions, their desires, their needs, their personality, and their concerns. In other words, people communicate to express their subjective culture. Through the process of communication, people link themselves to others. Usually communication is between people who have a similar understanding of the meaning of the symbols used in the communication. Sometimes the messages have slightly different meanings attached to them. Sometimes the meanings are so disparate that there is a great deal of confusion.

The majority of the members of any community or cultural group use the same modes of communication. One's own language, like one's cultural knowledge, is taken for granted. In communicating with members of a different cultural group, one of the most obvious aspects with which people must cope is the differences in communication patterns. Samover, Porter, and Jain identify eight specific components in the communication process.[3]

**1** The *source* of the message is usually a person who has a need to communicate. Regardless of the reason and context, the source is generally concerned with sharing some internal state of being while influencing the attitude and behavior of another. As a teacher, you have not only academic information to communicate, but attitudes, values, and skills as well.

**2** Because one's internal state cannot be shared directly it must be *encoded* in some form which can be communicated to another. *Encoding* is an internal process whereby the source selects particular verbal and nonverbal symbols, and, applying certain rules (grammar, syntax, etc.), strings them together in a particular manner and sequence.

**3** The result of the process of encoding is that the source now has a *message.* The message is the best attempt at conveying the source's original inner state and intent at that particular place and time.

**4** Next, the message must have a *channel* through which it can move from source to a receiver. In the case of written communication, the channel of communication is light. When listening to a speaker, the channel of communication is the air in which sound waves move.

**5** The next critical element in the communication process is the *receiver.* Receivers of the message may be those for whom the message is intended. However, others may also receive the message. The receiver now has a task opposite to the one that the sender or source had; that is, the message must now be interpreted.

**6** Upon receipt of the external stimulus it must be *decoded.* That is, the receiver must decode the message internally, and in so doing, make an attribution as to the meaning of the source's verbal and nonverbal behavior.

**7** Next to be considered is the *receiver response:* what the receiver decides to do about the message. Responses may vary from minimum (ignoring the message) to maximum (sending a message in return).

**8** Finally, *feedback* from the receiver enables the source to make some judgment about the effectiveness of the communication.

Figure 4.1 illustrates the communication process.

The communication process is complex, not least because, at each stage, cultural factors are at play that may determine, for example, what symbols are chosen, what ideas or concepts are chosen for encoding the channel through which the message is sent, and how the message is decoded. Samover, Porter, and Jain go on to identify four key characteristics of communication.[4] First, *communication is dynamic;* that is, it is an ongoing activity which is constantly changing. If messages are received and interpreted as intended, positive communication is maintained. If there is interference of some sort

**FIGURE 4.1**    The communication process.

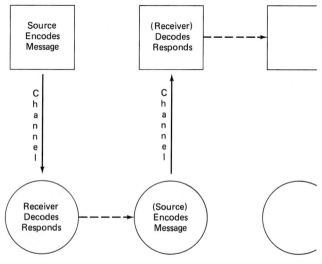

between the sender and receiver, communication may break down. Such interference may include the social or cultural context in which communication occurs as well as the particular language in which the message is sent.

Second, *communication is an interactive process.* Each person brings his or her unique background to the communicative encounter. For example, prior experience communicating with representatives of a social, gender, or socioeconomic group affects later communication.

Third, *communication is irreversible.* Once a message has been sent and received, regardless of how one feels after sending the message, it cannot be retrieved. This is important, especially in intercultural communication. It is possible, due to lack of knowledge or understanding of a culture's verbal and nonverbal communication patterns, to send an unintended message and to be totally unaware of having done so. While one may subsequently attempt to send messages to modify the negative effect, the fact remains that a negative message has been sent or received.

Fourth, *communication takes place in both a physical and a social context.* This is important, especially when we consider nonverbal factors. At the Paris peace talks during the Vietnam War, considerable time was spent in preliminary negotiation concerning the shape of the bargaining table. The eventual agreement to have a table with equal sides was important because it implied an equality of all parties at the table. While many Americans may tend to be somewhat relaxed about social hierarchies and the role of context in communication, people in some cultures place extreme importance on this dimension and the manner in which it is communicated to others. To some, the classroom or school context, with its authoritarian overlay, may be quite threatening. The fact that interactions occur in the context of the school or classroom environment may send certain unintended messages to parents and community. This alone may result in strained teacher-pupil-parent relationships.

Communication occurs through both verbal and nonverbal channels. Intercultural communication occurs whenever the sender and receiver are from different cultural backgrounds. Perhaps you can begin to imagine the problems inherent in the situation when a message encoded by a person with one cultural knowledge pattern must be decoded by a person with a different cultural knowledge pattern.

## VERBAL COMMUNICATION

Human beings are unique in their ability to make sounds which, when joined together in certain ways, can be understood by others. Through an extensive process of evolution, the human animal has developed the capability to produce, receive, store, and manipulate a variety of symbols and sounds. Humans, more than any other creature, depend on the production of sound in the form of language as their primary means of communication.

But words themselves are arbitrary. They may generate multiple meanings in people who speak even the same language, let alone a different one. Consider the word *tip.* Tip can mean to push something over or off an edge. It can also refer to payment for some services over and above the stated price. A *tip* can also refer to a good idea or suggestion that one person might communicate to another. A *tip* might mean a slender point at the end of something. Finally, in some parts of the world, a tip refers to a garbage dump. Such common words as *love, bread, chicken, turkey, bat, and top* all have many meanings. Linguists have estimated that the fifty most often used words in the English language can produce over fourteen thousand different meanings.[5]

It has also been estimated that more than 3,000 languages are spoken around the world—700 in Papua New Guinea alone and over 1,000 on the African continent! To a large degree, cultural experience determines the way a person acquires language, which language that person learns, and what meanings are attributed to words. Language and cultural knowledge are inextricably bound.

Language reflects the thought processes of a culture. According to Kaplan, English writing and thinking is linear.[6] That is, the speaker or writer tries to ''get right to the point,'' eliminating reference to issues and topics seemingly irrelevant to the message. The task is to communicate the message. Those who do not ''keep to task'' can be quite frustrating to English speakers. On the other hand, speakers of Semitic languages (Arabic and Hebrew) use various kinds of parallels in their thinking. References to past events, for example, are quite common and expected. Another important function of verbal communication among Semitic speakers, as well as many others, is the building of relationships.

No pattern of communication is ''right'' or ''wrong''; all have evolved to express and satisfy particular cultural patterns and needs. Some, however, may stress the development of interpersonal relationships more than others. If those interpersonal relationships are not expressed in the message (for example, when an American is speaking with an Arab), the person receiving the message may interpret it in a way that the speaker does not intend. The typical American linear speaker strives to get right to the point. In Figure 4.2, this is illustrated by the direct arrow. Arabic speakers, on the other hand,

**FIGURE 4.2**   Cross-cultural communication.

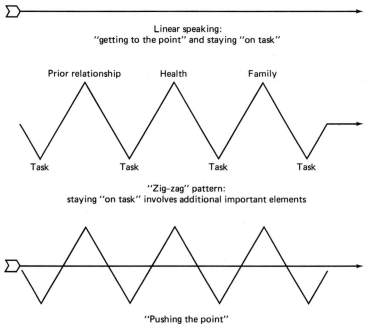

may think and speak in a "zig-zag" pattern, coming back to the main topic after brief discussions about the health of family members, the last time the two parties met, and significant events in one's life. To the Arab, these topics of discussion are just as important as the task at hand; they act to cement the relationship; place it in some historical context, thereby demonstrating commitment; and, by including reference to family members, demonstrate recognition of those who are important in the total life of the speakers. When the American continues to "push the point," important loops, or components, of communication are eliminated. The Arabic speaker may be left feeling cut off and rejected.

Language also plays a critical role in the maintenance of subcultures. Recall that ingroup membership is granted to those one feels comfortable with and with whom one has perceived similarities. One function language serves is to distinguish those who should be considered potential members of the ingroup from those who should be in the outgroup. Language serves to bind an individual to others by developing in the group a sense of real social unity. Maintenance and acceptance of their first language may serve to bind members of a minority group in the face of oppression, tension, and insecurity. Conversely, the existence of a growing movement across the United States to make English the official language might suggest a growing sense of threat to identity and a fear of loss of control on the part of a powerful majority group.

Translation is an important issue when people who speak different languages communicate. It is inaccurate to assume that one can easily translate from one language to another with the help of a good dictionary. Direct translation from one language to another can be quite difficult, if not impossible, to do accurately. Here are two quick examples. Many Americans became anxious and worried when they heard Nikita Kruschev say "We will bury you." In fact, the correct translation of his words should have been "We will survive you." President Jimmy Carter found himself in an embarrassing situation when visiting Poland, even though he used a highly skilled translator. Carter's desire to "learn your opinions and understand your desires for the future" was wrongly translated as "I desire the Poles carnally."[7]

Many factors contribute to the difficulties of translation. When a word has more than one meaning, it is often difficult to translate it accurately when the message is out of context. And some words are culture-bound; they *cannot* be directly translated into another language. The meaning of a word or phrase may also differ across cultures. For instance, in American English, the phrase *good neighbor* usually refers to those people who mow their lawn, shovel snow off their walks, and generally make sure that their yard or surrounding area appears to be in good order. In Italian, *good neighbor* refers to those people who do not throw trash out their windows. In the Soviet Union, a *good neighbor* is one who will watch a neighbor's children and feed them if needed. Words such as *peace, war, love, negotiation,* and *enemy* may elicit different meanings in the minds of others. Conceptual equivalence is a critical dimension in translation and must always be checked.

Finally, direct translation without knowledge of the culture can render some statements nonsensical. Consider translating the expressions "What's the matter? Cat got your tongue?" or "I'm all tongue-tied" into another language. To one who does not understand the cultural meaning behind the literal meaning of the words, translations of these sentences would make no sense whatsoever.

Read about Tony and his experiences interpreting language.

### Critical Incident: The Art Awards Ceremony

Tony, a African-American high school student, had an interest in art that he pursued on his own—visiting museums, reading books, sketching, and painting. His work reflected his African-American "roots." Tony enrolled at midterm in the predominantly white JFK High. He took an art class and was encouraged by his teacher to develop his talent. Tony entered several paintings in the school art show, received praise and attention for his work, and went on to enter the all city show, where he also did well. The longtime principal of his school, a middle-aged caucasian, Mr. Tarbell, was present at the awards ceremony, and was delighted that one of his students received rave reviews and an award. Congratulating Tony he said, "Good work, Tony. We are proud to have such a talented black student representing our school. You have an uncanny ability to paint."

Mr. Tarbell was surprised when Tony simply walked away from him with no comment.

How should this behavior be interpreted?

1 Tony was overwhelmed by all the attention and uncomfortable around someone in Mr. Tarbell's position.

2 Tony was offended by what Mr. Tarbell said.

3 Tony's friends likely motioned for him to come join them. Caught up in the excitement, he went on over.

4 Tony, embarrassed and not used to the praise he was receiving, especially from whites, left feeling uncomfortable.

### Rationales

1 You chose number 1. Although Tony may have been overwhelmed at the attention and aware of Mr. Tarbell's position, there is really no indication that he was uncomfortable. Please choose again.

2 You chose number 2. Although Mr. Tarbell thought he was complimenting Tony, his use of language—specifically, the phrase "uncanny ability to paint"—implies a stereotyping of blacks as not artistic. To a white student, he might have said, "You are a very talented young artist"—but Tony's ability to paint seems unnatural to him. Because of Mr. Tarbell's position Tony may have chosen to walk away rather than challenge him. You have selected the correct answer.

3 You chose number 3. His friends may have motioned him although there is no indication of this in the story. Choose another response.

4 You chose number 4. Although there may be something uncomfortable about the situation, nothing in the story really shows that Tony was embarrassed or uncomfortable. Choose another response.

## NONVERBAL COMMUNICATION

When you are speaking with another person, or just observing another person speaking, what do you attend to? Are you listening to what is said? Are you checking out the person's clothes? Are you noticing whether they have used a deodorant or not? Are you attentive to how close or far away the person is standing? Are you aware of the amount of eye contact between you and the other person?

You do, consciously or not, intentionally or not, attend to all these messages, and more, simultaneously. And whether you are aware of it or not, and whether they are intentional or not, you send a variety of messages to others in return. Consider the little girl who, while sitting cross-legged and turning red in the face, insists that she does not have to use the bathroom. There are many conflicting messages being sent in this situation. While you may be quite a sophisticated person who is able to conceal your thoughts fairly well, you always convey some of them through nonverbal messages.

It has been estimated that 50 to 90 percent of our communication occurs at the nonverbal level. Barnlund has stated:

> Many, and sometimes most, of the critical meanings generated in human encounters are elicited by touch, glance, vocal nuance, gestures, or facial expression with or without the aid of words. From the moment of recognition until the moment of separation, people observe each other with all their senses, hearing pause and intonation, attending to dress and carriage, observing glance and facial tension, as well as noting word choice and syntax. Every harmony or disharmony of signals guides the interpretation of passing mood or enduring attribute. Out of the evaluation of kinetic, vocal and verbal cues, decisions are made to argue or agree, to laugh or blush, to relax or resist, to continue or cut off conversation.[8]

Consciously or unconsciously we not only send and receive nonverbal messages, but we make judgments and decisions based on the messages we receive. Attending to both verbal and nonverbal messages strengthens our confidence in what we have observed and judged in others. Often we pay more attention to others' nonverbal messages than to their verbal ones, and attempt to read their underlying emotions from the nonverbal information. Fear or anxiety, for instance, is often inferred from seeing a person biting their nails, standing with a rigid posture, or pacing back and forth. Our intent is congruence between verbal and nonverbal messages, but we often fall short of that goal.

Our own learned behavior predisposes us to select and understand only part of what is communicated to us. Because of that, it is impossible to attend to all the nonverbal differences we might encounter. However, in our analysis of behavior we can begin to look at a number of kinds of nonverbal communication. We can consider personal appearance; kinesics, or body movement; eye contact and gaze; touch; and the way people orient themselves in time and space.[9]

## Appearance

People make judgments about others in the first seconds after a meeting takes place. These judgments are based on a number of factors, including appearance and dress. It is not accidental that job applicants spend considerable time learning to dress appropriately and make the correct initial greetings. First impressions are formed quite quickly by most people.

Standards of general appearance are subject to considerable cultural variation. What is beautiful by the standards of one cultural group may appear less beautiful, or even repulsive, to members of another. And we know that responses to another person are often influenced by that person's dress and appearance. It has been shown, for example, that well-dressed and well-groomed children (well-groomed by the teacher's standards) receive more of the teacher's attention than children who appear to be dirty and whose clothes are not neat and clean.

Appearance can affect the way we communicate with someone who is handicapped. The accompanying apparatus or the physical appearance of a handicapped individual often invites inaccurate attributions. That is to say, initial attention to a physical feature overpowers one's ability to make a sound and fair judgment about the individual. Skin color and other physical traits, the outward signs of ethnic or cultural differences, act in the same way—they tend to skew our attributions. Because this tendency exists, it is important to resist it: to avoid letting these stimuli trigger inaccurate attributions. We must learn not only to be *tolerant* of differences in appearance, dress, style, and mannerisms, but to *appreciate* them. It is better to begin with a nonjudgmental stance, perhaps to inquire about something one does not know or understand, and allow other characteristics to emerge before judgments are made.

## Kinesics and Eye Contact

The study of body movements is called *kinesics.* The nod of a head, certain hand gestures, and a glance at a watch all may convey certain messages to others. It has been estimated that human beings make over 700,000 separate physical signs, many of which are culturally determined.[10]

Caucasian-Americans, for instance, tend to demonstrate their liking of a person by standing parallel to that person and by facing him or her while engaging in eye contact. Leaning toward or away from another person signals interest or disinterest accordingly. African-Americans, on the other hand, tend to stand perpendicular to one another as a way to demonstrate interest or liking, and to avoid eye contact.

Gaze is a powerful cue in mainstream U.S. culture. Differences between African-American and caucasian-American communicators may lead to interactional problems and misunderstandings. African-American speakers tend to look at their communication partner more while speaking than while listening.[11] This is just the opposite of their caucasian counterparts.[12] In a typical conversation between a black person and a white person, a black listener is likely to look at the white speaker less than the white speaker expects. The white person may then make an inaccurate attribution of disinterest on the part of the black listener. On the other hand, when the black person is speaking, both parties in the conversation will be looking at one another more than either expects. Similarly, gazes that are perceived as lasting too long may result in the misattribution of hostility. The combined misattributions of hostility and disinterest may be the result of cultural patterning in power-related nonverbal cues.[13]

Eye contact itself has been shown to account for 30 to 60 percent of all communication in group situations. Among many African-Americans, Chicanos, Native Americans, and Puerto Ricans, children are taught to avoid eye contact out of respect for age and authority. In many Asian cultures, females are taught that it is taboo to look straight into the eyes of a man. Many Asian men, out of respect for this tradition, do not stare directly at women.

Body posture and how one positions oneself in relation to others also has an effect on interpersonal relationships. In the United States, for instance, people can be rather casual in the manner in which they sit. In Germany and Japan great effort is given to being formal. In these countries, to slouch in one's chair would be a sign of deliberate rudeness, or of ignorance of appropriate manners.

Seating arrangements can communicate such things as deference for authority or age. Students in many Asian countries deliberately do not sit close to the teacher as a way of showing respect. The positioning of furniture, too, may communicate strong messages to others. In American courtrooms, judges sit above other persons in the court, and witnesses sit facing the community—indicating that the truth must be spoken in front of all. The placement of a desk can be used to reinforce power relationships. In highly formal settings, the desk is usually placed between the person in authority and subordinates. In less formal societies, as in Latin America and Israel, desks are usually placed to one side so people can turn to face others to converse and interact. Where will the teacher's desk be placed in *your* classroom?

## Touch

From an early age, touch is used to communicate such messages as love, trust, and security. By early adolescence, most people have learned the rules that govern touching in their culture, including when it is appropriate to touch whom, in what manner, and where. We quickly learn such rules as that it is okay to shake hands with almost anyone, that we can hug some people but kiss only a few. We learn that what is considered acceptable in private, even within a group, may be quite different from what is acceptable in public. We also learn what kind of touch is acceptable and that what a touch means depends on the relationship between the people. One's response to touch would be quite different if the touch were from a parent, a friend, a teacher, or a stranger.

Factors such as location, duration, and the pressure of a touch may affect the meaning attached to it. In Thailand, for instance, the head is considered sacred. To touch the head of another is, therefore, a sin. Many a Thai student has been made uncomfortable by a "loving" pat on the head by a well-meaning teacher.

Context and prior experience may also determine what is appropriate and acceptable. To many people, for example, a touch would communicate concern and caring for someone who is crying. However, if a person grew up associating touch with sexual activity and learned that sex was wrong, or that touch was accompanied by physical abuse, the reaction to the touch might be quite negative. In general, people who are English, German, and British-American touch very little. Hispanic-Americans and Eastern European Jews, on the contrary, touch quite freely and often. Touch between the teacher and Hispanic children has been shown to increase academic achievement—a result of that culture's attitudes toward touch.

## Orientation in Time and Space

### Critical Incident: The Missed Meeting

Mrs. Conant, an eleventh-grade social studies teacher, was concerned that a newly arrived Lebanese student, Graciella, was having difficulty dealing with the material in her U.S. History textbook. After Graciella failed two consecutive tests, Mrs. Conant called Graciella's parents and arranged a conference for 9:45 A.M. on Thursday during her free period.

Before school on Thursday, Mrs. Conant prepared a list of her questions, concerns, and recommendations, and was looking forward to meeting the parents. After teaching her first class, she made certain that the central office secretary would direct the couple to her room, and then she returned there at 9:30 to await their arrival. As 9:45, and then 10:00, passed and no one showed up, Mrs. Conant became increasingly puzzled and irritated.

When the clock read 10:10, Mrs. Conant assumed the parents had forgotten about the appointment or had had car trouble. She decided to spend the remainder of her free period in the faculty lounge. On her way out the door, however, she met the parents, who introduced themselves and said how happy they were to have the opportunity to discuss their daughter's progress. They made no mention of their lateness and offered no apology or explanation.

Mrs. Conant, trying to hide her anger, told them that she had only a few minutes left and tersely explained her perceptions of Graciella's difficulties. As the parents began to give some feedback, the bell rang for the next class. Mrs. Conant cut them off, explaining that she had another class to teach. The parents, looking confused and insulted, left an angry Mrs. Conant walking back to the front of her classroom.

What is the best explanation of the problem underlying this unfortunate incident?

1 Mrs. Conant was overly concerned about Graciella's minor academic problems. A conference was really unnecessary, and the parents felt resentful about being summoned to school.

2 The parents were obviously at fault for being so late. Their lack of consideration indicates that they are just not very concerned about their daughter or the feelings of others.

3 The parents and Mrs. Conant have a different outlook on time and punctuality. Being 20 to 25 minutes late was no big deal to the parents, but it was very important to the teacher.

4 Mrs. Conant resents having to give up her free period to parent-teacher conferences.

## Rationales

1 Mrs. Conant's concern seems sincere and well founded, and the parents seem to appreciate it since they were immediately agreeable to the conference. The problem lies elsewhere. Please choose again.

2 Although the parents were late for the appointment, there is no evidence that they were intentionally insensitive or that they lacked concern for their daughter's progress. While "time" may be the main problem here, this attribution of motives and feelings is not justified by the evidence.

3 The differing views of time held by Mrs. Conant and the parents are the root of the problem and they best explain the hurt feelings on both sides. The working unit of time for Euro-Americans tends to be a 5-minute block. Mrs. Conant, therefore, would probably feel that a person who is 2 or 3 minutes late for a meeting need not apologize. After 5 minutes, a short apology would be expected. Being 15 minutes late—three "units" of time—would require a lengthy, sincere apology, or perhaps a phone call in advance.

Other cultures, however, do not place the same emphasis on time and punctuality as do Western cultures. Historical perspectives are important to Arab peoples. The working unit of time for many Arabs (as well as for Hispanics and Native Americans, among others) is a much longer block than it is for westerners.

Mrs. Conant and the parents are, therefore, victims of conflicting views of time and punctuality. This is the best response.

4 All the evidence suggests that Mrs. Conant is most agreeable to having conferences during her free period. Indeed, she initiates this meeting. Please choose again.

Behaviors related to spatial orientation and time perspective are classic examples of culturally determined behavioral patterns which can cause confusion and discomfort and can result in faulty attributions.[14] Except for feelings related to certain circadian rhythms of the body, a "sense of time" is not innate to the human species.

Hall differentiates three categories of time.[15] *Formal time* refers to such divisions of time as the days of the week or the calendar year. These divisions have quite rigid boundaries. *Technical time,* used by scientists and other technical specialists, is extremely rigid and precisely defined. *Informal time* includes the area of greatest human interaction. Phrases such as "wait a minute" or "I'll be here at 2:00" mean different things to different people. Many Europeans and mainstream Americans seem often to be bound by the clock. People spend time, waste time, and save time. Many American proverbs and catchphrases reflect this orientation: "Time is money," "Don't waste your time," and "The early bird catches the worm."

The American attitude toward time, emphasizing punctuality, promptness, and schedules, has been termed *monochronic*. Lives are punctuated by school bells, timeclocks, and appointment books. Even leisure time must be scheduled well in advance. Except when status differences are at play (e.g., it may be quite acceptable for a boss to be late for a scheduled meeting with a subordinate but it is not all right for the boss to be late for an appointment with a superior), punctuality is quite rigidly enforced in terms of the 5-minute "block" of time.

In some groups, *polychronic* time rules. In polychronic contexts, one is expected to be late. Tardiness may, in fact, be seen as a sign of respect. Time does not control the person or the day. This is the case among many Latin, Asian, and African cultures as well as those in the Middle East and Mediterranean region. Because the working unit of time is much larger in polychronic societies, people may schedule a meeting for 2:00 P.M., arrive at 4:00, and still be considered on time. Among the Sioux, there is no verbal structure for future and past; words refer only to the present.

The more relaxed attitude toward time of polychronic cultures is described by westerners in such phrases as "Hawaiian time" in Hawaii and "rubber time" in Malaysia. In the Philippines, "Stateside time" is a request that people be prompt for a particular gathering or event.

The way people orient themselves to others in space is also culturally determined. Not unlike the many species of birds who maintain a prescribed distance between themselves and others when atop a telephone wire, human beings show signs of territoriality. Witness the movement of people in the elevator as one exits at a certain floor; those remaining move away from one another in order to maximize the interpersonal distance.

The amount of distance maintained in interpersonal interactions is, to a great degree, learned behavior. The "comfortable" distance people maintain is quite constant among members of a given cultural group. The most comfortable distance for mainstream Americans in social gatherings is usually between 20 and 36 inches. Among many Hispanic-Americans, however, the comfortable distance is much smaller. To a caucasian-American this may bring about feelings of intrusion and violation of personal space. Imagine a scene in which an Anglo teacher and a Hispanic parent are engaged in conversation. The parent, wishing to establish an interpersonal distance that they feel comfortable with and that they feel is appropriate, will move rather close to the teacher. Because this close interpersonal distance invades the space in which the teacher is comfortable, the attribution the teacher might make is that the parent is being "pushy" or "aggressive." The teacher feels threatened and unconsciously moves away in an attempt to maintain the interpersonal space with which they are comfortable. The attribution the parent may then make is that the teacher is "cold," "distant," and "disinterested." Each individual in this interaction is making faulty judgments or attributions based on the simple fact that each is attempting to maintain the interpersonal space that is comfortable to them.

Read about Mrs. Klein's students.

> Two young women from Mrs. Klein's junior math class asked if they could talk to her for a few minutes after school. During the meeting, the girls complained to Mrs. Klein about the behavior of Juan, an exchange student from Guatemala, who had been attending their school for about 3 weeks. The complaints centered on what the girls described as Juan's "pushy," "aggressive," "overly friendly" behavior. "He puts his arm around me in the hallway and is just too close," complained one of the girls. "Everybody is getting tired of it," said the other.
>
> Mrs. Klein, who had already observed Juan's forward behavior in her own classroom, told the girls she would try to help. After putting things off for a few days, Mrs. Klein met with Juan and told him directly that touching or grabbing girls was totally unacceptable behavior. "If you want to be liked and accepted here, you cannot continue to be so aggressive," she warned him. When she asked him if he understood the situation, he nodded and left the room without saying anything.
>
> From then on, Juan no longer exhibited any "overly friendly" behavior, was noticeably more quiet, and became basically a loner at school. Although Mrs. Klein felt bad about Juan's apparent unhappiness, she was confident that she had done the right thing.

A cross-cultural misunderstanding, not the boy's aggressiveness, is at the center of this problem. For Juan, putting his arm around someone or getting close to them as he talks is merely a normal, acceptable show of friendship. Juan seems to be the victim of a misinterpretation, and Mrs. Klein has compounded the problem by not considering the relevant cultural differences during her talks with the girls and with Juan.

## COMMUNICATION BETWEEN ABLE-BODIED AND DISABLED PERSONS

Communication between able-bodied and disabled people can be thought of as cross-cultural communication, and the differences between the two groups create a unique set of communication problems. Nonverbal behavior of a disabled person is often misinterpreted and viewed as inappropriate. Similarly, nonverbal behavior of an able-bodied person may signal discomfort, confusion, or rejection to a disabled person, thereby further complicating an interaction. The behavior of one constrains the behavior of the other. A cycle of miscommunication is set up, and is difficult to break.

One function that communication received from others serves is the building of self-concept. Being different may become the main basis for the self-concept of a disabled individual.[16] When one becomes disabled later in life, a partial fragmentation of the self may result. Shearer relates Jack Ashley's experience of becoming totally deaf:

> He remembers the realization that he was wholly excluded from the conversation of his wife and brother-in-law as they drove him home from the hospital as ''one of the greatest shocks of my life.'' When he first tried to get back to work, to a job in which quick understanding and discussion are essential, he realized that he was unable to participate at all. ''I was cut off from mankind, surrounded by an invisible, impenetrable barrier. I could see people clearly, but they belonged to a different world—a world of talk, of music and laughter.'' . . . He had to give up aspirations of reaching the top of his career ladder.[17]

Many of the issues already referred to can be observed in able-bodied–disabled communication. Emry and Wiseman cite numerous conflicting social norms and demands which result in feelings of anxiety, uncertainty, and discomfort in interpersonal interaction between disabled and able-bodied communicators.[18]

Strong social norms demand that disabled persons be treated kindly and carefully. On the other hand, issues of independence and equity suggest that the disabled person is to be treated as an equal, as one would treat anyone else. The able-bodied person may feel discomfort in a situation brought on in part by trying to heed this mixed message. This may create further problems, since people tend to avoid situations that make them feel uncomfortable. If interactions between the able-bodied and disabled are fraught with discomfort, it is likely that people will engage in them as little as possible.

In general, human beings are drawn to explore—to look at, and perhaps stare at, whatever is novel to them as they try to understand their surroundings and reduce uncertainty. Part of the discomfort that arises in the able-bodied person when confronted by a disabled person comes from the conflict between a desire to stare and the fear of violating a social norm that discourages staring at other people.

Disabled persons also experience conflicting social norms. Disabled persons sometimes must depend on others to help them carry out their daily activities. Yet independence is a highly valued American ideal. Their conflict is especially evident in eating behavior. If a disabled person utilizes assistance, she or he can then be viewed as dependent upon others. Yet, if independence is insisted on, the person's behavior may be viewed as infantile and inappropriate. The tension for people with disabilities that arises between dependence and independence is found in such daily issues as personal hygiene, transportation, and dress.

Miscommunication between any two people occurs whenever efforts of one to communicate a specific meaning to the other are misinterpreted. Writing from the perspective of a disabled person, Paul Williams states:

> When one of us meets one of you, especially if it is for the first time, we are quite likely to lack many of the skills for successful communication. We may not be able to think of anything appropriate to say, or to put it into the right words, or to control our facial expression. But you also will show a great lack of skill. You will be embarrassed, you won't be able to think of

anything appropriate to say, you will tend to talk in an inappropriate tone of voice, you will tend to have a wide grin on your face and ask questions without really being interested in the answer. The handicap is a mutual one. Both of us have difficulty in communicating with and forming relationships with the other. The trouble is that you have lots of opportunities to go off and form relationships more easily. We don't. You can deny your handicap. We can't—we live with it all the time.[19]

Uncertainty regarding appropriate and inappropriate behavior may result in constrained behavior lacking the spontaneity and relaxed tone of "normal" interactions. Emry and Wiseman summarize some ways the able-bodied communicate differently with disabled people than with other able-bodied people:[20] Able-bodied persons tend to be more inhibited and nervous when communicating with disabled persons than when communicating with other able-bodied individuals. Able-bodied persons also demonstrate increased interpersonal distance, greater anxiety, and emotional discomfort when interacting with disabled persons. In addition, conflicting messages are often sent between able-bodied and disabled persons. Able-bodied individuals may communicate positive verbal messages yet nonverbally communicate rejection or avoidance. Overall, able-bodied persons tend to avoid communication with disabled individuals, are less likely to select disabled individuals as friends, and tend to negatively evaluate disabled individuals, or at least view them as being extraordinarily "different."

Disabled persons notice that, when compared to other disabled communicators, their able-bodied communicators glance away from them more frequently, stand further away from them, act more nervous, pretend to ignore the disability, and assume that the disabled person is more disabled than he or she actually is. All these are obvious barriers to effective communication.

## CROSS-GENDER COMMUNICATION

Consider the following situation:

### Critical Incident: "Unfeminine" Behavior Is Punished

Nine district principals, six men and three women, joined the school board president one Friday morning in an attempt to make a final decision on which university to hire as consultants for a major new curriculum development project. Board President Buford asked Mr. Dawson if he was prepared to summarize the pros and cons of entering into a contract with State University. He said that he was and briskly approached the flip chart in front of the room. With his feet planted firmly apart and with emphatic hand and arm gestures, Mr. Dawson detailed his position. Many heads nodded in agreement as he spoke.

"Good job, Dawson," replied Mr. Buford. "Now Ms. Williams, give us your summary of the arguments for and against entering into an agreement with City University."

Ms. Williams strode to the flip chart and gave an equally strong presentation. She did not receive any messages of agreement, however, even from the three people she knew agreed with her.

What, aside from honest disagreement, could have been responsible for this lack of support?

1 Mr. Dawson had the crucial advantage of presenting first.

2 Ms. Williams' strong body language is frowned upon as unbecoming a "lady."

3 The men resent having women as their equals.

4 Board President Buford had indicated his preference for State University, so the principals decided to fall in line.

## Rationales

1 Going first can sometimes be an advantage. However, in this case, only two choices were possible and those concerned with the decision were already familiar with the material. Some other dynamic is most likely at play here. Please choose again.

2 The commonly held belief that both men and women react negatively to a woman who uses an open stance, wide arm movements, and other "take charge" body language has been confirmed. These behaviors are part of those distinct differences that exist in what is considered acceptable behavior for men and women. In situations of power and persuasion, these differences often favor men, while putting women at a disadvantage. As women rise to top administrative posts, both men and women must become aware of the degree to which their judgments are based on norms that favor men. This is the most appropriate response.

3 While the possibility exists in any similar situation that some men might resent women in positions of power, there is no indication that this is the case in this incident. Please select another alternative.

4 Board President Buford does appear to be a forceful leader and a boardroom full of "yesmen" and "yeswomen" is, thus, a possibility. However, his preference is not mentioned in the story. An explanation based on this is, therefore, not justified. Please select another alternative.

One of the most interesting aspects of human communication patterns is the degree to which males and females are thought to "speak a different language."[21] Stereotypes of differences between male and female communication patterns are rooted in perceived differences in role, and, though largely unsupported by empirical research, are powerful factors in the way we perceive one another.

*Folk linguistics,* the folklore of male and female speech as expressed in jokes, cartoons, sayings, music, and literature, is an important key to understanding cultural perceptions about verbal communication among and between females and males and thus also a key to understanding the bases of miscommunication. This folklore perpetuates the perception of differences in male and female speech even though such empirical research as has been done indicates that the folklore is inaccurate and biased. One of the most commonly accepted beliefs about women's speech, for example, is that there is a lot of it. Yet, studies of talk in mixed-sex groups indicate that men speak at least twice as much, interrupt more often, and speak in ways that control both the direction of the talk and the overall situation in which people are speaking.[22] Indeed, Spender's research strongly indicates that a woman who is perceived to "talk a lot" is, in fact, talking about half as often as a man in the same situation.[23]

Another popular perception is that men curse and swear more than women. This is a particularly interesting belief because it persists in the face of nearly incontrovertible evidence to the contrary, particularly among the young. It is likely, for instance, that tape-recorded evidence of an hour spent among high school and/or college students in informal settings would show a kind of ''equality of language'' in terms of swear words. The point, of course, is that according to cultural norms, women are not *supposed* to swear. Rather, women are *supposed* to speak softly, to use the language well (be models for children and men), and to talk in ways that support the conversation of men.[24]

Despite a kind of cultural mandate to set an example, perceptions of differences between female and male speech patterns most often compare women's speech unfavorably to men's. Thus, as Kramer notes, ''Compared to male speech, the female form is supposed to be emotional, vague, euphemistic, sweetly proper, mindless, endless, high-pitched, and silly.''[25] In short, it can be discounted. When girls or women ''break'' this stereotype, it is usually noted that they are in some way less ''feminine.'' One of the saddest consequences of acting counter to this stereotype that we have ever heard is illustrated by this comment of a counselor in an adolescent treatment facility for disturbed young people: ''When one of our patients is a girl who acts out aggressively (as boys are supposed to do), who hits and uses foul language,'' he said, ''even the counselors don't want to have much to do with her.''[26] Of course, males can also suffer for ''unmasculine'' behavior. The language of boys and men is closely associated with our impressions of their masculinity. A boy who uses words like ''cute,'' ''sweet,'' and ''darling'' risks a major identity crisis brought on by the reactions of his peers and others.

Although we lack a significant body of empirical research on the subject, it appears that real differences in communication patterns of females and males may not be as important as perceived differences or stereotypes. As we have noted in earlier chapters, stereotypes serve in part to enable us to organize our experience on a daily basis without having to rediscover everything from scratch. When stereotypes enforce inequalities of power and influence, however, their unquestioned use may cause not only miscommunication, but also miscarriages of justice.

## INTERCULTURAL COMMUNICATION COMPETENCE

A discussion of interpersonal and intercultural communication cannot be complete without some reference to communication effectiveness and competence. Hammer discusses these concepts thoroughly, and highlights of his summary are presented here.[27]

*Communication competence* refers to the social judgments people make about others which are based on the behavior they observe. We have been using the word *attributions* throughout this book to refer to such judgments. *Communication skills* refers to the specific verbal and nonverbal behaviors used in any interaction. While communication skills themselves do not determine competence, they provide the basis for interactants' judgments of themselves and others.

The culture-general versus culture-specific distinction emerges in discussion of communication skills. The culture-specific approach assumes that communication competence can best be determined by the degree to which one becomes functional in the rituals and skills of verbal and nonverbal expression and reception practiced by a particular cultural group. This may be desirable in many circumstances, especially if one is teaching and living with people who belong to only one or two groups.

For those living and working in highly mixed settings, however, the number of specific skills to be learned may be overwhelming. In such circumstances, culture-general communication skills might be sufficient, or at least provide a base from which one can begin to develop specific knowledge and skill. The culture-general approach focuses on those dimensions of communication competence that can best be generalized to intercultural interactions.

While universal communication skills may exist, the specific behaviors that reflect those skills may vary across cultural contexts. Ruben says:

> While one can argue that the importance of communication behaviors such as empathy, respect, non-judgmentalness, etc., transcends cultural boundaries, the way these are expressed and interpreted may vary substantially from one culture (or one sub-culture) to another.[28]

This approach reinforces the notion of communication competence as a social judgment. It suggests that communication skill assessment must be made by all parties to the communication process.

Research in the area of intercultural communication has identified certain skills as important to both cross-cultural adaptation and intercultural effectiveness. Hammer, Gudykunst, and Wiseman identified three important dimensions of intercultural effectiveness: (1) the ability to communicate effectively, (2) the ability to deal with psychological stress, and (3) the ability to develop interpersonal relationships.[29]

Ruben also investigated specific behavioral skills of intercultural communication competence.[30] Seven specific skills or behaviors have been identified: (1) *display of respect,* or the ability to express positive high regard and respect for another person; (2) *interaction posture,* defined as the ability to respond to others in a nonjudgmental manner; (3) *orientation to knowledge,* or the ability to recognize that what we know is individual in nature, thereby reducing the likelihood of responding from a stereotypic perspective; (4) *empathy,* or the ability to see the world from another's point of view; (5) *self-oriented role behavior,* or the ability to function in both problem-solving and relationship-building roles; (6) *interaction management,* or the ability to take turns in discussions and to terminate the interaction based on a reasonably accurate determination of the needs and desires of others; (7) *tolerance for ambiguity,* already discussed, the ability to adjust quickly and with little discomfort to new and often ambiguous situations.

## Improving Intercultural Communication Competence

What we know about the specific skills which aid in intercultural communication indicates that if teachers begin to develop competence in these areas they will have more rewarding and more successful interactions, and will be better able to deliver instruction to children from a wide range of backgrounds.

There is no "best" way to go about improving one's intercultural communication competence, but attention to the six areas listed below should help you to do so.[31] First, *know yourself.* This means identifying the deeply held attitudes, biases, and opinions or subjective cultural elements you carry around. It means knowing how you come across to others, what impression you make on them. This may take considerable effort, in part because getting that information from others may be difficult. You must, therefore, be sensitive to the feedback you receive from others when you are engaged in interactions with them. If you believe you make one kind of impression, but others see you differently, you must work hard to change the image you present.

Second, *use a shared code,* i.e., a shared symbol and communication system, when speaking to those who regularly speak another language. Strive to "break the code" in the other person's head. Once this is accomplished, communication can take place. Ask questions, especially ones that use the concepts and vocabulary from the eighteen-theme culture-general framework as a point of reference.

Third, *take time.* People everywhere have a tendency to jump to conclusions. Effective communication demands that people suspend judgment and wait long enough to let others finish their sentences. Otherwise they risk putting their own ideas into others' mouths. Taking time to make decisions, especially when the parties are from different cultural groups, becomes very important. Each culture and each person has a unique communication style; you must allow people the time to communicate all they have in mind.

Fourth, *encourage feedback.* Feedback enables communicators to correct and adjust their messages as needed. Without feedback, there is no way to monitor the communication process. You should work to create an atmosphere that promotes feedback. Extended silence, after asking if people have any questions, is one way to encourage feedback. By becoming a model yourself, that is, by offering feedback to others, you may encourage others to do the same. Asking for clarification or further detail also invites others to expand on their communication. Statements such as "What do you mean when you say your son John is bored?" encourage expansion.

Fifth, *develop empathy.* The quality of empathy is essential to any communicative effort. When you cannot understand others' points of view or the perspective they speak from, you are probably unable to communicate effectively. At that moment, and from that moment on, a common frame of reference is lacking. One way to begin to develop empathy is to continuously stop and ask yourself what it might be like to have the experiences the other is relating. Try to put yourself in the other's shoes.

Sixth, *strive not to create stereotypes.* We have tried to avoid the creation of stereotypes in this book. However, when presenting examples of behavior in various cultural groups, there is always a danger of creating stereotypes in the minds of readers where they did not exist before. While some of these differences are important, it is what we have in common that, once identified and understood, can bring us to better understand those with whom we will live and work.

## ACTIVITIES

1 Arrange to do an observation of young children's play behavior at a nearby school. When observing preschool boys and girls, what gender differences are you able to observe? Think about the way they act, their choices of play activities, their responses to various stimuli. What happens when you ask boys and girls to play with a toy or game typically assigned to the other sex?

2 Engage in a series of role play situations involving nonverbal behavior. Small groups of students should each prepare one of the following role plays. Others should observe the interactions and interpret and evaluate the nonverbal messages *from different perspectives* (developed at a workshop at the East-West Center).

   a An American teacher in Japan repeats his question to a student whenever the student does not answer promptly.

   b A person from Greece keeps moving away from an American with whom he is having a conversation.

c An Ethiopian businessman is insecure with his business superior from the United States who regularly refers to dieting and is quite slim.

d Two male African students are frequently seen holding hands.

e An Indochinese child cowers in fright when he sees the teacher occasionally touch another child's head while helping them with their lessons.

f Lien from Vietnam was absent daily from gym class and when confronted begged to be excused.

g Mai came to school with red welts on her neck and down into her chest. When asked, she indicated they were caused by her parents and that now she is feeling better.

h An American homemaker visited her Laotian neighbor shortly after they moved in. She invited the woman to visit when she could. She was very distressed to have the Laotian neighbor drop in several times each day.

i Rai of Cambodia has shown exceptional ability on the school swim team but becomes very nervous and uncomfortable when he is asked to demonstrate something or when his skill is acknowledged.

## MORE CRITICAL INCIDENTS

### Why Are the Hispanic Teachers So Quiet?

Kaye Spanos is in her fifth month as principal of an urban school in Phoenix, Arizona. Kaye is an energetic person who encourages and desires staff input on the school's policies and curriculum. Generally, Kaye tries to facilitate staff participation with periodic printed surveys and by announcing during staff meetings that all comments are welcome. The middle school's teachers are about 50 percent Hispanic and 50 percent Anglo. Kaye has been disturbed lately by the dearth of input from Hispanic teachers. She is particularly interested in their ideas since 60 percent of the school's students are Hispanic. Although she feels she has been open to all, Kaye receives most of her feedback from the Anglo teachers.

How do you explain this situation?

1 The Hispanic teachers do not want to interact with Kaye because she is non-Hispanic.

2 The Anglo teachers dominate the Hispanic teachers and do not give them a chance to express their opinions.

3 The Hispanic teachers do not have opinions on the subjects Kaye includes in the surveys and meetings.

4 Kaye has taken an impersonal approach to eliciting opinions, whereas Hispanics favor a personalized approach.

### Rationales

1 You chose number 1. There is no indication that this is the case. The entire school population is mixed, and such a situation would make it difficult for Hispanic teachers to limit interaction with non-Hispanics. Also, there is no mention that Kaye feels she is the target of hostility. There is a better explanation. Please choose again.

2 You chose number 2. The story states that Kaye receives feedback both in meetings and through surveys. There is no way that Anglo teachers could dominate the

Hispanic teachers responses on the surveys. There is also no indication that there is domination rather than nonparticipation at the staff meetings. There is a more reasonable response. Please choose again.

3 You chose number 3. This is highly unlikely. These teaching professionals, like most others, will certainly have opinions about their workplace. Please choose again.

4 You chose number 4. Hispanic culture strongly emphasizes the affective side of interpersonal relationships. Personalized contact is thus very important to the Hispanic teacher. Although Kaye is genuinely interested in the opinions of all her teachers, she has approached them impersonally, through printed surveys and in the formal setting of a staff meeting. The Hispanic teachers would be more likely to respond if approached individually or addressed individually at a meeting. You chose correctly.

### Bad Calls on the Tennis Court

Pitchit is a 16-year-old Thai student who has been attending high school in Cleveland for the last year and a half. He tried out for the tennis team, and his obvious talent earned him a spot on the team as the second singles player. Coach Butler is impressed with Pitchit's play and the 7–1 record he has compiled.

During a match against one of the area's better players, Coach Butler watches as Pitchit wins the first set 6–3. Figuring that Pitchit will win the match easily, Mr. Butler goes to another court to watch one of his doubles teams play. Later he is surprised to learn that Pitchit lost the next two sets and the match. Another member of the team tells Mr. Butler that Pitchit's opponent made many bad line calls at crucial points in the match. He says that Pitchit knew he was being cheated, but he did not protest or challenge his opponent in any way. When the coach asked Pitchit about the match and why he did not stand up to his opponent's cheating, Pitchit said, "I just got beat; that's all."

How can Pitchit's reaction to an obvious injustice be explained?

1 Pitchit does not think winning is such a big deal.
2 Pitchit knows that he really lacks the talent to be the team's second singles player.
3 Pitchit resents the fact that Coach Butler did not watch his entire match.
4 Pitchit was not assertive enough to confront his opponent about the bad line call.

### Rationales

1 While this alternative may have some validity, it does not get at the underlying cause of Pitchit's behavior. Please choose again.

2 Pitchit's 7–1 record indicates that he has plenty of talent as a tennis player. There is no evidence that he feels at all inferior. Please choose again.

3 If Coach Butler had watched the entire match, Pitchit might not have been a victim of bad calls. This, however, has nothing to do with his passive reaction in this situation. Please make another choice.

4 This is the best response. In Thai and many other Asian cultures, assertiveness is not highly valued; it is often seen as a potentially disruptive trait. Socialization in such cultures encourages a certain passivity, a willingness to tolerate unpleasant situations without complaint to a much greater degree than is manifested in western cultures. Such passivity has its roots in both the religious (Buddhist) and other societal forces

that have shaped Asian culture. Pitchit, therefore, is hesitant to assert himself against his opponent, even though he knows he is being cheated.

### What Happened to Mariko?

Mr. Simms, chemistry teacher and moderator of the junior class, needed two more students to help as guides and hosts for the school's science fair. While walking through the cafeteria, he saw two of his better students, Julie and Mariko, an exchange student from Japan. When he asked them about helping at the fair, Julie responded with an enthusiastic "Yes." Mariko, however, hesitated and said that she felt her English was not good enough. Both Mr. Simms and Julie assured Mariko that her English was excellent and that she would do well as a guide. Mariko still appeared very hesitant, but said nothing else as Mr. Simms told the girls when to get to the fair on Saturday.

On the day of the fair, Mariko failed to show up. Mr. Simms and Julie were surprised and puzzled, and on the following Monday asked Mariko what happened. Mariko was vague and evasive, replying that she "just couldn't make it on Saturday."

What is the most plausible explanation for Mariko's behavior?

1 Mariko resented being "railroaded" into helping at the fair and not having the opportunity to explain why she was unable to attend.

2 She was reluctant to refuse the teacher's request because it would seem impolite and disrespectful.

3 Mariko felt that Mr. Simms and Julie were going out of their way to be kind to her. This caused her to feel embarrassed and somewhat angry. She was too proud to accept the extra help and attention they were offering.

4 Mariko felt that since the fair was not during school time, she had no obligation to attend or to explain why she was not there.

### Rationales

1 It seems that Mariko did have ample opportunity to explain to Mr. Simms why she could not or would not work at the fair. There is no evidence that she was really railroaded into this. Look elsewhere for the deeper reason for her hesitancy to tell Mr. Simms why she wouldn't attend.

2 This is the best response. Many cultures consider it rude to give a direct rejection or refusal. Hesitancy and ambiguity are used to convey reluctance and so avoid embarrassment to either party. Mr. Simms and Julie are undoubtedly puzzled by Mariko's lack of forthrightness. To Mariko, however, honesty is of lesser value than preserving dignity in interpersonal interactions, and one of the main sources of cultural conflict in this situation is the differing weights attached to honesty. While many western cultures view the direct and honest statement of intentions or opinions as a positive trait, others regard such behavior as discourteous.

3 While this face-saving motive has some plausibility, Mariko's hesitancy seems to have a different cause. There is no evidence here that Mariko's pride has been wounded or that she is in any way angry with Mr. Simms or Julie. Please choose again.

4 Mariko shows no resentment at being asked to do something outside of school time. Look elsewhere for an explanation of her hesitancy and evasiveness.

### Conversation at Lunch

Ranjani and Sathie are two female students from India studying at a large midwestern university. They often eat lunch together in the student lounge. They are both very pleased to have found another person from their country with whom they can share their concerns. They often have quite animated discussion, in English, giving each other help and advice.

David, an American student, usually sits nearby. One day, in a tone of frustration, he asks, "Why do you two argue so much?" Ranjani and Sathie look at him in astonishment and do not know what to say.

What do you think is at the root of the problem?

1 David feels left out of the conversation and wishes the women would include him.
2 David is trying to work and is angry that the women are talking so much.
3 David is a rude person who should not be eavesdropping on other people's conversations.
4 David misinterprets the women's conversation as an argument when in fact it is a friendly discussion.

#### Rationales

1 You chose number 1. There is nothing in the story to indicate that David wants to be included in the conversation. Please select another response.

2 You chose number 2. Although this is possible, David would probably not try to do his work in the lounge if he knew that these women were always in there at this time. Please select another response.

3 You chose number 3. There is nothing in the story to indicate that David is rude. The conversation is rude. The conversation was quite loud. Please select another response.

4 You chose number 4. This is the best choice. Indian women frequently have animated conversations in which they interrupt one another and give unsolicited advice. In David's experience, discussions with this tone, especially between women, are arguments. David has misinterpreted the conversation.

## REFERENCES

1 Brislin, R., Cushner, K., Cherrie, C., and Yong, M. *Intercultural Interactions: A Practical Guide*. (Newbury Park: Sage Publications, 1986).
2 Marshall Singer, *Intercultural Communication: A Perceptual Approach* (Englewood Cliffs, NJ: Prentice-Hall, 1987), p. 66.
3 Larry Samover, Richard Porter, and Nemi Jain, *Understanding Intercultural Communication* (Belmont, CA: Wadsworth, 1981).
4 Ibid.
5 Ibid.
6 Robert Kaplan, "Cultural Thought Patterns in Inter-Cultural Education," *Language Learning*, vol. 16, nos. 1 and 2, 1966, p. 15.
7 Paul Simon, *The Tongue-Tied American: Confronting the Foreign Language Crisis* (New York: Continuum, 1980), p. 9.
8 Dean Barnlund, *Interpersonal Communication: Survey and Studies* (Boston: Houghton Mifflin, 1968), pp. 536–537.

**9** Samover, Porter, and Jain, op. cit.

**10** Ibid.

**11** Marianne LaFrance and Clara Mayo, *Moving Bodies: Nonverbal Communication in Social Relationships* (Boston: Houghton Mifflin, 1978), p. 145.

**12** A. Kendon, "Some Functions of Gaze Direction in Social Interaction," *Acta Psychologica,* vol. 71, 1967, pp. 359–372.

**13** Michael Hecht, Peter Andersen, and Sidney Ribeau, "The Cultural Dimensions of Nonverbal Communication," in M. K. Asante and W. B. Gudykunst (eds.), *Handbook of International and Intercultural Communication* (Newbury Park, CA: Sage Publications, 1989), pp. 163–185.

**14** Edward Hall, *The Silent Language* (Greenwich, CT: Fawcett Publications, 1959).

**15** Edward Hall, *The Hidden Dimension* (Garden City, NY: Doubleday, 1966).

**16** Irving Goffman, *Stigma* (Englewood Cliffs, NJ: Prentice-Hall, 1963).

**17** A. Shearer, *Disability: Whose Handicap?* (Oxford: Basil Blackwell, 1984), p. 15.

**18** Robert Emry and Richard L. Wiseman, "An Intercultural Understanding of Ablebodied and Disabled Person's Communication," *International Journal of Intercultural Relations,* vol. 11, no. 1 1987, pp. 7–27.

**19** Cited in Shearer, op. cit., p. 54.

**20** Emry and Wiseman, op. cit.

**21** Cheris Kramer, "Folk-Linguistics: Wishy-Washy Mommy Talk," *Psychology Today,* vol. 8, no. 4 June 1974, p. 82.

**22** See, for example, Dale Spender, *Men's Studies Modified: The Impact of Feminism on the Academic Disciplines* (Oxford: Pergamon Press, 1981).

**23** Ibid.

**24** Cheris Kramer, "Women's Speech: Separate but Unequal?" *The Quarterly Journal of Speech,* vol. 60, no. 1 June 1974, pp. 14–24.

**25** Kramer, op. cit., ref. 21.

**26** Story related by a psychological counselor to one of the authors, Spring, 1989.

**27** Mitchell Hammer, "Intercultural Communication Competence," in M. K. Asante and W. B. Gudykunst (eds.), *Handbook of International and Intercultural Communication* (Newbury Park, CA: Sage Publications, 1989), pp. 247–260.

**28** B. Ruben, "Assessing Communication Competency for Intercultural Adaptation," *Group and Organization Studies,* vol. 1, no. 3, Sept. 1976, pp. 334–354.

**29** M. Hammer, W. Gudykunst, and R. Wiseman, "Dimensions of Intercultural Effectiveness: An Exploratory Study," *International Journal of Intercultural Relations,* vol. 2, no. 4, 1978, pp. 382–392.

**30** Ruben, op. cit.

**31** Samover, Porter, and Jain, op. cit.

# CHAPTER 5

# INFLUENCES ON LEARNING

*In America, as white children leave the home and move on through the educational system and then into the work world, the development of cognitive and learning styles follows a linear, self-reinforcing course. Never are they asked to be bicultural, bidialectic, or bicognitive. On the other hand, for children of color, biculturality is not a free choice, but a prerequisite for successful participation and eventual success. Non-white children generally are expected to be bicultural, bidialectic, bicognitive; to measure their performance against a European yardstick; and to maintain the psychic energy to maintain this orientation. At the same time, they are being castigated whenever they attempt to express and validate their indigenous cultural and cognitive styles. Under such conditions cognitive conflict becomes the norm rather than the exception.*

James A. Anderson

## INTEREST IN THE CULTURAL CONTEXT OF ACHIEVEMENT

Children entering school for the first time display a wide range of abilities and maturation levels, as well as a variety of mental ages, a wealth of language experiences and competencies, a diversity of early life experiences, and an inclination to learn in particular ways that are at least partially rooted in their socialization in the family.

One consequence of the reemergence of attention to cultural differences brought about by the civil rights movement was the suggestion that achievement in school might also be related to cultural elements in the lives of students. Clearly, some children did better than others in school, and school achievement did not seem necessarily to relate to native intelligence. The question was, Why do some groups of children always seem to adapt easily to school while others do not?

### Cultural Deprivation or Cultural Difference?

Most attention in the early years went to underachievement among the poor of various ethnic groups. The predominant explanation proposed for such differences was "cultural deprivation." The argument was that the poverty in which these students were socialized was, itself, a kind of culture that was at the root of their underachievement. The "poverty home" in which a child was raised was thought to retard development, thus leading to problems in school. Children raised in a "culture of poverty," so the argument went, never really acquired the cognitive skills or values requisite for success in school.[1] There was something wrong with the cultural background in which the child was raised.

Children from poverty homes were, and are still, often labeled as academically retarded, cognitively deficient, and unmotivated. Beck and Saxe suggested that these "socially disadvantaged" children were denied the experiences of "normal" children because they lacked toys and challenging objects with which to play as well as sufficient linguistic models to facilitate language development.[2]

In the ferment of the times, considerable attention was given to the possibility that genetics could explain perceived differences in learning ability, particularly those observed between black students and white students. Noting an IQ differential of about 15 points, for example, Arthur Jensen wrote that "genetic factors are strongly implicated in the average Negro-white intelligence difference."[3] He and others argued that such genetic differences would tend to work against African-Americans and against the "disadvantaged" generally when it comes to "cognitive" learning—abstract reasoning—which forms the basis for intelligence measurements and for the "higher" mental skills. Conversely, African-Americans and other children perceived to be "disadvantaged" tend to do well in tasks involving rote learning—memorizing mainly through repetition—and some other skills, and these aptitudes could be used to help raise their scholastic achievement and job potential.

Taking another position in the debate were those who argued that the proposition that some children were "culturally deprived" was simply an ethnocentric response to the observation that some children were not a part of the dominant cultural group. All people, they argued, have cultural knowledge, as exemplified by rich and elaborate languages and communication styles, organized behavior patterns, and value systems. *Cultural deprivation* was, therefore, an oxymoron. Cultural *difference,* on the other hand, was a much more reasonable explanation. These theorists suggested that the cognitive, learning, and motivational styles of many minority students were merely different from those required in the schools. Our nation, they asserted, had historically forced all children into a monocultural school culture, which favored white, middle-class values, behavior, and thinking skills. It was the school culture that needed to be substantially modified, not the minority students.

Moreover, Baratz and Baratz, noting that specific attention was centered on children who were both poor and black, argued that school programs based on the cultural deprivation model were examples of institutional racism.[4] Others asserted that this approach promoted historical assimilation models of schooling and thus violated the cultural integrity of students from diverse income and cultural groups.

Anderson cites two issues which are of major concern with respect to "deficit" explanations of difference in school achievement.[5] One is the assumption that Anglo-European notions about cognitive functioning, learning, and achievement are unquestionably the best and should be used as models of schooling. The second is an extremely ethnocentric assumption on the part of whites that minorities do not have a substantive, valid cognitive framework which may be somewhat different but equally effective. The burden of change, in a system that truly cares about its students, should not be placed on the individual child but on the school.

While the "deficit" position encourages insensitivity to individual strengths and differences, the "difference" position also has its problems. Not all cultural differences are related to school achievement. Indeed, not all cultural differences are benign, regardless of the setting. Furthermore, because cultural differences are often seen as negative and threatening to the status quo, we must be careful to specify the differences which truly make a difference in learning as it is supposed to take place in schools. Consider the following incident:

### Critical Incident: The Students Balk

Mrs. Allen teaches an elective class in English as a Standard Dialect. Her students (most of them African-Americans, with some Hispanics) have been identified by English teachers or guidance counselors as speaking an excessive amount of nonstandard English. The students and their parents have chosen to take advantage of this special class.

Mrs. Allen's classroom is supplied with library carrels and tape recorders, along with the usual desks arranged in slightly cramped quarters at one end of the room. Mrs. Allen has gone to a great deal of trouble to collect copies of written materials from a variety of sources and to make audiotapes for oral work. Each student took a placement test at the beginning of the year and received a binder full of individualized lessons geared to her or his particular needs.

On the days when the class stays together, working from their textbook, the students concentrate and participate. Other days, when they work individually, they complain, do not do much work, and some constantly visit others around the room. The only way Mrs. Allen can get individual work done is to act in a very authoritarian manner.

What should the teacher know about the students to help her understand what is going on?

1 Kids, being human, are naturally lazy. If Mrs. Allen does not keep them together and under constant supervision, they will do the least amount of work possible.

2 Students from some cultural backgrounds value learning and doing in groups rather than independent, individual efforts.

3 The students wanted attention from the teacher and discovered they could get it by being a "problem" for her.

4 The students resented studying this subject and expressed their resentment by not doing their work.

Rationales

1 You chose number 1. While there may be some truth to this response, depending on what teaching style the students are familiar with, it is not a valid maxim to teach by. In general, students, when motivated, can work well on their own. Please choose again.

2 You chose number 2. This is the most appropriate answer. The teacher was expecting that these students would enjoy working on their own. She did not realize that her students were from a background which has a group orientation and values joint work. Her students were far more comfortable not being singled out for individual programmed study.

3 You chose number 3. As many teachers know, this motivation is sometimes behind the activities of "troublemakers" in the classroom. However, as the behavior is widespread in the classroom, there seems to be something else going on. Please choose again.

4 You chose number 4. Teaching English as a Standard Dialect at the high school level is quite unusual, and the issues involved can be volatile. For these reasons it is quite plausible that students may resent studying this subject. However, the students seemed to work well when they worked as a whole class. In addition, this class is an elective, and there are no clues given which lead one to believe that students resent. Please choose again.

## The Difference between Education and Schooling

The moment a child enters the world she or he begins the task of learning the history, customs, attitudes, values, and behaviors that are the requirements of membership in a particular family, cultural group, and society. Such learning is, as John Dewey remarked, necessary to preserve the continuity of the social group, and consists in the "re-creation of beliefs, ideals, hopes, happiness, misery, and practices."[6] Such learning occurs in a variety of settings—at home, in the neighborhood, in church, and in voluntary associations such as clubs, street gangs, and athletic teams. It may be "taught" by a variety of people—parents, siblings, neighbors, friends, or adult group leaders, and it may take place formally or informally.

The distinction between formal and informal learning, which is often used by educators and others to distinguish between schooling and other forms of education, is both a help and a hindrance to understanding the nature of education in its broadest sense. It is a help when one is trying to distinguish between learning that occurs through daily experience and learning that occurs in schools. It is a hindrance, however, in that it tends to legitimize the belief that so-called informal learning can be easily discounted when discussing education. In fact, much of what is usually referred to as *informal learning* is quite deliberate. The processes of socialization, for example, can be said to have a curriculum, learning activities, and means of evaluation. Families clearly *mean* to teach their children knowledge and skills, as well as particular beliefs, attitudes, and values, and they do it in time-tested ways through sometimes ingenious activities. Moreover, learning that occurs through apprenticeship in settings other than schools has long been a staple of the educational enterprise.

One can make a distinction, however, between learning that takes place outside school and learning that takes place in school, and the differences may be quite apparent. For example, learning outside school is integrated rather than discrete; it is not broken down into "subjects" but rather flows in a more or less continuous stream. Such learning is characterized by *modeling*, in which the child typically first observes another person (parent, other adult, sibling, or peer) and is then invited and encouraged to attempt the task at hand. Instruction takes place in conversational rather than didactic form. The learner typically learns by doing rather than by reading. Questioning may very well take place, but critical inquiry (as in the scientific method) may not, and in some cases, may be actively discouraged because it is assumed that the "teacher" knows what she or he is doing and how to do it. (Unfortunately, in many cases critical inquiry is also rare in school!)

An important characteristic of learning outside schools is that it often occurs in an immediately meaningful, face-to-face context, and thus has an inherent affective component which tends to merge the emotional and cognitive domains. The things one learns from one's mother and father are not usually forgotten. In addition, in these contexts, the weight of responsibility for learning falls mainly on the learner. Whether one learns often depends on the value placed on the person giving the information, or on the reason for learning, not on the information itself. Maintenance of continuity, the group, and tradition are highly valued. Cooperation, not competition, therefore predominates.

Schooling, on the other hand, is set apart from the context of everyday life and has a normative set of beliefs, values, and behaviors—a culture of its own. Whereas much learning that occurs outside school is observational, with the learner observing the "teacher," schooling is characterized by intense emphasis on words, both spoken and read. Information is taught in discrete or separate "subject areas" without any particularly meaningful context, and skills are taught apart from their applications. For instance, in the in-context approach to teaching how to count, the child is given specific items to count which are important in a given situation—the number of plates that must go around the table or the number of rows of corn planted in the family garden. In out-of-context teaching, the child is taught how to count in the abstract—through symbols and in text material—with the assumption that the skill of counting will transfer to many situations in the real world. In school, language is the major means for transmission of knowledge; in the ideal case, inquiry and questioning are highly encouraged. Education in schools follows a highly structured curriculum, and the teacher (who in most cases is a stranger at first) rather than the learner is responsible for imparting the requisite knowledge. A relatively impersonal relationship develops, which, in many cases, is quite different from the personal kinds of relationships which direct learning outside schools. Moreover, change, discontinuity, and innovation are often highly valued in school and form part of the school culture, which may be quite different from the culture of the family and neighborhood. Consider the story of Jimmy, a young native Alaskan boy whose family moved to a large city.

## Critical Incident: From a Fishing Village to a School in Town

Jimmie and his family had recently moved to Seattle from a small fishing village outside Anchorage where he had spent most of his young life among his father's people, the Tlingits. Jimmie often accompanied his father while he made his living fishing for salmon and hunting for the winter food supply.

Jimmie's mother taught him at home and he pursued his studies on his own with her guidance. When he came to Seattle, he tested at grade level and was placed with other 9-year-olds in the fourth grade. In social studies, the class was broken into small groups, each given a different topic for group inquiry and presentation. Jimmie quietly sat at the edge of the group and did not share or discuss with them, even after several meetings, although he did seem to have his report outlined and completed. The group leader approached the teacher, complaining that Jimmie was not doing his fair share of the work.

What is an appropriate explanation for Jimmie's quietness?

  1 Jimmie is frightened of all the city children and is afraid to talk.
  2 Jimmie doesn't like his new school and misses his home in Alaska.
  3 Jimmie has always done his work on his own, and much of his learning has been on the job with his father.
  4 Because Jimmie has not been in public school, he is really unable to do the work.

### Rationales

  1 You chose number 1. There is no indication that this is his reaction. Jimmie may be unfamiliar with the setting of city and new children, but there is a more comprehensive response. Please choose again.

**2** You chose number 2. Though Jimmie may miss his home and may not be comfortable at the new school, it is not clear that this is so, and this does not explain Jimmie's behavior with the inquiry groups. Please consider the question again.

**3** You chose number 3. Jimmie has learned primarily by studying on his own and by practical application of skills in working and living. He has developed strong independent study skills and is not used to group involvement. Jimmie may need further guidance to adapt to group study. Perhaps he could begin by working with a partner, then move to small groups before a larger group project. He should also be encouraged to continue his independent work and may have much to offer the others in this area. This is the best response.

**4** You chose number 4. Jimmie tested at grade level, so he is clearly able to do the work. Choose again.

As we have seen, there are many differences between schooling and other forms of education. It is also important to note that incidental or unintentional learning can occur both in schools and outside them. Children often don't learn what we teach, wherever we teach it; they often do learn things from our teaching that we don't intend. Moreover, not all learning is of equal value. Children, for example, can learn to lie, to cheat, and to steal; Fagin, in Dicken's *Oliver Twist* was expert at teaching his boys to be pickpockets. Children can also learn that the world is not a sympathetic place for children and that they do not seem to "fit in" anywhere. This is learning, but it is not education—it is miseducation.[7] It is thus important, when considering *education* in its broadest sense, to understand that all learning (and all teaching) do not have positive consequences. Nevertheless, before making judgments about what children have already learned when they come to school, it is well to think about the context in which it was learned. Attitudes and skills that may appear reprehensible to us (lying, cheating, stealing) may in fact be survival skills to some children. In these cases, as in nearly all other cases, our job involves making connections between what children already know and new and more positive ways of surviving in the culture of the school and in the community.

### The Culture of the School

The American public education system has its roots in the Greek tradition. Certain characteristics and qualities of the schooling process have their beginnings here and have continued to this day. For instance, schools were not originally established to meet the needs of the individual. From early on, attempts were made to socialize young people into adult life and the society at large by striving to make the individual "fit" the group. The primary role of the teacher in this regard was to unify the individual students in the class. For this to happen, the child must develop loyalties outside the family and transfer some of them to the teacher, thus encouraging independence from the child's primary social group.

In order to succeed in school, one must learn to think and communicate by understanding and using abstract words and symbols that have been collected from chosen bodies of previously agreed upon knowledge. There is nothing innately correct about this system; it merely has been found to be a convenient method for carrying out a range of complex tasks in our society. The important point here is that the particular symbols used, the knowledge made accessible to others, and the preferred method of imparting that knowledge have been agreed upon by the majority of the members of a particular cultural group: in the case in the United States, dominant white middle-class males.

In accordance with one of the fundamental values of that group, the typical classroom is quite competitive. Another dominant value—individualism—characterizes the practice of teaching students as individual units even though there may be large numbers of students in any one classroom. Typical evaluation and assessment methods encourage competition. The standard bell curve demands that there be both successes and failures in any group. The success of one, then, is intimately tied to the failure of another.

The language of instruction in schools is also an important feature of school culture. In most schools, children learn in the language of the macro, or dominant, culture. In the United States, instruction is typically carried out in Standard English, although for many children, English is not the primary language. According to the 1980 census, 11 percent of all Americans are from non-English-speaking homes, and that figure is certainly higher today!

The characteristics of the school are, as in any cultural milieu, maintained by those who are themselves successfully socialized into the group, and, in part, wield the power. Thus, the culture of the school is maintained by successful teachers and administrators. Students in most schools are expected to learn in an out-of-context situation through words and symbols; display, or at least strive to develop, independence and the ability to compete; learn from, and be evaluated by, adults; obey school personnel in authority; be task-oriented; delay gratification of desires to win later rewards; and have a relatively high degree of fluency in the language of the macroculture. Those children socialized in families and neighborhoods where values, beliefs, and behaviors are congruent with the existing culture of the school stand a better chance of success within the system.

LeCompte suggests that there exist baseline conditions which reflect the social and structural demands of schools and transcend the idiosyncrasies of individual teachers.[8] Children who are successful in school learn the whole range of tasks presented to them. Others may learn some of what is required, but not all. In essence, there exists a culture particular to the school which must be learned and successfully negotiated by all participants.

Compared with some ethnic and/or socioeconomic groups, middle-class caucasian children are well socialized to be ready for school. Values articulated in the school, as well as skills expected for success there, are instilled in the child at home. LeCompte cites evidence that middle-class caucasian children beginning kindergarten have expectations which are quite congruent with those of the school.[9] Preschool children from middle-class families expect teachers to structure and organize their day, anticipate that they will learn to "work," and assume that teachers will control and discipline the classroom. In other words, these children are aware of the cognitive and authority demands of school before coming into contact with the institution. For many of these children, a relatively easy transition between home and school takes place, encouraging academic success. This does not appear to be true for many other ethnic, racial, and socioeconomic groups. In order to further understand this phenomenon, let's explore some of the stronger roots of school expectations.

## AMERICAN VALUES

American culture is complex, and it is difficult to identify a national culture, or "typical" American cultural patterns. Many Americans, in fact, think of themselves as having no culture, as being citizens of a nation too young to have really developed culture. Nothing could be farther from the truth. Every group of people with any history has created a culture which pervades their thoughts and actions. Since American cultural patterns associated with the white middle class are dominant in schools as representative of this society, these patterns will be analyzed in terms of the school experience and school readiness.

A brief reflection on American history suggests that those who colonized North America had relatively weak ties to their homelands. The extended family, important in the country of origin, was separated, leaving the nuclear family as the predominant source of strength and identity. This had a tremendous influence on the development of an "American" character, since people's orientation had to shift from the larger collective to the individual or nuclear family unit. The beginnings of an individualistic orientation emerge here. In addition, as people came to settle in America, the need to adjust to uncertainty, as well as to focus on change and development for survival, was paramount.

Over the years, a dominant white middle-class American culture has emerged which rests on six major values.[10] We can explore these values by looking at proverbs and sayings which have become part of our folk wisdom. Since such proverbs express the values of a people, they are an excellent indicator of the folk-knowledge that supports and integrates a society.

**1** *Americans have a tendency to view themselves as separate from nature and able to master or control their environment.* As a result, a high value is placed on science and technology as the predominant means of interacting with the world. This results in objectivity, rationality, materialism, and a need for concrete evidence. Proverbs and sayings such as "Necessity is the mother of invention" and "We'll cross that bridge when we come to it" reflect this belief. Can you think of any other proverbs or popular sayings which express a similar sentiment?

**2** *Americans are action-oriented.* As with number 1, this results in measurable accomplishments. There is emphasis on efficiency and practicality. Progress and change are important concepts. Our schools expect such an orientation, as evidenced by an emphasis on testing and measurement as well as a nearly religious belief in the efficacy of paperwork assignments. Proverbs such as "Seeing is believing" and "The proof is in the pudding" emphasize this cultural trait.

**3** *Americans have a future orientation; they believe in the promise that things will be bigger and better.* Middle-class Americans are seldom content with the present; they wish not to be considered old-fashioned, and they believe that effort applied in the present will affect their future. Progress is, in many ways, our most important product. Proverbs such as "I think I can, I think I can," "A penny saved is a penny earned," "From little acorns, mighty oaks grow," and even the more recent "No pain—no gain," reflect this tendency.

**4** *Americans are self-motivated and are comfortable setting their own goals and di-*

*rections*. From an early age, Americans are encouraged to reach out on their own, to attempt for themselves, to satisfy their own needs. Such proverbs as "Nothing ventured—nothing gained" and "If at first you don't succeed, try, try again" reflect this trait.

**5** *Americans have a strong sense of individuality*. They believe that the "self" is an individual separate from others. This results in a tendency to emphasize individual initiative, independence, action, and interests. Americans tend to believe that to be an effective person, one must be responsible, independent, and have an internal locus of control and set of standards. One should not depend on others for identity. Rather, people should maintain their individuality even within the larger group. American culture expects and encourages independence. From an early age, children are encouraged to make their own decisions and to develop their individual skills and abilities. The school expects children to work alone in their seats, rarely coming together with others to share in problem resolution and task assistance. How many of you have heard teachers say "Keep your eyes on your own paper" or "Don't talk with your neighbors"? A cursory review of most grade school report cards gives evidence of the emphasis on this trait: consider such statements as "Johnny is able to work independently," "Mary works well on her own," or "Shaun is a responsible student." The United States is one of the few countries where job seekers have a section on their resumes listing their interests and hobbies. Proverbs such as "Too many cooks spoil the broth," "Don't judge a book by its cover," and "God helps those who help themselves" stress this value.

**6** Finally, *Americans believe in the mutability of human nature*. That is, they subscribe to the notion that it is relatively easy to change and that people can be molded by their cultural environment. This belief underlies the assimilationist ideology which has pervaded American public education for so many years. "A stranger is only a friend you haven't met yet" and "Leaders are made, not born" may reflect this.

Cultural values, as well as certain skills needed for school success, are instilled in the child by the home and family of most middle-class caucasian Americans. Out-of-context teaching and learning which demands thinking in the abstract is supported by the future orientation of Americans. The mutability of human nature is assumed by the assimilationist ideology which emphasizes shaping the individual to a larger society. A technological and task orientation in our classrooms meshes well with the belief in our ability to control nature as well as our emphasis on accountability and testing. Achievement orientation encouraged at home is reflected in the middle-class child, although the gender of the child appears to influence the ways in which this orientation is expressed. A white middle-class boy, for example, often attributes success to effort and skill and failure to external factors, or perhaps to a lack of effort. A white middle-class girl is more likely to attribute success to luck and failure to lack of effort. In both cases, however, if a child fails at a given task, she or he is likely to try the task again, with the encouragement of a parent or teacher. Children from lower socioeconomic groups, who may also be members of ethnic minority groups, more often attribute failure at a task to lack of ability. This becomes an obstacle to the teacher who must try to motivate a child who is struggling with both the task in question and a belief in his or her own incompetence. The tendency for this child is not to attempt the task again and risk repeated failure.

## DIFFERENCES IN COGNITIVE STYLE

Students of psychology have long been interested in the relationship between a given stimulus and an organism's response to that stimulus. From these investigations two general approaches have emerged: the *stimulus-response* (S-R) and the *stimulus-organism-response* (S-O-R) models. The S-R model suggests that an organism's behavior can best be predicted by studying the functional relationships between stimuli and responses. The S-O-R model suggests that relationships between stimuli and responses are best predicted from information about the intermediating processes that occur within an organism.

Cognitive style has been proposed as one such mediating process. *Cognitive style* refers to the structure or process of thought rather than the content of cognitive activity. Kagan, Moss, and Sigel explain that *cognitive style* refers to stable individual preferences in perceptual and conceptual organization of the external environment.[11] It encompasses individual variations in how one perceives, thinks, solves problems, learns, and relates to others. This structure of thought is determined by one's socialization in the family and peer group as well as the local environment. It enters the educational context in discussions of learning styles.

*Learning style* refers to a biologically as well as a developmentally determined set of characteristics that make the same teaching method effective for some individuals and ineffective for others.[12] Learning style has been investigated in numerous studies, and these have resulted in the identification of a variety of dimensions which may vary across individuals and groups. Certain preferences of individuals seem to be biologically determined, while others are developed through experience. Learning style may include, for example, individual responses to the immediate environment, emotionality, social preferences, physiological traits, and cognitive-psychological orientation.[13] Responses to environmental influences include an individual's preference for quiet or noise, bright or soft illumination, or warm or cool temperature. Emotionality includes such factors as motivation, persistence at tasks, and sense of responsibility, as well as one's response to the structure of a given context. *Social preferences* refers to the degree to which the presence of others facilitates learning. Included in this category are the degree to which an individual prefers to work alone, in pairs, in cooperative groups, or with adults. Physical dimensions of learning style include preference for learning in verbal, tactile, or kinesthetic modes. Finally, the psychological dimension refers to the tendencies individuals have to be global versus analytic learners, right brain or left brain dominant, reflective or impulsive.

### Cultural Influences on Learning Style

Numerous influences may shape one's preference to learn in a particular way. In this section we will focus on only one—the cultural influences exercised through participation in a variety of social groups. People *learn* how to learn in a particular way. Socialization in any cultural milieu not only teaches one such things as what language to speak and what nonverbal communicative behaviors to use, but how to learn as well. This knowledge is often tacit—not articulated within the culture, and unknown to those outside it— as the teacher in the following story discovered!

### Critical Incident: Carefully Prepared Lectures

Robert, an agricultural engineering professor from New England, felt extremely fortunate to have been invited to spend 4 weeks in Texas training four groups of young English-speaking immigrant Mexican-American farmworkers in week-long sessions in the use and maintenance of some new farm machinery which they were excited about using.

Robert spent hours in the instructional lab constructing diagrams explaining the use of the machines and maintenance of their parts. He was especially pleased with the diagrams he made which explained possible problems and what to do when each occurred. These materials, combined with his extensive lecture notes, company operating manuals, films, books, and audio materials would assure the success of the program.

Much to his surprise, Robert found himself struggling through the sessions—and he saw that his students were struggling too. The first day always seemed to go well, but the remaining four seemed long and drawn out. The students often complained that they didn't understand. They were restless, talkative, and seemingly uninterested in what Robert had to offer. This confused Robert, who had assumed that they would be eager to learn the use of these machines, which would ultimately improve crop yield.

If you were asked to help Robert with his problem, where would you focus?

1 Robert's students were much younger than those he had initially been trained to teach.

2 Robert ignored the fact that most of his students speak Spanish (most commonly Tex-Mex) as well as English. He should have incorporated this in his presentation.

3 Migrant Mexican-American farmworkers are not accustomed to learning from books and papers. They often prefer to be taught with the real object.

4 The students resented Robert pushing his new technology on them and did not want this new machinery interfering with the methods to which they were accustomed.

### Rationales

1 You chose number 1. A growing body of literature is available that focuses on the adult learner, and it should be utilized when planning instruction for adults. However, the students in this story were not that much older than the students Robert was used to teaching. These young farmworkers would not require these kinds of modifications. Please select another response.

2 You chose number 2. Although these workers probably all speak Spanish, they also understand and regularly speak Standard English. This is not a critical factor here. Please select another alternative.

3 You chose number 3. It has been found that many Mexican-American farmworkers (as well as many other people from cultures without a long experience with a written language) typically teach each other and, therefore, learn in context rather than out of context. While Robert's professional training and experiences have stressed out-of-context learning of material (through books, films, lectures, and so forth), to be applied at a later time, many people learn more and become more involved and motivated when taught in an in-context situation. An out-of-classroom, hands-on approach would probably facilitate their learning process. This is the best response.

4 You chose number 4. There is no indication that the workers resented Robert or the fact that he was introducing new machinery. In fact, the text mentions that the workers were looking forward to using these machines. Please choose again.

The early investigation of cognitive style preferences is attributed to Witkin and his colleagues.[14] Witkin's investigations revolved around the ability of individuals to locate the upright in space. In one investigation, the "rod and frame test," subjects were asked to adjust a rod in a tilted frame until it appeared to be upright. In the "embedded figures test," subjects were asked to locate a hidden figure embedded in a more complex field.

In carrying out these experiments, Witkin noticed that there seemed to be individual differences in the ability of test subjects to perform the given task. The ability of some individuals to succeed at the tasks was found to be dependent upon the surrounding visual field, while others succeeded with no reference to outside influences. The terms *field dependent* and *field independent* were coined to describe these individuals. Field-independent individuals are able to adjust the rod upright regardless of the position of the frame. In other words, they can operate independent of the surrounding influences. Field-dependent individuals, however, are not able to adjust the rod upright. Rather, attending to additional factors in the surrounding field, they tend to follow the tilt of the frame and are unable to manipulate the rod independent of the frame. Field-independent individuals find it easier to locate an embedded figure than do field-dependent individuals. The latter get distracted by the extraneous visual field.

Field dependence and independence tend to be characteristics of individuals and may influence different aspects of life. Field-dependent individuals are more dependent on cues and the context of a learning field. They require the forest in order to see the trees, so to speak. A larger context is often required in order for field-dependent learners to achieve well in school. Students displaying field-dependent tendencies might be called *global learners,* since they derive meaning from broader concepts before focusing on details. Having better interpersonal skills, field-dependent individuals tend to be more adept in social situations. They are often perceived as better liked and as warmer and more considerate than field-independent individuals. Field-dependent individuals tend to prefer school subjects which have a human content.

Field-independent people, on the other hand, tend to focus on specifics; they can overcome extraneous stimuli and attend to discrete pieces of information. They have been called *analytical learners,* and tend to learn best when instruction occurs in small, incremental steps. Field-independent people tend to prefer more impersonal relationships and more abstract subject areas, such as music, math, and the sciences. Field-independent individuals are also able to impose structure on a rather messy field better than field-dependent individuals.

Many researchers have studied cognitive styles across various cultures and nations, and some of their findings are of interest to educators. Social groups such as the dominant American white middle-class male mainstream that encourage independence and autonomy and have a more open social structure have a tendency to socialize individuals to be field-independent. Social groups that encourage conformity and that have a more rigid social structure tend to socialize individuals to be field-dependent. Interestingly, Witkin's research in western societies has also suggested that women, regardless of ethnic identity, tend to be more field-dependent than men.[15] This may be because women have traditionally been less independent of the family than men, and have not been able to benefit from social mobility apart from fathers, husbands, and sons.

Similar studies have been undertaken among various American ethnic groups. Ramirez and Castaneda found Mexican-American children to be more field-dependent than their

Anglo peers (although they used the terms *field-sensitive* and *field-insensitive* in their work, as they think that the original terms have negative connotations).[16] While Mexican-American and Mexican children are more highly motivated in a cooperative classroom setting than are their Anglo counterparts, these studies also found that teachers use field-independent teaching styles most often and that they reward field-independent behavior.

Cohen[17] and Hilliard[18] have investigated this aspect of learning style among African-American students. Preferring the terms *analytic* and *relational* (for field independence and dependence, respectively), they found African-American students to be more relational and feeling-oriented than are most caucasian students.

Hilliard provides an example of how an analytical person would function in a relational task:

> If this person were asked to learn an Afro-American dance, the analytical is very likely to draw feet on the floor and to break the dance down into steps and to try to learn the dance piecemeal. It is also likely that the analytical person will establish a standard of performance which becomes "right" or "not right." On the other hand, if a relational is given an analytical task, a comparable translation will take place. Details are likely to be blurred, standards faintly adhered to, or the dance itself may be modified with no real concern for right or wrong so much as "fit" or "harmony."[19]

## Learning Style and the Classroom

### Critical Incident: Why Can't Rema Get to the Point?

Rema, a 16-year-old girl from Lebanon, came to the United States just one year ago. Although she still has some difficulty with speaking and writing English, her language use and understanding are sufficient for her to perform successfully in school. Midway through the eleventh grade at a highly regarded suburban school, Rema is achieving B's and C's in all of her classes.

Literature is Rema's favorite subject, and her teacher, Mrs. Mathews, is continually impressed with the breadth and depth of her reading. Rema reads voraciously and does not limit herself to the literature studied in class.

When the class takes a multiple-choice, true-false, or fill-in-the-blank test, Rema's grades are usually among the highest. When the class is assigned a composition in which they must interpret some aspect of the literary work, however, Rema's grade is always much lower. As Mrs. Mathews puts it, "Rema never really gets to the point; she tries to talk about everything at once."

Despite repeated efforts to remedy this writing problem, Rema continues to write confusing analyses.

How might Rema's writing performance be explained?

1 Middle Eastern and North American modes of thinking and communicating are very different.

2 Rema lacks the basic writing skills and vocabulary necessary to compose a composition of this length.

3 Rema has misunderstood or misinterpreted the main elements of the literary work she is studying.

4 Rema is not able to think clearly and express herself under pressure.

### Rationales

1 You chose number 1. In many cultures, including those of many African and Arab countries, communication is accomplished through associations. Everything that is associated with an idea is considered relevant when thinking about or communicating a concept. Such communication may be highly indirect. Whereas a typical North American will attempt to get right to the point, a person from the Middle East will often make many loops while on the way to making a particular point. (See Figure 4.2, p. 77.) Reasoning, thus, may appear more intuitive than analytic or deductive. Most western cultures communicate in direct terms and arrive at conclusions by step-by-step deduction or by following logically derived instructions. Rema's compositions are highly associative since this is the way one would demonstrate knowledge of a subject as well as intellectual ability in her culture. Once Rema and her teacher are aware of the differences in writing style, they can take some practical steps to improve the situation. This is the best response.

2 You chose number 2. Even though long composition assignments may be more complex and challenging than objective tests, Rema's overall academic performance indicates that she has decent skills in English vocabulary and writing. Her problems with written expression are probably not due to technical deficiencies. Please select another response.

3 You chose number 3. Since Rema reads widely and deeply, she has probably not misunderstood or misinterpreted the literary works studied in class. There is no evidence that Rema has any deficiencies in literary analysis and appreciation. Please choose again.

4 You chose number 4. Being under pressure is not mentioned anywhere in the story. There are no time limits or word minimums mentioned. Rema's problem appears to lie elsewhere. Please choose again.

It should be clear by now that the American classroom is populated by people from diverse backgrounds. And we know that the schooling system is the major point of entry into the mainstream society, and that the experience there is a major factor in later success. But this educational system is based on a Euro-Western worldview. For a variety of reasons, this system, *as it now exists,* seems to serve only certain populations well. Some of the students entering the classroom will come prepared, by the home and family, to satisfy the expectations and demands of the typical classroom. Others will not. What happens to the ''others'' as they participate in the culture of schooling is of critical importance to us all.

The closer the match between a student's learning style and the instructional style of the teacher, the greater the student's success in school. All indications are that students are likely to learn best in an instructional environment which is consistent with their preferred learning style. Cohen[20] and Hilliard,[21] for example, identified distinct school-related behaviors displayed by those who are field-dependent and those who are field-independent. Students whose strengths lie in the analytical realm (field independent) can often extract information embedded in text, may find linear relationships easily, may have longer attention and concentration spans, and may have greater perceptual vigilance. Students whose preference is relational (field dependent) often work to find special or personal relevance in content, may be more global in focus, often find more meaning in text, may tend to devalue linear relationships, may tend to exhibit emotive behavior, may have shorter attention and concentration spans, and often use strong and colorful expressions.

Since field-independent students tend to perform better at school-related tasks than field-dependent individuals, and since field-independence seems to be associated with the dominant white middle class, one might expect a majority of children from Mexican-American, African-American, Puerto Rican, and Native American backgrounds to be quite unfamiliar with the preferred learning and teaching style of the school when they first enter the school environment.

Schools tend to stress conformity, emphasize the memorization of facts, demand a logical and linear approach, emphasize the cognitive domain, be highly scheduled and task-oriented, be rule-oriented, and be hierarchically organized. Analytical thinkers tend to be rewarded in the school context.[22] Chiu, studying the relationship between cognitive style, academic achievement, and emotional responsiveness in fifty "analytic" and fifty "nonanalytic" Chinese fourth- and fifth-graders living in Taiwan, found that academic achievement of analytic students was significantly higher than that of nonanalytic students. At the same time, nonanalytic students scored higher on measures of anxiety than did their analytic counterparts.[23] These findings are consistent with observations made in the United States among both white and black populations. Students displaying field-dependent traits tend not to be reinforced in the school culture and may suffer as a result.

Using the Learning Style Inventory and the Group Embedded Figures Test, Jalali compared the learning and field-dependence and -independence characteristics of 300 culturally different fourth-, fifth-, and sixth-graders.[24] She found distinct differences in the learning styles of African-, Chinese-, Greek-, and Mexican-Americans. African-Americans preferred quiet, warmth, bright light, mobility, routine and patterns, frequent feedback from an authority figure, kinesthetic (action-oriented) instructional experiences, and afternoon or evening learning sessions rather than morning. Chinese-Americans preferred sound, bright light, morning, variety (rather than routines), and peer learning. Greek-Americans preferred learning alone, mobility, variety, and auditory instructions. Mexican-Americans preferred low light, structure, learning alone, tactile and visual instruction, and feedback from an authority figure. The majority of each group of students were field-dependent.

A word of caution is necessary here. Although dramatic differences can be found between cultural groups, research in this area indicates that there are as many within-group as between-group differences. Lumping all Hispanic students together, for instance, has its dangers. In addition, generational differences in learning styles have been found in some groups. First-generation Mexican-Americans, for instance, tend to be more field-dependent when compared with third-generation students. Even within families, parents, offspring, and siblings tend to be more different from than similar to each other. If we are to respond to students' learning styles, individual as well as group characteristics must be considered. Furthermore, although it is important to be able to adapt the learning environment to children with different cognitive and learning styles, it is also true that *new* learning styles can be suggested and encouraged. What is important is that what children bring with them to school be understood and valued, not ignored, deplored, or despised.

## CULTURE CLASH: A MODEL IN ACTION AMONG HAWAIIAN-AMERICAN CHILDREN

Children of color may begin the schooling process having been socialized in a way which may be in conflict with the expectations of the school; when this occurs, children and teachers may fail due to the *cultural incompatibility* between the culture of the school and the culture of the child. In this section, efforts to remedy the clash between the culture of the home and the culture of the school among one particular American minority group—Hawaiian-Americans—will be reviewed.

The cultural incompatibility approach has been the basis of considerable work at the Center for Development of Early Education (formerly the Kamehameha Elementary Education Program, KEEP), a privately funded, multidisciplinary, educational research and development program directed at remedying academic underachievement of native Hawaiians. As with many other ethnic minorities in American schools, poor school performance among Hawaiians was at first attributed to a variety of cultural and home deficiencies. This cultural deficit model, implying a superior-inferior dichotomy, is unfounded, unhelpful, and often rightfully labeled racist. All neurologically normal children have already learned a substantial amount of relatively complex material that is specific to their culture by the time they are of school age. Employing a cultural incompatibility model as opposed to a cultural deficit model implies that all children can learn prerequisite skills for any future need, including school readiness, if given the opportunity.

Researchers at Kamehameha schools proposed that a school environment that was compatible with the child's home culture could be developed.[25] This culturally compatible classroom might elicit from children those skills, attitudes, and behaviors that would contribute to the desired learning and help children achieve early school success.

While research findings are numerous and complex, some summary can be attempted here. To begin with, the Hawaiian socialization system teaches children to be contributing members of a family. For instance, even when adolescents work outside the home, rather than spend their hard-earned money strictly on themselves, they often contribute to the overall family resources. The family is not seen as a training ground for independence as is typical in many dominant culture families. Personal independence is not a goal; rather, interdependence is stressed. A collective orientation develops, as opposed to the individual orientation prevalent in middle-class caucasian society. This has implications for motivation and instructional strategies, as well as the reward structure in the classroom. For instance, the Hawaiian child may not be motivated by individual rewards (gold stars, grades) as much as a caucasian counterpart. Nor would a Hawaiian child desire to achieve independence from the group.

The sibling care system, whereby children from a very young age are placed in the care of older siblings, also promotes a high degree of interdependence by giving children early experience caring for younger children and carrying out many meaningful family chores. Adults tend to structure their relationships so they can relate to the sibling group as a whole, not to individuals on a one-to-one basis. As a result, children do not have as much one-to-one verbal interaction with adults. In addition, because Hawaiian children learn from peers from an early age, they are comfortable in the role of teacher as well as in the role of learner.

As a result, conditions in typical classrooms may not be sufficient to elicit and sustain appropriate learning strategies. Sibling care and interdependence may diminish the degree of authority alloted to any one adult. Peer orientation and affiliation, while frowned upon in the typical classroom, has been found to contribute to school success of Hawaiian children. Learning stations which consider this orientation facilitate learning. Reading instruction modeled after the culturally familiar "talk-story" activity improves reading skill and comprehension. Modification of instructional practice, classroom organization, and motivation management that takes into consideration the culture of the child has been found to make a significant difference in the achievement of Hawaiian children in school.

Figure 5.1 illustrates some aspects of mainstream culture which are congruent with the culture of the school but which may be in significant conflict with the cultural knowledge and attitudes of Hawaiian-American students.

Analysis of the classroom experiences of other minority children confirms the usefulness of the cultural incompatibility hypothesis. The KEEP model, for example, has been applied among the Navajo at Rough Rock. While not directly transferable, there is every indication that culture-specific modification of the program is possible. Efforts such as KEEP should be applauded. Even if not directly transferable to other contexts, the implications and motivations behind such work can be applied, especially where there is a large population of a single minority group in the schools.

## SOCIAL CLASS

We have said that differences in school achievement may be attributed to the cultural influences of race, ethnicity, and gender on learning style. Other aspects of human diversity may also be critical in determining school success. Such factors include motivation, aptitude and achievement, self-concept, peer pressure, family, health, teacher expectations, and socioeconomic status. It is to issues of socioeconomic status and its influence on school achievement that we now turn.

Most Americans believe they live in a classless, rather egalitarian society. At the least, American ideology promotes the idea that, through proper attention and diligence (and some luck, which Americans also believe in), an individual may "rise above" his or her social class. Part of what has been called an "American religion,"[26] this faith in the reality of upward mobility may account for the relative lack of attention to the concept of social class in the educational and psychological literature in the United States.[27] Certainly it accounts for the difficulty sociology professors encounter in helping young people understand the bases of class differences in this society. Nevertheless, as we all know, there are significant variations in standard of living, status of occupation, and extent of expectations of upward mobility among American citizens.

*Social class* has been defined in a number of ways, all of which refer to a hierarchical stratification, or "layering," of people in social groups, communities, and societies. Assignment to social class categories is one of a number of stratification systems that can be used to distinguish one individual or group from another in such a way as to assign "worth." The urge to organize people in layers almost appears to be a culture-general

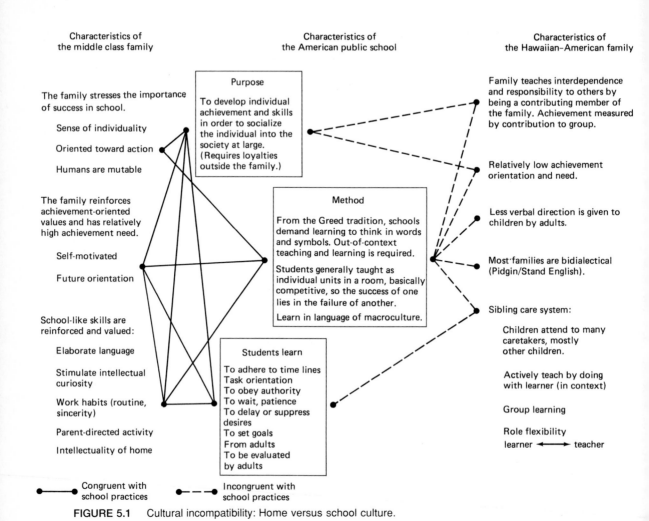

Characteristics of
the middle class family

Characteristics of
the American public school

Characteristics of
the Hawaiian–American family

The family stresses the importance
of success in school.

Sense of individuality

Oriented toward action

Humans are mutable

The family reinforces
achievement-oriented
values and has relatively
high achievement need.

Self-motivated

Future orientation

School-like skills are
reinforced and valued:

Elaborate language

Stimulate intellectual
curiosity

Work habits (routine,
sincerity)

Parent-directed activity

Intellectuality of home

Purpose

To develop individual
achievement and skills
in order to socialize
the individual into the
society at large.
(Requires loyalties
outside the family.)

Method

From the Greed tradition, schools
demand learning to think in words
and symbols. Out-of-context
teaching and learning is required.

Students generally taught as
individual units in a room, basically
competitive, so the success of one
lies in the failure of another.

Learn in language of macroculture.

Students learn

To adhere to time lines
Task orientation
To obey authority
To wait, patience
To delay or suppress
desires
To set goals
From adults
To be evaluated
by adults

Family teaches interdependence
and responsibility to others by
being a contributing member of
the family. Achievement measured
by contribution to group.

Relatively low achievement
orientation and need.

Less verbal direction is given to
children by adults.

Most·families are bidialectical
(Pidgin/Stand English).

Sibling care system:

Children attend to many
caretakers, mostly
other children.

Actively teach by doing
with learner (in context)

Group learning

Role flexibility
learner ←——→ teacher

●———● Congruent with
school practices

●- - -● Incongruent with
school practices

**FIGURE 5.1**   Cultural incompatibility: Home versus school culture.

characteristic; indeed, it has been said that whenever more than three people are in a group there will be stratification. While many Americans would identify class membership in terms of income,[28] it is important to understand that money alone does not determine one's social class. Rather, one's social class standing depends on a combination of prestige, power, influence, and income.[29]

Traditional class markers in the United States thus include family income, prestige of one's father's occupation, prestige of one's neighborhood, the power one has to achieve one's ends in times of conflict, and the level of schooling achieved by the family head. In other cultures, markers of social class may include bloodline and status of the family name, the caste into which one was born, the degree to which one engages in physical labor, and the amount of time which one might devote to scholarly or leisurely activities of one's choosing.[30]

For purposes of analysis, it is often helpful to divide American society into five social classes.[31] At the top there is a very small upper class, or social elite, consisting chiefly of those who have inherited social privilege from others. Second is a larger upper middle class, whose members often are professionals, corporate managers, leading scientists, and the like. This group usually has benefited from extensive higher education, and while family history is not so important, manners, tastes, and patterns of behavior are.

The third (or middle) social class has been called the lower middle class.[32] Members of this group are largely people employed in white-collar occupations earning middle incomes—small business owners, teachers, social workers, nurses, sales and clerical workers, bank tellers, and so forth. This is the largest of the social classes in the United States and encompasses a wide range of occupations and income. Central to the values of the lower middle class are a "desire to belong and be respectable. . . . [f]riendliness and openness are valued and attention is paid to keeping up appearances."[33]

Fourth in the hierarchy of social class is the working class, whose members are largely blue-collar workers (industrial wage earners), or employees in low-paid service occupations. Working-class families often have to struggle with poor job security, limited fringe benefits, longer hours of work, and more dangerous or "dirtier" work than those in the classes above them. It is not surprising, then, that members of the working class often feel more alienated from the social mainstream.

Finally, fifth in the hierarchy is the lower class—the so-called working poor and those who belong to what has been termed the *underclass*—a designation that refers to people who have been in poverty for so long that they seem to be unable to take any advantage at all of mobility options and thus lie "below" the class system. Clearly, poverty is both the chief characteristic and the chief problem of this group. Webb and Sherman point out that this simple fact needs to be underscored:

> Being poor means, above all else, lacking money. This statement would be too obvious to mention were it not for the fact that most Americans see poverty in other terms. Middle-class conversations about the poor often depict them as lazy, promiscuous, and criminal. Misconceptions about the poor are so widespread that it is difficult to appreciate fully what life is like at the lowest stratum of society.[34]

Complicating the issues of social class is the fact that in the United States there is a large overlap between lower-middle-class, working-class, and lower-class membership and membership in minority groups. African-Americans, Hispanics, Native Americans (including the Inuit and native Hawaiians) are the most economically depressed of all groups in the United States. These groups also have the highest school dropout rates. To the extent that social class status depends on income and occupation (and therefore, usually, prestige and power), women and children of all racial, ethnic, and religious groups constitute a large proportion of the lower classes. This is, in part, a consequence of the descent into poverty that characterizes the lives of women who are divorced and their children. At the present time, nearly 25 percent of all American children under 6 years old are members of households trying to exist below the poverty line.[35]

The working poor—those people who do work but in jobs that are minimum wage or slightly above, with no benefits, and hardly any job security—must also struggle to make it in today's society. To reach a middle-class lifestyle, a family of four in 1987 needed an annual income of about $31,000,[36] and inflation will continue to raise this figure. In many cases, to reach this level both husband and wife must work. Only 25 percent of men and women reach this level if only one partner in the marriage earns an income. Thurow states that

> although the dominant pattern today is a full-time male worker and a part-time female worker, the pattern is rapidly shifting toward a way of life in which both husband and wife work full time. . . . As an increasing number of families have two full-time workers, the households that do not will fall farther and farther behind economically.[37]

Brislin comments on the effect this reality has on women and children:

> The people left behind in the movement through social class levels include households headed by women, and these reached a staggering 31% of households in 1985. Dependence on one income, combined with the well-known fact of lower salaries earned by women, can result in poverty. Women and children constitute 77% of people living in poverty, and 50% of these poor people live in female-headed households with no husband present.[38]

Those of similar socioeconomic status, at whatever level, also share similar cultural knowledge, attitudes, and values. These can be seen in patterns of child rearing; attitudes toward and expectations about dress, food, and shelter; and beliefs about the necessity and value of schooling. Gordon suggests that the socioeconomic level of a family may be the strongest factor in determining differences between groups.[39] Of prime interest to us is the influence social class has on educational opportunity, behavior, and achievement.

Brislin has reviewed a number of useful sources in this area.[40] Kohn, for example, argues that parents from different class backgrounds emphasize different values when raising their children.[41] Parents in the middle classes tend to emphasize intellectual curiosity, self-control, and consideration of others. This leads to adult characteristics of empathetic understanding and self-direction. Working-class parents, on the other hand, stress neatness, good manners (often involving quietness and invisibility when adults are present), and obedience.[42] These emphases lead to a concern with external standards, such as obedience to authority, acceptance of what other people think of as good manners, and difficulty in articulating one's wishes to authority figures. The middle-class emphasis produces adolescents and adults who are relatively comfortable with self-initiated behaviors and at ease when interacting with those outside their immediate family or friendship networks. Kohn suggests that the skills children of the middle classes learn prepare them to assume professional and managerial positions that demand intellectual curiosity and good social skills.[43] In addition, Argyle suggests that the social skills learned by children of the middle classes may be central to success in the professions as they may have more weight than purely intellectual skills in many promotion and hiring decisions.[44] In contrast, the skills working-class children often acquire prepare them for wage labor jobs which are closely supervised and demand physical effort.

Lindgren and Suter suggest many reasons why students from middle-class backgrounds may do better in school than their working-class peers.[45] One is perceived parental expectation. Students from working-class backgrounds think their parents expect less of them with regard to future school achievement, even when this is not true. But children of parents who have attended college or had other postsecondary education are more likely to encourage their children to attend college than are parents who have not.

While family income may be a factor discouraging college attendance among the lower classes, the cultural context of schooling may also discourage many lower-income and inner city children.[46] Success in school, for example, demands linguistic competence. Children from working-class backgrounds may have less exposure, less expertise, and less confidence with language skills, and as a result may not understand teachers' questions as well as middle-class children. Gullo found that 3- to 5-year-old working-class children had more difficulty answering various "wh" questions (*who, when, where,* and *why,* but not *what*) than did middle-class children.[47] A considerable amount of teacher-student interaction consists of questioning, and it is conceivable that lower-class children may benefit less from lessons which employ questioning.

Another view, however, is taken by Knapp and Shields,[48] who seriously question the efficacy of emphasizing the so-called deficits of "disadvantaged children." To do so, they assert, is to

> risk making inaccurate assessments of children's strengths and weaknesses. . . . [to] have low expectations . . . and set standards that are not high enough to form the foundation for future academic success. . . . [and, in] focusing on the deficits of students from disadvantaged backgrounds . . . [to risk] overlooking their true capabilities. Finally, a focus on the poor preparation of disadvantaged children often distracts attention from how poorly prepared the school may be to serve these youngsters.[49]

While statistically there are significant differences in school performance of students from different class backgrounds, some students from working and lower-class backgrounds do quite well in school. Social class, *all by itself,* may not be the best predictor of school success. Rather, the relation of school success to social class appears to be mediated by a number of other factors, not the least of which is the teacher's perception of what social class *means.*

## TEACHER EXPECTATIONS

Teacher expectation regarding a student's potential for academic success is a critical factor in that student's achievement. *Teacher expectation* refers to the predictions teachers make about the future behavior or academic achievement of their students, based on what they presently know about them. *Teacher expectation effects* refers to student outcomes that occur because of the actions teachers take in response to their own expectations.[50]

An important type of teacher expectation is the *self-fulfilling prophecy,* a false belief which leads to behavior that causes that belief to become true. For instance, if false rumors begin to spread that the stock market is going to crash and millions of people rush to sell off their stock holdings, the market may in fact crash. The outcome, however, is not due to any event which was accurately predicted but to investors' responses to the false information.

In the classroom setting, teachers may have preconceptions about the probable success or failure of their students. For instance, let's assume that a teacher looks at her roster for the upcoming year and sees that she will have in her classroom a particular student, let's call her Sandra, whose sister, Sally, she taught two years earlier. Let's assume that

Sally had a difficult year. Not only did she struggle academically, but (perhaps as a result of academic failure) also had behavior problems. Our teacher, vividly remembering her problems with Sally, may expect that Sandra will repeat the pattern. Now, when Sandra walks into the classroom at the start of the year, our teacher may greet her coolly, may be hesitant to approach her, and may even avoid personal contact with her as much as possible. Such behavior on the part of the teacher may alienate Sandra, may make her feel as if she doesn't belong, may generate feelings of anxiety and uncertainty. These feelings may in turn cause Sandra to ''act out.'' Our teacher may then have set the stage for a self-fulfilling prophecy.

Now, just the opposite can also happen. A teacher may, for whatever reason, believe a certain child will be a good student, when in fact he or she may be just about average. This belief may translate into actions that demonstrate care and concern and an expectation of success to the student. The teacher may call on this student to read more than other students, may trust this student with major responsibilities, and may give her or him more attention and privileges; all this may result in increased achievement, an outcome which might not have happened without the teacher's high expectations.

A tremendous amount of research has been done over the past twenty-five years on the effect of teacher expectations on student achievement.[51] Many teachers expect students of color as well as those from lower socioeconomic groups to perform less well on school-related tasks than their middle-class peers. When these expectations are upheld, the teacher's beliefs are reinforced, thus perpetuating a vicious cycle.

It is a part of our folk wisdom that children tend to live up (or down) to those expectations that significant adults have for them. For some children, their teachers will be the only adults who may ever have high expectations for them. Clearly, to *automatically* discount the possibility of achievement because of the color of a child's skin or the evidence of a child's economic situation is discrimination of the most insidious kind because it is unspoken and largely invisible. It is perhaps not too much to say that the greatest gift that a teacher can offer a child is not knowledge, not skill development, not evaluation, but rather a fundamental faith that that child can acquire knowledge, develop skills, and demonstrate ability.

## ACTIVITIES

1 Generate a list of proverbs that were told to you while you were growing up. What underlying value was being transmitted through each proverb? How has this value influenced your life?
2 Go back and review the proverbs and American values listed in the chapter. How have these values influenced dimensions of American life other than schooling? For instance, how do these predominant American values influence people's orientation toward the environment? How does this help explain the current environmental crisis? How can we use this information to guide our efforts to correct this crisis situation?
3 Following are examples of proverbs from other cultures. Identify an underlying value expressed by each proverb and give a similar proverb from your cultural tradition.

*African*

He who sows nettles does not reap roses.
A horse that arrives early gets good drinking water.

By trying often, the monkey learns to jump from the tree.
Little by little grow the bananas.

*Japanese*

You will gain three moons if you wake early in the morning.

*Chinese*

Ice three feet thick isn't frozen in a day.
If one plants melons, one gets melons.
The plan of the year is in the spring. The plan of the day is in the morning. The plan of life is in hardship.

*German*

Joy, moderation, and rest shut out the doctors.
Young gambler, old beggar.

*Arabic*

An empty drum makes a big sound.
If you take off clothes, you are naked. If you take away family, you are nothing.
Doing things quickly is from the devil.
If you want to know somebody, look at his friends.

*Israeli*

Keep a small head.
If you're clever, keep silent.
Life is not a picnic.

*Indian*

I grumbled that I had no shoes until I saw a man who had no feet.
With every rising of the sun think of your life as just begun.

*Spanish*

One bird in the hand is worth one thousand flying.
Your getting up early doesn't make the sun rise earlier.

*Canadian*

Don't sell the bearskin before you kill the bear.

**4** From your knowledge of other cultural groups (verbal and nonverbal communication, values, etc.), what conflicts might you predict their children will face when they come into contact with the culture of the school? If you do not have sufficient culture-specific knowledge of any particular group, this is an opportunity to investigate all you can. Then, propose strategies which might be used to reduce or eliminate such conflict.

**5** Think of a town or city where you have lived. List the relative status levels of about five to seven neighborhoods. What are your rankings based on? Identify your neighborhood, or one most like yours. Now recall your ten closest friends from this town. Indicate which neighborhoods they are from. Finally, count the number of friends from your neighborhood or level and from one level above or below yours. What do your results indicate about friendship networks? What impact might this have on one's choice of a marriage partner? What other aspects of one's life and experience might this influence.[52]

6 Tell of a relationship you were able to develop with a person from a much higher or lower class background. Describe how the relationship developed. Identify any difficulties or pressures that others imposed which threatened the relationship. Did the relationship strengthen or weaken over time?[53]

7 Focus for a few moments on social skills, or what a socially skilled person is like, how they act, and what they might do. Think of the five most socially skilled people you know well. What do these people do for a living? What neighborhoods did they grow up in? What did their parents do for a living? People with a reputation for being socially skilled tend to come from the middle or upper levels of society. What experiences might they have, both in and out of school, which might give them social skills and prepare them to be comfortable in social situations?[54]

## MORE CRITICAL INCIDENTS

### The Chemistry Lab

Miguel, a 16-year-old Mexican student in Denver, has been in the United States for one year and can speak and understand English well enough to function in school. He has done well in his studies, carrying a 2.5 GPA with his highest grades in literature and history courses. He struggled through the first semester of chemistry, however, with D's and F's on most tests, which were based on class lectures. His lab reports salvaged his grade because they were always of the highest quality—a fact that his teacher Mr. Thompson attributed mainly to the influence and help of Miguel's lab partner, Dave, the best student in the class.

When everyone was assigned a new lab partner for the second semester, Miguel was paired with Tim, who was failing the course. Miguel's lab reports, however, continued to be excellent, and Tim's also improved significantly. Mr. Thompson was puzzled by Miguel's performance.

How might Miguel's performance in chemistry class be explained?

1 Miguel does not listen attentively to the class lectures and so cannot take adequate notes for the tests.
2 Miguel "freezes up" when taking tests.
3 Miguel learns better when he can discover things for himself and discuss his ideas with others.
4 Miguel lacks the analytic mind necessary to be successful in the study of science.
5 The lab sessions are less demanding than the material presented in the lectures.

#### Rationales

1 There is no evidence that Miguel does not pay attention or that he fails to take adequate notes. Please choose again.
2 Since Miguel has a 2.5 GPA, he must be doing well in tests in some of his courses.

Freezing up is, therefore, probably not the reason for his poor performance on chemistry tests.

3 Since Miguel consistently does well in the lab, he probably feels more comfortable and confident in such a hands-on, shared-responsibility learning situation. The emphasis there on activity, exploration, and group learning matches the learning style of Miguel's cultural background. This is the best answer.

4 Miguel's performance in the lab shows that he does have the analytic ability necessary to understand scientific concepts. This is not an adequate explanation of his performance. Please choose again.

5 No evidence indicates that the lab sessions are less demanding. Please choose another response.

### The Dream Home

Sam is an average student in Mrs. Grimes's third-grade class, though he has some difficulty with reading and receives special help for this. Early in the year his class was involved in a social studies unit on homes and housing. They were looking at styles of homes in the United States through history and up to the present time, considering log cabins and tepees as well as city apartments and country estates. Sam lives with his grandmother and sister in a small slatboard home at the edge of this predominantly middle-class suburban community. Mrs. Grimes made an assignment: the children were to go home and draw their own homes; the drawings were to be shared in class the next day. She drew her own apartment building to clarify the assignment. The next day Sam came in with a drawing of a large house with pillars and fountains and a circular drive through gardens.

How might Mrs. Grimes handle this situation?

1 She should reexplain the assignment to Sam as he may not have understood it.
2 She should not accept his drawing because he did not follow the directives of the assignment.
3 She should point out that there are many kinds of homes and encourage him to draw his own.
4 She should accept his drawing.

### Rationales

1 You chose number 1. It is likely that Sam understood the assignment, which was very specific. Although he may have some difficulty with reading, the assignment and its explanation were oral and included a demonstration. Choose another answer.

2 You chose number 2. Mrs. Grimes needs to consider the importance and purpose of the assignment in relation to the bigger issue that has emerged, the issue of Sam's feelings about his home. Choose another answer.

3 You chose number 3. Although her intention may be to help Sam be more comfortable by trying to create an acceptance of his own home, Mrs. Grimes needs to be sensitive to his feelings in the large-group setting of the classroom. She may want to talk with Sam personally about these issues and may at another time deal with the whole group, trying to sensitize them and break down class and status barriers and pressures. Pointing it out at this time, however, may increase troubled feelings for Sam. Please choose another answer.

4 You chose number 4. At this time and in this setting it is best to accept Sam's offering. Please read the discussion of number 3 above, as it points out the issue of shame or embarrassment about his home in comparison to the others' homes and how it can be dealt with compassionately. At another time group discussions can be carried out to sensitize the class on class and status issues. You have chosen the best answer.

## REFERENCES

1 James A. Banks, "The Influence of Ethnicity and Class on Cognitive Style: Implications for Research and Education," in W. Lonner and V. Tyler (eds.), *Cultural and Ethnic Factors in Learning and Motivation: Implications for Education* (Twelfth Western Symposium on Learning, Western Washington University, 1988).

2 J. M. Beck and Richard W. Saxe, *Teaching the Culturally Disadvantaged Pupil* (Springfield, IL: Thomas, 1969).

3 Arthur Jensen, "How Much Can We Boost I.Q. and Scholastic Achievement?" *Harvard Education Review,* vol. 39, no. 1, 1969, pp. 1–123.

4 S. S. Baratz and J. C. Baratz, "Early Childhood Intervention: The Social Science Base of Institutional Racism," *Harvard Educational Review,* vol. 40, no. 1, 1970, pp. 29–50.

5 James A. Anderson, "Cognitive Styles and Multicultural Populations," *Journal of Teacher Education,* vol. 39, no. 1, Jan–Feb. 1988, pp. 2–9.

6 John Dewey, *Democracy and Education* (New York: Macmillan, 1916), pp. 1–2.

7 Ibid.

8 Margaret LeCompte, "The Civilizing of Children: How Young Children Learn to Become Students," *Journal of Thought,* vol. 15, no. 3, 1980, pp. 105–128.

9 Ibid.

10 Larry Samover, Richard Porter, and Nemi Jain, *Understanding Intercultural Communication* (Belmont, CA: Wadsworth, 1981).

11 J. Kagan, H. Moss, and I. Sigel, "Psychological Significance of Styles of Conceptualization," in J. Wright and J. Kagan (eds.), *Basic Cognitive Processes in Children* (Chicago: University of Chicago Press, 1971).

12 Rita Dunn, Jeffrey Beaudry, and Angela Klavas, "Survey of Research on Learning Styles," *Educational Leadership,* vol. 46, no. 6, March 1989, pp. 50–58.

13 Ibid.

14 H. A. Witkin, *Psychological Differentiation* (New York: John Wiley & Sons, 1962).

15 Witkin, Ibid.

16 M. Ramirez and A. Castaneda, *Cultural Democracy: Bicognitive Development and Education* (New York: Academic Press, 1974).

17 R. A. Cohen, "Conceptual Styles, Cultural Conflict, and Nonverbal Tests of Intelligence," *American Anthropologist,* vol. 71, no. 5, Oct. 1969, pp. 828–856.

18 A. Hilliard, *Alternatives to IQ Testing: An Approach to the Identification of Gifted Minority Children,* Final report to the California State Department of Education, Sacramento, 1976, p. 39.

19 Ibid., p. 36.

20 Cohen, op. cit.

21 Hilliard, op. cit.

22 L. Chiu, "The Relation of Cognitive Style and Manifest Anxiety to Academic Performance among Chinese Children," *Journal of Social Psychology,* vol. 125, no. 5, 1985, pp. 667–669.

**23** Kagan, Moss, and Sigel, op. cit.

**24** F. A. Jalali, ''A Cross-Cultural Comparative Analysis of the Learning Styles and Field Dependence/Independence Characteristics of Selected Fourth-, Fifth-, and Sixth-Grade Students of Afro, Chinese, Greek, and Mexican-American Heritage,'' Ph.D. thesis, St. John's University, New York, 1989.

**25** L. Vogt, C. Jordan, and R. Tharp, ''Explaining School Failure, Producing School Success: Two Cases,'' *Anthropology and Education Quarterly,* vol. 18, no. 4, Dec. 1987, pp. 276–286.

**26** Robert N. Bellah, ''Civil Religion in America,'' in Alan Wells (ed.), *American Society: Problems and Dilemmas* (Pacific Palisades, CA: Goodyear Publishing, 1976), pp. 351–368.

**27** R. Brislin, ''Increasing Awareness of Class, Ethnicity, Culture and Race,'' In I. Cohen (ed.), *The G. Stanley Hall Lecture Series,* vol. 8, pp. 137–180. (Washington, D.C.: American Psychological Association, 1988).

**28** Gilbert and Kall, for example, suggest that in the United States, individual or family income is the central variable from which other opportunities follow. For instance, income generally controls the neighborhood in which one lives. This determines, to a great degree, the educational experience one has, in school and outside of it. The education one has then influences one's profession or occupation, which determines the prestige one obtains, and so forth. D. Gilbert and J. Kahl, *The American Class Structure: A New Synthesis* (Homewood, IL: Dorsey, 1982).

**29** Webb and Sherman, *Schooling and Society,* 2nd ed. (New York: Macmillan, 1989), pp. 397–398.

**30** Brislin, op. cit., p. 144.

**31** Webb and Sherman, op. cit., pp. 399–417.

**32** Ibid., p. 405.

**33** Ibid., p. 407.

**34** Ibid., p. 412.

**35** Nancy Gibbs, ''Shameful Bequests to the Next Generation,'' *Time,* October 8, 1990, p. 43.

**36** Brislin, op. cit., p. 145.

**37** L. M. Thurow, ''A Surge of Inequality,'' *Scientific American,* vol. 256, no. 5, May 1987, pp. 30–37.

**38** Brislin, op. cit., p. 146.

**39** J. Gordon, *Assimilation in American Life* (New York: Oxford University Press, 1964).

**40** Brislin, op. cit.

**41** M. L. Kohn, *Class and Conformity,* 2d ed. (Chicago: University of Chicago Press, 1977).

**42** Gilbert and Kahl, op. cit.

**43** Kohn, op. cit.

**44** M. Argyle, ''Interaction Skills and Social Competence,'' in M. P. Feldman and J. Orford (eds.), *Psychological Problems: The Social Context* (New York: John Wiley & Sons, 1980).

**45** H. C. Lindgrun and W. N. Suter, *Educational Psychology in the Classroom,* 7th ed. (Monterey, CA: Brooks/Cole, 1985).

**46** A. W. Boykin, ''The Triple Quandary and the Schooling of African-American Children,'' in V. Neisser (ed.), *The School Achievement of Minority Children: New Perspectives* (Hillsdale, NJ: Lawrence Erlbaum, 1986).

**47** D. Gullo, ''Social Class Differences in Preschool Children's Comprehension of Wh— Questions,'' *Child Development,* vol. 52, no. 2, June 1981, pp. 736–740.

**48** Michael S. Knapp and Patrick M. Shields, ''Reconceiving Academic Instruction for the Children of Poverty,'' *Phi Delta Kappan,* vol. 71, no. 10, June 1990, pp. 753–758.

**49** Ibid., p. 754.

**50** Thomas Good and Jere Brophy, *Looking in Classrooms,* 4th ed. (New York: Harper & Row, 1987).

**51** Ibid.

**52** Adapted from Brislin, op. cit., p. 146.

**53** Ibid.

**54** Ibid.

# PART TWO

# HUMAN DIVERSITY:
# POLICY AND PRACTICE

# CHAPTER 6

# PLURALISM AND EDUCATIONAL POLICY: A BRIEF HISTORY

*William James, the great American philosopher and psychologist, once divided all human minds into the tender minded and the tough minded. The former, James wrote, include those who, beginning with Plato, have declared unity and system to govern all things. The latter are those who, distrusting all unitary systems, find reality to lie in the concrete and the particular, in multiplicity and plurality rather than in unity.*

Robert Nisbet

## E PLURIBUS UNUM: THE GREAT DEBATE

When Noah Webster observed that ''our national character is not yet formed . . . ,''[1] he identified a central dilemma that still faces the United States, as well as many other multiethnic nations. This land of immigrants is, indeed, an odd land in which many may feel themselves to be strangers in their own country.

In the United States, one major solution to the problem of how to create one people out of many has been the public school system, which, for most of our history, has been part of the ''glue'' that holds us together. This helps to explain why the public schools have always been a battleground on which larger social issues have been contested. The way schools promote American pluralism has been publicly debated almost from the birth of the Republic to the present day. Educational literature over the past 160 years reflects profound disagreement about how to educate the young while forging a nation-state from a multiethnic population. Moreover, whatever the schools have achieved or failed to achieve has also been a source of continuous debate, with arguments ranging over a wide spectrum of issues of purpose and practice. What *is* certain is that advocates of all sorts have never been fully satisfied with the role of the school and the way it carries out its missions in terms of religious, cultural, and other forms of diversity. It will be useful for us to know something about the history of this debate. We will then look in some detail at the relatively recent legislation that has revolutionized educational policy regarding difference.

### We Have Been Different from the Beginning

One might argue that intolerance toward differences in the Americas began with the introduction of European culture in the 1490s. There is evidence that the Native American populations newly ''discovered'' in the ''new world'' exhibited far greater tolerance toward diversity of thought and lifestyle than did the arriving Europeans. The Taino people, for instance, greeted Columbus with food, shelter, and open festivity when the Spaniards first arrived on their small Caribbean island in 1492. At first intrigued with the Taino, Columbus wrote that ''their manner is both decorous and praiseworthy.''[2] The Taino's hospitality, however, was soon met with severe cruelty by the Spaniards. Within twenty years of Columbus's landing, the Taino were extinct as a people.

In fact, this tendency toward intolerance for both religious and cultural diversity on the part of the Spaniards may have prevented them from becoming the dominant culture in North America. So much energy was spent repressing and fighting the native populations that the northern spread of Spanish culture was halted in the desert southwest. The emergence of the English as the dominant force in the new lands may be partially attributed to their somewhat greater tolerance of and need for religious freedom. However, even though the English government allowed and even encouraged immigrants from a variety of ethnic backgrounds to settle in America, it was the white, English-born Protestants who, by the time the United States became a nation in 1776, had emerged as the dominant cultural group. This group, too, was fearful of "different" kinds of immigrants. In 1698, for example, South Carolina passed an act exempting Irish and Roman Catholics from new bounties.[3] In 1729, Pennsylvania placed a duty on all servants of Scotch-Irish descent. One official at the time wrote, "The common fear is that if they continue to come, they will make themselves proprietors of the province."[4] Ironically, the very people who originally had come to the new world to escape religious persecution were among those who actively engaged in the persecution of others for their beliefs, values, and ways of life.

### Industrialization, Immigration, and Religious Pluralism

In the early years of the nineteenth century, as an influx of European immigrants followed the industrial revolution across the Atlantic, the cultural, religious, and racial diversity of the United States began to be viewed as a "problem" for public schooling. Major battles were waged first, not around the issue of race, as is common today, but around the issue of religion.

Many new immigrants in this period were Catholic, and came to represent to native born citizens a threat to the stability of a largely Protestant republic—as well as competition for newly created industrial jobs. Many suspected that newly arrived Catholics owed a greater allegiance to the Pope than to the U.S. government, an issue that was not finally settled until the election of John F. Kennedy to the presidency in 1960. Second-, third-, and fourth-generation Protestants also opposed the emergence of Catholic schools, believing that they were intended to instill undemocratic values in Catholic children. Catholic parents, on the other hand, felt that a Catholic education not only was necessary to preserve their children's religious faith, but also was an important vehicle for maintaining Catholic communities.

Opposition to Catholic schooling often became violent both in word and deed. Political cartoonists had a field day with caricatures of the Pope as an ogre attempting to "swallow" the United States. More serious, however, were physical attacks on Catholic schools, exemplified by the burning of the Ursuline convent in Charleston, Massachusetts, by a Protestant mob in 1834.[5]

At the same time, the common school movement in the United States was gaining momentum. Elaborated and promoted by Horace Mann, Benjamin Rush, and Frances Wright, among others, in the 1830s, the idea of the common school was largely a Protestant invention, although its major intent was the creation of an educated citizenry that would be able to maintain the new forms of democracy being developed in the United States. Catholics, with some justification, believed that the common school would indoctrinate their children away from their religious faith. As the number of Catholic immigrants increased, and the network of Catholic schools began to provide a viable alternative to public schooling, Catholic parents began to insist that public funds raised through taxation to support public schools should also be used to fund private Catholic institutions. That debate continues to this day.

Catholics were not the only group who were feared and persecuted. In 1835, The Indian Removal Act saw the last vestige of Native American culture swept westward across the Mississippi River in the tragic roundup known today as the Trail of Tears; the last barrier to the right to vote for Jews was not abolished in New Hampshire until 1877; and in 1882 the immigration department passed an act that prohibited the entry of Chinese into the country.

### The Civil War: Freedmen's Schools and the Issue of Race

Issues of race in *public* education became important only after the Civil War. In the south before the Civil War, it was simply against the law to educate black slave children. Black children were not a schooling "problem" because they were not in school. In the North, blacks who had bought or had been given their freedom, achieved some education in the common schools, in African-American church communities, and through abolitionist efforts. After the Civil War, the education of black children still was not perceived to be a "national problem" by most whites because, where African-Americans were educated at all, they were educated in separate schools.

Southern states, notably resistant to providing public education for blacks, were not above taxing them for white schools. In some places—Florida, Texas, and Kentucky for example—black schools were built only after black citizens paid a second tax to build their own schools.[6]

In 1865, Congress established the Freedmen's Bureau to help freed slaves with the transition to citizenship. In 1866, the law was amended to assist in the provision of black schools. Many of the teachers in these schools were northern white women, often daughters of abolitionist families. Indeed, the story of the women who taught in the "Freedmen's Schools" is among the proudest in the history of teaching. By 1870, nearly 7,000 white and black "Yankee schoolmarms" were teaching 250,000 black students, and learning to cross the barriers of race and class that have characterized American history. The legacy of these teachers was enormous: not only did they educate children who became the teachers of segregated schools in the south into the twentieth century, but they educated a generation of free black leaders.[7]

Violence characterized the development of black schools after the Civil War as it had the development of Catholic schools earlier; the burning of buildings and harassment of teachers and students was commonplace. However, passage of the Fourteenth Amendment to the Constitution in 1868 made responsibility for civil rights a federal rather than a state function, and blacks began to gain more access to public education. Fully aware that education was a way out of poverty, black parents saw that their children got to school, one way or another. When they were needed on the farm, they took turns, as this Alabama boy describes:

> I took turns with my brother at the plow and in school; one day I plowed and he went to school, the next day he plowed and I went to school; what was learned on his school day he taught me at night and I did the same for him.[8]

Black children remained in segregated schools that were funded at minimal rates and often open for only part of the year. Indeed, despite efforts through the courts to equalize the rights of blacks in all spheres of public life, in 1896, in the *Plessy v. Ferguson* decision, the Supreme Court held that segregation was not prohibited by the Constitution. *Plessy v. Ferguson,* which upheld the doctrine that "separate but equal" facilities for blacks and whites were constitutionally permissible, justified separate (and often inferior) black education in both north and south until 1954.

## THE CIVIL RIGHTS MOVEMENT AND THE SCHOOLS: THE DEBATE CONTINUES

Perhaps the most dramatic efforts to come to grips with diversity in the society and in the schools occurred during the 1960s and 1970s, and were given momentum by the general social ferment engendered by the civil rights movement and the war in Vietnam. Educational reforms such as desegregation, multicultural and bilingual education, education in the least restrictive environment for individuals with special needs, and gender-equitable education called for a variety of programs that recognize the pluralistic nature of this society in a positive rather than a negative sense and were designed chiefly to help more students receive a better education within a pluralistic framework.

It is important to realize that these educational mandates were not achieved in isolation but as part of the larger human and civil rights struggles of the 1960s and 1970s. Thus, during this period, Congress passed a number of antidiscriminatory statutes: the Voting Rights Act (1963), dealing with voter registration; the Equal Pay Act (1963), which required that males and females occupying the same position be paid equally; the Civil Rights Act (1964), dealing with housing and job discrimination as well as with education; Title IX of the Education Amendments (1972), prohibiting sex discrimination against students and employees of educational institutions; and the Education of All Handicapped Children Act (1975), requiring schools to assume the responsibility for educating all children in the least restrictive environment possible. It was, in the words of one partisan observer, a period of "intensity of concern and commitment to do something about the problems in America stemming from the continued growth of its pluralistic character."[9]

In education the chief concerns were for access and equity: access to public education for excluded groups and a guarantee that such education would be equitable—that is, that it would be commensurate with the best that public education could offer. All these efforts rested on the belief that previously excluded groups had an inherent *right* to educational equity. Why was it important to emphasize the *rights* of racial and ethnic minorities, women, and persons with disabilities? Why was it important to enact legislation that protects their rights? Quite simply, because these rights had not been recognized in the past, and large numbers of people had experienced discrimination and unequal opportunity in a society that rests on the principle that all citizens are equal under the law. The civil rights movement was a reaffirmation of beliefs that form the very basis of American society and an insistence that we live up to our ideals in education as well as in other aspects of social life.

The debate about the precise way that public schooling should serve the interests of a diverse population did not end because a new generation of activists thought that schooling should be reformed. Indeed, political and educational reformers (who were often the same people) came up against old problems and old ideas. The first set of policy initiatives to be considered concerned children of racial, ethnic, and linguistic minorities who, it was asserted, were being discriminated against in public schools. To comprehend the difficulties encountered by reformers, a historical perspective is again useful.

## MULTICULTURAL EDUCATION: RACIAL, ETHNIC, AND LINGUISTIC DIVERSITY

During the years of massive immigration, from about 1870 to perhaps 1920, the "problem" of diversity in the schools was largely perceived as a problem of how to assimilate children of other nationalities. In short, it was thought to be the school's task to make immigrant children as much like white, Anglo-Saxon Protestants as possible in as short a time as possible.

### Anglo-Conformity and Assimilationist Ideology: The "Tender-Minded" View

Described by the terms *Anglo-conformity* or the *assimilationist model,* this view was typified by these words of a leading educationist, Ellwood Cubberly, written around the turn of the twentieth century about immigrant children and their families:

> Everywhere these people settle in groups or settlements to set up their national manners, customs, and observances. Our task is to break up these groups or settlements, to assimilate and amalgamate these people as part of our American race and to implant in their children so far as can be done, the Anglo-Saxon conception of righteousness, law and order, and our popular government and to awaken in them a reverence for our democratic institutions and for those things in our national life which we as a people hold to be of abiding worth.[10]

The assimilationist strategy was applied to each new ethnic group as immigrants poured through Ellis Island and other ports of entry: Jews, Poles, Slavs, Asians, Latin Americans—all became the "raw material" from which the "new American" would be made. Between 1860 and 1920, 37 million immigrants became naturalized citizens. Their sheer numbers changed the ethnic makeup of America. By 1916, for example, only 28 percent of San Francisco's population claimed English as its first language.

Yet, despite the high number of immigrants, the *dominant* American culture retained its English, Protestant identity. The nation's public schools, staffed as they were largely by white, middle-class, Protestant women, did little or nothing to encourage the expression of ethnicity or address the special needs of an increasingly diverse student population. Indeed, in large measure, it was the school's job to prevent such expression.

The nativist reaction at the turn of the century had a tremendous influence on the public school system. If one of the aims of the schools during the first half of the century was to assimilate children of all backgrounds into the greater American culture as quickly as possible, the idea of a melting pot was used to describe the result of assisting immigrants to shed their native languages, learn English, and to assimilate into the American culture at large.

The term *melting pot* actually came from the name of a play written in 1909 by Israel

Zangwill. The goal of creating one homogeneous culture from the many that arrived on the shores of the United States is captured in the following speech from the play:

> America is God's Crucible, the great Melting Pot where all the races of Europe are melting and reforming! Here you stand, good folk, think I, when I see them at Ellis Island, here you stand in your fifty groups with your fifty languages and histories, and your fifty hatreds and rivalries, but you won't be long like that, brothers, for these are the fires of God. A fig for your feuds and vendettas! Germans and Frenchmen, Irishmen and Englishmen, Jews and Russians— into the Crucible with you all! God is making the American . . . The real American has not yet arrived. He is only in the Crucible, I tell you—he will be the fusion of all races, the coming superman.[11]

James Banks suggests that assimilationists believe that one's identification with an ethnic group should be short-lived and temporary.[12] Identification with the group presents an obstacle to individual interests and needs. Assimilationists believe that, for a society to advance, individuals must give up their ethnic identities, languages, and ideologies in favor of the norms and values of the greater, national society. The goal of the school, from an assimilationist perspective, should be to socialize individuals into the society at large so all can function in an "appropriate" manner, thereby supporting the goals of the nation. Group identification, if it is to be developed, should be sought in small community organizations. The goal for assimilationists is to make it possible for everyone to be "melted" into a homogeneous whole.

### Pluralism: The Ideology of the "Tough-Minded"

The contents of the pot, however, never melted. In opposition to the assimilationist ideology came the call for *cultural pluralism* by a small group of philosophers and writers who argued that a political democracy must also be a cultural democracy,[13] and that immigrant groups were entitled to maintain their ethnic cultures and institutions within the greater society. The analogy they used was that of a salad bowl, arguing that the inclusion of other cultures would strengthen American society. An increasing number of people are beginning to accept and promote the idea of cultural pluralism: that is, that various groups can retain their heritage, and that this will not threaten, but indeed will enhance, American culture.

Pluralists view one's social group as critical to the socialization process in modern society. The group provides the individual with identity, a sense of belonging or psychological comfort, and support when faced with discrimination by the greater society. It is through one's group, usually the ethnic group, that one develops a primary language, values, and interpersonal relationships, as well as a particular lifestyle. Pluralists believe identity group(s) (racial, ethnic, religious, and so forth) to be so important that the schools should actively promote their interests and recognize their importance in the life of the individual. Pluralists assume a "difference" rather than a "deficit" orientation. As such, pluralists stress the importance of a curriculum addressing different learning styles and patterns of interaction, and recognizing students' cultural histories. The assumption is that the more congruent the school experience is with the experiences of the child, the better the child's chance of success.

One set of programs responsive to cultural and other forms of diversity fell under the umbrella term *multicultural education,* and included a number of efforts to address the needs of racial, ethnic, and linguistic minorities. In the context of the human and civil rights efforts of the 1960s, after many decades of educational discrimination rooted in long-standing patterns of social, political, and economic discrimination, America's visible minorities began seeking redress. Specifically, Spanish-speaking Americans in the southwest, Puerto Ricans on the east coast, Asian-Americans on the west coast, Native Americans on reservations and in urban settlements, and African-Americans throughout the United States began to seek their fair share of what America had to offer and demand that the nation live up to the ideals it professed. The powerful buildup of unrest and frustration born of the discrepancy between American ideals and American practices sought an outlet. From the *Brown v. The Board of Education of Topeka* decision in 1954 through the Civil Rights Act in the early 1960s and on to the Vietnam war, the most visible victims of educational inequity marched out of the ghettos and into court.

The start of these events is usually marked by the 1954 Supreme Court decision in *Brown v. The Board of Education of Topeka*. This landmark decision stated that segregated schools were inherently unequal and that state laws which allowed separate schools for black and white students were unconstitutional. Soon afterward, in 1957, the U.S. Commission on Civil Rights was established primarily to investigate complaints alleging the denial of people's right to vote by reason of race, color, religion, sex, or national origin.

From the first National Education Association study on the teaching of Spanish to Mexican-Americans in Tucson in 1966 to the American Association of Colleges of Teacher Education policy statement on pluralism, "No One Model American," in 1974, a series of investigative, judicial, and legislative moves directed toward ending educational discrimination in state after state demolished comfortable middle-class perceptions about cultural assimilation and helped to dim the embers under the American melting pot.

In the ten-year period from 1963 to 1973, private and governmental studies and hearings and a series of lawsuits regarding rights to native language instruction, placement of retarded children, and desegregation produced mandates for change in school administration, curriculum, and instruction for minority students. Concurrently, new educational strategies and new curricula, especially in bilingual and bicultural education, education for ethnic and racial diversity, and human relations, emerged and were instituted with varying degrees of preplanning and enthusiasm in districts across the nation.

The Civil Rights Act of 1964 made it illegal for public schools that received federal or state funds to assign students to schools based on their color, race, religion, or country of origin. The Bilingual Education Act was passed in 1968 as Title VII of the Elementary and Secondary Education Act. President Lyndon Johnson clarified the intent of this law in the following words:

> This bill authorizes a new effort to prevent dropouts; new programs for handicapped children; new planning help for rural schools. It also contains a special provision establishing bilingual education programs for children whose first language is not English. Thousands of children of Latin descent, young Indians, and others will get a better start—a better chance—in school. . . . "[14]

In 1970, the Office of Civil Rights Guidelines made efforts to provide non-English-speaking students with special training a requirement for public schools that receive federal aid. The office stated:

> Where inability to speak and understand the English language excludes national origin-minority group children from effective participation in the education program offered by a school district, the district must take affirmative steps to rectify the language deficiency in order to open its instructional program to these students.[15]

Passage of these laws, however, did not guarantee equality of educational opportunity to all American children. Frequently it was necessary to go to court to ensure compliance with congressional mandates. A significant case in the development of multicultural and bilingual education was *Lau v. Nichols,* decided by a 1974 Supreme Court ruling. This decision declared that a San Francisco school district violated a non-English-speaking Chinese student's right to equal educational opportunity when it failed to provide English language instruction or other needed special programs. An important consequence of the *Lau* decision was the declaration that school districts across the country must provide students an education in languages that meet their needs.

## PUBLIC LAW 94–142: RECOGNITION FOR THE EXCEPTIONAL CHILD

Special education has evolved historically in response to increasing recognition that students differ in learning style and rate. Learning is by definition an individual process influenced by a complex of individual characteristics. The question "What is *special* about special education?" prompts other questions: Do most students need "regular" education, but some, a minority, need "special" education? Are these two different things, and are there indeed two different types of students? Who decides who is "different" and who gets what? How do they decide?

From yet another perspective, the field of special education can be seen to have served as a sort of buffer between children considered exceptional and regular educators, indeed between exceptional and "typical" children. As in other areas of human difference, negative attitudes, fears, and stereotypes result from the lack of opportunity to interact on a personal level with persons with disabilities. Like other forms of "service" for people with disabilities, special education has often had the effect, whether intended or unintended, of segregating them—by assigning them to different classrooms and even different schools, with different teachers and curricula, and separate transportation, lunchrooms, and times for playground use.

Clearly, effectively addressing the challenge of human diversity is today a very high priority of American educators, but this was by no means always true. American schools have been characterized by such educational historians as Joel Spring as a "sorting machine,"[16] which serves a selective function, irrevocably determining the life course of the individual, assigning and confirming social roles, and ultimately, economic circumstances. Students with disabilities, although not the only ones relegated to restrictive experiences, certainly constituted a group at risk in consequence of this sorting process.

Although special education as a field has its roots in the nineteenth century and was influenced by even earlier events and practices, it has actually been part of the educational system for a relatively short time. The concept of a *special class,* a small, self-contained group of students believed to have certain characteristics in common that required the influence of a specially trained teacher, is of fairly recent origin. During most of the first half of the present century, there were relatively few such classes in American schools.

In the years following World War II such classes became more numerous, although special learning needs of a great many students with disabilities were not recognized, and many others were not served by the public schools at all. The tumultuous 1960s saw the concept of the special class spread, especially for students who were identified as mildly mentally retarded, emotionally or behaviorally handicapped, and (as they came to be labeled) learning disabled.

This trend was on a collision course with the civil rights movement. If "separate is not equal," as established by the Supreme Court in *Brown v. Board of Education,* the practice of screening and segregating groups of students was a violation of the law of the land.[17] In fact, disproportionately large numbers of African-American, Hispanic, and Native American children were among those "diagnosed" as exceptional, labeled mentally retarded or emotionally or behaviorally handicapped, and placed in special classes.[18] Key questions needing to be addressed by professionals and ultimately by lawmakers were: How were students determined to "need" special class placement? Were they helped by such placement? If they were helped, did they reenter regular education when they no longer needed special education?

Such questions arose from the prevailing view of the role of the school and a conception of the nature of teaching and learning. In recent years, however, some observers believe that schools have been moving from the *selective* (or sorting) mode to an *adaptive* one.[19] Thus, rather than assigning students to "slots" in the educational system, and therefore by implication in the society, educators have been modifying instruction in response to differences between students. Although the practice of finding a "placement" into which each student "fit" may have been a more humane, just, and responsible strategy than excluding all those who did not fit, a single-option approach to schooling now seems inadequate and ultimately impossible. Today, educators seek to adapt instruction to fit the needs of the student. To the extent that they can, students are neither doomed by their differences nor accorded status and opportunities denied to others.

The Education of All Handicapped Children Act of 1975 (P.L. 94–142) forms the cornerstone for the current definition of the educational rights of children and youth with disabilities. Many people associate P.L. 94–142 with the idea of *mainstreaming* students with disabilities within the regular classroom, even though this word is never mentioned in the law itself. It is accurate nonetheless to speak of P.L. 94–142 as "the mainstreaming law," since it establishes the right of children and youth with handicaps to a free, appropriate public education (FAPE), a right not previously guaranteed. This has both immediate and lifelong implications for access to the mainstream. First, the right to public education itself is established. Second, to the maximum extent appropriate, that education must be provided in "regular" or "typical" settings, with peers who are not handicapped. Third, to the extent that the education provided is appropriate to the needs of the student, it will enhance opportunity for full mainstream participation as an adult citizen.

Like other educational equity efforts, P.L. 94–142 was not enacted in a vacuum, but was a culmination of sentiments apparent much earlier. In 1948, for example, prior to the *Brown* decision that made the prohibition of educational segregation on the basis of race the law of the land, Congress prohibited discrimination against people with disabilities by the U.S. Civil Service Commission. In 1968, the Architectural Barriers Act prohibited construction of inaccessible facilities with government funds. With enactment of amendments to the Vocational Rehabilitation Act of 1973 (P.L. 93–112 and amended by P.L. 93–516), even more far-reaching policies were established. Section 502 of this legislation established the Architectural and Transportation Barriers Compliance Board (ATBCB) as a federal agency responsible for ensuring that federal funds were not used in connection with programs and services that were not accessible to people with disabilities. Section 503 affected the private sector in that contractors doing business with the federal government were prohibited from engaging in employment practices that discriminated against persons with disabilities.

The most familiar part of this legislation, Section 504, specifically prohibits any form of discrimination against persons with disabilities on the part of any agency receiving federal funds.

The impact of P.L. 93–112 was enormous. Not only were the nation's public schools affected, but all public institutions of higher education, all colleges and universities that receive federal financial assistance in any form (for example, research grants or student financial aid), and all public transportation systems, libraries, day care programs and numerous private sector business concerns that obtain any degree of federal funding were required to comply with the new regulations.

In addition to encompassing persons of any age—babies and children, youth, and adults—this legislation entails a very inclusive definition of *handicapped individual:* any person who (1) has a physical or mental impairment that substantially limits one or more of such person's major life activities, including learning; (2) has a record of such impairment; or (3) is regarded as having such an impairment. Thus, a person who has been provided special education while in school cannot be subjected to later discrimination—for example, in employment—for that reason.

The concept of *access* underlies Section 504 and associated policies. High curbs, stairs, and other physical barriers, for example, may make access to a college classroom building or a public library impossible for a person who uses a wheelchair. Therefore, we see curbcuts and ramps, a visual fire alert system makes *safe* use of the college library possible for a deaf student who could not hear a sound alarm, and appropriately wide stalls in public bathrooms, with a grab bar and toilet at appropriate height, permit access for wheelchair users.

In its admissions policies and its academic and student life policies, a college must ensure that there is no discrimination on the basis of disability. For example, students using wheelchairs cannot be denied the opportunity to study psychology because the psychology classes are taught on the second floor of a building that has no elevator.

While Section 504 prohibits discrimination against disabled persons in terms of access to jobs and education, it requires that disabled applicants be qualified for the job or educational program. An employer is not forced to hire a person *because* the person has a disability.

At the elementary and secondary school levels, Section 504 actually complements P.L. 94–142. While the latter requires that children with disabilities be schooled in the *least restrictive environment* (LRE), the former ensures that children are not placed in special education programs simply because they have disabilities. If a school system offers a special program for gifted students, a *qualified* student cannot be excluded because the student happens to have a disability. Before P.L. 94–142 was amended so that its benefits extended to preschool-age (3 to 5) children, certain states may have offered kindergarten but not required children to attend school until first grade. If schools were required by state mandate to offer kindergarten, however, schooling had to be made available to children with disabilities who were of kindergarten age. That is because, under Section 504, to do otherwise would have been discriminatory. Therefore, even if the state defined compulsory school age as beginning at age 6, schools with kindergartens were required to serve children with disabilities beginning at age 5. (It should be noted that, increasingly, states are mandating kindergarten attendance for all children; also, P.L. 94–947 made this issue moot by mandating preschool services for children eligible for special education.)

Since the passage of P.L. 94–142, it has been recognized that the cost of individually appropriate schooling for many students with disabilities is higher than the per pupil expenditure in any community. Additional personnel may be needed to provide ser-vices—such as speech and language therapy or occupational therapy. There may be special transportation needs. Some students with handicaps receive supplementary instruction and/or specialized instruction in smaller groups. The processes of determining a student's eligibility for special schooling and of developing an *individual education program* (IEP) for each student are both costly. In some instances, a school district may pay tuition for a student for whom the appropriate program is provided in another setting. P.L. 94–142 both establishes the right to an appropriate education and provides federal funding to assist schools in providing that education. Thus, whereas Section 504 is a civil rights law, P.L. 94–142 is also a grant-in-aid law.[20]

In order to be eligible for this funding, a state and school district must be in compli-ance with P.L. 94–142. This involves a number of specific requirements for the state department of education, or state education agency (SEA), and the local public school district, or local education agency (LEA). States must have appropriate policies, including special education rules and regulations, in place, and must monitor each school district's policies and practices. The basic requirements of the law have been effectively summa-rized by Turnbull and Turnbull as follows:[21]

> **1** *"Zero reject:* A rule of inclusion, a rule against exclusion of handicapped children and youth." In passing P.L. 94–142, the U.S. Congress was especially concerned about evidence that a great many children and youth in the nation were excluded from public schools because of handicapping conditions. Many states, for example, had policies stipulating that certain chil-dren could be excluded from school because of difficulties in learning associated with mental retardation, special health and medical needs, or behavioral problems. Some parents, of course, could afford to bear the brunt of costly private school programs, but most had no desirable alternatives.
>
> P.L. 94–142 changed that by mandating that every handicapped child must be provided a free and appropriate public education; no child could be excluded or "rejected" due to the nature or severity of a handicapping condition. No child could be regarded as "unable to benefit from education" or as "not educable." (Prior to this law, for instance, arbitrary criteria, most notably an I.Q. test score, were often used to separate children considered to be the school's responsibility from those who were not.) The basic requirement of the law applies not only to children living at home, but also to children who may live in an institutional or other setting, including children in hospitals or other medical care facilities.
>
> **2** *"Non-discriminatory evaluation*—a rule that schools must fairly evaluate students to de-termine if they are handicapped and, if so, the nature and extent of their handicap." The purpose of evaluation is to determine who is included rather than who is excluded. The specific re-quirements are intended to ensure that: 1) no single test or test criterion (such as I.Q. score) is

used as the sole basis for determining a child's need for special education services, the nature of those services, or the placement in which they are provided; 2) the *multifactored* evaluation process is carried out by a multidisciplinary team of appropriately qualified persons and addresses all areas related to the suspected disability (e.g., hearing, vision, communication, etc.); 3) tests employed as part of the multifactored evaluation process are administered in the child's native language, have been appropriately validated for the purpose for which they are being used, and are appropriately adapted to accommodate a child's sensory, motor, or communication impairment (e.g., use of sign language for a child who uses sign to communicate, and/or use of tests that have been normed and validated for children with such impairments).

**3** "*Appropriate education*—a rule that schools must adequately educate handicapped students, principally by designing a sufficient individualized education program (IEP) for them." The meaning of a free public education would seem to be a fairly straightforward proposition. But for children determined to be handicapped (using multifactored criteria), that education must also be appropriate for their individual needs. Prior to the enactment of the law, while many children with disabilities were unserved, many more were presumed to be inappropriately served (that is, special individual needs associated with a disability were not being addressed, or were not being addressed as effectively as they might have been). It has been observed, somewhat ruefully, that there is nothing new about "mainstreaming." A great many mildly retarded students were, indeed, in the regular classroom; however, many of these students experienced constant failure and many who did, dropped out.

Appropriate education for a handicapped student is defined as education based upon an Individualized Education Program (IEP), developed specifically for that student, based upon his or her unique individual needs determined through the multifactored assessment process. The IEP is presumed to represent the most valid state of what, for an individual pupil, is an appropriate education. To ensure that this is the case, it should represent the collective decision-making of all directly concerned—the professionals involved, the child's parent or parents, and, if 18 or older, the student. In practice, many younger students participate in the IEP process as well. IEPs are reviewed annually on the assumption that what is appropriate one year may not be appropriate the next.

**4** "*Least restrictive environment*—a rule that handicapped students should be placed in school programs with nonhandicapped students unless they cannot successfully be educated in such programs with the use of supplementary aids and services." By the 1985–86 school year, more than 90 percent of students identified as handicapped received their special education and related services in settings providing some degree of contact, integration, or co-learning with peers who were not handicapped. For more than 26 percent, special education was provided within the regular classroom itself, while 41 percent received some of their instruction and/or related services through resource rooms. More than 24 percent were taught in special classes located within regular schools, presumably permitting some degree of at least social, but not instructional, integration with nonhandicapped peers.

**5** "*Procedural due process*—a rule that parents and schools must be provided with a system of checks and balances to hold each other accountable for the decisions they make." The right to due process is a familiar and highly valued concept in a democratic society. In the past, parents were often simply informed that their child was going to be placed in a special class because school personnel had determined the child to be mentally retarded. This determination was probably made on the basis of an I.Q. test that was given in response to a teacher's referral. This notification was often the first time a parent was made aware that a problem had been detected, and parents were not routinely asked to approve diagnostic testing. It didn't always happen that way, of course, but quite often parents were indeed kept in the dark, and sometimes those parents who were consulted really had no opportunity to challenge the recommendation of school personnel.

This sort of scenario occurred especially often with students and parents who represented racial, ethnic, and linguistic minorities.[22] In addition, children who were placed in special classes early in their school careers were likely to remain in special education. There was no assurance that their placement status would be carefully reviewed on a regular basis, nor was there an individual plan that outlined the individual goals, objectives, and services uniquely appropriate to their needs.

**6** *"Parental participation*—a rule that parents must be given an opportunity to participate with the school's personnel in educational decision-making" for their child. It should be evident from the discussion of the IEP process and of procedural due process that P.L. 94–142 provides for an extraordinary degree of parental involvement in planning and decision-making that affects their children's education. In addition, the law encourages parental involvement in more broad and far-reaching forms of educational policy decision-making. That intent is realized, for example, in provisions that the state education agency (SEA) must conduct public hearings concerning proposed changes in rules and regulations affecting students with handicaps. At the local school district level, as well as in other community agencies, parents are increasingly represented on advisory and project planning committees.

Two very important further changes have occurred since P.L. 94–142 and Section 504 of the Rehabilitation Act were enacted. First, in 1990, Congress passed the Americans with Disabilities Act, to go into effect in 1992. This Act basically extends to the *private sector* provisions to ensure the rights of access and freedom from discrimination for persons with disabilities that had previously applied only to agencies receiving federal funds. For example, for buildings newly constructed or to be renovated or remodeled, provision for physical access for wheelchair users (e.g., pile height of carpet), visual alarm signals and telecommunication devices for persons with impaired hearing, specified percentages of drinking fountains, parking spaces, and tables in restaurants must be made. In addition, discrimination by employers based on disability is prohibited.

Second, the Education of the Handicapped Act (EHA) enacted in 1975 has been amended. An important change occurred in 1986, when Congress extended its provisions to eligible children beginning at age 3 and established a new section to enable states to provide family-based services for infants and toddlers with developmental delays (these changes are discussed further in Chapter 8). In 1990, the name of the law was itself changed to the *Individuals with Disabilities Education Act,* or *IDEA* (P.L. 101–476). This change is important because it substitutes the term *disabilities* for the term *handicaps,* puts "people first" (individuals with disabilities, not disabled individuals), and notes that the law does not apply only to "children," but rather extends its provisions through age 21. Some other important changes were included in these amendments:

**1** *Autism* and *traumatic brain injury* are identified as distinct categories of disability.

**2** A plan for *transition services* must be included in each eligible student's IEP no later than age 16 to address the transition from school to work and community living.

**3** A state can now be sued in federal court for violations of IDEA.

**4** Grant programs are authorized to enhance services for students with severe and multiple disabilities.

Taken together, these new provisions extend through force of law the concern of the society for those whose "difference" has traditionally excluded them from full participation in ordinary life. It is, perhaps, a mark of some maturity that, as a nation, we have come this far.

## TITLE IX: IS SEX A DIFFERENCE THAT MAKES A DIFFERENCE?

Discrimination in education on the basis of sex was addressed by Title IX of the Education Amendments of 1972. The preamble to this statute reads, in part:

> No person in the United States shall, on the basis of sex, be excluded from participation in, be denied the benefits of, or be subjected to discrimination under any education program or activity receiving federal financial assistance.

It was not until 1975, however, that the rules and regulations enforcing Title IX were published and sent to state departments of education and school districts. In the interim, there was heated controversy (and 10,000 written comments from citizens).[23] To understand why, it is necessary to become acquainted with a little of the history of male attitudes toward educating women.

Since the time of the ancient Greeks, enormous numbers of public figures—kings, statesmen, philosophers, educators, historians, scientists, writers, and clergy, almost all of whom have been men—have been writing, making speeches, sermonizing, and enforcing through public policy a concern about the education of women that borders on what, today, we might call paranoia. Negative attitudes toward the education of women have generally been based on three assumptions. First, it was asserted that women are intellectually inferior to men. Socrates noted that "all of the pursuits of men are the pursuits of women also, but in all of them a woman is inferior to a man."[24] His pupil Aristotle wrote: "The male is by nature superior and the female inferior, the male ruler and the female subject."[25] If the female mind were, in fact, of lesser quality and women had less aptitude for learning, why should they be educated at all? Erasmus puzzled over this question: "I do not know the reason, but just as a saddle is not suitable for an ox, so learning is unsuitable for women."[26]

A second rationale for not educating women—and perhaps the most important one—has been that "woman's place is in the home." Women did not, therefore, *need* education beyond instruction in household tasks. Moreover, literacy and tuition in the more advanced arts and sciences might very well make a woman dissatisfied with her life, impatient with men, and perhaps even infertile. Kant, for instance, declared that women would lose their value to men by becoming educated: "Even if a woman excels in arduous learning and painstaking thinking," he wrote, "they will exterminate the merits of her sex."[27] In 1871, the American physician Dr. James Clarke wrote a book on the education of women in which he insisted that women had only so much energy, and devoting it to the acquisition of higher learning would result in a shrinking of the reproductive organs and a consequent inability to bear children.[28]

A variation on the theme of women's "proper" place emphasized women's role, not as homemakers so much as pleasant companions for men. Goethe, for instance, wrote that "we love things other than the intellect in a young woman. We love what is beautiful, confiding, teasing, youthful in her; her character, her faults, her whims, and God knows what other undefinable things, but we do not love her intellect."[29]

Third, powerful men have asserted—an argument rooted in ancient male fears related to women's mysterious power to bring forth life—that women are inherently evil, and that to educate them would only enhance their power to create havoc in the lives and institutions of men.[30]

When the European inheritors of these ideas crossed the Atlantic and settled in what was to become the United States, they brought these ideas with them. The American experience, however—a nearly continuous frontier, the creation of a democratic state, and the need for a cheap labor force to help fuel the economic engine of the industrial revolution—altered the views of the men who have always been responsible for designing the schooling system in the United States. Perhaps the central theme in the continuing expansion of women's access to education in America has been the need to provide a "place" for women in the democratic state,[31] to give them a *political* role while maintaining their place in the home. The American solution was ingenious: women would become the primary educators of the Republic, first at home as instructors of new generations of democratic citizens, and later in the schoolhouse, as teachers in the common school. For this job, of course, they needed schooling—but not too much. (Women were denied access to higher education until the latter half of the nineteenth century, and as recently as 1960, only 15.4 percent of all women 18 to 24 years old were enrolled in college.[32])

Women, then, should become regular pupils in the new common schools—and for the first time in western history, girls were admitted to schools on the same basis as boys.

Benjamin Rush, one of the architects of the common school, argued vigorously for allowing women access to schooling:

> I beg pardon for having delayed so long, to say anything of the separate and peculiar mode of education proper for WOMEN in a republic. I am sensible that they much concur in all our plans of education for young men, or no laws will ever render them effectual. To qualify our women for this purpose, they should not only be instructed in the usual braces of female education, but they should be instructed in the principles of liberty and government; and the obligations of patriotism, should be inculcated upon them. The opinions and conduct of men are often regulated by the women in the most arduous enterprises of life; and their approbation is frequently the principal reward of the hero's dangers, and the patriot's toils. Besides, the *first* impressions upon the minds of children are generally derived from the women. Of how much consequence, therefore, is it in a republic, that they should think justly upon the great subjects of liberty and government![33]

The rapid spread of the common (elementary) school across the nation in the nineteenth century created, in turn, an immediate need for teachers. While prior to this time the role of schoolmaster had been primarily a male one, men in the first third of the century were being lured into the new factories, where they could make considerably more money. This created an enormous gap in the teaching force, and women were designated as indisputably the best pool of labor to fill it. Male educationists, however, were careful not to stray too far from the conviction that women's "natural" role was a predominantly maternal one. Jill Conway writes of three arguments for the recruitment of women into the teaching profession:[34]

> [Women] manifest a livelier interest, more contentment in the work, have altogether superior success in managing and instructing young children, and I know of instances, where by the silken cord of affection, have led many a stubborn will, and wild ungoverned impulse, into habits of obedience and study even in the large winter schools (Henry Barnard, *Second Annual Report* [Connecticut School, 1840], pp. 27–28).

[Women] are endowed by nature with stronger parental impulses, and this makes the society of children delightful, and turns duty into a pleasure. Their minds are less withdrawn from their employment, by the active scenes of life; and they are less intent and scheming for future honors and emoluments. As a class, they never look forward, as young men almost invariably do, to a period of legal emancipation from parental control. . . . They are also of purer morals (*Fourth Annual Report* [Boston Board of Education, 1841], pp. 45–46).

In childhood the intellectual faculties are but partially developed—the affections much more fully. At that early age the affections are the key of the whole being. The female teacher readily possesses herself of that key, and thus having access to the heart, the mind is soon reached and operated upon (Assemblyman Hurlburd, *New York State Education Exhibit* [World's Columbian Exposition, Chicago, 1893], pp. 45–46).

Many young women in the nineteenth century "kept school" at 16 or 17 years of age, having only just a bit more schooling than their pupils. In general, a woman worked as a schoolmarm only until she married; marriage remained the "normal" occupation of women. But it became understood that teaching was a female profession, and it lost both status and financial rewards because it was associated with "women's work." Nevertheless, the opening up of teaching to women did provide girls with considerably more opportunities for schooling, and eventually served as a wedge into the world of higher education.

The inclusion of girls in elementary schooling did not, however, significantly diminish the power of old ideas either that women were intellectually inferior to men or that learning would ruin their value in the home. Writing in 1805, for example, an essayist known only as "Sophia" bitterly satirized some prevailing views of education for women:

A woman who is conscious of possessing more intellectual power than is requisite in superintending the pantry, and in adjusting the ceremonials of a feast, and who believes she is conforming to the will of the giver, in improving the gift, is by the wits of the other sex denominated a learned lady. She is represented as disgustingly slovenly in her person, indecent in her habits, imperious to her husband, and negligent of her children. And the odious scarecrow is employed, exactly as the farmer employs his unsightly bundle of rags and straw, to terrify the simple birds, from picking up the precious grain, which he wishes to monopolize. After all this, what man in his sober senses can be astonished to find the majority of women as they really are, frivolous and volatile; incapable of estimating their own dignity, and indifferent to the best interests of society?[35]

While the language is somewhat different from that used today, the sentiments criticized are still prevalent: distrust of the highly educated woman and the suspicion that she cannot possibly be doing justice to her home and family. Indeed, women in the last part of the twentieth century, who *have* gained access to higher education and to the workplace, are still expected to do the major share of the work of keeping the home and raising the children. That is a problem that the next century will have to solve.

Although access to schooling and to higher education has increased considerably in the United States over our history, there is still a long way to go in ensuring equity—commensurate treatment in and outcome of schooling—for girls and women. In other words, schooling in many cases does not have the same *meaning* for women as it does for men. Girls do not bring the same socialization patterns with them to school, nor are many teachers and other school personnel able to transcend their own gender socialization—their own ideas of what is "right" and "proper" for young boys and girls. Thus, the educational experience of boys and girls in school differs, regardless of race, class, religion, health, or disability. Indeed, one of the most important tasks of the next several years will be to assess the ways in which membership in these social groups serves to mediate the experience of gender in teaching and learning.

During the 1960s, members of the women's movement and others began to pressure the Congress to enact legislation that would guarantee equitable educational experience for girls and women. The result was Title IX of the Education Amendments of 1972. The intent of Title IX was to prohibit discrimination in elementary and secondary schools on the basis of sex. Areas of particular interest in the interpretation of Title IX are the following:[36]

**1** *Comparable facilities:* Although the law allows separate facilities for males and females, toilet, locker, and shower facilities for each sex must be comparable. Facilities for physical education and athletics must be comparable.

**2** *Access to course offerings:* Schools must allow students of both sexes free access to any course offered by the school, including physical education, health education, vocational education, home economics, industrial and business education, advanced placement courses, and adult education. Students may be separated by sex for physical education and courses in human sexuality; they may also be grouped by ability in physical education classes if objective standards of assessment are applied regardless of sex. Schools may also set vocal requirements for participation in single-sex or mixed choruses.

**3** *Access to vocational education:* Local school districts may not deny, on the basis of sex, admission to any vocational school or program.

**4** *Counseling and counseling materials:* Schools may not use counseling assessments and/or materials to discriminate on the basis of sex. Furthermore, schools are required to ensure that counseling materials are "sex fair"; this includes tests, pamphlets, and books on opportunities for further education, careers, and occupations, and on personal growth and aspirations. Counseling may not be used to guide, direct, or encourage students to enroll or not enroll in particular courses on the basis of cultural beliefs about the "proper" place of males and females in society.

**5** *Financial assistance:* Schools may not award financial assistance, grants, or merit awards on the basis of sex. While this provision applies most often to institutions of higher education, high schools are also affected. For example, high schools may not award money, or allow community organizations to award money, to students when gender is an eligibility requirement. Exclusions to this rule may be made, however, in some circumstances. Schools can award athletic scholarships to members of single-sex teams, so long as comparable awards are available for single-sex teams of the other sex. In addition, academic scholarships that are restricted by the donor to members of one sex are permitted, provided that the pool of scholarship funds is otherwise equitably distributed.

**6** *Student health and insurance benefits and services:* Schools must ensure that insurance policies offer the same coverage for male and female students and that insurers who contact parents directly also do not discriminate in coverage offered.

**7** *Marital and parental status of students:* Schools may not discriminate against students in academic or extracurricular activities on the basis of sex in matters related to their marital or parental status. Pregnant students may not be denied access to any class or school-sponsored activity, nor can the school require that pregnant students attend special classes designed for their future needs as parents.

**8** *Athletics:* Equal opportunity and equal dollar expenditures for both sexes are required in interscholastic athletics, school clubs, and intramural games sponsored by the school. Membership in single-sex teams must be based on competitive skills. Girls must be allowed to try out for noncontact team sports unless a separate team for girls is provided in the same sport. When a school does provide separate teams for male and female students in the same sport, girls may compete for the boys' team with the superintendent's or principal's approval, but boys may not participate on the girls' team.

**9** *Education programs and activities:* Equal access to educational programs receiving federal assistance, and equal treatment once enrolled, are required. Schools and other education agencies also may not cooperate with any organization, agency, or individual that discriminates on the basis of sex.

**10** *Employment:* Schools may not discriminate on the basis of sex in employee recruitment and selection; job advertising, upgrading, promotion, tenure, layoffs, termination, rates of pay, or classification; or in collective bargaining, leave, fringe benefits, financial support for training, preemployment inquiries, pregnancy, marital or parental status, and employer-sponsored activities.

Like P.L. 94–142, Title IX requires the establishment of grievance procedures, self-evaluation, and remedial and affirmative action policies in the schools. Unlike P.L. 94–142, Title IX has suffered a significant weakening since its passage. Federal dollars allocated to school districts for technical assistance in its implementation have evaporated, as has funding to hire overseers to guarantee compliance. Title IX has been responsible for the creation of more opportunity for girls, particularly in physical and vocational education; however, many schools are notorious for spending considerably less time, effort, and money on girls' athletics and athletic equipment. Interestingly, this may be particularly significant in terms of girls' ability to achieve success in the still predominantly male world of business. As women climb the corporate ladder, many who do are finding that one of the things they have in common is early participation in team sports.

Schools have been somewhat less than enthusiastic about implementing other features of Title IX. For instance, not many schools that offer parental leave to female employees also offer this fringe benefit to male employees.[37] Furthermore, some schools are willing to enforce Title IX provisions for students but not at all for adult employees.[38] In general, a lack of commitment on the part of federal and state governments, coupled with a growing disinclination on the part of school districts to invest scarce resources in additional programming and benefits, has resulted in a sharp decline in Title IX policy initiatives.

## DIVERSITY AND EDUCATIONAL POLICY IN THE 1990s

It is instructive to reflect on the very different outcomes of the several mandates for equal educational opportunity legislated in the 1960s and 1970s. Why, for example, did

P.L. 94–142 take root when bilingual education programs and anti-sex discrimination policies did not? While a number of factors are involved—a new economic picture in the country, a disenchantment with the nation's ability to live up to its ideals in the aftermath of the Vietnam War, and an assortment of government scandals—it seems relatively clear that the differences are due principally to deep-seated beliefs about the function of schools in American society and the roles of women and minorities.

In the past decade we have seen a powerful resurgence of the belief that the primary function of schooling is academic rather than social—that is, that schools are to teach "knowledge" and not try to change the society. Moreover, with dawning awareness of the magnitude of the demographic changes taking place in the United States, schools are once again viewed by many as a major agency of assimilation. An issue of scale may also be at work here. Children and adults who qualify as "exceptional" represent a relatively small minority of the population, while the members of minority culture groups and the lower classes are increasing rapidly in number, and females constitute more than half the population. To alter educational programs—both academic coursework and extracurricular activities—is a time-consuming, expensive process. When that must be done across the board to address concerns of multitudes of students and school employees, it appears to be an overwhelming task.

The definition of equal educational opportunity is also a problem. For some, equal educational opportunity means an *equal chance* to participate in acquiring an education. The major responsibility for actually acquiring it then lies with the student; the function of government and other public agencies is merely to ensure access. If the student cannot, or will not, do what is required to obtain the education, it is unfortunate, but neither the school nor the community have an obligation to do anything about it. In contrast, some believe that equal educational opportunity means an *equal share* in education. Responsibility for effective education lies principally with the government and the school. If students cannot or will not do what the school requires, schools must be restructured in such a way that they can and will. Public educational policy should focus on the outcomes of schooling, and measures should be taken to ensure that most, if not all, students receive the benefits of a good education.

Ironically, it may be that the very issue of demographic change that has historically been used to support assimilationist arguments for the role of the school as a political socializer of the young will in the end provide the most powerful impetus for more pluralist approaches to schooling. Educational policy may rise and fall on the very number of culturally and economically different students sitting in the nation's classrooms. We simply cannot afford to let one-third to one-half of our children "fall through the cracks." Clearly, the attitudes that underlie any changes in American schools will be critical to what kind of changes are made and to the success with which they are institutionalized. If we alter schooling in ways that separate students according to race, ethnicity, religion, social class, health, or disability, we will be doing what we've done before. Remediation, tracking, and cosmetic programs such as Black History Month and Women's History Month often result not in integration but in isolation and segregation. If we approach educational reform in terms of a positive commitment to the strengths that a recognition of diversity can bring, we may succeed in creating schools in which all children can flourish and be culturally enriched.

Stating the choices in such a simple (some would, perhaps, say "simplistic"!) way does not, of course, imply that the work to be done will be easy. We have not eliminated a single practical problem by outlining the issues. It is important to understand, however, that in the United States educational policy arises finally from the beliefs and values of its citizenry. A thoughtful and thorough examination of those beliefs and values is therefore a major starting point for educational reform.

## ACTIVITIES

1 Federal and state policies are ultimately carried out in many different ways by various schools and communities. Interview personnel at a nearby school to find out what impact recent federal and state legislation has had at the school level.

2 Review recent newspapers and magazines for attention given to issues related to multicultural education, gender-sensitive education, and special education. What does your survey imply about the concerns of the nation? Of nearby communities? Of parents, teachers, and students?

## REFERENCES

1 Robert Frost, "The Gift Outright," in *The Witness Tree* (New York: Henry Holt, 1942), p. 1.41.1.

2 D. A. Brown, *Bury My Heart at Wounded Knee* (New York: Holt, Rinehart and Winston, 1970), p. 1.

3 L. Dinnerstein and D. M. Reiners, *Ethnic Americans: A History of Immigration and Assimilation* (New York: Harper Row, 1975).

4 Ibid., p. 2.

5 Eugene F. Provenzo, Jr., *An Introduction to Education in American Society* (Columbus, OH: Charles E. Merrill, 1986), p. 90–91.

6 Rodman B. Webb and Robert R. Sherman, *Schooling and Society,* 2d ed. (New York: Macmillan, 1989), p. 524.

7 Nancy Hoffman, *Women's 'True' Profession,* (Old Westbury, NY: The Feminist Press and McGraw-Hill, 1981), pp. 90–197.

8 Quoted in Meyer Weinberg, *A Chance to Learn: A History of Race and Education in the United States* (New York: Cambridge University Press, 1977), p. 46.

9 William A. Hunter (ed.), *Multicultural Education through Competency-Based Teacher Education* (Washington, DC: American Association of Colleges of Teacher Education, 1975), p. 17.

10 Cited by Rupert Trujillo in "Bilingual-Bicultural Education: A Necessary Strategy for American Public Education," in *A Relook at Tuscon '66 and Beyond,* report of a National Bilingual Bicultural Institute (Washington, DC: National Education Association, 1973), p. 21.

11 Israel Zangwill, *The Melting Pot* (New York: Macmillan, 1909), p. 37.

12 James Banks, *Multiethnic Education: Theory and Practice,* 2d ed. (Boston: Allyn Bacon, 1988).

13 Ibid.

14 Cited in Pamela L. Tiedt and Iris M. Tiedt, *Multicultural Teaching: A Handbook of Activities, Information, and Resources,* 3d ed. (Boston: Allyn Bacon, 1990), p. 9.

15 Ibid.

16 Joel Spring, *The Sorting Machine: National Educational Policy Since 1945* (New York: David McKay, 1976).

17 B. M. Caldwell, "The Importance of Beginning Early," in J. B. Jordan and R. F. Dailey (eds.), *Not All Little Wagons Are Red: The Exceptional Child's Early Years* (Arlington, VA: Council for Exceptional Children, 1973).

**18** J. R. Mercer, *Labeling the Mentally Retarded: Clinical and Social System Perspectives on Mental Retardation* (Berkeley, CA: University of California Press, 1973).

**19** M. C. Reynolds and J. W. Birch, *Teaching Exceptional Children in All America's Schools: A First Course for Teachers and Principals* (Reston, VA: Council for Exceptional Children, 1977).

**20** H. R. Turnbull and A. P. Turnbull, "Public Policy and Handicapped Citizens," in N. Haring (ed.), *Exceptional Children and Youth,* 3d ed. (Columbus, OH: Charles E. Merrill, 1982), pp. 21–44.

**21** Ibid., pp. 32–33.

**22** Mercer, op. cit.

**23** Anne O'Brien Carelli, "What Is Title IX?," in *Sex Equity in Education: Readings and Strategies* (Springfield, IL: Charles C. Thomas, 1988), p. 85.

**24** Gary Clabaugh, "A History of Male Attitudes toward Educating Women," *Educational Horizons,* vol. 64, no. 3, Spring 1986, p. 130.

**25** L. Glenn Smith, "From Plato to Jung: Centuries of Educational Inequities," *Educational Horizons,* vol. 60, no. 1, Fall 1981, p. 5.

**26** Clabaugh, op. cit., p. 128.

**27** Ibid., p. 133.

**28** Smith, op. cit., p. 8.

**29** Clabaugh, op. cit., p. 134.

**30** Barbara Walker, *The Crone: Women of Age, Wisdom, and Power* (New York: Harper Row, 1985).

**31** Linda Kerber, *Women of the Republic: Intellect and Ideology in Revolutionary America* (New York: W. W. Norton, 1980).

**32** Barbara H. Solomon, *In the Company of Educated Women* (New Haven, CT: Yale University Press, 1985), pp. 63–64.

**33** Benjamin Rush, "A Plan for the Establishment of Public Schools and the Diffusion of Knowledge in Pennsylvania; to which are added Thoughts upon the Mode of Education, Proper in a Republic. Addressed to the Legislature and Citizens of the State." (Philadelphia: Printed for Thomas Dobson, 1786), pp. 13–36.

**34** Jill Conway, "Politics, Pedagogy, and Gender," *Daedalus,* vol. 116, no. 4, Fall 1987, p. 141.

**35** Kerber, op. cit., pp. 196–198.

**36** This description of the major provisions of Title IX is adapted from Carelli, op. cit., pp. 88–92.

**37** Ibid., p. 92.

**38** Paul Thurston, "Judicial Dismemberment of Title IX," *Phi Delta Kappan,* vol. 60, no. 8, April 1979, p. 595.

# CHAPTER 7

# MULTICULTURAL AND BILINGUAL EDUCATION

*In the community where I lived as a child, my neighbors were Japanese, Chinese, Hawaiians, and Portuguese. Nearby there were Filipinos and Puerto Ricans. As I grew up, I did not ask why—why were we from so many "different shores," from Asia and Europe as well as Hawaii itself . . . My teachers and my textbooks did not explain the reasons why we were there.*

*After graduation from high school, I attended a college on the mainland where I found myself invited to dinners for "foreign students." I politely tried to explain to my kind hosts that I was not a foreign student; still they insisted that I accept their invitations. My fellow students (and even my professors) would ask me where I learned to speak English. "In this country," I would reply. And sometimes I would add, "I was born in America, and my family has been here for three generations." Like myself, they had been taught little or nothing about America's ethnic diversity, and they thought I looked like a foreigner.*

Ronald Takaki

Our discussion of multicultural and bilingual education begins by considering some of the problems faced by schools and teachers, as well as by speakers of a second language, in areas with a fast-changing population. Let's begin by looking at these data on the Dade County, Florida, schools in the late 1980s:[1]

**1** From July 1, 1988 to September 12, 1989, 24,062 foreign-born students entered Dade County's public schools. This number is more than the total school enrollments in 47 of Florida's 67 counties. Among that number, 8,385, or 34.8% were Nicaraguan.

**2** As of October, 1989, Dade County's schools had 278,153 students—72,249 were foreign-born.

**3** In July, 1989, statistically a fairly typical month for the registration of foreign-born students, 1,432 new students registered representing 62 different countries.

**4** Most of the foreign-born children entering the schools are at an educational level two years behind their age group. It is estimated that it will take at least two years to overcome this, as well as the adjustment problems the students are encountering. Most of these children are considered "at-risk" students. They speak very little or no English, and as such are in need of bilingual programs and programs relating to dropout prevention. Such programs, as school personnel state, are costly to provide.

The classroom environment plays a significant role in how a child perceives himself or herself, both linguistically and academically. A child who comes to school speaking a language different from that expected in the school is often made to feel inferior by both peers and teachers. Typically there are contradictory views among parents and teachers concerning the child's use of their home language in the school (usually Spanish in the case of the Dade County schools). Because of language and other cultural barriers, parents often feel alienated from the school, a feeling teachers sometimes inaccurately interpret as disinterest. Children, as a consequence, find it difficult to acquire a positive identity because they do not fully identify with either the school or the home.

Teachers are a critical link in student's successful adjustment in the classroom. They must be sensitive to the child by providing materials that capitalize on and enrich the child's cultural and linguistic differences. Teachers must place a positive value on the child's cultural differences in order to encourage development of self-esteem. Teachers should also make an effort to reach out and involve families as much as possible. In most instances, when teachers encourage students to use their native languages, school-work, attitudes, and self-esteem improve. At the same time, teachers must enable students to acquire the attitudes, values, and skills that they will need to fully participate in the public culture. How this has been, and is being, attempted is the focus of this chapter.

## MULTICULTURAL EDUCATION: IDEA TO PRACTICE

In the first half of the twentieth century American education effectively ignored the culture and needs of those generally considered not to fit the mold of the white, Anglo, male model American. And while assimilationist efforts were successful for many who shared northern European roots, discrimination still barred most people of color from full participation in the American dream.

All attempts at multicultural education seem to have been efforts to respond to the educational needs of children who do not belong to the majority group. If one reviews the expanding literature on multicultural education programs, certain common purposes can be seen. Multicultural education programs have had some or all of the following aims: to combat the ethnocentricity of school culture and to legitimize the presence of other cultures in the school; to educate children in such a way that they do not come into conflict with their parents—in other words, to ensure continuity between the school and family; to present learning about languages and cultures as a positive acquisition rather than an imposed discipline; to eliminate prejudice and discrimination in teaching; to bring about equal opportunities for all; to guarantee the pluralism of educational systems; and, to respect the rights of children.[2]

In his early work, Banks addressed ethnic identification and proposed a typology of expanding ethnic identification which he suggests individuals move through in their development into reflective citizens.[3] More recently, in part due to perceived similarities in the goals of international and multicultural education, this typology has been expanded to include development toward national and global citizenship. This typology is hierarchical; that is, individuals can enter at any stage and, if provided sufficient experiences, should move upward. However, it should be noted that they can also move downward. A typology such as this can become the cornerstone for an effective multicultural education program.

In stage 1, *ethnic psychological captivity,* the individual believes the negative myths about his or her group that society has institutionalized. Stuck at this level, the individual is typically ashamed of his or her group, and as a consequence, develops low self-esteem, often accompanied by self-rejection.

In stage 2, *ethnic encapsulation,* the individual spends a disproportionate amount of time with her or his own group. As a result, a high degree of ethnocentrism emerges, alienating the individual from others. Intense negative feelings toward those who are different may emerge, especially if an individual feels that her or his group is being threatened in some way. A strong ingroup orientation develops.

Banks calls stage 3 *ethnic identity clarification.* At this stage the individual has accepted him or herself and has a rather clear sense of their own group. Because the individual has a more fully developed sense of self, they are able to respond positively to others.

In stage 4, *biethnicity,* the individual has developed the skills necessary to participate fully in two ethnic cultures. Many Jewish Americans or African-Americans have learned to function effectively in a highly integrated workday setting while returning to private lives which may be reflective of their own ethnic group. Members of other ethnic or religious groups have also achieved this level of biethnicity and benefit from the rewards that participation in several ''worlds'' can offer.

Stage 5 Banks calls *multiethnicity and reflective nationalism.* At this stage, the individual is able to function effectively in several ethnic cultures within his or her nation. One can understand, appreciate, and share the values of several groups. While individuals at this level strongly identify with their own group, they also have a strong commitment to the pluralistic nation and its values of human rights and dignity for all. Banks suggests that most people never have experiences sufficient to achieve this level. He cautions that while many may participate at superficial levels, such as eating at ethnic restaurants or listening to music from other cultures, few ever fully understand the values, symbols, and traditions of many others, or gain the skills necessary to function in other groups.

Finally, at stage 6, *globalism and global competency,* the individual has developed the skills necessary to function not only in other groups within one's own nation, but with others in other parts of the world as well. Banks suggests that individuals at this level have ''the ideal delicate balance of ethnic, national, and global identification, commitments, literacy, and behaviors. This individual has internalized the universalistic ethical values and principles of humankind and has the skills, competencies, and commitment needed to take action within the world to actualize personal values and commitments.''[4]

The general thrust of efforts under the rubric of multicultural education in recent years has broadened, moving from an assimilationist ideology to a more pluralistic model. Still far from achieving its goals, multicultural education is striving to restructure schooling for empowerment in terms of racial, social, and gender equity.

## All Multicultural Education Programs Are Not the Same

In their analysis of multicultural education in the United States, Sleeter and Grant find five distinct categories of efforts described under the label *multicultural education.*[5] While there is clearly some overlap between them, they represent the variety of approaches used to date by educational pluralists attempting to advance the cause of a positive approach to cultural diversity.

**1** *Teaching the culturally different:* The main purpose of these programs is to counter the cultural deficiency orientation while assisting individuals to develop and maintain their own cultural identity. They attempt to help individuals develop competence in the culture of the dominant group while developing a positive self-identity. The focus of such efforts tends to be on aspects of the culture and language of specific target groups which a teacher can build upon, not on issues of social and power relationships. Few of these efforts extend beyond attention to culture (in the traditional sense), race, and ethnicity; there is generally no attention to gender, exceptionality, or social class.

**2** *Human relations:* Designers of programs in this category view multicultural education as a means by which students of different backgrounds learn to communicate more effectively with others while learning to feel good about themselves. Such efforts provide practical ideas for how teachers can improve their communications with others while helping students understand their culturally different peers.

**3** *Single-group studies:* Programs in this category provide instruction that focuses on the experience and culture of a single group. In response to the early demands by those seeking inclusion in the curriculum, courses that reflected the heritage, contributions, and perspectives of these ''forgotten'' groups were developed in many schools and universities across the nation. Such courses as African-American History, Chicano Literature, and Native American Culture were developed and taught, for the most part, by members of the target ethnic group. Those who took the courses were also typically members of that group. The primary goal of these courses was twofold: (1) to develop a content dimension, since exclusion from mainstream material typically resulted in a lack of readily available information about the group; (2) to help students develop a more positive self-perception and self-image.

**4** *Multicultural education*: It soon became apparent that the adoption of single-group courses was not in itself sufficient to enable many minority students to achieve in school at levels comparable to most of their majority counterparts. A slow shift in direction began to occur that offered a new approach, a new way of looking at the question of what appropriate multicultural education is. Broader issues of school reform were raised, and attention focused on the total school environment. As more and more ethnic groups began to make similar demands, the pressure on schools and universities to develop and deliver courses that reflected the experiences of many different groups increased. As similarities in people's experience and perspective became evident, schools, colleges, and universities began to offer courses that attempted to link the experiences of various ethnic groups while developing a conceptual core. Such course offerings as Ethnic Minority Music, Minority Literature, and The History of Minorities in America became popular.

These courses helped to raise the consciousness of a number of people about various cultures and their contributions to a variety of disciplines and causes. Underlying all these approaches was a focus on such issues as the value of diversity in a pluralistic nation, the acceptability of alternative life choices, social justice and equal opportunity, human rights, and equitable distribution of power among members of all ethnic groups.

Meanwhile, other reformers attempted to address the needs of women, religious groups, individuals with handicaps, and those from less prosperous regions of the country, such as white Appalachia. Teachers who employed such a multicultural approach in their teaching would utilize material, concepts, and perspectives of many different individuals from diverse groups. English literature, for instance, would not be limited to a study of the literature of the so-called dead white men, but would include works by women, as well as by female and male writers from a variety of ethnic and cultural groups. In addition, the works selected for study would be ones identified as relevant by members of that particular group.

**5** *Education that is multicultural and social reconstructionist:* Even these approaches did not seem to have an impact sufficient to empower most people to make a difference in their lives. A mismatch between the curriculum of the school and the daily experiences and cultural backgrounds of many people of color is assumed to exist which is nearly impossible for many to transcend. Essentially, the schools succeed at placing certain individuals at an advantage while successfully suppressing many others.

Sleeter and Grant speak of providing education that is multicultural and social reconstructionist.[6] This approach goes beyond multicultural education, attempting to help students critically analyze their circumstances and the social stratification that keeps them from full participation in the society. The phrase "education that is multicultural" means that the entire educational program should be designed to address the needs of students of every race, ethnicity, culture, religion, exceptionality, or gender. This approach also strives to provide students with the skills necessary to become socially active—to work to create the necessary changes. This approach is designed to enable individuals to shape their own destinies, hence the term *social reconstructionist.*

Sleeter and Grant cite four practices unique to education that is multicultural and social reconstructionist.[7]

**1** Schools and classrooms that adopt such an approach are organized in such a way that democracy is put into action. That is, children are not told what democracy should be like; rather, they are given the opportunity to participate in constructing a system that exemplifies democracy in action. Students participate in such activities as determining the rules and consequences of classroom interaction, may participate in determining portions of the curriculum, and may be included in various aspects of program evaluation (see Chapter 13).

**2** Students learn to analyze their life situation and to become aware of societal inequities that affect their lives—for example, unequal pay for equal work—and of false assumptions that the educational system may have promulgated—for example, that an education automatically improves one's social and economic status. On this latter point, Ogbu relates the experiences of a disenfranchised individual:

> White people have always felt that they are superior to all other groups. And when the minority people begin to protest and challenge this superiority complex the white people begin to shout the slogan of "law and order." But the only solution to the problem, you say, is education. Education will do it. All right, now you take my wife. She has four years of college and yet she can't get a job. Now education is not the only answer. It is one of the answers but not all the answer.[8]

**3** Students learn social action skills so that they are prepared to act on their knowledge and concerns in the political, economic, or social arena. Only then can significant social change occur.

**4** Finally, attempts are made to encourage groups to coalesce so that the efforts of smaller groups can be concentrated in the fight against oppression and discrimination. It is then that a large social movement can form. That is, when large numbers of people come together in their efforts to promote or resist change in society, formal organizations may be born. The feminist and civil rights movements of the past few decades resulted in the formation of many organizations that direct their efforts and make significant change.

## THE IMPACT OF MULTICULTURAL EDUCATION ON STUDENTS

Since the early part of this century social scientists have known that children as young as 3 years of age are able to differentiate human physical characteristics such as skin color.[9] Children also, from about age 5, make attributions about others based on their skin color, associating black with negative value and white with positive value.[10]

Banks provides a comprehensive survey of the effects of multicultural education on the racial attitudes of children.[11] A variety of multicultural education efforts have been observed to have positive effects; these include curriculum units and courses developed around specific ethnic and/or cultural groups (e.g., African-American History);[12] multiethnic social studies readings; integrating multicultural activities into social studies, English, and reading;[13] and use of multiethnic readers in the language arts program.[14] Certain instructional strategies may also have positive effects. For instance, studies rather consistently suggest that positive racial attitudes can result among students of different ethnic groups when they utilize cooperative learning activities.[16] The results of the cooperative learning studies suggest, as Banks reminds us, that factual content may not be as important as how it is taught and how the concepts are communicated to students, parents, and community.[17] (See Chapters 12 and 13 for further discussion.)

In general, studies conducted since the 1940s demonstrate that curriculum interventions can have a positive impact on student attitudes. However, the results of such studies have not been consistent. Some possible reasons for the inconsistent findings are differences in the nature and structure of the intervention, duration of exposure, individual student characteristics, such school characteristics as degree of cooperation versus competitiveness, characteristics of the community where the school is located, as well as characteristics of the teachers.[18] There is also a need to analyze the long-term effect of such interventions.

Over the years, a number of writers have analyzed the wide variety of multicultural education programs developed in the 1960s and 1970s and categorized them in ways that might help us to understand their purposes and practices. Cameron Mitchell, for example, provides a slightly different typology than does Banks or Sleeter and Grant (although perhaps you will be able to ''see'' Banks in Mitchell's work). Writing about the assumptions, expectations, and practices of various multicultural education programs, he argues that most, if not all, of them are premised on one of the following three models.[19]

*1   Models of cultural understanding:* The basic approach of programs based on this model is to emphasize improving communication between ethnic and cultural groups. Assumptions made by proponents of this model include the recognition that the United States is a culturally diverse nation-state where cultural diversity has helped to create a powerful society through the contributions of all Americans. The schools, however, have not acted to promote this view of American society with the result that prejudice and discrimination against particular racial and ethnic groups exist. In order to remedy this situation, schools and teachers should ''positively endorse cultural diversity and foster an appreciation and respect for 'human differences' in order to reduce racial tension and estrangement of minority groups in the school and in society.''[20]

In this approach, all social and ethnic groups are assumed to be relatively ''equal'' in worth and ethnic identity is thought to be ''a matter of individual choice or preference—the language of the shopping mall''[21] or the banquet table. Proponents of this model are advocates of the elimination of racial and sexual stereotypes, and, moving beyond awareness of cultural differences in food, dress, and so forth, emphasize that students should develop positive attitudes toward minority and disadvantaged groups. In other words, attitudes should change. Mitchell argues that these programs "take a 'benign' stance towards racial inequality in schooling";[22] consequently, they focus most of their attention on the development of racial and ethnic harmony.

Expecting that schools will actively promote the cultural enhancement of all students, these programs place primary responsibility on the classroom teacher to provide information and enrichment activities designed to reduce prejudice. Mitchell indicates that these programs have not been very successful in changing attitudes; indeed, in some cases attitudes among white students toward African-Americans and other minorities have deteriorated. The lack of success of these programs has been attributed in part to problems with both content and methods.[23] In addition, these programs may in fact foster stereotyping by clustering individuals together on the basis of only one characteristic—race, ethnicity, religion, and so forth. Differences *within* these groups are little emphasized.

*2  Models of cultural competence:* Proponents of models of cultural competence suggest that it is not enough to appreciate other cultural groups; one must first come to terms with one's own cultural identity, and then move beyond that to become "at home" in more than one cultural system.[24] Advocates of this kind of program believe that traditional assimilationist approaches such as the "melting pot" idea served to preserve Anglo dominance, and that cross-cultural interaction will assist in the survival of minority language and culture, as well as help decrease discrimination and prejudice.[25]

Minority students are encouraged not only to be proud of their own heritage, but also—in the case of those whose groups lack power and are subject to prejudice—to become fluent in the dominant or public culture. Pluralism in education is regarded as a twofold entity: on one hand, one should gain one's identity from one's family (group, community) or origin; on the other, one should be able to participate in the public culture by virtue of one's competence in that culture's language, habits of thought, customs, and values.

Critical of the idea of "cultural deficits" and of programs that stress remediation, advocates of cultural competence programs argue for inclusive curricula in which knowledge and values rooted in minority cultures are examined. Mitchell asserts, however, that the twofold approach to cultural identity contains a fundamental contradiction. By affirming minority culture, these programs challenge dominant society norms that are promoted in the school. At the same time, encouraging students to "build bridges" to the public culture—often by stressing language adaptation—seems to carry with it the danger of placing those students on the road to assimilation.[26]

*3  Models of cultural emancipation and social reconstruction:* Advocates of models of cultural emancipation share with proponents of other models the belief that cultural diversity in the United States is a positive element of the society and that fostering positive self-concepts among minority students is a valuable enterprise. They differ with their colleagues, however, in that they focus on attitudes of teachers and other school personnel and on the culture of the school, which, they claim, acts to suppress the development of ethnic and racial identity and is partially responsible for underachievement among minority students. They link schooling opportunities and achievement to the economy, and suggest that improving achievement among minority students will help them "break the cycle of missed opportunity created by a previous biography of cultural deprivation. The labor market is expected to verify emancipatory multicultural programs by absorbing large numbers of qualified minority youth.''[27]

This view of multicultural education assumes that there is a basic conflict between traditional school curricula and the life experiences of minority students based on what might be called the ''white, middle class privilege bias'' of most American schools. Schools therefore play an active role in creating differing ''educational opportunities and life chances for minority and majority youth.''[28] It is thus incumbent on school personnel to act in ways that will redress past injustices and increase educational opportunity for minority students.

Critics of this model point out that it may be unduly optimistic to believe that improved school achievement based on an inclusive curriculum will translate into better job opportunities for minority students. Prejudice and discrimination exist outside the school as well as in it, and the school has little power to alter pervasive attitudes in the larger community. In addition, the complexity of the school culture itself has not been sufficiently addressed by emancipatory multiculturalists who

> tend to ignore the complex social and political relations that are constituted in the internal order of the schools. Issues of policy formation, decision-making, trade-offs, and the building of alliances for specific reformist initiatives have not really been addressed within multicultural frameworks. For these reformist educators educational change hinges almost exclusively upon the reorganization of the content of the school curriculum.[29]

You may find it useful to reflect on these models. Which do you think makes the most sense? Which of the criticisms above seem to be the most important? Which category do you think this book falls into?

## BILINGUAL EDUCATION

I take it you already know
Of tough and bough and cough and dough?
Others may stumble but not you,
On hiccough, thorough, laugh, and through.
Well done! And now you wish, perhaps,
To learn of less familiar traps?

Beware of heard, a dreadful word
That looks like beard and sounds like bird,
And dead: it's said like bed, not bead—
For goodness' sake don't call it ''deed!''
Watch out for meat and great and threat.
(They rhyme with suite and straight and debt.)

A moth is not a moth in mother
Nor both in bother, broth in brother,
And here is not a match for there
Nor dear and fear for bear and pear,
And there's dose and rose and lose—
Just look them up—and goose and choose,
And cork and work and card and ward,
And font and front and word and sword,

And do and go and thwart and cart—
Come, come, I've hardly made a start!
A dreadful language? Man alive.
I'd mastered it when I was five.

*T.S.W.*

(From a letter published in the *London Sunday Times,* January 3, 1965)

There are over 300 different languages in everyday use in the United States. This number includes over 200 Native American languages, the languages of the colonizers (English, French, and Spanish), languages of the immigrants—both old and new—and a variety of dialects spoken in various regions of the country. Many children bring these languages with them to school as first languages (L1).

Language not only is a critical key to understanding the culture and experience of others, but also enables people to develop a sense of belonging and acceptance in a particular group. It is through language that complex concepts and ideas are transmitted. It should come as no surprise that competency in the language of the school is critical to achievement in school.

Four basic language skills that must be mastered in order for a nonnative speaker of a language to communicate successfully in that language are listening, reading, speaking, and writing. The goal in developing listening comprehension is for the student to acquire the ability to comprehend unstructured native language 2 (L2 = English for non-English speakers in the United States) when used at normal speed. The goal in developing reading skill is acquisition of the ability to read in the second language without strain, and eventually of the ability to comprehend it without translation into the native tongue. In developing speaking ability, the individual seeks to acquire the ability to communicate effectively in the verbal mode with a native speaker of the language. Finally, the goal in development of writing skills is the ability to send a written message that a native speaker can understand.

Each of these skills can be subdivided. If we consider vocabulary, grammar, pronunciation, meanings, and style, as subdivisions of the four major categories, we produce twenty possible dimensions of language use. Thus, when judging speaking skills, we might consider the size of a person's vocabulary, their pronunciation, and their ability to use correct grammar.

In addition to the twenty dimensions of language described above, five culture-related domains must be mastered for an individual to be considered competent in the communication process in any language. *Discourse* is the manner in which language is organized in speech and writing beyond the level of the sentence. *Appropriateness* refers to the kind of language used in a social context, from relatively relaxed and informal language to that used in more formal contexts. *Paralinguistics* includes aspects of nonverbal communication such as gestures, facial expressions, interpersonal distance, intonation, volume, and pitch. *Pragmatics* unites discourse, appropriateness, and paralinguistics with such cultural norms and expectations as when it is appropriate to speak with whom and how (including taking turns and appropriate topics for conversation). Finally, *cognitive-academic language proficiency* considers the degree to which language must be mastered to facilitate learning of abstract concepts.

It should be clear by now that *language differences* refer to much more than differences in vocabulary, grammar, and pronunciation. Learning to communicate in one's first language is difficult enough. Developing the full complement of skills necessary to achieve cognitive-academic language proficiency in a second language may take years. Teachers should understand the complex demands faced by children who come to school speaking a language other than Standard English. Equally important is to consider the emotional experiences of children who do not have full competence in the language of the school. Issues of anxiety, belonging, and ambiguity, discussed earlier in the book, are all critical to the experience of English-language-deficient children in our schools.

## THE BILINGUAL DEBATE

Issues related to bilingualism and bilingual education seem to center around two broad questions. The first is whether children will suffer if they become bilingual. A commonly held misconception is that the brain has only so much room and that knowledge of two languages means less room for other school-related knowledge. This belief is accompanied by the further misconception that the two languages of a bilingual person will be only half-developed compared to the one fully developed language of a monolingual person.

The second question is whether children will suffer if their education is carried out in two languages. The assumption of many parents and teachers is that children cannot achieve full mastery in the disciplines in the bilingual context. Children, it is thought, cannot cope with the demands of schooling in two languages.

### Just Who Is Bilingual?

Before one can address these two basic questions, one must first define *bilingual*. While someone may be able to speak in two languages, use of one of those languages may be more or less restricted to a particular setting. One's native language, for example, may be used at home or among other speakers of that language, while one's second language may be used at school or at work. No definitive cutoff points can be identified that distinguish a monolingual from a bilingual.[30] The 1984 Bilingual Education Act defines limited-English-proficient (LEP) individuals as those not born in the United States, those whose native language is not English, those from environments in which English is not the dominant language, and members of the various Native American groups who commonly use languages other than English.[31] It is estimated that there are between 3.5 and 5.5 million limited-English-proficient students in our schools today, fewer than two-thirds of whom receive the support they need to succeed in school.[32]

### Types of Bilingual Programs

Bilingual education for language minority students has three basic goals: (1) Students should attain high levels of proficiency in the English language; (2) students should achieve academically in all context areas; (3) students should experience positive personal growth. To achieve these goals, schools in the United States have adopted one of four models of bilingual education: submersion, English as a second language, Transitional bilingual education, and structured immersion. The distinctions between these models are somewhat blurred, but they can be discussed generally in terms of their primary emphases and methods.

In *submersion* programs, language minority children are placed in the regular classroom with native speakers of English. This can accurately be described as a "sink or swim" approach. Some unexamined myths commonly exist about the effectiveness of the submersion experience. It is quite common to hear statements such as thus: "My parents or grandparents came to this country without speaking a word of English. They received their education only in English, and they didn't suffer." Those who make such statements are probably ignorant of the actual feelings of their ancestors. Language use plays a critical role in identity, both for the group and the individual. Most people have a strong need to use their first language as a means of self and group preservation, particularly first- and second-generation immigrants.

The Supreme Court decision in *Lau v. Nichols* found submersion programs unlawful. In most instances, *English as a second language* (ESL) programs have replaced the typical submersion approach. In ESL instruction, English is taught by attempting to integrate the student's background and cultural experiences through language learning, through vocabulary and language development that stresses the student's language needs, and with techniques from second-language learning that can be applied to the subject matter and the teaching of English. In ESL programs, children are kept in the regular classroom for most of the day as in submersion programs, but are "pulled out" at various times for English instruction.

In *transitional bilingual education* (TBE), efforts are made to phase out one language while developing facility in English as quickly as possible. The thinking behind TBE is that unless children's skill in English develops rapidly they will soon fall behind their English-speaking counterparts in the regular classroom. In such programs, the child's first language is used only as an interim medium in instruction.

In *structured immersion* programs students are taught by teachers who are fluent in the native language of the child. While students are allowed to speak with one another and with the teacher in their first language, the teacher usually responds in English. In this way, students receive instruction in subject matter that is comparable to their English-speaking peers while simultaneously learning to speak English.

The distinction between submersion and immersion programs is important. Baker provides a helpful analogy.[33] If language learning is compared to learning how to swim, submersion is like throwing a nonswimmer into the deep end of a pool. In submersion programs, students are forbidden to use their home language. The entire school program is presented in the majority language. Suppose that when you throw someone into the deep end of a pool, you assume that they will be among skilled swimmers who will help them. In submersion programs the second-language learner is assumed to be with competent users of the language. The child learning a second language, however, is likely to have considerable difficulty keeping up with the ideas of fluent speakers and interacting with them.

In immersion programs, as in more traditional approaches to learning to swim, the student gradually moves from the "shallow" to the "deep" end of the pool. Pupils are allowed to splash about using their first language while slowly being taught the skills necessary to acquire the second language. Slowly moving into deeper and deeper water, the swimmer eventually learns all four strokes and is able to swim unaided. In immersion programs, students can listen, speak, read, and write in either language as needed. They generally are homogenous in their ability to use the new language; they are all non-swimmers. Slowly, as ability and confidence grows, they naturally switch to the second language. Successful immersion programs enable children to dive into either language pool equally well.

### Explaining Bilingual Functioning

Cummins maintains that it is possible to propose a scientifically valid theory of bilingual education.[34] Yet many remain frustrated by the indecision and vagueness of American policymakers with regard to bilingual education. More than twenty years after the passage of the Bilingual Education Act of 1968, agreement has not been achieved on the goals and methods of bilingual education. The various Supreme Court rulings that have arisen from the Act have also not resolved these questions. As the Harvard Encyclopedia of American Ethnic Groups states:

> The Bilingual Education Act, like most congressional legislation, was passed in response to demands of diverse interest groups and was, of necessity, sufficiently vaguely worded to satisfy advocates with conflicting views. It has no commonly agreed-upon purpose. At a minimum it aimed to use the native tongue of non-English-speaking children for a limited number of years in order to ensure the acquisition of basic skills such as arithmetic and writing. At the maximum its goal was not only the provision of temporary help to children in the process of linguistic assimilation, but also linguistic and cultural maintenance—the preservation of the language and value of foreign culture.[35]

Various theories intended to explain bilingual functioning and to explore the extent to which bilinguals develop cognitively have been proposed. Two of these will be considered below.

### Balance Theory

*Balance theory* is the one intuitively held by many people. The assumption that they make is that "increasing" one language automatically causes a "decrease" in the second language. The brain is thought to have only so much room for language skills. The analogy of balloons being inflated in the head by the entrance of knowledge and skill is often used. A bilingual person is pictured as having two half-filled balloons, while a monolingual person has one completely filled balloon. The consequence of bilingualism is lowered proficiency in both languages—in thinking, reading, vocabulary, and knowledge. This theory assumes that the two languages are "kept separate" from one another.[36] Unfortunately, it can also be used to argue against foreign language instruction for English-speaking students.

Balance theory has not been substantiated by research. Indeed, Baker says that this theory is misconceived and psychologically incorrect, as balanced bilinguals do not suffer cognitively.[37] In fact, the true bilingual may have certain cognitive advantages over the monolingual. In addition, bilingual education that fosters two languages to a good level of proficiency has no effect on first-language skills.

## Thresholds Model

The *thresholds model* contends that there is a critical level of competence which must be attained in each language, first to avoid any negative effects of bilingualism, and second to experience its possible positive consequences. The child may experience either positive, negative, or neither positive nor negative cognitive effects, depending on whether the child has developed limited, proficient, or partial bilingualism.

This model views the child as simultaneously climbing two ladders representing language proficiency.[38] If not enough steps are climbed, the child stays on a lower rung that is characterized by potential negative cognitive effects. With limited linguistic skills, academic learning and cognitive growth are reduced. The child reaches the first threshold when age-appropriate proficiency in one language is achieved. At this point, both negative and positive cognitive effects due to being bilingual are unlikely. The second threshold is reached when the child is relatively balanced and proficient in two languages. The potential for cognitive gains is great here.

Threshold theory can also help explain why in early immersion programs there are temporary lags in achievement when instruction is carried out in the second language. Until the child has reached a level of mastery of the second language sufficient for conceptual learning to occur (which may require up to five years or more!), below average performance can be expected. While the threshold theory helps us understand why immersion education is successful, it also suggests that minority children taught in their second language, who fail to develop sufficient competency in that language, will not benefit from second-language instruction.[39] Negative effects of this situation are cumulative, with children falling progressively further behind in academic and cognitive skills because their proficiency in the second language is not sufficient to allow them to develop necessary cognitive skills. In other words, if they are not able to think ''fluently'' in the second language, they cannot learn to think effectively, either.

## Outcomes of Bilingual Education Efforts

Baker and de Kanter reviewed over 300 studies of transitional bilingual programs in the United States and abroad.[40] They concluded that special programs in schools *can* improve the achievement of language minority students. However, they found no evidence that any particular program should be preferred by the federal government.

Given these findings, Baker suggests that immersion-type programs would be preferable to transition or submersion programs as they provide support for the home culture and language.[41] Transition and submersion programs imply assimilation into an English-only society. Immersion programs aim to foster bilingualism, biculturalism, and a pluralistic nation. Educators will have to do some deep soul-searching as the debate over immersion or transition-type programs continues. To date, at least twenty-three states in the United States have passed ''English as an official language'' laws. This is expected to generate considerable debate over bilingual education in the United States.

## SOME PROBLEMS AND OPPORTUNITIES THAT SCHOOLS FACE

In its review of multicultural and bilingual education policy and practice in the United States, the Organisation for Economic Cooperation and Development summarizes three major issues.[42] (1) The history of the adoption of multicultural education in the United States is marked by social concerns which have arisen primarily from the problems of minority integration. Because an expansion of the nation's welfare programs occurred at the same time as the demand for equality in the schools and the development of multicultural education, an association between the two has persisted. This, perhaps, has held back development of the field. (2) The introduction and evolution of multicultural education has been strongly influenced by many lobbies (African-American, Hispanic, etc.), but the various lobbies have never been able to present a united front in support of their various educational demands. Interests diverge and there is no unanimity, even within each community. It is in situations like this that the culture-general framework can help advocates conceptualize common needs and experiences. (3) Like multicultural education, the implementation of bilingual education programs is highly controversial due to the ambiguity of objectives. Education departments at both the state and federal levels do not seem to be opposed to bilingual education provided that it continues to move in the direction of assimilation. Other groups see bilingual education as a means of preserving the identity of minority cultures.

### Public Responses to Multicultural and Bilingual Education Reforms

In terms of schooling mandates, educationists and the public have responded to multicultural efforts in various ways. In direct conflict were two major groups: those who advocated special programs such as bilingual and multicultural education and those who believed (1) that the American educational system in its "traditional" form had always provided for the upward mobility of culturally diverse peoples who were "willing to work," and (2) that the nation-state would be destroyed if the schools did not continue offering a monocultural and monolinguistic education. In the latter group, some moralize that pluralistic approaches to education, especially bilingualism, can "handicap a child— perhaps permanently—by offering him a crutch that won't hold up in the work-a-day world in which he must live in later life."[43] Others worry that hiring of "ethnics" will now be mandated for available (and scarcer) teaching positions. Still others warn that ethnic and racial identity movements serve to weaken the "glue" that holds the nation together and aggravate tensions and differences that the schools, for at least seventy-five years, had been at some pains to diminish.

A third group, composed primarily of educators and speaking in a somewhat softer voice, asserted that pluralism in education was not a remedial effort, nor a form of reparation, but rather the affirmation of a substantial social reality. Pluralism, in their view, was not an ethnic or racial property, but a national characteristic, long ignored in education. Rudolf Schmerl at the University of Michigan, for example, observed:

> Intercontinental origin is still much more apparent in our electoral process than in our educational system. Our politics cultivate the immigrant and ethnic ethos as a matter of simple realism. Our educational system seems to be capable, so far, of no more than cursory, half-embarrassed hints about the diversity of our origins and experience, memories, and loyalties, fears, hopes, bitterness, and pride.[44]

And the American Association of Colleges of Teacher Education policy statement on pluralism states:

Multicultural education affirms that schools should be oriented toward the cultural enrichment of all children and youth through programs rooted to the preservation and extension of cultural diversity as a fact of life in American society. . . . To endorse cultural pluralism is to understand and appreciate the differences that exist among the nation's citizens. . . . Cultural pluralism is more than a temporary accommodation to placate racial and ethnic minorities.[45]

This view, however, has not dominated the educational scene. While nearly forty years of advocacy has produced a legacy of judicial and legislative mandates aimed at educational equity, their realization in practice is still a long way off. More than a decade ago, James Boyer of Kansas State University, speaking at a conference exploring issues in teacher education, described the status of multicultural education this way:

Perhaps more than any other aspect of the characteristics of American education, concepts of multi-culturalism have had difficulty gaining both academic respectability within teacher education and within the context of instructional delivery in public elementary and secondary schools. Not only has the topic been mis-used, misunderstood, and under-studied, it has been rejected as a critical entity because it forces us to re-examine so many of our practices, policies, and research endeavors.[46]

## Reaction in the 1980s

The 1980s saw a retrenchment from the ideals of educational equity and equality and a resurgence of old assimilationist arguments in new costumes. We have seen these arguments masked by a call for "excellence" in the face of "mediocrity," and read plans for curricula based on the old European-, white-, male-oriented classics. Frequently, calls for the traditional model of education have been made explicitly at the expense of attention to diversity. President Ronald Reagan, for example,

claimed that one reason that the schools were failing was the attention that had been focused on female, minority, and handicapped students. He asserted that, if the federal government and educators had not been so preoccupied with the needs of these special groups of students, education in the U.S. might not have succumbed to the "rising tide of mediocrity." What the President failed to note is that, if these three groups of students are eliminated, only about 15% of the school population remains.[47]

At present, programs in multicultural education, global or international education, gender-equitable education, and education for exceptional individuals continue to develop, although in a political climate that is far from congenial. Unfortunately, children from diverse backgrounds are still, more often than not, forced into a single, more manageable class group by teachers who are stressed by the demands of a difficult job. The model for this group of students still is usually conceived of as Anglo, middle class, and experientially enriched. Significant changes still must be adopted and integrated into the fabric of American education.

## ACTIVITIES

1 Reflect on your experiences in school. What attention, if any, was given to issues related to multicultural education? To bilingual education?
2 Interview some teachers in various schools. What efforts related to multicultural or bilingual

education have they participated in? Under which of the categories identified by Grant and Sleeter would these efforts fall? In your opinion, is this the most appropriate level of involvement? If not, what else might be attempted?

3 Interview someone who attended school in this country but whose first language is not English. What were his or her experiences in school like? In your interview, consider the U-curve hypothesis of adjustment that was introduced in Chapter 2. Can you identify particular points of frustration and success? When did this person finally feel as if they were at home, or really belonged to the local community? What role did teachers play in the adjustment? What role did language learning play in the adjustment? What was this student's language learning experience like? Which category of bilingual education would best describe the experiences?

# REFERENCES

1 From a memorandum written by Dade County Public Schools Superintendent, Dr. Joseph A. Fernandez, October 3, 1989.

2 Organisation for Economic Cooperation and Development, *One School, Many Cultures* (Paris: Organisation for Economic Cooperation and Development, 1989).

3 James A. Banks, *Multicultural Education: Theory and Practice,* 2d ed. (Boston: Allyn Bacon, 1988).

4 Ibid., p. 201.

5 Christine Sleeter and Carl Grant, "An Analysis of Multicultural Education in the United States," *Harvard Educational Review,* vol. 57, no. 4, November 1987, pp. 421–444.

6 Christine Sleeter and Carl Grant, "Educational Equity, Education That Is Multicultural and Social Reconstructionist," *Journal of Educational Equity and Leadership,* vol. 6, no. 2, 1986, pp. 105–118.

7 Ibid.

8 J. Ogbu, *The Next Generation: An Ethnography of Education in an Urban Neighborhood* (New York: Academic Press, 1974), p. 99.

9 E. Frenkel-Brunswick, "A Study of Prejudice in Children," *Human Relations,* vol. 1, no. 3, 1948, pp. 295–306.

10 Ibid.

11 James A. Banks, "Multicultural Education: Its Effects on Students' Racial and Gender Role Attitudes," in James Shaver (ed.), *Handbook of Research on Social Studies Teaching and Learning* (New York: Macmillan, 1990).

12 D. W. Johnson, "Freedom School Effectiveness: Changes in Attitudes of Negro Children," *The Journal of Applied Behavioral Science,* vol. 2, no. 3, 1966, pp. 325–330.

13 O. L. B. Shirley, "The Impact of Multicultural Education on Self-Concept, Racial Attitude, and Student Achievement of Black and White Fifth and Sixth Graders," Ph.D. dissertation, The University of Mississippi, 1988.

14 J. Litcher and D. Johnson, "Changes in Attitudes toward Negroes of White Elementary School Students after use of Multiethnic Readers," *Journal of Educational Psychology,* vol. 60, no. 2, April 1969, pp. 148–152.

15 R. Slavin, "Cooperative Learning: Applying Contact Theory in Desegregated Schools," *Journal of Social Issues,* vol. 41, no. 3, 1985, pp. 45–62.

16 Ibid.

17 Banks, op. cit.

18 Ibid.

19 Cameron Mitchell, "Multicultural Approaches to Racial Inequality in the United States" (Baton Rouge: Louisiana State University, 1989), typescript.

**20** Ibid., p. 13.

**21** Ibid., p. 10.

**22** Ibid., p. 12.

**23** Ibid., p. 16.

**24** Ibid., pp. 19–20.

**25** Ibid., pp. 20–21.

**26** Ibid., pp. 22–23.

**27** Ibid., pp. 25–26.

**28** Ibid., p. 27.

**29** Ibid., pp. 30–31.

**30** Colin Baker, *Key Issues in Bilingualism and Bilingual Education* (Clevedon, United Kingdom: Multilingual Matters, 1988).

**31** H. Hernandez, *Multicultural Education: A Teacher's Guide to Content and Process* (Columbus, OH: Charles E. Merrill, 1989).

**32** Ibid.

**33** Baker, op. cit.

**34** J. Cummins, "The Influence of Bilingualism on Cognitive Growth: A Synthesis of Research Findings and Explanatory Hypotheses," *Working Papers on Bilingualism,* vol. 9, 1976, pp. 1–43.

**35** Stephan Thernstrom, *Harvard Encyclopedia of American Ethnic Groups* (Cambridge, MA: Belknap Press, 1980).

**36** J. Cummins, *Bilingualism and Minority-Language Children* (Ontario: Ontario Institute for Studies in Education, 1981).

**37** Baker, op. cit.

**38** Cummins, op. cit. (ref. 34).

**39** Ibid.

**40** K. A. Baker and A. A. De Kanter, *Effectiveness of Bilingual Education: A Review of Literature* (Washington, DC: Office of Planning, Budget, and Evaluation, U.S. Department of Education).

**41** Baker, op. cit.

**42** Organisation for Economic Cooperation and Development, op. cit.

**43** "Two Language Teaching," editorial in the *Albuquerque* (New Mexico) *Tribune,* May 19, 1975, p. 54.

**44** Rudolph B. Schmerl, "The Student as Immigrant," in Dolores E. Gross, Gwendolyn C. Baker, and Lindley J. Stiles (eds.), *Teaching in a Multicultural Society* (New York: The Free Press, 1977), p. 45.

**45** American Association of Colleges of Teacher Education, "No One Model American," *Journal of Teacher Education,* vol. 24, no. 4, Winter 1973, pp. 264–265.

**46** James B. Boyer, "The Essentials of Multi-Culturalism in the Context of Teacher Education Research: A Projective Overview," paper prepared for the 1979 conference Exploring Issues in Teacher Education: Questions for Future Research, University of Texas at Austin, 1979.

**47** Carol Shakeshaft, "A Gender at Risk," *Phi Delta Kappan,* vol. 67, no. 7, March 1986, p. 499.

# CHAPTER 8

# EXCEPTIONALITY IN THE
# CONTEXT OF DIVERSITY

*A gust of irritability is blowing through me just now because there has been a recurrence of a tendency in some people to try to run my affairs. This seems all the stranger to me because since I was seventeen I have arranged my own life. At the age of twenty-two I began working very hard for whatever money I have earned during the past thirty-four years. Of my own accord I have undertaken public responsibilities in America and other lands. After Teacher's health broke down I worked very much alone with Polly's hand to furnish information and her voice to reinforce my halting speech. Yet there are still those who appear to think it is incumbent upon them to alter my life course according to their own ideas! There was some excuse when I was young and bewildered in the search of something worth doing. But mother and Teacher knew me better than any one else ever did, and never dictated the course of action I should follow. There have always been other friends and power to advance the work for the blind, and they respect my desire as a human being to be free. It is beautiful to consider how their cooperation has increased my happiness and rendered possible whatever I have accomplished. However, unless I keep on my guard against uncalled-for though well-meant interference, they cannot help me any more than they can help any other person who readily surrenders his will to another.*

Helen Keller

In this chapter we address a dimension of human diversity that bears some similarities to other dimensions—cultural membership; racial, ethnic, and linguistic identification; gender; and age—but also presents some differences. *Exceptional* individuals may be members of all these groups. It has been noted that "unlike Hispanic and Black Americans, the disabled subculture does not form a distinct cultural community nor are disabilities transmitted in a way parallel to racial characteristics." Exception to this statement can be taken on two counts, however. First, it may not be appropriate to apply the term *subculture* to persons with disabilities because they ordinarily are more different than they are similar. Second, some groups of handicapped individuals may constitute "distinct cultural communities." Thus, for example, we speak of the culture of the Deaf, because hearing-impaired people have created a language, have developed customs related to the enhanced use of some senses (e.g., vision), and have banded together to create organizations and institutions designed to serve their special needs.

The term *exceptionality* itself encompasses very diverse "groups," which in many cases actually are not groups at all in the traditional sociological sense, since each of these cuts across other categories. The term *exceptional* is often used to refer to persons with disabilities; however, exceptionality encompasses persons who are considered gifted as well. Although many gifted individuals may also have disabilities, such as impaired vision or hearing, cerebral palsy or other physical impairments, a specific learning disability, or serious emotional problems, the majority, of course, do not—just as a majority of those whose intellectual or other abilities are characterized as "average" do not have disabilities. By definition, it is difficult to generalize about human exceptionality and highly misleading to do so.

However, one generalization can be made with some safety: persons considered exceptional are individuals who experience many needs, feelings, beliefs, hopes, and dreams that are similar to those that others experience. Each of these individuals, like every person who is "nonexceptional," has a sense of self—an identity—and each presents to others many characteristics that help to define her or him as a unique person. Some of these characteristics may be associated with or influenced by the dimension on the basis of which the person is considered exceptional. But it is not exceptionality—a disability or giftedness—itself that defines the person. Identifying someone as "a blind lawyer" is just as inappropriate as it is to speak of "a woman doctor," "a black teacher," or "an Iranian student." It is both unjust and inaccurate to suggest that the single most important characteristic—the defining characteristic—of a certain physician is that she happens to be female. *As a physician,* her defining characteristics will be her training, her skill, her choice of a specialty or her decision to engage in family practice. Similarly, the *student* who happens to have cerebral palsy may do outstanding work in math, do average work in English, enjoy rock music, be a member of student government, and have an after-school job in a fast food restaurant.

## WHO IS EXCEPTIONAL?

As you can tell, in this chapter, the term *exceptionality* is being used in a special way. Clearly there are many ways of being exceptional, and a person can be exceptional in some respects but not in others. The concept of exceptionality implies a range of normality, or "nonexceptionality." However, we can't really say that individuals who do not "qualify" as exceptional should therefore be considered *average.* A familiar example is the ability of students to achieve in academic subjects. Many students whose apparent school learning ability in a subject is neither exceptionally high nor exceptionally low have above-average or below-average ability. This implies a continuum, a range, where the term *exceptional* would be reserved for those at or near the extremes. However, not all forms of exceptionality can be most appropriately defined on the basis of a continuum based on some quantitative index—certainly not a single measure (such as IQ, muscle coordination, central vision acuity). As we shall see, a number of considerations enter in, some involving quantitative measures (e.g., test scores) and others involving qualitative issues that require judgment.

The concept of exceptionality itself misleadingly implies a qualitative distinction between those who are "normal" and those who are "different." There is a further implication, equally erroneous, that everyone with a certain type of "differentness" constitutes a homogeneous group, while all those without that differentness are identical with respect to that particular dimension. For example,

• All people not considered hearing impaired hear well and are able to communicate with others effectively under all conditions; all hearing-impaired people must read lips or use sign language.
• All people who are not visually impaired read normal-size print comfortably; all visually impaired people use braille.
• All nondisturbed children behave appropriately and exercise good self-control at all times; all emotionally disturbed children behave inappropriately and have difficulty with self-control.

• All non-learning-disabled students read, write, and calculate with maximum efficiency; all students with specific learning disabilities perceive or produce symbols in a distorted fashion.

• All persons who are not mentally retarded remember well and solve problems well under all conditions; all persons who are mentally retarded cannot remember information or apply reasoning to solve problems.

• All nonautistic people welcome change and interact with others with grace and enthusiasm; persons experiencing autism cannot tolerate any change and do not communicate with or respond to other people.

These generalizations are all obviously inaccurate. In fact, it may be that the subliminal recognition of the universality of the experiences of persons with disabilities—the recognition that we all share these experiences to some extent—accounts in some measure for the emotional reactions nondisabled people sometimes have in social encounters with disabled people. For example, a person who needs corrective lenses to read a newspaper knows what it's like to try to make sense of the unintelligible pattern of blurred images that she sees when her glasses have been misplaced. What would it be like if, even with the glasses, things were always just a blur?

Exceptionality, then, "depends on both the *degree* and the *frequency* of deviation from the norm. Exceptional people are those who differ from the norm so significantly and so repeatedly as to impair their success in very basic social, personal, or educational activities."[1]

Attempting to define *exceptionality* as a dimension of human diversity leads to a tangle of conceptual complications, since exceptionality is a matter of attributions as well as attributes. The perceptions of others, as well as those of the exceptional individual, define exceptionality at least as much as do "objective" characteristics. It is true that "differing from the norm" is a key aspect of exceptionality; however, the social and psychological consequences of such differences are more crucial than the differences themselves. Although the term *handicapped* is employed in legislation in order to define eligibility for certain benefits, it is more accurate to use this term in reference to a social context. Most authors make these distinctions:

**1** An *impairment* is a medically diagnosed structural defect or loss of physical function which can sometimes be restored; for example, a person who has lost a limb may use a prosthesis.[2]

**2** A *disability* may result from an impairment to the extent that a person's life functioning is affected.

**3** A *handicap* involves the responses of other people, in terms of opportunities that might be denied or negative or unaccepting attitudes expressed, and the person's own psychological adjustment.[3]

## WHO IS HANDICAPPED?

John Updike has described his own perceptions of handicaps in a personal way:*

* From *The Centaur* by John Updike. Copyright © 1962, 1963 by John Updike. Reprinted by permission of Alfred A. Knopf, Inc.

Had the world been watching, it would have been startled, for my belly, as if pecked by a great bird, was dotted with red scabs the size of coins. Psoriasis. The very name of the allergy, so foreign, so twisty in the mouth, so apt to prompt stammering, intensified the humiliation. "Humiliation," "allergy"—I never knew what to call it. It was not a disease, because I generated it out of myself. As an allergy, it was sensitive to almost everything: chocolate, potato chips, starch, sugar, frying grease, nervous excitement, dryness, darkness, pressure, enclosure, the temperate climate—allergic, in fact, to life itself. My mother, from whom I had inherited it, sometimes called it a "handicap." I found this insulting. After all, it was her fault; only females transmitted it to their children. Had my father, whose tall body sagged in folds of pure white, been my mother, my skin would have been blameless. "Handicap" savored of subtraction, and this was an addition, something extra added to me. I enjoyed at this age a strange innocence about suffering; I believed it was necessary to men. It seemed to be all about me and there was something menacing in my apparent exception. I had never broken a bone, I was bright, my parents openly loved me. In my conceit I believed myself to be wickedly lucky. So I had come to this conclusion about my psoriasis: It was a curse. God, to make me a man, had blessed me with a rhythmic curse that breathed in and out with His seasons.[4]

Although the word *handicapped* is used for legal purposes as though it referred to objective conditions, who is handicapped and what their handicap means really depends on the individual as well as on the society and its institutions. For example, in preliterate societies, the notion of *specific learning disabilities* would have had no relevance. However, in the United States today, students identified as having specific learning disabilities constitute the largest group of those needing and receiving special education services. In Sparta, infants born with birth defects were destroyed, and *infanticide* has been practiced, and is still practiced, in numerous societies, for survival, military prowess, and sharing of economic resources.[5] In ancient Egypt, on the other hand, infanticide was not practiced, and there are indications that useful roles in the society were found for many persons with impaired sensory function or other physical limitations.

The question "Who is handicapped?" may prompt a variety of responses, including some arising from unconscious associations. If you were asked this question, it is possible that you might first think of a particular person, perhaps a famous one. For example, lovers of classical music may think immediately of Itzak Perlman, and admirers of Ray Charles or Stevie Wonder are also legion. You might remember a former classmate, or one you now know or have seen, who uses a wheelchair. A first association some may make is with the Special Olympics. Others may believe there is a distinction between physical and mental disabilities and associate the word *handicapped* with the former: some people are handicapped, other people are mentally retarded.

Do you associate impaired hearing with being handicapped? If you yourself have a slight hearing loss, do you consider yourself handicapped? Are the many middle-aged and elderly people who experience lessened hearing or visual acuity handicapped? What about the many people of all ages who use corrective lenses? What about those people whose license plates, car window stickers, or dashboard placards entitle them to park closer to shopping mall entrances or stores? Do you think of a person as *becoming* handicapped or being so throughout life? Can someone *stop* being handicapped? Can one be handicapped under certain conditions but not others?

What emotions do you associate with this word? Pity? Admiration? Discomfort? Guilt? Would you associate any other words—*courage, charity, contribution, care, determination, different, problem, helping, helpless, dependent, special,* or others?

Are you beginning to think, "This has gone far enough!"? We're talking about a tremendous variety of individuals and circumstances! In all likelihood, you were aware of that diversity before you opened this book. However, that would have been far less likely in the not so distant past, even though there were famous blind musicians in your grandparents' day as well, and most people have at least heard of Helen Keller. Today, however, sign language interpreters are prominent at public gatherings, outstanding (and some mediocre) movies and television specials have featured persons with physical and mental impairments, and some television advertising portrays attractive, competent people who use wheelchairs. However, you also know that not all wheelchair users or leg amputees climb mountains or are marathon runners, nor are all blind persons talented pianists or vocalists. Although you have been importuned on the street or at an airport, you do not think, surely, that most blind or deaf people beg or play on your sympathy to get you to buy items you don't want, as many had to do in the past.

Perhaps you yourself have a disability. Although, like most of your peers, you hope, and expect, to be successful in your future role, you may not think of yourself as "talented" and headed for stardom or for prominence among the movers and shakers of business or international politics. On the other hand, you may indeed some day be famous, powerful, influential in your field, and rich! Your disability does not mark you as "special" in the sense of being endowed with superior resources of talent and character, but neither must it relegate you to paths of lesser opportunity than those for which your *abilities* qualify you.

## Visible and Invisible Handicaps

A graphic representation of a wheelchair is the international symbol for disability. It is used to indicate that a rest room is accessible to persons with visible disabilities (i.e., wide door, grab bar), but also to identify, among other things, dedicated parking spaces for persons who may or may not have apparent disabilities. Although the nature of a disability may not be apparent, a person's *use of a wheelchair makes visible the person's disability*. A person seen leaving an automobile in a Handicapped Only parking space and walking unassisted in a "normal" fashion might get angry looks, at least until the dashboard placard, coded license plate, or other symbolic indicator revealed that their use of the space was legitimate. Possibly, the person seen walking from the car to the mall has a chronic, serious heart condition—an invisible disability. Do you think that people with invisible disabilities should wear some kind of large badge so they won't be misunderstood?

One form of disability that has been much misunderstood is specific learning disability. In fact, the child whose learning disability has not been recognized as such has been referred to as "the misunderstood child." Before the concept of specific learning disability came into general use, this child's problems were often attributed by teachers and parents to lack of motivation, negativism, being a "slow learner," or just being a "problem child."

Teachers, parents, and peers might attribute academic learning difficulties, inattention, and other problems that a student with a visible physical or sensory impairment had in school to that impairment—very often erroneously! But typically, the student with a learning disability looks just like other nondisabled students, and in many instances may demonstrate good verbal skills in conversation. There are no symbols or artifacts—wheel-chair, hearing aid, walker, white cane—or other visible signs of the disability. Note that the misunderstanding we are talking about works both ways: the student whose problem is invisible is expected to do well and is blamed if he or she doesn't, while the student who has a visible impairment may be pitied, not expected to do well, and be excused for inappropriate behavior.

### Eligibility and Stigma: The Labeling Dilemma

Recall that people need to categorize the world around them, to simplify their experience by grouping things together. Some ways of designating aspects of human differences have probably served to distance people from each other, rather than to foster mutual acceptance and understanding. For example, reference to "the poor," "the disadvantaged," or "the elderly" implies a notion of "them" as distinct from *us*. Such references are often accompanied by a statement about what "they" need, do, are like, believe, or want. The implication is that behavior patterns, motives, aspirations, etc., are the same for all members of that group. Clearly, this is never true. Another problem with the way certain groups are identified is that their differentness, rather than their "person-ness," is underscored.

The paradox is that in attempting to identify a group in order to accomplish something positive on their behalf—for example, to provide affordable medical care or housing—members of that group are identified on the basis of *deviance criteria*,[6] and their individuality is treated as less important than their shared characteristic. The price of individual identity and of inclusion as part of "us" may be forgoing certain benefits.

These concerns are particularly relevant with respect to "the handicapped." What is missing in that designation is reference to *people*—or better, individuals—who may indeed be eligible for certain benefits, indeed whose *right* it is to have these benefits. What is implied by a label like "the handicapped" or "the disabled" is that certain people are worthy of attention and concern, not because of their individual merit, but because of their collective limitations.

The issue of eligibility both complicates and simplifies the matter of defining who is exceptional. One problem is that the definition process can become circular. For example, we might define special education as a range of services provided in schools for students who are exceptional. And which students are exceptional? Those who need special education!

One of the most problematic aspects of practice in the field of special education is, in fact, that of definitions and criteria.[7] And one of the most serious problems experienced by persons considered exceptional, in school and in the broader society, is the problem of *labels*. Exceptionality labels, such as *disabled, handicapped, emotionally disturbed,* and *learning disabled,* have no doubt been helpful in generating public awareness of special needs and giving people access to services. But these benefits may come at a high price. In his summary of the results of a massive project in which ninety-three leaders investigated issues in the classification and labeling of children, Nicholas Hobbs listed numerous possible negative consequences, including peer rejection, permanent stigmatization, misdiagnosis, loss of educational opportunities, and unwarranted segregation in institutions.[8]

The concept of human exceptionality has traditionally encompassed various forms of "deviation from the norm,"[9] including special abilities as well as disabilities. Would you speak of an extraordinarily bright child as "a deviant?" It would be as appropriate to do so as to refer in this way to a person whose measured intellectual ability and observed day-to-day adaptive skills suggest mental retardation. If you were either of these people, you would certainly rather be valued and respected for who you are than be assigned a label, especially the label "deviant."

A great many children and youth have difficulties with certain aspects of school learning, and for some, school seems overwhelming. Some of these children may eventually be officially designated as having a handicapping condition. But for others, no matter how real the problems may be, there is not sufficient basis to attribute them to a handicapping condition. This may seem somewhat arbitrary; two students may be experiencing problems of a very similar nature, and seem clearly to need some kind of extra assistance, but only one may qualify to be considered *handicapped* and thus eligible for special education.

Many professionals, indeed, think it is arbitrary. For example, distinguishing students who have specific learning disabilities from those who don't satisfy the criteria for the "passport" that label constitutes is often a matter of judgment, rather than hard evidence.[10] Judgments of this sort are clearly risky business! And the label "learning disabled" is itself problematic. Suppose that you as a student in school found certain academic areas of instruction extremely difficult, seemingly beyond your capability. (As a matter of fact, perhaps you did!) It wasn't a question of your not being "bright" enough (for example, to read long passages of difficult text material with sufficient comprehension, and to do so rapidly and every day; to put your ideas together on paper, again rapidly, with correctly spelled words; or to handle tasks requiring computation, again rapidly), but rather that something in the way you "processed" information, interpreted symbols, or translated what you saw or thought into the printed word made these things hard for you. If you could have used a pocket calculator in math, a typewriter or computer, or a tape recorder, how much easier your life in school might have been! You might have been permitted to use such aids, or a teacher could have given you the added time that would make the difference, or helped you break down a complex problem into the component steps, or used an alternative way of presenting information. Such things made a big difference for Albert Einstein. Maybe you could have been another Einstein!

But this would have cost you something. You would have had to accept a label, something that would have set you apart from your friends. The extent to which you might have been handicapped by being helped would have depended mainly on (1) your degree of comfort with yourself, as you are, and (2) the attitudes of others.

Another aspect of the labeling dilemma involves the associations people make with labels. It has been suggested that one explanation for the dramatic increase in the number of students identified as learning disabled, with a parallel decrease in the number identified as mentally retarded, is that the former label is more readily accepted by parents than the latter. It is okay to have a child with a learning disability, because it is understood today that such a problem is consistent with average, above-average, or even superior intellectual ability. Many famous and highly successful people are known or believed to have been "LD kids"; one can believe that "my child is like Nelson Rockefeller, Winston Churchill, Thomas Edison, Albert Einstein . . ."

Research on teachers' attitudes is informative in this regard. As the mainstreaming mandated by P.L. 94–142 (see Chapter 6) has progressed, researchers have tried to determine how receptive "regular" teachers are to having students identified as handicapped in their classes. Generally, it appears that teachers are far more receptive to having students with specific learning disabilities mainstreamed into their classes than those with other "labels." Next in order of preference, depending on the study, are students with speech problems and students with orthopedic or other health impairments. Last are students labeled as mentally retarded or students labeled as behavior disordered or emotionally disturbed. The reasons for these preferences are self-evident. Appropriate social behavior, including compliance with classroom rules, and intellectual ability sufficient to succeed with the standard curriculum are high-priority concerns for teachers. The associations brought to mind by the labels "behavior disordered" and "mentally retarded" suggest that these could be areas of concern. The label "learning disabled" is less likely to provoke these associations.

## EXCEPTIONALITY AND SUCCESSIVE LIFE STAGES

In the past, students preparing for careers in the field of special education typically began the specialized portion of their preparation with a course titled something like Introduction to Exceptional Children or Psychology of Exceptional Children. Today, professionals are aware of the need for life span approach, so that decisions affecting even a young child are guided by the criterion of ultimate function,[11] that is, what skills a person will need in order to function effectively as an adult. Additionally, there is awareness that disabilities are unlikely to be "cured" or "fixed" in elementary school, and the developmental needs of people of high school and postsecondary age are very different from those of young children. Finally, there is now systematic service provision for preschool-age children with disabilities, as well as for eligible infants and toddlers from birth; in each case the law recognizes the unique needs associated with that developmental period. Let us examine briefly the experience of exceptionality in a developmental context.

### Infancy

The presence of exceptionality at birth is generally associated with biological anomalies that may place the newborn at risk. The extent of risk may be unknown, as in the case of many children born significantly preterm and at exceptionally low birthweight. The baby is considered to be at *established risk*[12] if a biological condition that is highly likely to result in some degree of disability is present. Examples are cerebral palsy, spina bifida, and congenital blindness. Such risk factors may result from any of a variety of *prenatal* causes, including genetic defects and some possible hereditary influences not yet well understood, but also including injury associated with maternal infection (e.g., rubella), or use of drugs or alcohol. There may also be *perinatal* causes, including difficulties in delivery that result in temporary deprivation of oxygen flow to the brain.

*Congenital impairments* are those present at birth, although they are not always diagnosed at birth. For example, this is still often—and tragically—the case with hearing loss. And Duchenne muscular dystrophy (the most common type) is often not manifest until the child is 3 or 4 years old. When congenital impairments are diagnosed immediately, major concerns initially center around medical care and, in many instances, necessary surgery. Associated with these needs of the newborn are family needs—for support, information about resources, and guidance in providing for the baby's needs. The term *early intervention,* now familiar in the context of exceptionality, implies a coordinated plan, potentially involving diverse resources in the community, for *family-focused services,* called an Individualized Family Services Plan (IFSP).

Many children who do not present indications of established risk at birth—both those considered at biological risk and those who are not (e.g., birthweight and gestational age within normal range, no evidence of respiratory distress, normal reflexes, etc.)—may suffer impairments as a result of *postnatal* causes associated with illness or injury. These may be incurred during the first years of life (the infancy and toddler periods), or later.

*Developmental disabilities* are, by definition, acquired during the *developmental period,* the first eighteen years of life. However, hearing or vision loss may occur at any time during life, and serious injury to an adult (for example, head injury incurred in a motor vehicle accident) can result in a person's becoming permanently disabled. Although the majority of young children (birth through age 2) who can and increasingly do benefit through early intervention programs, have biologically based impairments that were present at birth and diagnosed at (or even prior to) birth or soon thereafter, some present acquired impairments. There are many other children, however, whose exceptionality is not definitively established, in many instances not even suspected, and in others not yet present, until later.

### The Preschool Period

Social policy (P.L. 99–457) has made specific distinctions between the infant-toddler period (birth through age 2) and the next phase of early childhood, ages 3 through 5. This *preschool period* is considered to involve unique characteristics and needs distinct from those of both younger and older children.

Increasingly, the term *preschool* is a misnomer, however, since in the United States most 5-year-olds, a majority of ''4's,'' and a great many ''3's,'' as well as even younger children, are enrolled in some type of daily program, increasingly often provided by or in association with the schools.[13] Before this major change in American society took place, the majority of children referred for consideration of special educational needs were first observed to present problems in school. The social and cognitive demands of school revealed or confirmed suspicions of special needs. Increasingly, that identification can and does occur earlier, which creates the possibility of early educational intervention to lessen the handicapping effects of a disability and enhance the child's compensatory skills. Since crucial developmental events occur during the preschool period—in language, thinking, self-esteem, learning of social and self-care skills, and other important areas—it presents unique opportunities. While many young children present continuing needs for medical care, they are most significantly unique because of what they share with their agemates who are not disabled. That principle applies, of course, to subsequent periods of development as well.

One difference involves *where* preschool-age children identified as exceptional may be ''in school.'' There are a very few special programs provided for preschool-age (and also primary-age) children identified as gifted; there are, however, model programs for very young children identified as both gifted and disabled.[14]

While the majority of older students with disabilities attend schools with nondisabled peers (that is, "regular" school), receiving services based on individually determined needs, but increasingly as "regular" class members, there are fewer mainstreaming opportunities for preschool-age children in the public schools. Students (now including 3- to 5-year-olds) identified as eligible for special education must be served, at no cost, by the public schools; thus a young child with disabilities may participate in a special preschool program. However, integrated experiences with nondisabled peers are generally recognized as critically important. Conversely, experiences with children with disabilities are important for "typical" children.[15] Therefore, various options have been developed, including public school or other public programs (e.g., community preschool, kindergarten, day care) and early childhood special education (ECSE) programs; ECSE programs that include "typical" (nondisabled) preschool children; and ECSE programs located in public school buildings.[16]

## Elementary and Middle School

As academic demands increase over the school years, the potential for problems increases as well, both for children considered exceptional and for those who are not. Among the many children at risk for school failure are those of cultural and linguistic backgrounds presenting differences from the majority culture of the school, as well as children whose home and family do not provide optimal emotional security and support for learning. There is risk, too, associated with being a girl in school, and risk associated with being a boy as well. Highly capable learners are placed at risk to the extent that their learning opportunities fail to challenge and motivate them and nurture their gifts. Students with diverse learning styles are at risk to the degree that such diversity is not recognized and valued. Like all of these students, those with physical, intellectual, or social-emotional disabilities are also experiencing changes associated with physical, mental, and emotional development. For many of these children, certain adaptations—e.g., in the physical environment of the classroom, in time requirements, in instructional materials, in teaching technique—represent the key to success. For some, supplementary assistance—e.g., supplementary tutoring, speech or language therapy, arrangements for their bathroom needs—is necessary. And for some, an alternative or modified curriculum for some portion or for all of the academic program may be indicated. For each child eligible for special education because of a handicapping condition, the plan is specific to the assessed needs of the child and established through an Individualized Education Program (IEP).

## Secondary School and Transition to Adulthood

Though the right to a free, appropriate public education (FAPE) for students identified as handicapped extends through age 21, a disproportionately large number of these students drop out before they have reached that age or receive a high school diploma.[17] The academic nature of the secondary curriculum, together with the subject matter orientation of secondary teachers, increases the difficulty of successful instructional mainstreaming for many students. A long-standing problem has been the dearth of instructional materials specifically geared to the needs of older students—for example, reading materials that are appropriate in terms of both level of difficulty and level of interest.

Smaller proportions of students with certain types of disabilities are likely to be served at the secondary level through special classes. For example, an early but still relevant study revealed that, in California, nearly half the junior high students and nearly two-thirds of the high school students with physical disabilities were mainstreamed,[18] compared to just 14 percent of the elementary school students, only half of whom were fully mainstreamed. Although this finding could be interpreted as suggesting that great gains had occurred, it appeared that availability of programs (more at the elementary level) rather than needs of students accounted for what Best suggested was "mainstreaming by default, rather than by design."[19] Although that study was completed prior to required implementation of P.L. 94–142, there continues to be concern that we may not provide as well for students with handicaps at the secondary level. Programs for students with special learning disabilities were put in place later at the secondary than at the elementary level, and development of appropriate practices has been slow. Initially, it was believed that effective intervention in elementary school could remediate many, if not most, specific learning problems, so that special programming in high school would not be required. We now know that this is often, perhaps most often, not the case. A learning disability is likely to be a continuing problem, at least through the high school years, and in many cases at the postsecondary level as well.

An even more basic problem has been the frequent failure to recognize the changing developmental needs of children with disabilities. This is perhaps reflected in the traditional generic use of the word *children* in college course titles, titles of textbooks for those courses, and in fact in federal and state special education legislation. (Remember, P.L. 94–142 was titled the Education of All Handicapped Children Act, although it applies to students up to 22 years old!) Is it common usage to speak of high school students, including those old enough to vote, as "children?"

You may feel that too much is sometimes made of semantics. However, it is instructive to explore the connotations of the language used to describe people with disabilities.[20] Persons identified as mentally retarded, in particular, have been described with words and phrases suggesting perennial childlikeness. An extremely effective national advocacy organization, the Association for Retarded Citizens (ARC), was until recently named the Association for Retarded Children. Some community agencies that provided services to youth and adults as well as children had titles identifying them with services to children, and often their logo and fundraising approach (e.g., "poster child") identified their services with children.

Possible reasons for this are many. A cynical interpretation of an agency's highlighting children in its fundraising efforts, even when funds will support adult services as well, is that images of children are more likely to evoke pity, and, consequently, charitable impulses. What's wrong with that? Nothing, perhaps, except the association implied between persons with physical or mental disabilities (of any age) and children.

Have you heard an individual with mental retardation spoken of as having "the mind of a 6-year-old," although the individual is an adult? Such a description conveys a very vivid picture: most people recognize that a child of 6 thinks quite differently than an adult! But it is misleading. A person at age 13, or 15, or 18, or 22, or 46, has needs very different from those of a young child and, irrespective of his or her IQ score, very different abilities. This is not to suggest that people with significant degrees of mental retardation achieve the same levels of cognitive sophistication that persons of average or above-average measured intelligence achieve; they do not. To consider Piaget's theory of successive stages of cognitive development, for example, people with a significant degree of retardation (severe, or profound) may not attain the level of *formal operations*.[21] That has implications with respect to certain academic subjects, such as algebra. It does *not* imply that people with identified mental retardation cannot attain varying degrees of functional independence and engage in productive work in the community.

The *transition* from school to work and community living continues to be probably the highest priority with respect to young people with disabilities. A great many high school students with disabilities will go on to pursue higher education, because their *abilities* qualify them to do so. The goal of independence, for example, for a bright student with significant physical involvement associated with cerebral palsy, may involve completing college, earning a law degree and passing the bar, beginning a practice or joining a firm, and pursuing a legal career. Along the way, this person may be handicapped to the degree that physical or attitudinal barriers stand in the way, while daily living may involve ongoing challenges. Many people with learning disabilities may continue to be challenged by the requirements of living in our complex society; increasing numbers, however, do go on to college. The present authors are acquainted with people with advanced degrees who continue to need to compensate for a learning disability.

Not everyone, with or without disabilities, has the intellectual ability to pursue higher education, however. It is a question of ability, not disability. Federal law requires that "no otherwise qualified handicapped individual in the United States shall, solely by reason of his handicap, be excluded from the participation in, be denied the benefits of, or be subjected to discrimination under any program or activity receiving federal financial assistance."[22] This regulation (Section 504 of the Vocational Rehabilitation Act Amendments of 1973) clearly affects higher education, as well as elementary and secondary education. The key phrase is *otherwise qualified*.

Some students with disabilities are not "otherwise qualified" for higher education. (Many people who are qualified and disabled choose not to go to college; for a great many the expense of a college education is the principal barrier.) For students experiencing mental retardation, transitional needs involve preparation for maximally independent community living, work that is satisfying, productive, and remunerative, and successful and satisfying relationships with other people. This preparation is not suddenly initiated as the student prepares to leave high school, or when public education's responsibility is about to end. Instead, it is reflected in the student's school planning virtually from the beginning.

## Adulthood

Development is a lifelong process, as Erik Erikson's familiar description of the stages of personal and social development people experience in the course of their lives suggests.[23] You as a young adult are a different person than you were in your early teens or than you were as a child, although threads of continuity clearly have run, and will continue to run, through your life. That "child" is part of the adult you. But as an adult you have priorities, needs, and aspirations that are different from those you used to have. Also, society has different expectations for you than it had when you were younger. (You may be all too conscious of this hard fact!)

The concept of *normalization* can serve as both a guide for those who provide services and the basis for a philosophical position on the role and status of exceptional individuals in society. *Normalization* was originally defined as "making available to all mentally retarded people patterns of life and conditions of everyday living which are as close as possible to the regular circumstances and way of life of society."[24] Today, normalization is a guiding principle underlying all services for everyone with disabilities, and indeed all forms of human services, including health care, residential arrangements for elderly persons, and programs for persons experiencing poverty. This principle pertains to persons of all ages with any form or degree of disability. Many adults with disabilities may not require special services, but if services such as supported employment are needed, they should be provided in accordance with the principle of normalization. *Normalization* is a term closely associated with contemporary recognition of the rights and the personhood of individuals with disabilities. In the context of education, it is closely identified with the concept of the least restrictive environment (LRE) and the practices of integration and mainstreaming.

The normalization philosophy emerged from work with people who had been labeled mentally retarded. Society's treatment of persons so labeled historically has demonstrated in dramatic ways the opposite of normalization to an even greater degree than has been the case with persons with other disability labels. Human beings were segregated from the rest of society, deprived of human rights and rights of citizenship, often incarcerated in institutions in which dehumanizing conditions prevailed—human warehouses, they have been called—subjected to brutal physical treatment, and even put to death, not only in the distant past but also in Hitler's mad quest for "racial purification." Protection and care of people identified as mentally retarded resulted from humanitarian efforts of reformers, but better "services" neither eliminated abuses nor accorded personhood. It is important to recognize that *normalization* does not mean pretending that everyone's needs and abilities are the same, that disabilities really don't exist, or that physical or mental impairments can be "fixed" or "cured" by education, training, medical treatment, or special therapies. It means that a person with a disability is a person, a member of society and of the community. To enable people with disabilities to be maximally independent and to have productive, contributing lives is good for the community and the society as well as for the person herself or himself.

## EXCEPTIONALITY AND GENDER

Certain problems are associated with gender. For example, Duchenne muscular dystrophy occurs much more frequently in males than females. However, many types of physical impairment occur with equal frequency in children of both sexes.

The broad issue of gender-related inequalities in education will be addressed in Chapter 9; in this section, we address one puzzling set of phenomena bearing on the relationship of gender and exceptionality. While some forms of exceptionality are associated with known impairments (certain medical syndromes or impaired vision or hearing), the vast majority of placements of students for special education do not involve impairments that can be identified with perfect objectivity and reliability. In these instances, judgments are made. An initial judgment may be made by a teacher who decides whether or not to initiate a referral and, if so, to whom and on what basis. If a possible handicap (as defined in federal law and state regulations) is suspected, judgments are made concerning what types of assessment data are needed. The professionals conducting the *multifactored assessment* must decide what questions need to be addressed, with what instruments, and in what setting.

Once all the assessment data are obtained, a description of the student's levels of functioning, including discussion of any special needs, is constructed as part of the Individualized Education Program planning process. That Individualized Education Program will then reflect a series of decisions made by the professional team and parents about individual goals and objectives, type of placement, and any needed services.

This chain of events is sometimes set in motion if a teacher (or parent, or other adult) suspects a problem involving vision, hearing, or physical health. If such problems have been ongoing, however, they should have been identified earlier. Most teacher referrals involve suspected problems in learning (possible mild mental retardation or specific learning disabilities) or social-emotional well-being (possible emotional or behavioral handicaps). These are the "judgment handicaps," and they comprise (with speech and language problems) the vast majority of the students referred for and ultimately provided special education.

The compelling question is: Why are so many more boys referred for such problems, and ultimately provided special education, than girls? To what extent is the higher rate of referral and placement of boys than girls a reflection of inherent gender differences, and to what extent is it related to societally determined sex role and social expectations? Is the ratio of boys with learning disabilities to girls *really* four or five to one? Is that actually the approximate ratio of boys with serious emotional-behavioral problems to girls, and is the nature of typical expressions of these problems for girls and boys different?

It has been noted for some time that many school referrals that may lead to placement on the basis of severe emotional (behavioral) handicap involve *acting-out behavior*.[25] Although other manifestations are addressed by the federal definition, a special class placement is made more often if unacceptable social behavior is present than otherwise. (It should be noted that awareness of a student's emotional problem may suggest the need for another form of help, such as counseling for the child and possibly the family.) So we have two facts: (1) More students who act out—for example, in the form of verbal or physical aggression—than students who do not are referred and placed in special education, even though others may give evidence of unreasonable fears, inability to form relationships, inability to concentrate on and succeed in school learning, or psychosomatic problems; (2) more boys than girls fall into the "acting out" category.

A study conducted in the early 1970s may shed some light on this issue.[26] Based on teacher ratings used to identify possible emotional problems in 3- to 7-year-old children, the researchers found two major factors, or problem categories: factor I, *interaction-participation versus apathy-withdrawal*, and factor II, *cooperation-compliance versus anger-defiance*. A factor I problem might involve a child's lack of interest or participation in tasks or play activity, possibly reflecting extreme fear of rejection or failure, or simply preoccupation with one's own thoughts or fantasies. Factor II problems included belligerent or bullying behavior, resisting adult control, and being a destructive influence on group activity, so that a child might be feared by peers.

Teachers identified many more factor II problems, and these much more frequently involved boys than girls. When girls were identified, the problems most frequently involved factor I-type behavior, such as apathy and withdrawal. However, this study involved children of preschool, kindergarten, and primary age. Some combination of gender-specific characteristics and social expectations may be more operative for this age group than for others.

It would be wrong to infer that girls do not engage in acting-out behavior, as teachers of the fourth through ninth grades in particular can attest. Belligerence toward adults, fighting among peers, theft (especially shoplifting), and "status" offenses such as truancy and running away are frequent among girls around the time of puberty and early adolescence. Some clinicians have long observed that acting-out adolescent girls ultimately seen in residential treatment situations actually pose greater management difficulties than boys in similar settings.[27] It was William Glasser's work with girls in such a treatment setting that led him to develop his reality therapy approach.

The definition of *serious emotional handicap* as a special education category contains an "excluder" with respect to maladaptive or undesirable social behavior: social maladjustment is not to be regarded as symptomatic unless it is caused by serious emotional handicap. Inappropriate or undesirable social behavior on the part of a child may indeed precipitate a teacher referral, however. If that referral leads to comprehensive (multifactored) assessment, the child may be determined to be eligible for and in need of special education services on the basis of any criteria in the three "high-incidence" categories (learning disability, mild mental retardation, or emotional handicap). Although teacher referrals occur at all grade levels, those leading to consideration of the child for special education occur most frequently at the kindergarten and primary level. Thus, we really do not know to what extent the higher rates of referral and placement for boys may mean that more boys than girls have problems, and to what extent sex-role expectations may be involved. Are young boys more likely to engage in behavior that prompts teacher to refer them? If so, are boys, and girls as well, behaving in a manner congruent with cultural expectations? Do teachers *expect* to see more boys with problems than girls?

Many authors have noted that, in the past, although by no means all potentially eligible students were placed in school programs serving students with educable or mild mental retardation, those who were most often evidenced behavior problems in the classroom.[28] Thus, the sex-role expectancy factor may have been operative. It is therefore important to learn whether males outnumber girls in these placements, as they do in placements for specific learning disability and serious emotional handicap.

A study of characteristics of students served in "educable" or mild mental retardation programs in the 1985–1986 school year found that the composition of their sample, in a medium-sized midwestern city, was 55 percent male and 45 percent female.[29] This difference is not so dramatic as that typically found in the other two "high-incidence" areas, but any difference would seem important. These authors noted that the number of students in mild mental retardation programs has decreased in recent years and that students now served in these programs comprise "a more patently disabled group" than in the past.[30] If intellectual ability, and therefore the prevalence of mental retardation, is equally distributed among males and females, differential rates of referral and placement would be based on other factors, such as classroom behavior. If students served in mental retardation programs today are "more patently disabled" than was true in the past, it may be that referrals are less frequently influenced by judgment and expectancy. Yet, boys appear to outnumber girls in this type of placement as well.

## CULTURE, LANGUAGE, AND EXCEPTIONALITY

What is considered exceptional varies both within cultures and from one culture to another across time and social class.[31] It may be that the current emphasis on and high prevalence rate of learning disability in the United States is primarily a reflection of the emphases of a technologically complex society that is very concerned about literacy. In developing nations, specific learning disabilities among otherwise nonimpaired children, youth, and adults are not likely to be the object of priority concern.

Within the pluralistic context of American education, several general concerns have been associated with exceptionality. Principal among these has been the disproportionately large representation of ethnic and linguistic minorities among students referred for and placed in special education, especially the high-incidence categories of educable and mild mental retardation, emotional-behavioral handicap, and speech-language handicap. Observations that inordinately large percentages of African-American, Hispanic, and Native American children were placed in special classes for students with mild mental retardation led Dunn and Mercer to question the special class model (a segregated form of education). These observations also led to the legally mandated requirements for non-biased and multifactored assessment and procedural due process in placement decisions.[32] Despite these legally mandated reforms, declining prevalence of identified mild mental retardation overall, and increasing questioning of the viability of the segregated special class model, placement rates for minority students continue to be disproportionately high.[33] In the study by Epstein and coworkers cited previously, a large percentage (42 percent) of the placements for mild mental retardation were of minority students, even though a majority of the students in the community were white.[34]

A brief review of the history of intelligence testing in American society may shed some light on the problem of identification and labeling across culture groups. Once American psychologists discovered the procedure developed in France by Binet and Simon for comparing measured abilities, they set about applying the new tests to a number of practical problems. In addition to applications with school-age children, testing of adults seemed to present potentially important uses. Thus, mass testing of servicemen was begun around the time of World War I (with startling results; until appropriate adjustments were made in the way the IQ was calculated, it appeared that the majority of our "doughboys" were somewhat retarded!).

A practice that today seems appalling was the testing of newly arrived steerage immigrants at Ellis Island. As Sarason and Doris remind us, ". . . this was a period of American history when racist attitudes were at high, e.g., one need only recall that it was the period of the revival of the Ku Klux Klan and of extended and intense agitation for restrictive immigration—the restriction to be based not on numbers but on ethnic and racial origin."[35]

At that time, H. H. Goddard was among the best known and most widely respected authorities on mental retardation, or "feeblemindedness" as it was then termed. A passionate believer in the hereditarian view of mental abilities, Goddard expressed grave concern about the "threat" to society he believed was posed by "the moron," that is, persons functioning just above the level of severe retardation. Not only did they drain society's resources but, according to Goddard, they were inclined to criminality and promiscuity. Although Goddard and other advocates of restriction on immigration believed these "undesirable" persons were inevitably present in any society (he advocated confining them to colonies), he was convinced their number in America was increasing drastically due to immigration. The interrelationship between racism, eugenics, anti-immigration sentiments, and compulsory sterilization of the "feebleminded" is epitomized in Goddard's writing and public statements. As Stephen Jay Gould suggests:

> Once Goddard had identified the cause of feeble-mindedness in a single gene, the cure seemed simple enough: don't allow native morons to breed and keep foreign ones out. . . . Goddard's women tested thirty-five Jews, twenty-two Hungarians, fifty Italians, and forty-five Russians. . . . Binet tests on the four groups led to an astounding result: 83 percent of the Jews, 80 percent of the Hungarians, 79 percent of the Italians, and 87 percent of the Russians were feeble-minded—that is, below age twelve on the Binet scale. Goddard himself was flabbergasted: could anyone be made to believe that four-fifths of any nation were morons?[36]

Goddard saw these results as suggesting a clear and present danger to the United States and urged that the Congress take restrictive action, which it did. As Gould notes, "Goddard rejoiced in the general tightening of standards for admission. He reports that deportations for mental deficiency increased 350% in 1913 and 570% in 1914 over the average of the five preceding years."[37]

To Goddard, language translation would have taken care of any possible cultural bias in the test. Today, it is recognized that culture bias involves more than linguistic differences, important though they are. As Gould reminds us, the people being tested were not "upper deck" passengers;[38] they were indeed "your tired, your poor," the majority of whom had had little, if any schooling, and none of whom had ever been in an IQ testing situation. No doubt most were frightened, as well as exhausted.

Cultural bias in tests is posed by either content or the testing situation itself, or both. P.L. 94–142 addressed the problem of misidentification of students as handicapped on the basis of culture-biased tests by (1) requiring multifactored assessment, but only with informed parental consent, and (2) stipulating that tests must be administered in the child's native language. Also, generally accepted psychometric principles stipulate that individuals to whom a test is administered must have been appropriately represented in the norming done for that test. Alternative approaches have also been proposed in the attempt to reduce cultural bias, the best known of which is the System of Multicultural Pluralistic Assessment (SOMPA).[39]

## A LOOK AT THE PAST AND HOPES FOR THE FUTURE

For a time in America, many of those who came to be known as WASPS (white Anglo-Saxon protestants) entertained, and freely expressed, views of "foreigners" that are now nearly universally considered repugnant. Every nationality or ethnic group had at least one nickname, and most of these nicknames were derogatory. This name-calling, however scurrilous, was but a minor manifestation of the negative attitudes of many people who, ironically, referred to themselves as "native Americans!" Supported by the nationalism of the times, and coupled with ill-informed and inappropriate applications of Darwinism, imperialist and expansionist policies on the one hand, and calls for restrictions on immigration to the United States on the other hand, represented an Anglo-Saxon form of racism, or Anglo-Saxonism, so virulent as to be nearly incomprehensible today (to most people, at any rate).[40] But vestiges remain, even among people who have witnessed the Holocaust in Europe and who increasingly think of themselves as part of a global society.

At that time, many people did not draw clear distinctions between ''feeblemindedness'' and flawed moral character or mental health. ''They'' (waves of immigrants arriving from southern and eastern Europe) were believed to pose a severe threat to ''us,'' so much so that in 1894 a group of young Harvard graduates formed the Immigration Restriction League. Their movement was soon joined with another growing movement, eugenics:

> In 1911, Prescott Hall, a leader of the Immigration Restriction League, in conjunction with his old Harvard classmate Charles Davenport, arranged to have a committee on immigration attached to the Eugenics Section of the American Breeders Association. The first report of the committee appeared in the *American Breeders Magazine* in the following year. The report advocated more rigorous enforcement of existing restrictions on the admission of the alien insane and feebleminded and a further tightening up and extension of these regulations. The feebleminded were viewed as perhaps an even greater menace to public health than the insane, for the latter were more likely to be segregated in institutions.[41]

However, it was not only those persons known to be mentally defective or mentally ill that were of concern. It was believed that a much greater number of immigrants were of subaverage mental and physical ability, thus constituting a significant threat in terms of the ''genetic stock'' they brought with them.

The fear of the ''feebleminded'' resulted in the period of what has been called The Indictment. The views of the average citizen on the subject were unenlightened to begin with, and ''experts'' like Goddard and Davenport were able to convince a large segment of the American public that the mentally retarded constituted a serious threat to the society. This threat was represented not only by those whose intellectual functions were severely impaired (''idiots'' and ''imbeciles,'' in the parlance of the times), but even more seriously by those of higher mental function—''morons''—described by Goddard as promiscuous, violent, and conscienceless. Against this threat, two major policy responses were advocated—and carried out. Compulsory sterilization laws were enacted in nearly all states, and permanent institutional placement became the fate of multitudes of children *suspected* of being slow to develop.

That was then, this is now. Today, women vote, people of Slavic descent retain intact the surnames they had at birth. Professional football teams have black, as well as white, quarterbacks. Both women and men of various ethnic heritage hold elective office. And persons with intellectual, as well as physical, disabilities are regarded as individuals. The compulsory sterilization laws have been repealed, the institutions are closing, and increasingly persons identified as mentally retarded are people who live in your neighborhood, work at McDonalds or another business in your community, are part of your religious congregation, or, if they are of school age, attend the public elementary, middle, or high school. If you are a teacher, these once feared ''menaces'' may be among the students in your class, or at least may be members of your school community.

Not so long ago, people with disabilities were seen as objects of pity, if they were "seen" at all. Uncomfortable in the company of a blind or deaf person, a person with no legs, a person whose speech was hard to understand, people who were not disabled would often avoid those who were. One could feel good about contributing to a worthy cause, and these charitable impulses and feelings of pity could be, and still are, exploited through fundraising efforts. What is provided through charity, however, can be withheld as well. There is great difference between being a recipient of charity and being recognized as a person of ability, with a contribution to make, a person with rights.

In some societies even today, infanticide is practiced; in the distant past, it was the rule in most societies for infants born with birth defects, and many societies also practiced female infanticide. In the area of exceptionality, as in the area of gender, a prolonged period, extending well into the modern age, of neglect followed. Altruistic, humanitarian efforts brought about positive changes. But for persons with disabilities, as for white women and people of color, being "done for," though preferable to being "done to," was, and is, not enough.

As we near the end of the twentieth century it becomes increasingly hazardous, though tempting, to prognosticate about human life in the future. On the one hand, new technological miracles continue to be revealed, while on the other hand, many people (the majority of them children) go to bed hungry. Many will die of hunger or hunger-related illnesses. Babies survive who only a few years ago could not have survived; babies die who ought to survive. Diseases have been conquered in the past, and no doubt the means of prevention or cure will be found during your lifetime for diseases or birth defects that presently challenge the courage of those afflicted, and their families, and the talent, intellect, and determination of those involved in research. When will cystic fibrosis be conquered? What progress will be made in the fight against cancer, especially as it affects children? And how will we deal with AIDS?

The incidence of both vision and hearing impairments, as distinct phenomena occurring in otherwise intact children, has decreased, but the incidence of these impairments in combination with other developmental problems is increasing. This is apparently due in large measure to increased survival rates of infants born significantly preterm and presenting a variety of risk indicators.[42] For many infants, who first experience life in a neonatal intensive care unit and who may go home equipped with life support apparatus, the future is uncertain. In the past, most professionals would communicate to parents of a baby born with spina bifida or Down syndrome a very pessimistic message. That is less likely to be so today, for we see these children experiencing successful and satisfying lives to a degree unimaginable only a few years ago.

What does the future hold for increasing numbers of newborns weighing slightly more than one pound at birth? What forces will shape that future? Among these babies with problematic futures are increasing numbers of infants with fetal alcohol syndrome (FAS), babies born to cocaine-addicted mothers, and babies with AIDS. These children reflect etiological circumstances which, although to some degree present, were virtually unknown until recently. Will addicted babies represent an increase in the numbers of future adults with disabilities, or will they represent a change with respect to the nature of disability itself? Which of these babies who are at risk for disability will in fact experience disability as they progress through childhood into adulthood?

Key civil rights legislation on behalf of persons with disabilities was enacted in the

1970s and 1980s (see Chapter 6). The future will no doubt hold other positive changes from the standpoint of social policy.

In terms of education for exceptional children, the model through history has been the residential school, frequently under the auspices of religious organizations, but since the early to mid-nineteenth century increasingly under public auspices. Ultimately, the administration of educational programs for children and youth with disabilities came to be regarded as the responsibility of educational, rather than medical or other agencies. It was recognized that children with disabilities could live at home and attend school during the day in their communities. Special schools and special classes, under public school auspices, began to emerge, but still most exceptional students were not beneficiaries and many were not served at all. Those who were received an education through what soon became a separate component of the educational enterprise, special education. Typically, these students had little opportunity to interact with their nondisabled peers, who in turn had little exposure to students with disabilities.

Although the special class model developed rapidly, at no point did, or could, special classes provide appropriately for special learning needs of a majority of students with disabilities. To what extent the special class is a viable alternative for significant numbers of students identified as exceptional remains a subject for debate. But since the enactment of P.L. 94–142 in the United States, and similar policies in other countries, in the 1970s, ever increasing numbers of students with identified handicapping conditions have participated partially or fully in the educational mainstream, receiving instruction appropriate to their individual needs.

The issues of the future for exceptional students, in the United States at any rate, are intertwined with those involving public education generally. These include growing concern about educational challenges presented by, and for, vast numbers of students who experience difficulties but do not ''fit'' into the present exceptionality categories. There has been a trend toward attempting to identify steadily growing numbers of students as learning disabled in order to address their needs, so that the number presently so identified more than doubles the expected number, while many more are found not eligible on the basis of criteria employed. At the same time, the trend toward mainstream participation for students who are identified as handicapped continues. The Regular Education Initiative (REI) may well portend the end of the separation between special and regular education.

As efforts continue to eliminate vocational discrimination against the disabled, the ability of even individuals with severe disabilities to engage in productive, community-based employment is being recognized. The future will no doubt hold ever increasing opportunities for productive and satisfying work for people who only yesterday received custodial care and who today participate to some degree in sheltered work training situations.

The ability of individuals with severe disabilities to live independently, to communicate with others, to work, to enjoy recreational activities, and to enter the mainstream has been immeasurably enhanced through technology. Given the wonders that have been achieved, who can foretell what the future may hold? Through implantation of electrodes and laborious effort, people with severe motor impairment have been enabled to use their limbs. A wide variety of increasingly affordable devices and materials enable people to use the telephone, and are like FAX machines, in widespread use, if not already ubiquitous.

Societal attitudes and social policy concerning exceptional individuals have undergone radical changes within an extraordinarily short period of time. Children, youth, and adults with disabilities are now seen in the context of the diversity that characterizes society both in the United States and in the world community. These changes can, in large measure, be attributed to self-advocacy on the part of the community of persons with disabilities, as well as to advocacy by parents and creative work by professionals.

We are now only at the threshhold of a revolution, a revolution that has served to place people before their disabilities, that identifies persons with disabilities as individuals rather than as groups or categories, and that has established the rights of the person with a disability access to appropriate education and full citizenship. This revolution has, rightly, placed the primary responsibility to ''adapt'' to individual characteristics and needs with the institutions of society, including the school.

## ACTIVITIES

1 Interview a parent of a child who receives special educational services. In what ways has the child been helped? What improvements are still needed in the education the child receives? What recommendations does the parent have for you as a future teacher regarding what you might provide children who have special needs?
2 Interview a teacher, focusing on how they have been affected by educational policy directed at children with special needs. What modifications have they had to make in their teaching? What special preparation have they received to help them make the necessary changes? What do they feel is still needed?
3 Ask to observe a conference where an Individual Educational Plan is developed for a student with special needs. Analyze the perspectives and needs of each of the parties at the meeting. What concerns were addressed by parents? Teachers? Administrators? Psychologists? Student? What concerns were left unattended?

## REFERENCES

1 Haring (ed.), *Exceptional Children and Youth,* p. 1.
2 H. D. Love and J. E. Walthall, *A Handbook of Medical, Educational, and Psychological Information for Teachers of Physically Handicapped Children* (Springfield, IL: Charles C. Thomas, 1977).
3 C. Deloach and B. G. Greer, *Adjustment to Severe Physical Disability: A Metamorphosis* (New York: McGraw-Hill, 1981); M. B. Langley, ''Working With Young Physically Impaired Children, part A: The Nature of Physical Handicaps,'' in S. G. Garwood (ed.), *Educating Young Handicapped Children: A Developmental Approach* (Germantown, MD: Aspen, 1979).
4 John Updike, *The Centaur* (New York: Knopf, 1963), pp. 52–53.
5 R. C. Scheerenberger, *A History of Mental Retardation* (Baltimore, MD: Paul H. Brookes, 1983).
6 R. Bogdan, ''The Sociology of Special Education,'' in R. J. Morns and B. Blatt (eds.), *Special Education: Research and Trends* (Elmsford, NY: Pergamon Press, 1986).
7 J. E. Ysseldyke and Algozzine, *Critical Issues in Special and Remedial Education* (Boston: Houghton, Mifflin, 1979).

**8** Nicholas Hobbs, *The Futures of Children* (San Francisco: Jossey-Bass, 1974).

**9** Haring, op. cit., p. 1.

**10** Hobbs, op. cit.

**11** L. Brown, J. Nietupski, and S. Hamre-Nietupski, "The Criterion of Ultimate Functioning and Public School Service for Severely Handicapped Students," in M. A. Thomas (ed.), *Hey, Don't Forget About Me! Education's Investment in the Severely, Profoundly, and Multiply Handicapped Child* (Reston, VA: Council for Exceptional Children, 1976).

**12** T. Tjossem (ed.), *Intervention Strategies for High Risk Infants and Young Children* (Baltimore, MD: University Park Press, 1976).

**13** J. Glazer, "Kindergarten and Early Education Issues and Problems," *Childhood Education,* vol. 62, no. 1, Sept.–Oct. 1985, pp. 13–18.

**14** M. B. Karnes and L. J. Johnson, "Identification and Assessment of Gifted/Talented, Handicapped, and Nonhandicapped Children in Early Childhood," in J. R. Whitmore (ed.), *Intellectual Giftedness in Young Children: Recognition and Development* (New York: Haworth Press, 1986), pp. 35–54.

**15** P. L. Safford, *Integrated Teaching in Early Childhood: Starting in the Mainstream* (White Plains, NY: Longman, 1989).

**16** M. McLean and S. Odom, "Least Restrictive Environment and Social Integration," White Paper, Division of Early Childhood, Council for Exceptional Children, Reston, VA, 1988.

**17** Office of Special Education Programs, *Eleventh Annual Report to Congress on the Implementation of the Education of the Handicapped Act* (Washington, DC: U.S. Dept. of Education, U.S. Office of Special Education and Rehabilitation Services, 1989).

**18** G. A. Best, "Mainstreaming Characteristics of Orthopedically Handicapped Students in California," *Rehabilitation Literature,* vol. 38, nos. 6–7, June–July 1977, pp. 205–209.

**19** Ibid., p. 209.

**20** See, for example, D. Biklen, *The Complete School: Integrating Special and Regular Education* (New York: Columbia University Press, 1985).

**21** B. Inhelder, *The Diagnosis of Reasoning in the Mentally Retarded* (New York: John Day, 1944, reprinted 1968).

**22** Section 504, Vocational Rehabilitation Act Amendments of 1973, 20 U.S.C. 794.

**23** Erik Erikson, *Childhood and Society,* 2d ed. (New York: W. W. Norton, 1963, reprinted 1972).

**24** B. Nirje, "The Normalization Principle," in R. B. Kirgel and A. Shearer (eds.), *Changing Patterns in Residential Services for the Mentally Retarded,* rev. ed. (Washington, DC: President's Committee on Mental Retardation, 1976), p. 231.

**25** W. C. Morse, R. L. Cutler, and A. H. Fink, *Public School Classes for the Emotionally Handicapped: A Research Analysis* (Washington, DC: Council for Exceptional Children, National Education Association, 1964).

**26** M. Kohn and B. L. Rosman, "A Two-Factor Model of Emotional Disturbance in the Young Child: Validity and Screening Efficiency," *Journal of Child Psychology and Psychiatry,* vol. 14, no. 1, March 1973, pp. 31–56.

**27** W. Glasser, *Reality Therapy* (New York: Harper & Row, 1965).

**28** D. L. MacMillan, *Mental Retardation in School and Society,* 2d ed. (Boston: Little, Brown, 1982).

**29** M. H. Epstein, E. A. Polloway, R. M. Foley, and J. R. Patton, *Special Services in the Schools,* vol. 6, nos. 1–2, DeKalb, IL., Northern Illinois University, 1990, pp. 121–134.

**30** D. L. MacMillan and S. Borthwick, "The New EMR Population: Can They Be Mainstreamed?" *Mental Retardation,* vol. 18, no. 4, 1980, pp. 155–158.

**31** R. B. Edgerton, *The Cloak of Competence: Stigma in the Lives of the Mentally Retarded* (Berkeley: University of California Press, 1967).

**32** L. M. Dunn, "Special Education for the Mildly Retarded—Is Much of It Justifiable?", *Excep-*

*tional Children,* vol. 35, no. 1, Sept. 1968, pp. 5–22; J. Mercer, *Labeling the Mentally Retarded* (Berkeley: University of California Press, 1973), pp. 5–22.

**33** P. M. Brady, J. L. Manni, and D. W. Winnikur, ''Implications of Ethnic Disproportion in Programs for the Educable Mentally Retarded,'' *The Journal of Special Education,* vol. 17, no. 3, Fall 1983, pp. 295–302.

**34** Epstein et al., op. cit.

**35** S. B. Sarason and J. Doris, *Psychological Problems in Mental Deficiency,* 4th ed. (New York: Harper Row, 1969), p. 302.

**36** Stephen Jay Gould, *The Mismeasure of Man* (New York: W. W. Norton, 1981), pp. 164–166.

**37** Ibid., p. 168.

**38** Ibid., p. 167.

**39** J. R. Mercer and J. Lewis, *System of Multicultural Pluralistic Assessment Conceptual and Technical Manual* (Riverside: University of California, Riverside, 1977).

**40** R. Hofstadter, *Social Darwinism in American Thought,* rev. ed. (New York: Braziller, 1959).

**41** Sarason and Doris, op. cit., p. 291.

**42** G. L. Ensher and D. A. Clark, *Newborns at Risk: Medical Care and Psychoeducational Intervention* (Rockville, MD: Aspen, 1986).

# THE EXPERIENCE OF GENDER: WHAT IT MEANS TO BE MALE AND FEMALE IN SOCIETY

*If women were the recognized social equals of men, we should see a very different state of society from that which now exists. . . . men and women wearing nearly or quite the same dress . . . performing substantially the same duties . . . pastimes, recreations and pleasures. If the equality of the sexes were recognized, we should see both sexes educated alike . . . both accorded the same rights, not only in political affairs. Under the head of rights may be ranged all the sexual inequalities, and still higher rights as well: the right to themselves, the right of controlling their own persons, the possession of their own bodies.*

Lester Frank Ward

## THE DEVELOPMENT OF SEX ROLE IDENTITY

One of the most important, and earliest, tasks engaged in by an individual in our society is the development of a sense of self, or identity—the knowledge that she or he is separate from mother, father, family. This perception begins when an infant is about 7 or 8 months old and continues to develop over the lifetime of the person, who may add to or even significantly change that sense of identity several times during his or her life.

One's feeling of identity—of personhood—is composed of physical, psychological, social, and cultural elements. Your perception of your size, for example, is partly a function of actual height and weight, but is also determined by what your ethnic, social, or cultural group has decided is "a good size." In the United States, the Anglo ideal of tall and slender—or "fit"—(as well as blonde and fair-skinned) is the traditional model for beauty. If you are short, and perhaps a little overweight, and/or dark-haired and dark-skinned, those facts are a part of your perception of your identity—and you may think of yourself not only as a certain size, but also as less than beautiful or handsome.

An extremely important part of one's identity, and one that begins at least at birth, is one's self-identification as either a male or a female. It is thought that identification in terms of sex begins about 18 months of age, and we know that it is clearly internalized by the age of 3.[1] But sexual identity is more complex than simply "knowing" that you are male or female. More important to your sense of self is your identification as a member of a *gender* group—"I am a girl"; "I am a boy." While sex is a biological characteristic, gender is a social one. In all cultural groups, gender identity includes knowledge of a large set of rules and expectations governing what boys and girls should wear, how girls and boys should act, how boys and girls should express themselves, and the "place" of girls and boys or men and women in the overall structure of the society. Knowledge of these rules is knowledge of one's role as a member of a gender group, and provides us with the ability to deal with many social situations without having to stop each time to figure out what to do. Sex role identity, however, also limits us—limits the range of choices in, and sometimes the very quality of, our lives.

## SEX ROLE SOCIALIZATION: PUTTING LIMITS ON BEHAVIOR

Because in the United States, as elsewhere, primary socialization and sex role learning usually occurs in the family through intimate relationships with parents, other adult rel-

193

atives, siblings, and playmates, the rules associated with one's sex role may vary by race, by ethnicity, by social class, by religion, and even by geographical region. This socialization takes place in a variety of different ways, many of them small and incremental—simple routines of daily life and language. The process of sex role learning has been described as having three parts:

**1** The child learns to *distinguish* between men and women, and between boys and girls, and to know what kinds of behavior are characteristic of each.

**2** The child learns to express appropriate sex role *preferences* for himself or herself.

**3** The child learns to *behave* in accordance with sex role standards.[2]

### Sex Role Socialization: A White, Middle-Class Bias in Research

While this process of internalizing one's knowledge of and identification with sex role is a part of all children's lives, it has been most studied in the lives of middle-class white children. In addition, this research has focused more on the effects of sex role socialization on girls than on boys. This is significant for at least two reasons. First, it reflects the predominant characteristics of the researchers themselves, many of whom have been white, middle-class university scholars, often feminists interested in discovering the reality of women's lives. Because the focus has been on girls, the consequences of sex role socialization for boys, which are great, have often been minimized.

Second, studies primarily located in the white middle class have reflected the dominant social group in the United States. Because dominance is often equated with universality, norms related to sex role socialization are often thought to apply to *all* American girls and boys—indeed, to *all* girls and boys everywhere. New research, which attempts to look at the sex role socialization of various racial, ethnic, religious, and national groups is beginning to discover significant differences between white, middle-class socialization practices and those of other groups, something we will discuss a little bit later in this chapter.

Research on differences in sex role socialization of boys and girls, biased toward the middle-class white child though it is, has been instrumental in bringing both the nature of sex role socialization and the inequities associated with it to our attention. It has provided a consciousness-raising tool necessary to the further exploration of a fascinating and critical stage in our lives, the time when we develop an important part of our sense of self. Because all social groups are to some degree influenced by norms of the dominant society, this research also has outlined *some* practices of sex role socialization that are common to diverse groups. Therefore, in this chapter we are going to explore the general outlines of sex role socialization as they have been delineated for white, middle-class children. We will also attempt to outline some of the newer findings about children who belong to other racial, ethnic, and class groups.

### Sex Role Socialization for the Middle Class

For the white middle class, differences in socialization practices for boys and girls are many and obvious, if you look. Florence Howe describes some of them this way:

We throw boy babies up in the air and roughhouse with them. We coo over girl babies and handle them delicately. We choose sex related colors and toys for our children from their earliest days. We encourage the energy and physical activity of our sons, just as we expect girls to be quieter and more docile. We love both our sons and daughters with equal fervor, we protest, and yet we are disappointed when there is no male child to carry on the family name.[3]

## Agents of Sex Role Socialization

Sylvia Kramer has suggested a number of socialization agents in early childhood.[4] The first, of course, is parents. Studies have demonstrated not only that infant boys are handled more roughly than their sisters and that infant girls receive more verbal attention, but also that young boys are given more freedom to explore than young girls, who are often kept closer to the supervising parent, and that girls receive more help on tasks than boys, who are encouraged to "figure it out for yourself." Research also shows that parental reaction to the behavior of their children tends to be more favorable when girls and boys are behaving in ways traditionally associated with their sex.[5] Thus parents shape the expectations and abilities of their children not only by overt behavior but also by rewarding them with approval when they behave "appropriately."

A second socializing agent in the lives of young children is television, which bombards children with stereotypical images of boys and girls and women and men. Both programming and commercials project ideas associated with gender role, but perhaps commercials are among the most powerful socializers. Commercials, for example, present women as inordinately concerned with their looks, and with cleanliness. As Kramer notes, wryly, "Dirt, in any form, distresses them."[6] Invisible male voices "instruct" housewives in the use of household products from toilet cleaners to air fresheners, thereby promoting the idea that although women do the work, men "know" the best products and methods to use. Commercials also present traditional expectations of children's behavior. As recently as 1989, a series of commercials for first aid products of an American company showed a mother saying to a little boy who had fallen and scraped his knee, "Hush . . . big boys don't cry," followed by a father holding a little girl with the same injury and saying, "Daddy will kiss it and make it all better."

A third influence on young children's development of sex role identity is children's books. Although increasing numbers of nonsexist books are being published today, the "classics" are still being read with enthusiasm. Traditional fairy tales, such as Cinderella, Little Red Riding Hood, Snow White and Rose Red, and Sleeping Beauty present "heroines" who are browbeaten, tricked, chased, put to sleep by wicked witches (another ever popular female character), and/or eaten. Release from such vicissitudes, when it occurs, is always at the hands of a (handsome) young man who finally shows up at the end of the story to whisk the young girl away on *his* horse, to live out her days in *his* castle.[7] In many favorite children's stories, boys build things, explore the unknown, rescue animals, climb trees and mountains, and save girls from infinite kinds of disaster. Girls, in these same stories, help boys, help their mothers, wait for their fathers to come home, wait for pets to be rescued, are occasionally invited to bring food into the playhouse built by their brothers, and wait to be saved.

A fourth important gender socializer of children is toys. If the inclinations of parents and relatives to buy "sex-appropriate" toys is not sufficient to the task, manufacturers

provide useful clues to the gender of the child expected to use the toy on its package. Kramer notes that "with few exceptions, blocks, cars, trains, manipulative games, chemistry sets, doctor's kits, work tools, building games, and of course balls of all kinds show boys on the package. Dolls, kitchen or cleaning toys, needlework or sewing equipment, and nurse's kits show girls on the package."[8]

Boys' toys are relatively more complex, more varied, and more expensive than girls' toys,[9] and frequently have no counterpart for girls. Consider, for example, the range of remote-control cars, boats, and airplanes for sale, as well as electronic sports and adventure games that are marketed for boys. Of course, one can spend a great deal of money buying fashion accessories for Barbie and her minions, but even then, there is Ken to consider (and buy and dress). While there is no *law* preventing parents and others from buying "cross-sex" toys, most people still feel a bit uncomfortable doing so. Even in the 1990s, we buy toy lawn mowers for little boys and toy shopping carts for little girls, and seldom do the reverse.

Other socializing influences on young children may be observed in a variety of everyday places and activities. From nursery rhymes, we learn that young girls are frightened of spiders while young boys are nimble and quick. In Bible stories we observe that young boys are brave and able to do away with giants, while women have a tendency toward evil actions such as cutting off a man's hair and robbing him of his strength. From familiar proverbs and sayings we become aware that sometimes objectionable behavior on the part of boys must be excused on the grounds that "boys will be boys" (did you ever hear "Girls will be girls"?), and that "It's a man's world." And from children's songs we learn that John Henry built a railroad while Suzannah was waiting for her young man to return from Alabama.

### Masculine and Feminine Behavior

If traditional sex roles seem to limit girls more than boys, it may be only that our society favors the active, the adventurous, and the aggressive. There is a high price to be paid by boys for all their "freedom." First of all, boys are socialized much earlier to what is perceived to be "manly." A girl who participates in boys' activities, plays with boys' toys, is impatient with dresses and ribbons and lace, and in general eschews "girlish" things is called a tomboy and is regarded with some tolerance by most adults at least until adolescence. At that point, they feel confident, chances are good that she will "grow out of it." But boys who want to play with dolls, spend time with their mothers in the kitchen, cry easily, like to stay clean, and avoid contact sports are called sissies—a much more negative label—often from the age of 3 or so. Adults viewing such behavior even in very young boys often become enormously uncomfortable and worried that "he is moving in the wrong direction." Adult intervention in these "girlish" activities is usually swift, direct, and unmistakable.

Second, boys are punished much more harshly for deviation from the norms of "masculine" behavior and at an age when they are too young to really understand the source of their "problem" or the reasons for adult distress. Hartley argues that:

To make matters more difficult, the desired behavior is rarely defined positively as something the child *should* do, but rather, undesirable behavior is indicated negatively as something he

should *not* do or be—anything, that is, that the parent or other people regard as "sissy." Thus, very early in life the boy must either stumble on the right path or bear repeated punishment without warning when he accidentally enters into the wrong ones.[10]

One result of this socialization is that boys very early come to regard anything having to do with girls' play and behavior as something to be avoided at all costs, and this attitude increases during the elementary years until most boys would rather "drop dead" than play with girls. This is commonly regarded as a "natural" stage of development rather than the result of intensive socialization,[11] and thus little is done to alter practices that lead to separation of the sexes and the disdain for the "feminine" which often lasts a lifetime.

That such lessons are well learned is inarguable. Hartley asked a representative group of boys (8 and 10 years old) to describe what boys and girls have to be able to know and do. Boys, they said,

> have to be able to fight in case a bully comes along; they have to be athletic; they have to be able to run fast; they must be able to play rough games; they need to know how to play many games—curb-ball, baseball, basketball, football; they need to be smart; they need to be able to take care of themselves; they should know what girls don't know—how to climb, how to make a fire, how to carry things; they should have more ability than girls . . . they are expected to be noisy; to get dirty; to mess up the house; to be naughty; to be "outside" more than girls are; not to be cry-babies; not to be "softies;" not to be "behind" like girls are; and to get into trouble more than girls do.[12]

Thinking about the roles boys must assume, it is hard not to question, with Hartley, "not why boys have difficulty with this role, but why they try as hard as they do to fulfill it."[13]

### Sex Role Stereotyping: The Power of Norms

One answer to "why they do it" is that sex roles are *normative*—that is, the ideas about what attitudes, values, and behavior are associated with one's gender have been coded by the social group into norms or stereotypes. A *norm,* as you probably know, is a rule of conduct based on attitudes and values which are usually internalized through socialization until they become "of course" statements.[14] Webb and Sherman note that:

> Most of us learn [normative] lessons so well that deviation from [them] seldom occurs to us. If you are a female, you do not whisper reminders to yourself to behave like a woman. Your womanly behavior is part of your womanly self. You *are* a woman. Part of this fact is no doubt biological, but we know from the study of other cultures that females go about being a woman in very different ways. Much of female [or male] behavior is not biological at all; it is learned.[15]

Because these norms are so much a part of us, they seem "natural" and "right" and we take them very much for granted. That sense of "naturalness" is probably the most powerful force operating to encourage obedience to norms. However, there are other factors involved in encouraging normative thought and behavior. In all societies, there are *sanctions,* or punishments, for deviation from norms. In terms of sex role, an important sanction for "unwomanly" or "unmanly" behavior is the belief that such behavior means that one is simply not a man or a woman.

In our society, sex role stereotypes include the belief that boys and men are aggressive, independent, strong, logical, direct, adventurous, self-confident, ambitious, and not particularly emotional. Girls and women are passive, weak, illogical, indirect, gentle, and very emotional. Boys, the stereotypes say, are good at math and science, and girls are good at language and writing. Boys are loud and girls are quiet. Girls play with dolls and boys play with balls. While it is true that not every single boy or girl believes or adheres to these stereotypes, it is generally the case that *society* attempts to enforce them, even in the face of contrary evidence, such as the fact that girls and women are now participating in nearly every aspect of life once "owned" by boys and men.

Sex role stereotypes not only contain particular content, but—in almost every society—stereotypic content is differentially valued. In other words, it is often the case that not only are boys and men perceived to be *different* from girls and women, their behavior is also more highly valued. This differential value is expressed in a variety of ways, an important one being language. We have already mentioned the difference in value implied in the words *tomboy* and *sissy*. There are others. An aggressive man, for example, is often praised for being a "go-getter," while an aggressive woman is referred to as a "bitch." A woman who alters her behavior, and frequently her plans, to accommodate another person is described as "caring," while a man who does the same thing is often called a "wimp." Sex stereotypes "genderize" traits which either males or females are *able* to display in favor of one gender or the other.

The power of sex role stereotypes is enormous and frequently costly to girls and women. A classic study of the way clinical psychologists define mental health done in the late 1960s assessed their beliefs about traits associated with the healthy male, the healthy female, and the healthy adult. A list of 122 bipolar items (e.g., aggressive-passive) associated with stereotypical masculine and stereotypical feminine characteristics was given to three groups of male and female psychologists.

> Each group was given a different set of instructions: One was told to choose those traits that characterize the healthy adult male; another to choose those of the healthy adult female; the third, to choose those of the healthy adult—a person. The result: The clinically healthy male and the clinically healthy adult were identical—and totally divergent from the clinically healthy female. The authors of the study concluded that "a double standard of health exists for men and women." That is, the general standard of health applies only to men. Women are perceived as "less healthy" by those standards called "adult." At the same time, however, if a woman deviates from the sexual stereotypes prescribed for her—if she grows more "active" or "aggressive" for example—she doesn't grow healthier; she may, in fact . . . be perceived as "sicker."[16]

Another way to say this is that if a woman behaves like a man she is perceived to be "unwomanly," while if she behaves like a woman, she is perceived to be "childish."

Sex role stereotypes are equally hard on boys and men, but in a somewhat different way. As the woman's movement has succeeded in opening up to women public roles that have traditionally been taken by men, women have learned to assume those roles more or less well, and the sex role socialization of young girls has changed somewhat to accommodate their broader life chances. The same is not true of boys and men. Cooper Thompson tells the following story that illustrates the point:

> I was once asked by a teacher in a suburban high school to give a guest presentation on male roles. She hoped that I might help her deal with four boys who exercised extraordinary control

over the other boys in the class. Using ridicule and their status as physically imposing athletes, the four wrestlers had succeeded in stifling the participation of the other boys, who were reluctant to comment in class discussions.

As a class, we talked about how boys got status in that school and how they were put down by others. I was told that the most humiliating put-down was being called a ''fag.'' The list of behaviors that could elicit ridicule filled two large chalkboards; the boys in the school were conforming to rigid, narrow standards of masculinity to avoid being called a fag. I, too, felt this pressure and became very conscious of my mannerisms in front of the group. Partly from exasperation, I decided to test the seriousness of these assertions. Since one of the four boys had some streaks of pink in his shirt, and since he had told me that wearing pink was grounds for being called a fag, I told him that I thought *he* was a fag. Instead of laughing, he said, ''I'm going to kill you.''

He obviously didn't and, in retrospect, I think that what I said was inappropriate. But, in that moment, I understood how frightening it is for a boy to have his masculinity challenged, and I realized that the pressure to be masculine was higher than I ever would have expected. This was, after all, a boy who was a popular and successful athlete, whose masculinity was presumably established in the eyes of his peers; yet because of that single remark from me, he experienced a destruction of his self-image as a male.[17]

Thompson goes on to say that much of the definition of masculinity adhered to by these boys was based not on what boys *should* do, but rather on what they *should not* do, and that what they should not do was to be anything like a girl. Two forces that, in our society, help to enforce male and female stereotypes are misogyny and homophobia. Simply stated, *misogyny* is the hatred of women and *homophobia* is the fear of homosexuality and homosexuals, often accompanied by repugnance and hostility. Thompson argues that while these forces seem to target different kinds of people, they are really different aspects of the same thing. ''Homophobia is the hatred of feminine qualities in men, while misogyny is the hatred of feminine qualities in women.''[18] In both cases, feminine qualities are devalued, even contemptible.

Thompson's story may seem almost melodramatic, but it reflects a fundamental set of values in our society, values that—often unconsciously—guide our thinking, our behavior, and our public policy. Carelli has made an effective distinction between sex role stereotyping, sex bias, and sex discrimination. She writes:

> Whenever specific behaviors, abilities, interests, and values are attributed to one sex, then sex role stereotyping is taking place. . . . Behavior that results from the underlying belief in sex role stereotypes is referred to as ''sex bias.'' . . . Any action that specifically denies opportunities, privileges, or rewards to a person or a group because of their sex is termed ''sex discrimination'' if the action is against the law.[19]

Calling another boy a fag because he is exhibiting ''female'' qualities is an example of sex bias—an action based on sex role stereotypes. If that boy were prevented from, say, taking art classes on the grounds that drawing is a ''feminine'' activity and that all artists are fags, that would be sex discrimination, since denying access to specific educational activities is against the law.

Clearly, the power of sex role stereotypes is great, and the cost is high for everyone: boys and girls, women and men. Sex role stereotypes prevent girls and boys from having valuable human experiences; they limit growth and development both by denying these experiences and by creating anxiety in children; and they create social and institutional

barriers against the development of interests, goals, and talents in young people that may be outside sex role "parameters." The human cost in terms of discouragement, sadness, fear, and alienation is incalculable. Sex role stereotypes also contribute to the organization of schooling and to the subtle and not so subtle messages that boys and girls absorb about their identities, their expectations, and their futures.

### Variations in Sex Role Socialization Patterns

We said earlier that much of the research on sex role socialization has been done in terms of white, middle-class children. It is important to keep in mind that their story is not the whole story and that other socialization patterns are alive and well in our society. Culturally determined variables include the age at which sex role socialization begins, the degree to which the socialization to sex role is enforced, the actual content of the sex role socialization, and the people and situations most influential in the socialization process.

According to some researchers, working- and lower-class children learn to differentiate sex roles earlier, as indicated by awareness of sex-typed toys, and parents in these families are more concerned that traditional sex role stereotypes be enforced.[20] This research indicates that "middle class girls not only showed later awareness of sex typing than working class girls, but were less traditional in their sex role concepts."[21] Thus, if any children are going to "break the mold" of sex stereotypes, middle-class girls will have the best chance and working- and lower-class boys will suffer the most from attempting to do so.

Among nonwhite groups, Ladner's research suggests that independence is a higher value for black girls than for white. Black girls appear to identify more often with the image of the "'strong black woman'—the resourceful, hardworking, economically independent female."[22] Teenage black girls tended to see this image in two ways—the mother who kept the family together by struggling for life's necessities, and the upwardly mobile, middle-class black woman who provided a role model for escape from the ghetto.[23] Weitzman, discussing Ladner's research, writes that although the socialization of black girls begins at home,

the home is quite different from that in which the white girl is socialized. The black girl is more likely to live with a single parent or in a three-generational household than is the white girl. Her parents may be in the home less frequently, and from an early age she may be cared for by older siblings, other relatives, or neighbors. Consequently, socializing agents other than the parents are likely to influence her development. As Ladner points out, peer groups and various adult female relatives and acquaintances take on great significance as role models and reinforcers of appropriate sex-role behavior.[24]

The complexity of variation in sex role socialization patterns is illustrated beautifully in a study of Appalachian girls by Borman, Mueninghoff, and Piazza.[25] Like their black sisters, Appalachian girls are socialized to identify with strength in women; like that of their white, middle-class sisters, the image of women is also passive and accepting. Unlike that of their black sisters, who carry with them the slave history of being moved arbitrarily from place to place, the Appalachian ideal incorporates a strong sense of place—a particular and very deep attachment to the mountains that gives them a sense of pride and belonging:

Young Appalachian women possess a strong cultural heritage emphasizing their identification with place, their strength, and their ability to manage family and other social relations with particular ability and energy. . . . Women in Appalachian literature are repeatedly pictured as strong and earthbound, life-giving and nurturing, passive and accepting. The novelist Emma Bell Miles, for example, ''sees the woman as passive, internal, deep, reflective, stable,'' an individual who also knows her life is dedicated to service and inevitably to suffering.[26]

Further exploration of such variations in sex role socialization in the family and neighborhood will broaden and deepen our understanding of the complexities of the process and may also begin to deepen our appreciation of the experience of gender in American society. Another set of socialization processes—perhaps equally important and certainly more easily studied—occurs in the school. It is to the set of attitudes, values, and practices that schooling contributes to the experience of gender that we turn now.

## DIFFERENTIAL TREATMENT OF BOYS AND GIRLS IN CLASSROOMS: THE EXPERIENCE OF GENDER IN SCHOOL

If stereotyping according to sex role is a major part of the socialization of children at home, it is also an integral feature of schooling. Far from being places where ''all children are treated alike,'' the school and the classroom are continuing sources of gender differentiation which reinforce deeply held and mostly unexamined cultural beliefs about appropriate ideas, values, and behavior for girls and boys. Although twenty years of research and scholarship on differential treatment of boys and girls in classrooms has raised educators' consciousness of gender equity issues, changes have been slow, often grudging, and frequently difficult to see. The Wheat People and The Grainers were not alone in finding it hard to accept new ideas. Furthermore, in recent years the renewed and almost paranoiac emphasis on ''excellence'' in the schools generated in the political arena has served to draw attention away from issues of racial, class, and gender equity. Charol Shakeshaft does not exaggerate when she writes that:

Since the call for excellence was first sounded in 1983 in *A Nation at Risk,* a lot of loose talk has blamed the so-called lack of excellence in the schools on the pursuit of equity. . . . As troubling as it is to hear political and educational leaders falsely blaming the mediocrity of the school system on those who seek a system that offers women, people of color, and handicapped students a fair shake, it is even more disturbing to chart the failure of the public to see the reliance of excellence on equity. At best, the two are described as ''twin goals''; at worst, the importance of equitable practices to excellence in education is flatly denied.[27]

### Factors That Prevent Attention to Gender Bias in Schools

Part of the problem is that with increased awareness of differential practices and outcomes for girls and boys in school, and with the passage of Title IX, which presumably guaranteed equal access of both sexes to curricular and other school offerings, many people believe that ''the problem has been taken care of.''

Another factor is that the past two decades have spawned an almost unprecedented set of interventions and programs designed to alleviate or prevent an astonishing variety of health and human service related problems that have an impact on teaching and learning. As the school has been asked (and often, required) to participate in wider and wider areas of students' lives, many teachers have come to regard any suggestion that they take account of yet another "problem" as simply an additional burden.

Some people concerned with issues of gender in schools empathize with teachers:

> You are a teacher. You are in your classroom. You are responsible for the academic, social, emotional, psychological, and physical well-being of thirty students. You may, indeed, be responsible for at least 100 students during one school day. You have to prepare interesting, challenging lessons to compete with television, MTV, and other media. You should be watching for signs of drug and alcohol abuse, or other potential student problems. You must be aware of the signals of possible suicide, pregnancy, physical abuse, drop-out, or signs of depression. . . . You are acutely aware of your paycheck, your status, and the demands of the community on your time and your psyche. . . . But now they want you to do "sex equity."[28]

A third factor that operates to prevent teachers and administrators from attending to issues of gender as they play themselves out in the schools is that schools reflect the society of which they are a part—indeed, one important job of schools is to pass on the "general" culture to the next generation. In our society, despite twenty years of the woman's movement, a number of antidiscrimination laws, some hard won adaptations of language (we now routinely say *mailperson* and add *she* to *he* when we speak of unnamed persons), and increasingly sophisticated media attention, the sexes are still seen to occupy largely separate spheres. Sex role socialization practices do not continue more or less unchanged for no reason. Thus, if it is true that boys and girls have different experiences in school, the most likely reaction of parents, teachers, and the public is that different experiences are acceptable because they prepare children for the lives they will probably lead.

A final reason for major disinterest in sex-equitable education in schools is that nowhere in the recent major critiques of public schooling has gender been made an issue of any importance. As Foxley notes,

> In no other era in our history have so many public and private organizations issued reports recommending reform in American education. . . . With all of this attention on the need to increase the quality of American education, none of the major reports address in any substantive way the need to improve educational equity for male and female students. If the topic is mentioned at all, it is done very briefly. . . . And without some impetus and encouragement at the national level, few educators and administrators at the local level will bother to be concerned about sex equity.[29]

Lack of any real concern about gender issues in education results in a kind of generalized apathy on the part of the public and of school professionals as well. Those educators who are concerned with and spend a good part of their professional life working to achieve sex-equitable education quickly get used to all sorts of clever comments from their colleagues: "How are things in the woman's world?" they hear, or "Oh, no, not that 'women's stuff' again!" or even, "Well, boys will be boys, you know."

## Gender: A Difference That Makes a Difference

Yet the fact is that an enormous amount of research has documented both the ways in which girls and boys are treated differently in schools and the differential outcomes that result from such treatment. The end result of the research is the finding that, in general, boys and girls have significantly different educational experiences, experiences that emerge from differential teacher-student interaction, from differential teaching practices and expectations, from sex bias in curriculum materials, and from an unmistakable but unexamined male bias in the culture of the school.

## Academic Differentiation

We know, for example, that girls start out ahead of boys in a variety of attributes, notably verbal ability, eye-hand coordination, and, indeed, mathematical ability.[30] We also know that, by the seventh grade, they begin to fall behind boys in achievement on standardized tests and that this decline continues and even accelerates during high school.[31] At the same time, girls generally receive better grades in school than boys. Some scholars believe that grades may ''be one of the rewards [girls] get for being more quiet and docile in the classroom.''[32] We know that boys are awarded 64 percent of all National Merit Scholarships and that they outperform girls on all subsections of the American College Testing Program Examination (ACT), the Scholastic Aptitude Test (SAT), the Graduate Record Examination, the Medical College Admissions Test, and the Graduate Management Admissions Test (GMAT).[33]

We know that girls with high mathematical ability are less likely than boys to be identified, and that even when they are identified they are less likely than boys to participate in accelerated math classes.[34] On the other hand, we know that girls with learning disabilities are also less likely than boys to be identified and that when they are, interventions are made at a later age.[35]

Insofar as American schools are concerned, girls constitute a population that is nearly invisible. Sadker and Sadker note that ''girls are more likely to be invisible members of classrooms. They receive fewer academic contacts, less praise, fewer complex and abstract questions, and less instruction on how to do things for themselves.''[36] Indeed, Shakeshaft asserts that the most ignored person in the classroom is the high-achieving female.[37]

At the same time, boys are more likely to be corrected for academic mistakes and encouraged to ''do it until they get it right.'' Again, Shakeshaft observes that ''boys learn to handle criticism because they have opportunities to respond that allow them to grow. Boys also have more opportunities to build self-esteem because they speak more and are more often praised and told that they have ability.''[38] At the same time, boys are more likely to be identified as learning disabled and more likely to receive remediation.[39] There is a darker side to the academic experience of boys, just as there is to their sex role socialization: boys are more likely to receive lower grades, to repeat grades, and to leave high school before completion.[40] Although girls, as a group, get better grades than boys, they are less likely to think that they will do well in college.[41]

By the time they finish high school, girls exhibit a decline in career commitment,[42] a finding commonly attributed to social helplessness,[43] and to a notion that boys will disassociate themselves from ''smart'' girls.[44] Studies reveal that a majority of both male and female college students believe that characteristics usually considered to be masculine are more highly valued and more socially desirable than those characteristics ordinarily associated with femininity.

## rricular Materials

Girls' experience of invisibility (or helplessness or devaluation) is reinforced by curricular materials. Several examples may be sufficient to make the point.

In the early grades, girls who appear in reading and arithmetic text books are most often portrayed in stereotypical sex roles. Howe, for example, asks us to imagine arithmetic problems in which boys and girls are occupied in the following ways:

1 girls playing marbles; boys sewing;
2 girls earning money, building things, and going places; boys buying ribbons for a sewing project;
3 girls working at physical activities; boys babysitting and, you guessed it, sewing.[45]

One of the more insidious elements of this form of stereotyping is that, although some progress has been made in very recent years in expanding the activities of girls in reading and math books—so that we might perhaps find girls playing marbles, playing in sports, and earning money—we would still be quite shocked to find boys sewing and buying ribbons. Girls in textbooks, like their real life mothers, get to do twice the work.

Perhaps you may think that, after all, the examples in these elementary textbooks are not that important since most girls and boys today see many examples of women (usually their mothers, and often their sisters, grandmothers, aunts, and neighbors) working in all kinds of occupations. We would argue that early, repetitive impressions are more significant than is often assumed. Certainly there is evidence that, even when confronted with direct evidence to the contrary, children stick to sex role stereotypes with amazing tenacity. The following story surprised us; perhaps it will surprise you too.

"Boys are doctors. Girls are nurses," insisted the kindergarten class. Amazed that young children could be so firm in their stereotype, the teacher took the twenty-two youngsters on a field trip to a nearby hospital. She introduced them to a female doctor and a male nurse who talked with them about their jobs and gave them a tour of the hospital.

Upon returning to the classroom, the teacher emphasized her point. "Now you can see that boys can be nurses. Girls can be doctors."

"No they can't," the students insisted.

"What do you mean?" The teacher was stunned. "We visited the hospital and met a man who is a nurse and a woman who is a doctor. You saw them. They talked with you."

"Yes," chorused the children triumphantly, "but they lied."[46]

*start here* →

Persistent images of boys and girls in stereotypical roles are not the only problem with text materials. Another one is the absence of women in history and social studies texts, an absence that helps to establish the inaccurate but firm impression that women have done very little of importance in the history of the nation. Summarizing a study of high school social studies texts done during the 1970s, Trecker described the impression these books give of women and their lives this way:

Based on the information in these commonly-used high school texts, one might summarize the history and contributions of the American woman as follows: Women arrived in 1619. . . . They held the Seneca Falls Convention on Women's Rights in 1848. During the rest of the nineteenth century, they participated in reform movements, chiefly temperance, and were exploited in factories. In 1920 they were given the vote. They joined the armed forces for the first time during the second World War and thereafter have enjoyed the good life in America.

Add the names of the women who are invariably mentioned: Harriet Beecher Stowe, Jane Addams, Dorothea Dix, and Frances Perkins, with perhaps Susan B. Anthony, Elizabeth Cady Stanton, and, almost as frequently, Carrie Nation, and you have the basic text.[47]

Although during the 1980s writers and publishers eliminated a good deal of the sexism in text materials, there is a considerable way to go. While recent studies of mathematics texts, science texts, and Newberry Medal books show less sexist language and less stereotypic portrayals of girls and women, improvements in history texts have not been as great, despite a large amount of new research in women's history.[48] You might try evaluating your own college texts, or texts that your younger brothers and sisters are using in grade school and high school. Sadker and Sadker have developed the following description of six forms of bias in curricular materials that you can use as a guide:[49]

**1** *Linguistic Bias.* Referring to the use of masculine terms and pronouns in curriculum materials, linguistic bias is one of the easiest forms of sex bias to detect and eliminate. In history texts, terms such as *caveman, forefathers,* and *mankind* inherently deny the contributions of women. Similarly, masculine occupational titles such as *mailman, policeman,* and *businessman* are labels that deny the participation of women in our society. So does use of the pronoun *he* to refer to all people.

Another form of linguistic bias occurs when women are identified in terms of being someone's wife or possession, as in this sentence: "Winston Williams and his wife and children moved to New York." When this is reworded to read, "The Williams family moved to New York," all members of the family are considered equally.

**2** *Stereotyping.* Many studies indicate that children and adults have been stereotyped in textbooks. Boys typically are portrayed as exhibiting one set of values, behaviors, and roles, whereas girls are drawn with a different set of characteristics. In reading books, boys routinely have been shown as ingenious, creative, brave, athletic, achieving, and curious. Girls have been portrayed as dependent, passive, fearful, and docile victims. Adults have also been stereotyped in roles and careers. In a study of seventy-seven basal readers published between 1980 and 1982, Britton and Lumpkin found a total of 5,501 careers depicted; 64 percent were attributed to Anglo males, 14 percent to Anglo females, 17 percent to males of color, and 5 percent to females of color. The most common careers shown for Anglo males were soldier, farmer, doctor, and police officer. The most frequently shown role models for males of color were worker, farmer, warrior, Indian chief, and hunter. The most common careers for white women were mother, teacher, author, and princess. For females of color, mother and teacher also headed the list, followed by slave, worker, porter, and artist.[50]

**3** *Invisibility.* Women have made significant contributions to the growth and development of the United States, yet few have appeared in the history books children are assigned to read. This form of sex bias—invisibility, or omission—has characterized not only history books, but also texts in reading, language arts, mathematics, science, spelling, and vocational education. For example, a 1972 study of science, math, reading, spelling, and social studies textbooks found that only 31 percent of all illustrations included females and that the percentage of females decreased as the grade level increased.[51]

In another study, researchers analyzed 134 elementary readers and found males pictured twice as often as females and portrayed in three times as many occupations.[52] A 1970 study of history texts found that students had to read more than 500 pages before they found one page of information about women.[53] When girls and women are systematically excluded from curricular material, students are deprived of information about half the nation's people. Even though studies in the 1980s show that significant improvement has been made, women and girls are still underrepresented on textbook pages.

**4** *Imbalance*. Textbooks perpetuate bias by presenting only one interpretation of an issue, situation, or group of people. Often this one-sided view is presented because the author has limited space or decides that it is not feasible to present all sides of an issue in elementary textbooks. History textbooks contain many examples of imbalance, mostly minimizing the role of women. For example, Janice Trecker studied the most widely used history textbooks and found more information on women's skirt lengths than on the suffrage movement.[54] As a result of such imbalanced presentation, millions of students have been given limited perspectives concerning the contributions, struggles, and participation of women in U.S. society. Although more recent textbook studies show improvement, problems remain.

**5** *Unreality*. Many textbooks have presented an unrealistic portrait of U.S. history and contemporary life experience by glossing over controversial topics and avoiding discussion of discrimination and prejudice. For example, almost 50 percent of all marriages end in divorce, and one-third of all children will live with a single parent during part of their lives. Yet many textbooks portray the typical American family as one having two adults, two children, a dog, and a house in suburbia. When controversial issues are not presented, students are denied the information they need to confront contemporary problems.

**6** *Fragmentation*. Textbooks fragment the contributions of women by treating those contributions as unique occurrences rather than integrating them into the main body of the text. In fragmented texts, the contributions of important women are often highlighted in separate boxes or are contained in a separate chapter. Fragmentation communicates to readers that women are an interesting diversion but that their contributions do not constitute the mainstream of history and literature. Fragmentation and isolation also occur when women are depicted as interacting only among themselves and as having little or no influence on society as a whole. For example, textbook discussions of feminism often talk about how women are affected by this contemporary movement, but there is little analysis of the effect of the women's movement on other groups and social issues.

## The Culture of the School

A number of factors influencing differential experience for boys and girls in school are related to school organization and staffing patterns, and the perceived purpose of schooling itself. One concern expressed with some frequency is that the school is a "feminized" institution and is thus not a good place for boys. The "feminization of schooling" argument relies on the fact that the majority of teachers—particularly in elementary school when socializing influences on children are particularly strong—are women. Its proponents then state that the folkways of schooling regarding behavior—walk, don't run, be quiet, be polite, sit still, don't talk, be respectful of authority—have much the same content as the more general socialization of girls; they are thus presumed to be detrimental to boys' development in traditional male ways. Influenced by this argument, some educators have decided that schools are good places for girls but bad for boys.

Other educators argue that, in fact, schools are organized, staffed, and governed precisely for the benefit of boys. They cite the fact that the grade structure of schools, for example, is based on male development patterns.

Although females mature earlier, are ready for verbal and math skills at a younger age, and have control of small-motor skills sooner than males, the curriculum has been constructed to mirror the development of males. Decisions about the grade in which students should learn long division, read *Huckleberry Finn*, or begin to write essays are based on the developmental patterns of boys (and primarily white boys), not on the developmental patterns of girls (or of minority students).[55]

A second observation about schools made by those who are unimpressed by the feminization of schools position is that although research indicates that girls do better in single-sex schools, nearly all public schools are coeducational. Such an environment is thought to be ''better'' for boys because it provides a second curriculum in social interaction which girls receive nearly from birth.[56] Shakeshaft notes that ''two messages emerge repeatedly from the research on gender and schooling. First, what is good for males is not necessarily good for females. Second, if a choice must be made, the education establishment will base policy and instruction on that which is good for boys.''[57]

Staffing patterns of schools also give students the clear message that women are workers and men are leaders, supervisors, and bosses. In the past forty years, the number of women in positions of leadership and authority in schools and school districts has actually declined,[58] and while there is some evidence that more women are entering the graduate programs which prepare them for administrative positions, it is still harder for a woman to get hired as a principal or superintendent. One exception to that rule has been mentioned by Biklen, who finds that women frequently are hired as principals in large, urban districts which may have a number of ''difficult'' schools.[59]

Finally, it has been argued that schools are designed to serve the public world associated with male roles, not the private one associated with female roles. Education, this argument goes, is primarily for public life—that is, education is in many ways a preparation for work. This is an interesting point, especially since women are increasingly participating in that public world. On the surface, the very ''public'' character of schooling should be of benefit to both males and females. However, this conclusion misses the point, which is that, to a great extent, in order to participate fully in public life, girls and women have to learn to *be like boys and men*. Women's experience and women's knowledge do not find a place in either the school or the workplace.

### Models for Achieving Sex Equity in Schools

Earlier in this book we suggested that Title IX addresses, in part, the issue of whether or not sex is a difference that makes a difference in education. Perhaps you have concluded that, if sex does not, then gender certainly does make a difference. If you have, reaching that conclusion is only a first step in the process of thinking through what can or should be done to increase educational equity for boys and girls. Not all of those who propose strategies for educational equity in terms of gender believe that a child's sex is fundamentally important when it comes to teaching and learning. That is, they tend not to believe that it *determines* educational outcomes. Others subscribe to the view that sex is or may be a significant variable and should be recognized as such.

Anne Bennison and some of her colleagues have developed a categorization of models for achieving sex equity in schools based on varying philosophical views of the nature of boys and girls.[60] They argue that the assumptions that differentiate various programs can be divided into three categories: (1) assumptions about the characteristics of learners; (2) assumptions about what the goals of education for different groups and individuals should be; (3) assumptions about the structure of programs aimed at promoting educational equity. As you examine them, reflect on which ideas make the most sense to you and which you think would be the most workable in the classroom.

**1** *Assimilationism:* This model assumes that sex is not a difference that makes a difference, at least in terms of the abilities boys and girls have when they enter school. Proponents of this model argue that while some inherent biological differences between males and females exist, they are unrelated to learning. Differences that appear to be sex-related (e.g., in math, verbal, and spatial ability) are small, with much variation and overlap between groups. For these people, equal educational opportunity means similar educational treatment. The position is that if you treat students alike, the outcomes of their education will be similar. Equity assimilationists tend to favor education for androgyny:

> The way to achieve androgyny is by providing truly equal educational opportunities to girls and boys. Such provisions include eliminating sex-role stereotypes in textbooks and other curriculum materials; changing the teaching and advising practices of teachers, administrators, and school counselors; and having similar expectations of success for both sexes.[61]

**2** *The deficit approach:* The deficit model characterizes differences between males and females as important in the educational process, and assumes that the differences render the sexes unequal in terms of learning. Most advocates of this model would subscribe to the belief that existing differences are primarily the result of differential socialization practices for boys and girls. They argue that the value of the different behaviors taught to boys and girls is arbitrated by the dominant culture and tends to favor males. The focus of these models is on the role of the school in ensuring equal educational outcomes for all children. In order to do this, different educational environments for different children are usually required—for example, compensatory education. Indeed, a central feature of these models is an emphasis on helping students to "compensate for deficits that society identifies as important."[62] Compensatory programs, however, also assume that the goal of the school is to help all children achieve in terms of currently accepted standards of performance; they do not criticize those standards.

**3** *The pluralist model:* Proponents of the pluralist models of gender equity also believe that differences related to sex or gender are important to the success of all children. Pluralists celebrate differences between boys and girls and actively seek to provide different educational programs which produce unique educational outcomes:

> The compelling conclusion here is that women's culture should not be ignored simply because it has not been salient in the discussion of male-dominated educational systems; moreover, it should be possible to develop a female-based epistemology that would perceive and acknowledge the reality of women's lives.[63]

Contrasting strongly with the assimilationists' encouragement of androgyny as an educational ideal, pluralists tend to favor separate educational programs (e.g., single-sex education) and emphasize multicultural and bilingual efforts, which they believe should be the norm for all children.

**4** *Social justice model:* Advocates of the social justice model believe that sex *may* be a difference that makes a difference in schooling, that people are both alike and different and should sometimes be treated in the same way and sometimes differently. This raises the immediate question of how one decides whether or not a gender difference is educationally important. Social justice proponents would use justice as the deciding criterion: that is, they declare that "differences in educational treatment can best be justified in terms of how such differences enable people to secure their basic human rights and allow equal access to social goods."[64] Social justice advocates argue that "in an unjust society in which disadvantages and inequalities in power can be linked to sex, these characteristics are no longer irrelevant differences."[65] Quite often, proponents of the justice model find themselves advocating almost a case-by-case judgment about the necessity for developing alternative educational treatments for children.

These four models can be helpful in analyzing various approaches to sex equity in schools. It is well to remember that most programs fall somewhere along a continuum, but nevertheless there are clear distinctions between the attitudes and values espoused by these approaches. It is therefore a good idea to try to establish your own position— although that position *may* combine assumptions from more than one model—so that you can support the decisions you make and the actions you take in the classroom.

## A FINAL WORD: GENDER AND THE IDEAL OF THE EDUCATED PERSON

Jane Roland Martin has made a perceptive observation about the nature of education as we have historically defined it, and that is that formal education, in content and practice, stresses attitudes and values that are associated primarily with the *productive processes* of society—political and economic activities as well as the creation of art, music, dance, and drama. The *reproductive processes* of society—activities that generally involve caretaking of homes, children, the ill, and the elderly—are not important areas of learning in school, nor are they included in the criteria ordinarily used in delineating the ideal of the educated person.[66]

Martin argues that both kinds of processes are essential for the continuation of a healthy society, and that, indeed, the reproductive processes may be even more important if we are to succeed in solving the family, health, and environmental problems we face at the end of the twentieth century. She writes:

> The statistics on child abuse and domestic violence in our society today belie the assumption that the knowledge, skills, attitudes, and traits of character necessary for effectively carrying out the reproductive processes of society occur naturally in people. Education for these processes is not only as essential as education for society's productive processes but also has an overarching political, social, and moral significance.[67]

In short, Martin argues that the knowledge and experience of women, which arise in part from the nature of their traditional roles in society, is knowledge and experience we sorely need and must be included in any consideration of educational policy and practice. A number of other authors have begun to explore the nature of this knowledge in some detail, and while the area is too extensive to go into in great detail here, work in two areas is important to mention.

First, Carol Gilligan has studied the moral development of girls extensively, and finds significant differences in the development of moral and ethical thinking in boys and girls. Boys, she asserts, develop an "ethic of rights," with a heavy emphasis on law and justice, while girls develop an ''ethic of care,'' which places more importance on connection, and the nurturing of relationships. One is not necessarily better than the other in her view, but they are decidedly different. Girls and women, she says, ''speak in a different voice.''[68] Research on the way children play games provides one illustration of this difference. Lever, for example, has found that when disputes arise in playground games, boys will argue, negotiate, even change the rules on the spot in order to keep the game going. Girls, on the other hand, are likely to end the game if it means arguing, which they perceive as threatening to the relationships between the children engaged in the game.[69]

A second important study focused on women's ways of acquiring and processing knowledge.[70] Here, the authors studied college women of a wide range of ages in a variety of types of postsecondary institutions. For many of these women, silence—literal and figurative—was an apt description of their experience. The process of ''finding a voice'' was both frightening and exhilarating to them, and was often associated with nontraditional forms of teaching, forms that the authors called ''connected education.'' Teachers who practice ''connected knowing'' are extremely interested in how students are experiencing the ideas and information in the subject matter and what students are thinking. Trust is an important issue:

> As a teacher, she must ''trust'' each student's experience, although, as a person or a critic, she need not agree with it. To trust means not just to tolerate a variety of viewpoints, acting as an impartial referee, assuring equal air time to all: It means to try to *connect*, to enter into each student's perspective. But, again, subjectivity is disciplined: like the participant-observer, the connected teacher is careful not to ''abandon'' herself to these perspectives. A connected teacher is not just another student, the role carries special responsibilities. But it does not entail power over the students.[71]

Other authors are beginning to explore the relation between women's experiences in caregiving and the process of teaching and learning. The work of Madeleine Grumet, for instance, focuses on the experience of motherhood as a model for teaching,[72] and Nancy Hoffman has provided us with a historical account of the nurturing role of women in the history of teaching.[73] Taken together, the work of these scholars provides not only new models for understanding the experience of gender in educational processes, but, perhaps more important, new directions for education itself.

## ACTIVITIES

1  Using a week's worth of your campus or local daily newspaper, circle every headline in which females or males are mentioned. Compare the number of mentions of each. Compare the number of roles associated with males and females (e.g., husband, wife, banker, politician, daughter, son, athlete). In what sections of the paper are males and females referred to most often? Is there a difference between the campus newspaper and the local one?

2  Examine your textbooks in teacher education and in arts and sciences. Look for evidence of the types of bias discussed in the chapter. (One interesting project is to count the number of males and females listed in the index.)

3  Interview someone who is a member of the same sex and who attended a school that was different from yours in terms of type of population (e.g., coeducational versus single sex).

Compare academic experiences, extracurricular activities in which you both participated, dating patterns, and dress.

4 Make a list of the chores you were expected to do at home as you were growing up. If you have brothers or sisters, were their chores similar or different? If you were an only child, or had only siblings of the same sex, talk to someone else who had siblings of the opposite sex.

5 Do a study of your classmates in terms of the number and kinds of math and science courses you each took in high school. Is there any difference between the males and the females? Ask your classmates if they can describe the reasons for taking or not taking math and science courses, and compare their reasons.

# REFERENCES

1 L. C. Pogrebin, *Growing Up Free* (New York: Bantam Books, 1980).

2 Lenore J. Weitzman, "Sex-Role Socialization," in Jo Freeman (ed.), *Women: A Feminist Perspective* (Palo Alto, CA: Mayfield, 1975), p. 109.

3 Florence Howe, "Sexual Stereotypes Start Early," in Laurie Olsen Johnson (ed.), *Nonsexist Curriculum Materials for Elementary Schools* (Old Westbury, NY: Feminist Press, 1974), pp. 25–32.

4 Sylvia Kramer, "Sex Role Stereotyping: How It Happens and How to Avoid It," in Anne O'Brien Carelli (ed.), *Sex Equity in Education* (Springfield, IL: Charles C. Thomas, 1988), pp. 5–23.

5 See, for example, B. Fagot, "The Influence of Sex of Child on Parental Reactions to Toddler Children," *Child Development,* vol. 49, no. 2, 1978, pp. 459–465; S. Dronsberg, B. Fagot, R. Hagan, and M. D. Lleinback, "Differential Reactions to Assertive and Communicative Acts of Toddler Boys and Girls," *Child Development,* vol. 56, no. 6, 1985, pp. 1499–1505.

6 Kramer, op. cit., p. 9.

7 For an insightful analysis of the impact of several fairy tale "heroines" on the socialization of children, see Madonna Kolbenschlag, *Kiss Sleeping Beauty Goodbye: Breaking the Spell of Feminine Myths and Models* (New York: Bantam Books, 1981), p. 7.

8 Kramer, op. cit., p. 11.

9 "A Report on Children's Toys," in Judith Stacey, Susan Bereaud, and Joan Daniels (eds.), *And Jill Came Tumbling After: Sexism in American Education* (New York: Dell, 1974), pp. 123–125.

10 Ruth E. Hartley, "Sex Role Pressures and the Socialization of the Male Child," in Stacey, Bereaud, and Daniels (eds.), *And Jill Came Tumbling After: Sexism in American Education* (New York: Dell, 1974), pp. 186–187.

11 Kathleen Barry, "View from the Doll Corner," in Elizabeth S. Maccia (ed.), *Women and Education* (Springfield, IL: Charles C. Thomas, 1975), p. 121.

12 Hartley, op. cit., p. 90.

13 Ibid., p. 91.

14 Robert S. Lynd and Helen Merrell Lynd, *Middletown in Transition* (New York: Harcourt, Brace 1937), p. 402.

15 Rodman B. Webb and Robert R. Sherman, *Schooling and Society,* 2d ed. (New York: Macmillan, 1989), p. 56.

16 Howe, op. cit., p. 28.

17 Cooper Thompson, "Education and Masculinity," in Anne O'Brien Carelli (ed.), *Sex Equity in Education: Readings and Strategies* (Springfield, IL: Charles C. Thomas, 1988), p. 47.

18 Ibid., p. 48.

19 Anne O'Brien Carelli, "Introduction," in Anne O'Brien Carelli (ed.), *Sex Equity in Education* (Springfield, IL: Charles C. Thomas, 1988), pp. xiii–xv.

20  See, for example, Melvin L. Kohn, ''Social Class and Parental Values,'' *American Journal of Sociology,* vol. 64, no. 4, January 1959, pp. 337–351; and Meyer L. Rabban, ''Sex Role Identification in Young Children in Two Diverse Social Groups,'' *Genetic Psychological Monographs,* vol. 42, 1950, pp. 81–158.

21  Weitzman, op. cit., p. 119.

22  Joyce A. Ladner, *Tomorrow's Tomorrow: The Black Woman* (Garden City, NY: Doubleday, 1971), pp. 120–176.

23  Ibid.

24  Weitzman, op. cit., p. 120.

25  Kathryn M. Borman, Elaine Mueninghoff, and Shirley Piazza, ''Urban Appalachian Girls and Young Women: Bowing to No One,'' in Lois Weis (ed.), *Class, Race, and Gender in American Education* (Albany, NY: State University of New York Press, 1988), pp. 230–248.

26  Ibid., p. 234.

27  Shakeshaft, ''A Gender at Risk,'' *Phi Delta Kappan,* vol. 67, no. 7, March 1986, p. 499.

28  Carelli, op. cit. (ref. 19), p. xi.

29  Cecelia H. Foxley, ''Sexism: Still an Issue in Education,'' in Anne O'Brien Carelli (ed.), *Sex Equity in Education* (Springfield, IL: Charles C. Thomas), p. 97.

30  Eleanor Maccoby and Carol Jacklin, *The Psychology of Sex Differences* (Stanford, CA: Stanford University Press, 1974).

31  Glen Harvey, ''Finding Reality among the Myths: Why What You Thought about Sex Equity in Education Isn't So,'' *Phi Delta Kappan,* vol. 67, no. 7, March 1986, pp. 509–512.

32  Myra Sadker, David Sadker, and Lynette Long, ''Gender and Educational Equity,'' in James A. Banks and Cherry A. McGee (eds.), *Multicultural Education: Issues and Perspectives* (Boston: Allyn Bacon, 1989), p. 115.

33  Ibid., pp. 114–115.

34  Lynn H. Fox, ''The Effects of Sex Role Socialization on Mathematics Participation and Achievement,'' in Lynn H. Fox, Elizabeth Fennema, and Julia Sherman (eds.), *Women and Mathematics: Research Perspectives for Change,* NIE Papers in Education and Work, no. 8 (Washington, DC: National Institute of Education, 1977).

35  Shakeshaft, op. cit., p. 502.

36  Myra Sadker and David Sadker, *Sex Equity Handbook for Schools* 2d ed. (New York: Longman, 1990).

37  Shakeshaft, op. cit., p. 501.

38  Ibid.

39  Ibid., p. 502.

40  Jere Brophy and Thomas Good, ''The Feminization of American Elementary Schools,'' *Phi Delta Kappan,* vol. 54, no. 8, April 1973.

41  Sadker, Sadker, and Long, op. cit., p. 115.

42  Jacquelynne S. Eccles, ''Gender Roles and Women's Achievement,'' *Educational Researcher,* vol. 15, no. 6, June–July 1986, pp. 15–19.

43  Carol Dweck and N. Neppucci, ''Learned Helplessness and Reinforcement Responsibility in Children,'' *Journal of Personality and Social Psychology,* vol. 25, no. 9, January, pp. 109–116.

44  Peggy Hawley, ''What Women Think Men Think,'' *Journal of Counseling Psychology,* vol. 18, no. 3, May 1971, pp. 193–199.

45  Howe, op. cit., p. 27.

46  Myra Sadker, David Sadker, and Susan Klein, ''Abolishing Misperceptions about Sex Equity in Education,'' *Theory into Practice,* vol. 25, no. 4, Autumn 1986, pp. 219–226.

47  Janice Law Trecker, ''Women in U.S. History High School Textbooks,'' in Janice Pottker and

Andrew Fishel (eds.), *Sex Bias in the Schools: The Research Evidence* (Cranbury, NJ: Associated University Presses, 1977), pp. 146–161.

**48** Sadker, Sadker, and Long, op. cit., p. 109.

**49** Ibid., pp. 107–109.

**50** Gwyneth Britton and Margaret Lumpkin, "Females and Minorities in Basal Readers," *Interracial Books for Children Bulletin,* vol. 14, no. 6, 1983, pp. 4–7.

**51** Lenore Weitzman and Diane Rizzo, *Biased Textbooks* (Washington, DC: The Resource Center on Sex Roles in Education, 1974).

**52** Words and Images, *Dick and Jane as Victims: Sex Stereotyping in Children's Readers* (Princeton, NJ: Women on Words and Images, 1975).

**53** Trecker, op. cit.

**54** Ibid.

**55** Shakeshaft, op. cit., p. 500.

**56** Ibid.

**57** Ibid.

**58** Louise Bach, "Of Women, School Administration, and Discipline," *Phi Delta Kappan,* vol. 57, no. 7, March 1976, pp. 463–466.

**59** Sari Knopp Biklen, "Introduction: Barriers to Equity—Women, Educational Leadership, and Social Change," in Sari Knopp Biklen and Marilyn B. Brannigan (eds.), *Women and Educational Leadership* (Lexington, MA: Heath, 1980), pp. 1–23.

**60** Anne Bennison, Louise Cherry Wilkinson, Elizabeth Fennema, Vandra Masemann, and Penelope Peterson, "Equity or Equality: What Shall It Be?" in Elizabeth Fennema and M. Jane Ayer (eds.), *Women and Education: Equity or Equality?* (Berkeley: McCutchan, 1984), pp. 1–18.

**61** Ibid., p. 6.

**62** Ibid., p. 8.

**63** Ibid., pp. 9–10.

**64** Ibid., p. 14.

**65** Ibid.

**66** Jane Roland Martin, *Reclaiming a Conversation: The Ideal of the Educated Woman* (New Haven: Yale University Press, 1985), p. 6.

**67** Ibid., p. 6.

**68** Carol Gilligan, *In a Different Voice* (Cambridge, MA: Harvard University Press, 1982).

**69** Janet Lever, "Sex Differences in the Games Children Play," *Social Problems,* vol. 23, 1976, p. 482.

**70** M. F. Belenky, B. Clinchy, N. Goldberger, and J. Tarule, *Women's Ways of Knowing: The Development of Self, Voice, and Mind* (New York: Basic Books, 1986).

**71** B. M. Clinchy, M. F. Belenky, N. Goldberger, and J. Tarule, "Connected Education for Women," *Journal of Educational Thought,* vol. 167, no. 3, 1985, p. 44.

**72** Madeleine Grumet, *Bitter Milk: Women and Teaching* (Amherst, MA: University of Massachusetts Press, 1988).

**73** Nancy Hoffman, *Women's "True" Profession: Voices from the History of Teaching* (Old Westbury, NY: The Feminist Press and McGraw-Hill, 1981).

# CHAPTER 10

# EXPANDING EDUCATIONAL BOUNDARIES

*We are living in a new age which itself is defined by the fact that the challenges we face do not respect any conventional boundaries. They don't respect geographical boundaries and they don't respect old definitions.*

Richard F. Celeste

## A QUESTION OF BOUNDARIES

In many ways, this book is about boundaries; boundaries that we impose on ourselves, that we impose on others, and that are imposed on us all by factors often beyond our direct control. It is a book about physical boundaries, about boundaries of language, about boundaries of gender, race, ethnicity, and religion. It is about political boundaries and economic boundaries and social boundaries of many kinds. More important, it is also a book about crossing boundaries, and about getting rid of some of the ones that get in our way.

In today's world, old boundaries are fading away and new ones are emerging. In Germany, the Berlin Wall has disappeared; in eastern Europe and the Soviet Union, ethnic boundaries are reappearing. In the Middle East, political and religious boundaries shift and harden. Around the globe, the antagonism of political ideology that pitted east against west has given way to antagonisms based on economics as the countries in the southern hemisphere struggle to survive in the face of an inequitable distribution of resources weighted toward those in the northern hemisphere.

Now, as we have said, social boundaries do not arise arbitrarily. They help us understand the world we live in; they offer the comfort of familiarity; they allow us to proceed through our days without having to identify and reidentify everything and everybody over and over again. Social boundaries help to give meaning to our lives. They are also often responsible for sustaining hatreds, for enabling human beings to turn away from human suffering, and for the occurrence of war.

But today, old boundaries and old definitions are becoming increasingly dysfunctional. It is necessary, in the face of new circumstances, to rethink some of our old ideas and to find ways to cross the boundaries that separate people. We may not like it; indeed, many of us today are reacting to change by pulling back, by hardening our resolve to "keep things as they were." It is quite likely that we will see much more of this kind of response in the years ahead, but in the end, change will have its effect. Whether that effect is positive or negative is up to us. And teachers may play a very important part in the process, because teachers have the power to engender new ideas and new ways of doing things in the children they teach.

In this chapter, a number of ideas that we believe are helpful in leading us to remove, change, or bridge old definitions or theories that may stand in our way as we attempt to bring ourselves into the next century will be discussed. In particular, we will be talking about rethinking three major areas of social life: culture, community, and education. Our focus is a relational one: that is, we will be looking not only at the relations between these three areas, but also at the relations that comprise them.

## NEW BOUNDARIES AND NEW DEFINITIONS: THE CONCEPTS OF CULTURE AND COMMUNITY

The question of the relation of culture to education—particularly the role that one's cultural knowledge, habits, values, and attitudes play in the way one learns and the way one teaches in American schools is a question that has occupied educational thinkers in the United States almost from the beginning. So far, we have attempted to describe and explain some of the history associated with that question, as well as to offer some alternative ways of looking at aspects of culture as it influences human social behavior, especially in schooling. In some ways, however, this approach is like trying to solve a jigsaw puzzle with only individual pieces in hand; it is difficult to put the puzzle together without some indication of what the whole picture might look like when we get through. In this case, the "whole picture" is an idea of what "American culture" really is.

### The Monoculturist View

There are, of course, a number of ideas about what the "final" picture of the nation is or should be. We may call these ideas *images,* or *models,* of American culture. What we actually "see" when we look at any kind of social behavior depends a great deal upon what we think we are going to see. Thus, for example, the American culture that many people see is one with a single central set of characteristic knowledge, habits, values, and attitudes. For people who view American culture this way—let's call them *monoculturists*—those characteristics are the following: "real" Americans are white and they are adult; they are middle-class (or trying very hard to be); they go to church (often Protestant, but sometimes Catholic as well although that is a bit suspicious); they are married (or aim to be) and they live in single-family houses (which they own, or are trying to); they work hard and stand on "their own two feet"; they wash themselves a good deal, and generally try to smell "good"; they are patriotic and honor the flag; they are heterosexual; they are often charitable, only expecting a certain amount of gratitude and a serious effort to "shape up" from those who are the objects of their charity; they eat well; they are not interested in "highfalutin" ideas found in books by overly educated people; they believe in "good old-fashioned common sense"; they see that their children behave themselves.

Now, of course, this is a composite picture. Not all "real" Americans have every single characteristic. But in order to "qualify," they must have many of them. And divergence from some of them (for example, heterosexuality) almost automatically disqualifies a person even if that is the only way in which he or she differs. For people who see American culture this way, those who do not share these characteristics are clearly not "real" Americans, whether they happen to have been born here or not. They somehow do not really "belong" in the picture as they are. Moreover, their difference makes them dangerous to the maintenance of America as it is "supposed" to be. It is therefore a primary role of schooling to make the children of the culturally different into "American" children—that is, to teach these children those ways of thinking, behaving, and valuing that will allow them to fit harmoniously into the "real American" culture. Children of "real Americans," of course, do not need such help because they already match the model.

As we have seen, American schools do in fact perform this role: they use various methods to try to make all students fit the "real American" image.

## The Multiculturist View

There are other people who see American culture in a very different way. For these people—let's call them *multiculturists*—"American culture" is a mosaic, or a "tossed salad," made up of many groups with different characteristics. For the multiculturists, the "real American" of the monoculturists is only one of many kinds of American, although one who often has considerably more power than others. For people who see American culture this way, each group is valuable in and of itself and all contribute to the strength and dignity of the society we call America. Therefore they believe that it is the role of schooling to encourage, preserve, and protect differences.

For the multiculturist, the "real American" is one who has benefited from association with two (or more) cultural groups, perhaps speaks more than one language, and appreciates the value of his or her own group and remains loyal to it in both adversity and success. If one is a member of a minority group that is also oppressed (not all minorities are oppressed; for example, the English in this country are a minority group, but not oppressed because of it), the multiculturist would expect that person to do whatever possible to help other members of that group.

Often, especially in recent years, the educational practices recommended by multiculturists include emphasizing curriculum content for special groups of children that educate them about the history, literature, music, and ideas of their culture of origin. Thus, for example, African history may be taught to African-American children, Hispanic music to Chicano children, Native American stories to the Sioux in the Dakotas. The issue of *parity*—or equality with the dominant culture group—is also often of central concern. Thus, a middle-class black or an English-speaking Mexican-American who has achieved economic parity with the middle class and learned to speak fluent Standard English, has presumably lost some of his or her "ethnic" status and no longer needs special educational programs.

Old boundaries of cultural identity and old definitions of the term *culture* inform the thought of both monoculturists and multiculturists. In each case, *culture* is viewed as a unitary phenomenon, one that can be described by a single set of characteristics that apply to all members of a cultural group and not to members of others. This perception of culture is similar to a notion of culture first proposed by the anthropologist E. B. Tylor in 1871: "Culture, or civilization, taken in its wide ethnographic sense, is that complex whole which includes knowledge, belief, art, morals, law, custom, and any other capabilities and habits acquired by man as a member of society."[1]

Tylor's notion of culture has had a remarkably strong influence on our thinking about culture, whether or not we are familiar with his work. Moreover, as we pursue a new definition of culture, it is interesting to us in at least two ways. First, it emphasizes that culture is a "whole" phenomenon; it is a *single set* of identifiable characteristics. People who belong to a cultural group have particular knowledge, beliefs, art, morals, laws, and customs associated with *that* group. Second, cultural knowledge is *learned* by an individual as a member of a social group.

We would argue here that while the second statement is accurate—individuals do acquire cultural knowledge as members of groups—the first part of Tylor's definition is no longer accurate, particularly for citizens of modern nation-states. His definition was based upon observations of people—often preliterate people—living in social groups that had a number of characteristics in common. Among them were (1) relatively small territorial boundaries, (2) continuous face-to-face interaction, (3) shared symbol systems, and (4) a "we-feeling" sense of community. In such circumstances, knowledge, and beliefs, as well as more material constructions, such as clothes, houses, food, objects of art, which we refer to as *cultural* were developed together by the people in that place, were passed down from generation to generation, and came to be associated with them by themselves and by others.

### The Distinction Between Cultural and Political Communities

The problem with this definition of culture with respect to both modern nation-states and to what sociologists call *subcultures* within them is that it does not recognize the complexity of cultural influences that can affect either. The definition sets up *cognitive boundaries* that hinder our investigation of the ways in which cultural elements are *at work* in the lives of individual people.

One way to get at this problem is to think about Tylor's definition of culture in terms of the concept of community. Now, the word *community* also has a number of meanings. As Leichter has pointed out, it can mean a physical place with geographical boundaries (the community I live in), a group of people or institutions who carry out a particular function (the medical, business, or military community), "those who communicate directly on a face-to-face basis" (the workplace community) or "those who share information and ideas across geographical space" (the scientific community), and "those who have a sense of belonging or a sense of common heritage" (an ethnic or religious community).[2] In general, however, *community* usually means a geographical (and often political) entity or a sense of "we-feeling," of belonging to and identifying with a particular group of people. Sometimes, although it is increasingly rare, these two meanings are joined: one feels a part of, identifies with, and receives comfort from living in a particular geographical community.

For most of the history of the United States, small American towns matched Tylor's definition of cultures. What can be called *cultural communities* developed in these towns as they had done in Europe. The United States was a rural nation. Travel was an arduous undertaking; communication between localities was difficult and took a long time. Many, many people were born, grew up, and died in the same town—sometimes in the same house—and never traveled more than twenty miles in any direction. Very different cultural communities—for example, Ipswich, Massachusetts, with its small white clapboard houses, its seafaring economy, and its Puritan heritage, and Williamsburg, Virginia, with large manor houses, a plantation economy, and an aristocratic heritage—developed relatively unhampered by national concerns. Although people of different races and social classes lived in these towns, as Stanley has noted, "The members of the community tended to share not only common information and common knowledge, but a common point of view hammered out on the anvil of debate and supported by local public opinion."[3]

In contrast, the *political community* that was the United States was relatively far removed from local concerns and interests. It may be helpful here to stop for a moment and think about the difference between a political and a cultural community. Perhaps the simplest way to differentiate the two is to say that a cultural community is based on a shared history, on shared daily experiences and—perhaps more important—shared meaning emerging from those experiences, whereas a political community is based on an agreement to coexist under law. The United States can be seen as a political community that rests on the Constitution. As you know, the Constitution was framed by people who differed in many respects; it is a *political* document stating a set of rules based on a common interest in protecting their very different attitudes and values. As Sarason suggests, the members of the Constitutional Convention achieved their ends,

> not by assuming that shared values were necessary and sufficient for success, but by contriving and inventing ways which might protect these values against man's tendencies to act rashly, selfishly, and corruptly; not by deluding themselves that the end product of their labors was adequate for all time but by specifically providing for change and orderly change which in principle could undo all they had done.[4]

In creating the Constitution, they created an overarching *political community—a framework in which all Americans are more or less equal before the law.* While the ideals of democracy and freedom are shared by most Americans, within that framework Americans experience life worlds that can be fantastically different. Indeed, the very meaning of *freedom* can vary for American citizens. For our purposes, these life worlds—in which knowledge, experience and meaning are shared—constitute a cultural community that may be based on historical and contemporary experiences, shared stories, customs, art, habits of thought, and symbolic meanings transferred from generation to generation through face-to-face interaction. And we are back to Tylor's definition of culture but situated in a local community or even a neighborhood setting.

In a period when time and distance separated cultural communities in the United States, conflict between these cultural communities and between any local cultural community and the national political community developed slowly. Indeed, it took almost two hundred years for conflict over slavery to explode in the horror of the Civil War. After about 1840, however, the character of the population of the United States underwent increasingly rapid change. Immigration added millions of people from new racial, ethnic, and religious groups to the population; industrialization, urbanization, and the development of technology threw them together in competitive situations; the United States emerged as a world power; and relatively easy means of communication and travel became available. Under these circumstances, two things happened: conflict became more acute, and the processes of cultural diffusion were enhanced. Not only were diverse groups competing with one another for economic security, but individuals were exposed to ideas, values, habits, and knowledge different from those of their own cultural community.

Increasing diversity was perceived as a threat to national stability at a time when the country needed a strong identity. The development of loyalty to the political community became a primary role of the school; in the process, the distinction between political and cultural communities was repressed. ''American culture'' was defined solely in terms of the dominant cultural community: the Anglo, Protestant, middle-class cultural community. Schooling was programmed *as if* a single cultural community existed within the political community, *as if* a single symbol system were shared by all citizens, and *as if* those who for some reason did not share it were deficient or "culturally deprived."

As the society changed, the unity of the local geographical community often broke down. If, in an earlier America, the basic social unit molding attitudes and values and providing support for the individual was the small town, today improved communications, transportation, industrialization, specialization, and urbanization have fundamentally altered the foundations of social organization. Industrial growth and corporate specialization have created interest groups that cross national as well as local boundaries. Urbanization may result in social isolation even in the midst of a multitude of social groups and voluntary organizations. Advanced communication brings instant awareness of events and attitudes that originate far from the listener while simultaneously presenting a cultural message all its own. Independence of the individual in this situation may be a physical fact, but it is not a psychological one. As Stanley stated, "minds and characters are increasingly shaped by attitudes and thinking peculiar to particular interests rather than by those common to the entire community."[5]

Each interest group has developed some sort of social philosophy—its own conception of what is good for the commonwealth. Those concepts influence individual and family perceptions of reality, which are acquired by each of us in intimate face-to-face interaction. Moreover, as we move outside the family circle to the neighborhood, the school, the religious institution, and the variety of voluntary associations available to us, and as we learn the meaning of nationhood interpreted both by the school and by our diverse associations, we each develop a somewhat unique pattern of cultural capabilities and habits. Feinberg recognized this social reality when he said:

> Breaking it down into subsystems, we may find that no two Americans have precisely the same culture. If we define culture as a system of symbols and meanings, we probably will find that every individual carries thousands of cultural units around with him all the time.[6]

In the United States, as in many countries around the world, the truth is that we are all in some sense multicultural. At the same time, the picture is further complicated by the fact that what we might call the disaggregation of American culture (some refer to this phenomenon as *balkanization*) has not proceeded uniformly across the nation. What this means is that some, but not all, individuals have access to a wide variety of cultural contexts. In complex nation-states like the United States, characterized by multiple ethnic populations, a highly sophisticated communications network, and an intricately stratified social structure, access to significantly different cultural knowledge may be as close as the next block or as far as Wall Street is from an Appalachian hollow. The cultural community that was the small town continues to exist: it can be rather dramatically observed in Amish communities in Pennsylvania and other midwestern states, or in Mexican towns in Texas and other southwestern states, or in all white suburbs and towns across the country. It can also occur in ethnic enclaves in large cities—for example, in Chinatown in New York and San Francisco, in "little Italys," or Slavic "villages,"— or in black neighborhoods in cities, suburbs, and towns everywhere. The experiences that individuals share, the experiences from which they learn who they are, may develop within these cultural communities, and the people who live in them may, in fact, be monocultural.

Access to a limited variety of cultural contexts may be as problematic as access to many such contexts and may explain, in part, the recent reemergence of stereotypes that so plague racial, ethnic, and religious minorities. Limits on access may be imposed in a variety of ways, by others, or by oneself. Many of us, for example, limit our contact with disabled individuals as a matter of choice. We are usually unsure how to act, and what to say.

When limits are externally imposed, however—as when we accept uncritically the views of people around us or when we simply lack contact with people in other groups—these limits may become so rigidly defined that stereotypic myths emerge. Some of our most enduring stereotypes—the mountain man, the cowboy, the dancing minstrel, the southern belle—emerged from a time in our history when access to distant regions of the country was difficult. As rapid communications and easy travel have blurred the lines of regional culture, other stereotypes have emerged. These stereotypes tend to represent not regional characters but economic and political ones: the blue-collar worker, the feminist, the ghetto black, the Yuppie. One reason for this is that, while geographical boundaries in modern societies have become more permeable, economic strata have solidified.

For this reason, it is cruel to assume that a vast potpourri of cultural learning is available to anyone in America with some gumption and an eye for the future. A potential Horatio Alger, born black in Bedford-Stuyvesant in 1973, may even now be looking in vain for that job that is the "first rung up the ladder." Economic stratification may now limit, in the same way geography used to limit, one's access to diverse cultural learning. Economic stratification works in both directions, too. That is, those in the "higher" social classes often have little access to the poor. It is often difficult, for example, for members of mainstream, middle-class church congregations to identify people in need of the kind of assistance that many of them see as their ministry. They often have to go to agencies for names and addresses!

At the same time, for some individuals access to significantly different cultural contexts is not only possible, it is awesome in its profusion and complex in its results. The contributions of middle-class American youth to the civil rights movement and to ending the war in Vietnam exemplifies the kind of profound change that is possible when access to plural worlds is available.

We are led to conclude that the social, personal, and educational implications of congruence or dissonance in one's cultural experience must become a matter of intense study.[7] If we say that all Americans are multicultural, we are speaking, at least in part, potentially. Some of us are, indeed, predominantly monocultural. Yet because we live in a society where the potential for participating in multiple life worlds is extensive and becoming more so, there is a need to seriously investigate the cultural patterns of our lives.

We need to examine the degree to which cultural knowledge, attitudes, and values are *at work* in our experience. Moreover, we must not only investigate the *nature* of our cultural experiences as teachers and students but we must also begin to look at the ways in which various cultural learnings *mediate* the development of a personal cultural milieu. Being female, for example, is only one characteristic: what does it mean to be a black female? An old female? A black, old, handicapped female? Think of the possible combinations in *your* life, and in the lives of people you know. It can be a fascinating exercise.

We have argued that individuals in the United States today may or may not have access to a number of cultural options. Educational, familial, occupational, institutional, and leisure worlds all provide contexts in which individuals grow and develop. In what particularity do yours exist? We would like to suggest that the *experience* of American pluralism is the experience of participating in a network of social relationships through which the individual develops cultural knowledge, skills, attitudes, and values. The universality of such distinctions as work-leisure, family-peer group, public-private selves, and interpersonal-mass communications suggests that we are tacitly, if not consciously, aware of the "plurality of life worlds in which the individual typically lives in modern society."[8]

## The Communities of Education

The focus of our attempt to make new definitions of culture and community has shifted from a consideration of the characteristics people acquire by virtue of their membership in groups, to a consideration of the *relationships* between various cultural learnings that they have so acquired. This shift rests on a relational view of society, one perhaps best stated by John Dewey when he wrote that "society *is* individuals-in-their-relations. An individual apart from social relations is a myth—or a monstrosity."[9] A similar view has been put forth by the anthropologist Clifford Geertz, when he writes that "man unmodified by the customs of particular places . . . could not in the very nature of things exist."[10]

The multifaceted nature of modern social life has been thoughtfully examined by J. W. Getzels, who notes that today both geographical and symbolic communities influence the practice of and participation in educational activity. He writes:

> Of whatever kind, communities are at once settings for educational institutions [schools] and instruments of education in their own right. On the one hand, they determine the structure and curriculum of their schools. On the other, they provide the cognitive and affective experiences on which their inhabitants grow up. To be reared in Hoboken is not the same *educationally* as to be reared in Malibu Beach, even if the schools in the two places were the same. Schools are only one of the many contexts in which the child is educated.[11]

Some of the differences between Hoboken and Malibu Beach are due to differences in the nature of the symbolic communities present in them, communities that expose children to different cognitive and affective norms and values and that "also make available or emphasize divergent cognitive experiences and resources."[12] On these grounds, Getzels argues that "a simplistic notion of the community as a single-scaled autonomous phenomenon is not tenable."[13] Traditional formulations and studies of the community and education

> typically visualized the school and the child as embedded in a community conceived as a culture with a certain ethos defined by its constituent values. The quality of the school's roles and the quality of the children's personalities were related to the ethos of the community, and the specific role expectations and pupil dispositions to its values.[14]

In other words, according to the standard definition of *community,* the nature of the community determines in large measure the nature of the learning individuals who live in it acquire. But the modern community is not often a single entity. Indeed, contemporary communities—particularly urban communities—are much more often composed of a variety of neighborhoods which may be extremely different, to the extent that simply crossing the street takes one into another world. To say that the "children of Hoboken" have all acquired the same learnings by virtue of living in Hoboken is not sensible: it all depends on where in Hoboken one lives and how many other places in Hoboken (or elsewhere) one may visit.

Ronald Lippett takes a different approach. Defining *community* very broadly, he then describes a set of communities that serve as socialization agents.[15] Think about how many you have participated in, and what you learned.

**1** *Formal education agencies, public and private:* Where did you go to school? Was it a large school or a small one? What difference did that make? Was the school public or private? If it was private, was it affiliated with a church? What did you learn there that may have been different than the child next door who went to public school?

**2** *Religious organizations:* We have already mentioned the strangeness you might have felt upon going to church, synagogue, or mosque with a friend if it were very, or even a little, different from your own, or if you had never been to any organized religious activity before. All religious organizations have education programs of some kind that stress certain attitudes and values, and they teach, as well, a particular kind of behavior in the conduct of the service.

**3** *Leisure time (nonschool) child and youth service agencies:* Usually emphasizing recreational activities, leisure organizations play an important role in socializing children, often to citizenship roles and other forms of "character" education. But think of the variety of voluntary leisure activity groups to which a person can belong: the Scouts, an athletic club, a motorcycle gang, a street gang, a neighborhood house basketball team, Little League baseball, a tap-dancing class, a computer club. Are there differences in the learnings that are associated with these activities apart from the stated purpose of the organization? What kind of differences? What might a child learn in each of them?

**4** *Legal enforcement and protection agencies:* These might include police juvenile bureaus, juvenile courts, traffic safety agents, and truant officers. Perhaps you have been to juvenile court. Were you a defendant or a visitor on a field trip? Does it make a difference?

**5** *Therapeutic, rehabilitative, and resocialization services:* A variety of professionals in what are sometimes called the "helping professions"—doctors, nurses, social workers, therapists, and counselors—also have responsibilities educating the young. Have you had considerable experience in hospitals? Is there a particular "culture of the hospital"? What is it? What did you learn there?

**6** *Employers and work supervisors of the young:* Especially for teenagers, employers often significantly influence what is learned about the economic system and the job market, and one's future employment prospects. Where a young person works may often make a difference in what they think about the economic system. Have you worked? Where? What did you learn there? Do you have friends or acquaintances who worked in a very different kind of place? What difference did it make?

**7** *Political socializers:* While the school is often regarded as the primary political socializer of the young, it is the case that in the United States very little responsibility for that function is given to politicians or governmental units. Nevertheless, it is possible that you participated in a government-official-for-a-day activity, or that your parents are politically active. Do you belong to the same political party as your parents? Why?

**8** *Parents:* Clearly, parents are influential teachers of their children; some believe that they are by far the most influential. We have already discussed education in the family at length. However, it might be well to think about exactly what kind of things you have learned from your parents. You have also probably learned some significant things from parents of your friends. Can you think of anything?

**9** *Older and like-age peers:* Friends are powerful socializing agents, perhaps more so than parents at certain ages. What have you learned from *your* friends?

**10** *The mass media:* The potential of the mass media—television, the recording industry, radio, and the print media—to teach the young is enormous and growing. Some believe that it rivals parents and schools as an educating agency. The sheer amount of time you spend watching television or listening to tapes and CDs (when you are not doing anything else), as well as *what* you watch or listen to, may be significant in forming your attitudes and values. What television programs do you watch regularly? What music do you listen to? Many students claim that the content of lyrics or television programs has no impact on them. Do you believe that too? Why? Suppose two young people of the same sex (male) and the same age (16) are stranded in a small airport by a snowstorm. They have no one to talk with except each other and must wait an undetermined amount of time before their plane can take off. One of these young men lives in a small town, and has spent most of his free time at home during the past three years watching television (MTV, World Championship Wrestling, broadcasts of sports events) or listening to heavy metal groups. The other, who lives on a farm, has spent most of his time helping his parents work the farm, raising a calf through the 4-H Club in his area, and volunteering in the local old age home. He also watches television and has a stereo (we don't want this to be *too* removed from reality!).[16] What do you think these two young men will talk about during the long, snowy hours?

The picture of culture and the community that emerges from these considerations is clearly a complex one, perhaps more complex than we have imagined. All human beings are creatures who create meaning and order from the diverse material and ideational worlds in which they find themselves. Cultural knowledge does not exist apart from the meanings it has for real people living out their lives in real social and geographical settings. The United States today is not merely a complex whole, or even a set of complex wholes. It is, rather, a myriad of cultural patterns and human possibilities.

## A NEW UNDERSTANDING OF EDUCATION: THE CONCEPT OF SOCIAL NETWORK

How, then, are we to understand the role of culture and community in the educational process? And how are we to relate the larger processes of socialization, acculturation, and enculturation to education in schools? Many caring and concerned educators, aware of the changing boundaries of social life and the new demographic realities of the United States and of its new place in a global economy, have focused on a variety of forms of multicultural education as a means both to address important issues of cultural difference among students and to assist them in gaining access to more of the society's resources.

However, multiculturists too have often assumed old boundaries and old definitions of culture and community. In a critical review of multicultural objectives, for example, Tice observed that such education

> has, at least implicitly, regarded individuals as if they came to school in solid cultural blocks, such as "plain old America," "the blacks," "Puerto Ricans," and "welfare people." The belief was that individuals should leave the way they came, with perhaps an added understanding of "other points of view."[17]

Multiculturists' efforts to create specialized or altered ethnic-based curricula may have been less than effective, in part because they also categorize students according to single rather than multiple cultural identities. The African-American, or Vietnamese-American or Hispanic-American child—no matter what her or his background—is not *precisely* the same child, culturally, as the Nigerian child, or the Vietnamese child, or the Puerto Rican child. Ethnicity has a different meaning when it is hyphenated. Moreover, these programs most often have been aimed only at minority students, not at the entire student population. Criticizing such an approach, Robert J. Cottrol writes that:

> Multicultural education should not simply be a program designed for minority students. There is a temptation to believe that multicultural education can somehow provide a quick fix for the ills that plague inner-city education. If only we teach inner-city students about the African Kingdom of Mali in the Middle Ages instead of dwelling on Medieval England, if we present less Abraham Lincoln and more Frederick Douglass, if we offer more of the writings of Malcolm X and less discussion of the Eisenhower administration, then students who previously had been turned off by school will suddenly become scholars, enthusiastic and interested in their school work.[18]

The problem with the ethnic-based approach is that it is too simplistic to apply to the lives of modern American children. While it is *of course* a good idea to broaden curriculum content—to make curricula more representative of the story of the world's families—it is insufficient. As Cottrol notes:

> The students most at risk—those from decaying inner city neighborhoods, those from broken families, those who join gangs in fear of their lives, those who are the heirs of a culture of despair that has developed in all too many of our ghettoes in the last generation—will not be inspired nor have their lives radically changed by the addition of a multicultural dimension to their educations, however much we might hope so.[19]

## The Complexity of Actual Social Life

What is required, rather, is a more sophisticated understanding of the ways in which *cultural elements* of racial, ethnic, religious, economic, gender, and health identity work together in the life of a child, and in the life of the child's teacher as well, and of the ways in which these elements mediate one another and are mediated by the culture of the school. And if we are to understand the multiple influences of culture, community, and education on each other in a more sophisticated way, we need a conceptual framework in which the various strands of our cultural lives can be related to one another and to schooling. For example, as educators interested in developing effective ways of dealing with human diversity in the classroom, we must have concepts that will allow—even encourage—us to think about membership in multiple cultural milieux. No one is *just* an African-American, or *just* a Korean, or *just* female, or *just* poor. We are, all of us, the product of associations in many social milieux and we cross social boundaries all the time. What, if any, are the connections between our various identities, and how do we think about utilizing those connections and creating new ones?

Our framework must enable us to cross old categorical boundaries such as race, ethnicity, class, gender, religion, health, and disability. In addition, we need to be able to cross *disciplinary boundaries* to find the concepts and ideas that may help us. This latter will be even more crucial for us because education as a field of study depends to a large extent on other disciplines—particularly psychology and sociology, but also history, economics, political science, anthropology, and literature—for its informing knowledge.

Psychology, which focuses on the individual more or less outside the context of the social group or groups, has had a marked influence on our thinking. Sarason, for example, notes that educational theory has acquired much of its character from psychology, educational psychology, child development, and certain elements of psychiatry. He argues that, while valuable knowledge has been gained by this focus,

> what has escaped notice . . . is that the theories generated by these studies have been, for all practical purposes, asocial. That is to say it is as though society does not exist for the psychologist. Society is a vague, amorphous background that can be disregarded in one's efforts to fathom laws of behavior.[20]

Conversely, sociology, also an important resource for educational theorists, focuses on group characteristics, and ignores individual differences. Craven and Wellman describe the process of the sociologist with respect to urban social life in terms that may be familiar to you:

> The rich, and often bewildering, complexity of social life in the city is such that the sociologist who would seek to understand it has always had to adopt some strategy . . . by which to guide his inquiry. More often than not, he has approached this problem by way of a simple "sorting" strategy. He has grouped individuals and institutions into various pigeonholes, representing their individual social or organizational characteristics, so that people might be sorted into slots such as "middle class"; institutions might be classified as "social agencies"; localities might be tagged as "suburbia." Once the units have been sorted into categories according to their independent characteristics the sociologist classically proceeds to make sense of the classification scheme through the comparison of inhabitants of different slots.[21]

The problem here is that *individual* members of sociological categories do not always have all the characteristics that are attributed to the *group*. Not all African-Americans speak Black English at home; some poor people are well read because they spend a lot of time at the library; not all handicapped individuals require special education; not all females are soft-spoken, passive, and nurturing. In part, these descriptions refer to stereotypes of these groups. The problem with getting rid of stereotypes, of course, is that they ordinarily contain a kernel of fact. Many African-Americans—especially city dwellers—do speak Black English; many poor people are not good readers; many handicapped individuals do require special education; and many women—especially white women—are soft-spoken, passive, and nurturing. The "facts" that we think we know about a particular group, then, are often the result of the attribution of traits found to be more or less true of the *group*. Some people have argued that such an emphasis on group characteristics also diminishes and distorts the individual's role as a choicemaker.[22] Clearly, if we wish to emphasize the availability of cultural options for teachers and students, we must be able to take choice into consideration.

## Special Problems of Educators

Unlike psychologists, sociologists, anthropologists, and other academicians, educators must always deal with the concrete presence of students in classrooms. They thus have the special problem of putting information garnered from the social sciences into a real, dynamic human context. As Harold Dunkle has observed:

> Education . . . both as a field of theoretical study and as an area of practical activity, must lie close to the concrete. . . . To be sure, the sciences which investigate particular facets of the student's existence do tell the educator many facts about the student, but each seems to be a somewhat partial truth as far as the educator's task is concerned. [The teacher] feels the need for some means to put Humpty Dumpty together again in order to treat the student as the concrete individual which [she or] he is.[23]

It is always necessary to filter through the concepts that come to us from other disciplines through the lens of educational practice. We are not psychologists or sociologists or anthropologists—or mathematicians, historians, grammarians, or scientists. We are educators, and that requires a special kind of thinking.

John Dewey offers perhaps the most useful comments to those whose business it is to use ideas from the social sciences and humanities:

> There is not subject-matter intrinsically marked off, earmarked so to say, as the content of [education]. Any methods and any facts and principles from any subject whatsoever that enable the problems of administration and instruction to be dealt with in a bettered way are pertinent.[24]

These methods and facts do *not,* however, provide rules of practice for educators. Rather, they give us *ideas* which, with reflection, may alter our vision or our attitudes. It is up to us, then, to create rules of professional practice for our classrooms.

Our criteria for developing new ways of looking at human diversity should emerge not only from academic knowledge but also from a consideration of the characteristics of educational practice. Four such criteria that seem critical to us are:

**1** Whatever ideas are used as resources must be *concrete* in their application; that is, they must be centered on the individual and must relate to actual people or instances.

**2** Conceptual resources must be able to deal with *complexity.* Not only the individuals who participate in the teaching-learning process, but the process itself is characterized by multiple elements.

**3** Concepts and models must be able to take *inconsistency and ambiguity* into account. One of the ways individuals succeed in their attempts to integrate diverse influences is by learning to encompass inconsistencies and to tolerate ambiguity. If we are honest, we must acknowledge that it is often the unexamined inconsistencies in individuals and situations that either enhance the teaching-learning process or prevent our making the connections on which effective education depends.

**4** Finally, our conceptual resources must be able to accommodate *change.* If there is one thing we seem to be agreed on it is that education is a developmental process, and all educational theory should have a dynamic character as well.[25]

Clearly, unless the nature of the role of American pluralism in education is understood with attention to particularly *educational* criteria, it is unlikely that we will be able to alter our practice very much.[26]

## Education as a Network of Relations

Mitchell has noted that "the apparent complexity of social phenomena frequently bespeaks a lack of theoretical concepts available for their analysis."[27] In other words, we have few notions that let us think and talk about complex issues. This is, in part, because one purpose of the social sciences is *simplification*: they attempt to abstract from real life ideas that provide insights and help to explain certain aspects of the phenomenon in question, but do not attempt to describe the whole of whatever they are looking at.

In contrast, the educational enterprise can be viewed, in all its complexity, as a *network of relationships*—a web of educational goals and settings that begins to surround the baby in the cradle and extends, over time, to include all those educative influences, including the school, that impinge on the child's life and within which the child exercises choice.

Emerging concurrently in a number of disciplines in the period since World War II, concepts rooted in the idea of social network have developed in response to a number of new problems in the study of complex phenomena.[28] As seems to be the case with all large ideas, the concept of social network has been used in a variety of ways. However, all who use it agree that a *social network* is a distinct type of social unit that differs significantly from any other: for example, a group or system. Sarason outlines some of these differences this way:

> Every unit in a network does not interact with every other unit in a network. . . . Both group and system conceptualizations, in contrast, specify that the component units have interdependent roles related to the functioning of the group as a whole. . . .
>
> [A] network is not surrounded by a clear boundary. Rather a network extends far out in numerous directions into the environment through indirect ties and can never be fully described and a boundary drawn. . . . Groups and systems, on the other hand, are both defined in part through specifications of their boundaries. . . .
>
> The only characteristic that all members of a network have in common is their relationship (direct and indirect) to the ego [or person who is at the center of the network]. The members of a network do not necessarily share common aims, a distinctive subculture, or other traditional social science categorical features generally attributed to both groups and systems. *Whereas groups and system conceptualizations are employed to simplify the complexity of social phenomena by clustering individuals according to distinguishing social characteristics, network conceptualizations allow the description of the actual complexity of societal phenomena.*[29] (Italics added.)

In other words, the idea of a social network enables us to think about an individual (child or adult) in terms of the web of social relationships in which that person lives. It fosters the image of a person who has meaningful and significant relationships with a variety of people, who may or may not be a part of the same ethnic, religious, social

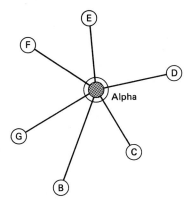

FIGURE 10.1    Social network: First-order star.

class, or racial group. Through those relationships, as through communication wires that link the information systems of a technological age, flow a variety of elements including knowledge, attitudes, values, habits, ways of approaching and understanding the world—in short, learning.

The network idea also enables us to investigate actual relationships between organizations or other social units. Network theorists often use a visual representation consisting of dots and lines to aid in their analyses. J. A. Barnes, who is credited with the original use of this technique in a study of modern social life, describes his model this way: "The image I have is of a set of points, some of which are joined by lines. The points of the image are people, or sometimes groups, and the lines indicate which people interact with one another."[30] Personal social networks are usually "drawn" around a central person; Barnes refers to this person as the *ego* or *Alpha* of the network (see Figure 10.1). Further, network drawings can represent two sorts of phenomena. Figure 10.1 indicates a person (Alpha) and six other people who stand in a particular relationship to him or her—perhaps family, or good friends, or coworkers, or people in the neighborhood. Barnes calls this network a *first-order star,* because it consists of only the relationship

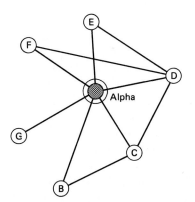

FIGURE 10.2    Social network: First-order zone.

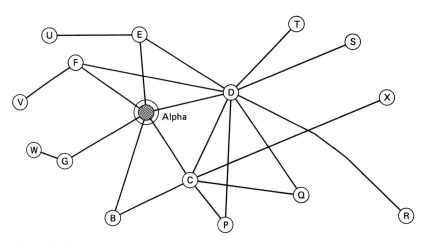

**FIGURE 10.3**    Social network: Second-order star.

between Alpha and a set of other people. You can play with this drawing in a variety of ways. Try putting yourself in the middle as Alpha, and indicate people (perhaps your closest friends) in your social network; there can be more than six, but keep it simple at first.

Not only do individuals carry on continuing relationships with other people, but at least some of the people anyone knows also have relationships with one another. This characteristic of social networks—the degree to which those in one's social network also have relationships with one another—Barnes and others have called *density*. A number of attributes are associated with the density of a network: for example, information travels faster in a dense network, and the influence of network members on the behavior of Alpha is likely to be stronger. Figure 10.2 indicates which of the members of Alpha's network also have relationships with one another. This drawing represents what Barnes calls a *first-order zone*, or a picture of *all* the relationships in Alpha's primary network. Now try indicating on your own network sketch which of the people in your network also know and relate to one another.[31] Do your friends all know one another, or are there some who live in a somewhat different world than others?

Figure 10.3 represents what Barnes calls a *second-order star*, or a picture of Alpha's network, as well as the network of one person who is a member of Alpha's network.[32] Here, we begin to see what a "friend of a friend" looks like in a network (for example, in Figure 10.3, R is a friend of D, who is a friend of Alpha). Figure 10.4 illustrates what Barnes calls a *second-order zone*, or all the relationships in the network of Alpha and one of her or his first-order contacts.[33]

Perhaps you can begin to see how the notion of social network helps one visualize the degree to which one's associations can extend across boundaries. It also helps us to comprehend the complexity of our social relationships: if we kept playing with these drawings, we would soon run out of paper, time, and patience! Of course we already knew that we relate to many people; the point is that the idea of social network helps us actually map our existence in social space.

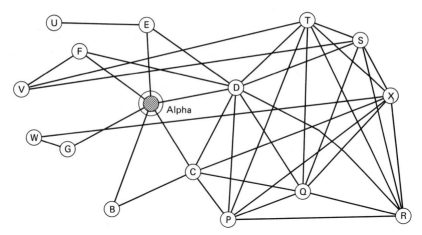

**FIGURE 10.4**    Social network: Second-order zone.

The concept of social network can be used to map relationships in terms of roles and status positions as well as at interpersonal, organizational, community, and societal levels. A person can have more than one kind of relationship with any other person—for example, a child whose father is also his scoutmaster, or a person whose sister-in-law is also her employer—and the network approach offers one way of investigating the ways in which different relations—between people or between any social units—mediate one another.

What the notion of social network allows us to do is to consider the actual linkages that a person has and to trace actual resources available or not available to that person. The focus in a network is "not on the attributes of the people in the network but rather on the characteristics of the linkages in their relationships to one another, as a means of explaining the behavior of the people involved in them."[34]

Consider Grant and Sleeter's example of a male, middle-class Hispanic child in a classroom.[35] Because of his ethnic identification, such a child might be considered a member of an oppressed minority. Indeed, Hispanics, as a group, are oppressed in our society. Because of this identification, expectations of that child might differ from expectations of white, middle-class children, and placement of that child in academic programs might differ from placements of white, middle-class children. However, this particular child is also a member of two groups that oppress others: he is male, and he is middle-class. In order to understand how cultural knowledge is at work in his life, one can use the notion of social network to investigate exactly how and where and probably from whom he has acquired knowledge and values related to gender, ethnicity, and social class, and pretty much exactly what that knowledge and those values are. An investigator will then be able to decide where in his network he (or you, as the teacher) might turn for additional resources or where in his network there are omissions that he or you might need to find. In other words, the idea of social network allows us to begin to understand the ways in which this particular child has integrated or not integrated his communities of education, and we have a good chance of being able to understand the reasons and to be able to predict his behavior.

The term *social network* has been used in other ways, each of which can be useful in rethinking education. It has, for example, been used as a *metaphor* for the organization of social life: "Our associations with other human beings are a *network*." Other terms, such as *web* and *social circle* are commonly used in everyday language and suggest similar ideas. While it is not wise to take metaphors too seriously, these metaphors *suggest the interrelatedness* of our social lives and guides us toward a more accurate perception of our socially significant relationships. Such metaphors also suggest that society itself is interconnected and that we can never be either alone or totally free.

A second use of the term *social network* is to describe an *analytical construct*. We have already seen some results of using the idea of social network to analyze the relationships of our Hispanic youngster. Networks other than personal ones can also be analyzed. For example, we can trace out the network of associations between educative agencies in a community (the family, the school, the library, the museum, the street gang) to see where connections do or do not exist and to understand the congruence or conflict in the content of education offered in these settings.

Social networks, in an analytical sense, have been found to have a number of characteristics in common. First, they *cut across* the geographical and symbolic boundaries that map the social space of daily life. Second, they consist of *person-to-person* relationships, although these need not always be face-to-face relationships. One could, for example, count the author of a book or an essay or a poem as a significant member of one's network, as does this respondent in one of Studs Terkel's interviews: "It's amazing, even in the backwoods of Alabama, there's a classic tucked away in some country school. It's funny, poetry has a way of molding people. There's a buried beauty—"Gray's Elegy" changed my life."[36] How could we explain the ability of a backwoods girl from Alabama to become, say, a professor of literature unless we knew that the eighteenth-century poet Thomas Gray had become a member of her social network?

Third, although relationships in a social network may not be face-to-face and immediate, they are nevertheless *conceived as ties* which may be normative, affective, or instrumental. In the above instance, they must have been all three: the tie between the girl and Thomas Gray set a standard, was infused with wonder, and helped her to transcend her cultural community.

Fourth, as has been already mentioned, the boundaries of networks are *dynamic,* both internally and at their farther reaches. People come and go in social networks: they move into the neighborhood; they appear at school; they move away; they die. Thus, one's network is always changing at least to some extent. At the edges of one's network, where friends-of-friends-of-friends reside, there is always a chance that someone will appear to make that single contribution that redirects a life—the person who can serve as a translator for the small Hmong child who sits quietly and disconsolately in a corner of the classroom; the person who may know that a deaf child has been raised to depend on visual clues; the person who understands that young black girls are taught to be more aggressive than young white girls and that Latoya is not acting up or acting out but simply organizing her world as she has been educated to do.

Finally, a social network *as a whole* may have identifiable characteristics which may be related to the behavior of its members. One's network, for example, may be dense, which means that all or most of its members know one another and communicate often. News travels fast within the network, but it does not leave the network rapidly nor does new information enter easily (in such a network there are few people who have connections to other networks). So the teacher who does not adopt innovations quickly may not be slow, or intransigent; she or he may simply not be in a network where many innovative ideas appear.

A third use of the term *network* describes a social unit that is chiefly seen by its members as a means of obtaining their goals and objectives. While a person's behavior is often seen as an outcome of one's network environment, it can also be seen in part as a result of individual choice-making. Investigators have studied at least three ways in which networks are used instrumentally: help-seeking behavior (using one's network to learn about job opportunities); behavior which seeks to provide help (activity in a network that supports a person who needs assistance, such as people who are ill, or hungry, or homeless); and activity within a network designed to introduce innovation and/or produce change. After the passage of P.L. 94-142, for example, a number of networks of people were created in regions, states, school districts, and schools in order to facilitate the diffusion of information about the law and about practices associated with mainstreaming disabled students. *Networks* of this kind and the process of *networking* may be the most familiar to the general reader, since this use of the term has become ubiquitous in recent years.

Implied in this meaning of *social network* as a tool is a view of society as a set of overlapping personal networks. Direct and indirect ties in these networks may be activated selectively or new linkages may be created for the achievement of individual or group goals. Thus, the concept of social network as a tool both extends the meanings of the analytical concept and transforms the network into a resource for action.

Metaphorical, analytical, and strategic uses of the term *social network* all rely on an initial conception of networks as interpersonal. They consist of relationships between people. At a more inclusive level, the idea of social network has also been used as both a descriptive and prescriptive model of society. We have talked a great deal in this book about changes that have occurred and are occurring in American society and in this society's relations with other societies on the planet. Some of these changes are related to an increasing interconnectedness between people and events facilitated by our increasing ability to travel and communicate. The injunction "Think globally, act locally," means, in part, that our local efforts are linked not only to local outcomes but to global efforts and global outcomes.

The idea of social network as a model of society has been described by a number of authors, sometimes with great optimism about the results of increasing interconnectedness. The philosopher Teilhard de Chardin, for example, writes:

> No one can deny that a network (a world network) of economic and psychic affiliations is being woven at ever increasing speed with which envelops and constantly penetrates more deeply within each of us. With every day that passes it becomes a little more impossible for us to act or think otherwise than collectively.[37]

Others have described the situation in a sadder tone, reflecting a sense of loss. The physicist Robert Oppenheimer, whose thinking mirrors the statement at the beginning of this chapter, writes:

> In an important sense this world of ours is a new world, in which the unity of knowledge, the nature of human communities, the order of society, the order of ideas, the very notions of society and culture have changed and will not return to what they have been in the past.[38]

Caution against sailing too optimistically into the ''new order'' is urged even more eloquently by Sarason, who looks at new kinds of boundaries and new definitions with some hesitancy. He reminds us that from the point of view of the individual, the world is not a village where everyone knows everyone else. Rather, it is a very large, infinitely complex, and extremely diverse planet on which unknown forces appear to influence one's behavior in mysterious ways. Thus, a sense of loss of control may be pervasive:

> World War II and its aftermath took the concept of ''one world'' out of the realm of rhetoric and apparent utopian idealism and placed it in the daily lives of people. We know, as man has never known before, that our individual lives can be altered by people and events, near and far. It is ironic that we have reached this world view, which some individuals over the centuries dreamed about and longed for, with foreboding as well as nostalgia for the past. Unprecedented interrelatedness has been accepted more as a fact than as a value, because the consequences of interrelatedness conflict with traditional modes of organization and their underlying values. There is a part of each of us that knows how inescapably interrelated and interdependent our world has become, but there is another part that feels impotent and puzzled about how to salvage our individualities as we see ourselves caught in a world net the strands of which seem endless, endlessly strong, and ever growing.[39]

The difficulties implicit in reconceptualizing long held ideas of culture and in redirecting schooling toward a more realistic and equitable view of American children are unquestionably great. Clearly, the concept of social network is not a panacea for improving education in an increasingly interconnected and pluralistic society. At issue, however, may be not only the fate of large numbers of children, but also the future of democracy in a pluralistic nation. Moreover, it has been pointed out that:

> The materials for a truly multicultural approach to what should be a multicultural curriculum are all around us; in our names, our families, our towns and cities, our aspirations, and our memories. In their conjunction lies the hope of building a sense of community. The school's opportunities to contribute to that effort are practically limitless.[40]

It seems that we know where we want to get to; we are less certain about how to get there. Any approach to public education that does not take into account the abilities as well as the needs of all children will necessarily evolve into a deficit approach. Optimal learning of *all* children *must* be the goal of all in the educational process.

The concept of social network provides the beginnings of a framework teachers can use to work toward this goal—by acquiring skills to accurately assess the multicultural composition of their classrooms, by identifying the needs and strengths of each child based not only on their natural abilities and personalities but also on the cultural knowledge and resources they bring with them, and by implementing a perspective on personal behavior and instructional activities that can be incorporated into the daily lessons, both formal and informal, of the classroom.

In later chapters, we will be relying both implicitly and explicitly on a network perspective as we describe cognitive and material resources for the kinds of curriculum and pedagogy we believe are needed in the next century. We will begin with a network view of the educative community in which schools exist, and culminate with a discussion of schools that are already changing in ways that make a difference. Now we would like to leave this section as we began, with a view of what is necessary for schooling in a new age:

We are slowly coming to realize that many of the principles and models that have guided such things as our economic development, land use, energy use and distribution are anachronistic. As we come to better understand the irrelevance of these principles and models, we will presumably align our practices with more appropriate theories. The same thing must occur with regard to education. . . .[41]

## ACTIVITIES

**1** Do a survey of 15 people, asking each of them what the term "community" means to them. Compare their answers. Do you notice any themes?

**2** Using Figure 10.1, draw a network with yourself as ego. The people in your network might be family, or friends, or co-workers, or fellow-church members. Still using Figure 10.1 as a model, draw a network with yourself as ego, and include all of the people you can think of with whom you have regular or familial relationships that are at least relatively close. Using Figure 10.2, draw lines between the members of your network who have similar kinds of relationships with one another apart from you. Using Figure 10.3, draw a "Figure 1" network of a close friend or family member. Now, draw lines connecting the people in the two networks who have relationships with one another. What can you say about the density of your social network? Do the people in your social network have many of the same characteristics, or do they have different characteristics?

**3** Using Lippett's typology of 10 socialization communities, think about your own experiences (or lack of experiences) in each. Given those in which you have had some experience, think about what you have learned by participating in that "community." Make a list of these learnings and compare it with a list from someone in your class. What similarities or differences do you find?

## REFERENCES

**1** E. B. Tylor, *Primitive Culture* (New York: Harper Torch Books, 1958), p. 1.

**2** Hope Jensen Leichter, "Families and Communities as Educators: Some Concepts of Relationship," in Hope Jensen Leichter (ed.), *Families and Communities as Educators* (New York: Teachers College Press, 1979), p. 15.

**3** William O. Stanley, *Education and Social Integration* (New York: Bureau of Publications, Teachers College, Columbia University, 1953), p. 8.

**4** Seymour B. Sarason, *The Creation of Settings and Future Societies* (San Francisco: Jossey-Bass, 1978), p. 17.

**5** Stanley, op. cit., p. 10.

**6** Richard Feinberg, "Schneider's Symbolic Culture Theory: An Appraisal," *Current Anthropology,* vol. 20, no. 3, September 1979, p. 547.

**7** We are indebted to our colleague, Normand R. Bernier, Professor of Cultural Foundations of Education at Kent State University, for the idea that it is an important function of schooling to examine the variations among life worlds of teachers and students. See Normand R. Bernier, "Beyond Instructional Context Identification," in Judith L. Green and Cynthia Wallat (eds.), *Ethnography and Language* (Norwood, NJ: Ablex, 1981), pp. 291–302. A related concept of his, the role of the school in *negotiating* life worlds, will be discussed in a later section.

**8** Peter Berger, Brigitte Berger, and Hansfried Kellner, *The Homeless Mind: Modernization and Consciousness* (New York: Random House, 1973), p. 12.

**9** John Dewey and John C. Childs, "The Underlying Philosophy of Education," in William N. Kilpatrick (ed.), *The Educational Frontier* (New York: Appleton-Century, 1933), p. 291.

**10**  Clifford Geertz, *The Interpretation of Culture* (New York: Basic Books, 1973), p. 35.

**11**  J. W. Getzels, "The Communities of Education," in Hope Jensen Leichter (ed.), *Families and Communities as Educators* (New York: Teachers College Press, 1979), p. 101.

**12**  Ibid., p. 115.

**13**  Ibid., p. 107.

**14**  Ibid., p. 108.

**15**  Ronald Lippett, "The Socialization Community," in William M. Cave and Mark A. Chessler (eds.), *Sociology of Education* (New York: Macmillan, 1974), pp. 338–352.

**16**  Adapted from a suggestion by Normand R. Bernier that two students who *look* very much alike may, in fact, be quite different in orientation, belief, value, and behavior, Kent State University, Seminar in Multicultural Education, Summer, 1979.

**17**  Terrence N. Tice, "Multicultural Objectives: A Critical Approach," in Dolores E. Cross, Gwendolyn C. Baker, and Lindley J. Stiles (eds.), *Teaching in a Multicultural Society* (New York: The Free Press, 1977), p. 126.

**18**  Robert J. Cottrol, "America the Multicultural," *American Educator,* vol. 14, no. 3, Winter 1990, p. 19.

**19**  Ibid., pp. 19–20.

**20**  Seymour B. Sarason, *Psychology Misdirected* (New York: The Free Press, 1981), p. 15.

**21**  Paul Craven and Barry Wellman, "The Network City," *Sociological Inquiry,* vol. 43, nos. 3–4, Summer 1973, pp. 57–58.

**22**  Barry Wellman, "Studying Personal Communities," in Peter V. Marsden and Nan Lin (eds.), *Social Structure and Network Analysis* (Beverly Hills: Sage Publications, 1982), p. 64.

**23**  Harold Dunkle, *Whitehead on Education* (Columbus: Ohio State University Press, 1965), pp. 19–20.

**24**  John Dewey, *The Sources of a Science of Education* (New York: Liveright Publishing, 1929), pp. 48–49.

**25**  Averil E. McClelland and Jeanne Williams, "Approaches to Cultural Diversity: Culture at Work in Human Behavior," paper presented at the annual conference of the American Educational Studies Association, Boston, November 7, 1981, pp. 4–5.

**26**  Ibid.

**27**  J. C. Mitchell, "Theoretical Orientations in African Urban Studies," in Michael Banton (ed.), *The Social Anthropology of Complex Societies* (New York: The Association of Social Anthropologists, Monograph no. 4, Praeger, 1966), p. 41.

**28**  Seymour B. Sarason et al., *Human Services and Resource Networks* (San Francisco: Jossey-Bass, 1977), p. 126. The authors list the following as disciplines and fields in which the network concept has been developed: sociology, anthropology, psychiatry, psychology, administrative sciences, geography, city planning, and communications engineering.

**29**  Ibid., pp. 128–129.

**30**  J. A. Barnes, "Class and Committees in a Norwegian Island Parish," *Human Relations,* vol. 7, no. 1, February 1954, p. 3.

**31**  Adapted from J. A. Barnes, "Networks and Political Process," in J. C. Mitchell (ed.), *Social Networks in Urban Situations* (Manchester, England, Manchester University Press, 1969), p. 59.

**32**  Ibid., p. 60.

**33**  Ibid., p. 61.

**34**  J. C. Mitchell, "The Concept and Use of Social Networks," in J. C. Mitchell (ed.), *Social Networks in Urban Situations* (Manchester, England: Manchester University Press, 1969), p. 2.

**35**  Carl A. Grant and Christine E. Sleeter, "Race, Class and Gender in Education Research: An

Argument for Integrative Analysis,'' *Review of Educational Research,* vol. 56, no. 2, Summer 1986, p. 196.

**36** Studs Terkel, *American Dreams: Lost and Found* (New York: Pantheon Books, 1980).

**37** Pierre Teilhard de Chardin, *The Future of Man* (New York: Harper & Row, 1964), p. 177.

**38** Robert Oppenheimer, ''Prospects in the Arts and Sciences,'' *Perspectives USA, II,* Spring 1955, pp. 10–11.

**39** Sarason et al., op. cit., pp. 1–2.

**40** R. Schmerl, ''The Student as Immigrant,'' in Dolores E. Gross, Gwendolyn C. Baker, and Lindley J. Stiles (eds.), *Teaching in a Multicultural Society,* (New York: The Free Press, 1977), p. 57.

**41** John I. Goodlad, ''Study of Schooling: Some Findings and Hypotheses,'' *Phi Delta Kappan,* vol. 64, March 1983, p. 470.

# HUMAN DIVERSITY: EMERGING THEORY AND PRACTICE

# CHAPTER 11

# THE EMERGING
# EDUCATIONAL COMMUNITY

*Every day in every part of the world people set out to teach something to others or to study something themselves or to place others or themselves in situations from which they hope desirable changes in knowledge, attitudes, skills, or appreciations will result.*

Lawrence Cremin

## EDUCATION IN MULTIPLE SETTINGS

Part Three of this book will focus on strategies designed to assist teachers in thinking about and actively pursuing educational goals for themselves and their students that address the issues of human diversity which have been discussed throughout this book. In most cases, pursuit of such goals will mean change: change in the way we select and write curricula; change in the way we think about teaching and actually teach; and change in the attitudes, norms, and values of the school as a social setting—what we have referred to as the culture of the school.

One strategy that seems to us fundamentally necessary if we are to achieve these goals is an alteration in the way we think of and define education itself. In past chapters, we have alluded to the idea that education is a broader concept than schooling. We have also tried to use the two terms carefully: when we mean schooling, we say *schooling;* when we mean education in a broader sense, we say education.''

It is obvious that education—defined as teaching and learning—occurs nearly everywhere. Indeed, one of the difficulties that we all encounter in talking about education at all is that it is pervasive in human life. Not often emphasized, however, are the actual settings, apart from schools, in which education occurs and the precise nature of teaching and learning in those settings. Neither are the relationships between educational settings much studied or understood, particularly the relationships between schools and other educational settings.

Yet in an increasingly interrelated and interdependent world, those relationships are important. Schools do not exist apart from the other institutions and organizations that comprise the communities in which they operate. There is no wall around a school that keeps the people in it invulnerable to political, social, and economic factors outside its offices, gyms, cafeterias, and classrooms. Similarly, schools are not (or should not be) isolated from the instructional activities outside the school in which children (as well as teachers, administrators, and other school personnel) participate. Therefore, it would serve us well to be able to understand the school as an important *but not isolated* part of the total educational effort in American society. To do so is to be able to begin to see the relationships between educating agencies and the often overlapping educational networks in which individuals move.

## GROVER'S CORNERS: A THOUGHT EXPERIMENT

Rather than focus on the whole of the society, we will begin by considering the educational enterprise at the level of the political unit we call the city, town, or community.

We will be using the term *community* in several ways and will generally try to specify which way we are using it. In order to make our discussion as clear and as concrete as possible, we will set up what we call a "thought experiment." In this experiment, we will posit an imaginary, freestanding (not a suburb), medium-sized town of about 60,000 people—let's call it Grover's Corners, after the town in the famous American play *Our Town,* by Thornton Wilder.[1] Now, conditions in such a town will vary, depending on its ethnic and religious composition, its economic base, and its location (Is it in New England? the deep south? the midwest? the mountain states of the west? the southwest? the northwest?). The size of Grover's Corners is also important. If it were a city of several million, conditions would differ (although one can argue that 60,000 people might constitute a fair-sized neighborhood in a major urban center). If it were a community of 10,000 or less, conditions would also be different. In our thought experiment, Grover's Corners may assume a variety of characteristics; play along with us, and let's see what we can learn.

To begin with, our imaginary Grover's Corners is clearly a *community* in the sense that it is a town. It has city limits; it has a mayor and a city council. It has its own set of laws, as well as being under the jurisdiction of its state and of the nation. It has a wealthy residential section, a number of middle-class neighborhoods, and at least one poor section. It has some industry, a number of churches, synagogues, and a mosque. It has several day care centers, a museum, a relatively large public library with several branch libraries, a television station, several radio stations, and a daily newspaper. It has department stores, bars, neighborhood convenience stores, and numerous commercial and service businesses. It has a municipal park and a Class A professional baseball team with its own ballpark, a YMCA and YWCA, a welfare department, a child welfare department, and a juvenile reformatory for boys. It has a community theater, several malls, and a downtown business district. It has an adequate number of lawyers, doctors, dentists, accountants, architects, and other professionals. It has both public and private elementary schools, middle schools, and high schools. And, in addition, let's put in a community college.

## The Educational Community in Grover's Corners

Within the geographical community that is Grover's Corners is an *educational community*. The term *community* here means those people of all ages who are actively engaged in instruction and learning and those organizations and settings in which deliberate and systematic teaching and learning occur. *Community* used in this way can refer to those who carry out any function—in this case, it's education. It will perhaps not surprise you to learn that we are going to investigate this educational community using a network perspective. Two aspects of network theory will be paramount: we will talk about *personal educational networks,*[2] or networks of relations between individuals, and we will talk about networks of educative settings, what have been called *interorganizational networks* or *fields.*[3] Discussion of each can be used to illuminate the educational enterprise in Grover's Corners; they are, of course, related, but they can be examined separately.

### The Educational Field in Grover's Corners: Or, What Educational Resources Are Available in This Town?

In what we are going to call the *educational field* in Grover's Corners, there are at least two major components. The first of these is made up of the *institutions in the community,* among which are the family, the church, and, perhaps surprisingly, the economic basis on which Grover's Corners rests. We will use Robert Bierstedt's definition of the term *institution:* "a formal, recognized, established and stabilized way of pursuing some activity in society."[4] Thus, for example, the family is the institution largely responsible for the physical care and primary socialization of children, for the regulation (with varying degrees of success) of sexual practices and mate selection, and for the regulation of the inheritance of private property.[5] The institution of religion functions in large measure to fulfill human spiritual and ethical needs, and the institution of the economy functions to regulate production, trade, and finance.

Lawrence Cremin, perhaps more than anyone else in the United States, has noted the ways particular institutions relate to one another at particular times and in particular places in terms of the educational messages they create and the effect of those messages on the people who come into contact with them. Social institutions, he asserts, have varying kinds and degrees of influence on one another, such that in a particular time and place they form what he calls an *educational configuration* that can and should be studied. He writes:

> Relationships among the institutions that constitute a configuration of education may be political, pedagogical, or personal. There may be overlapping lines of support and control—one thinks of the hold of Protestant missionary organization on the families, churches, and schools of Ohio Valley towns during the nineteenth century, or of the interlocking influence of a genteel upper class on the museums, libraries, and scientific societies of eastern seaboard cities during the twentieth century. Or there may be substantial pedagogical influence extending from one institution to another within the configuration—consider, for example, the spread of entertainment styles from cinema and television to churches, colleges, and adult education organizations during our own time. Or, indeed, there may be decisive personal influence deriving from the same people moving as teachers or students through more than one institution—such has always been the case with the configurations of education maintained by small sectarian communities like the Mennonites, the Hasidic Jews, and the Black Muslims.[6]

The relationships between the institutions of an educational configuration may be consonant or dissonant. That is, the lessons taught may reinforce or undermine one another. Consonance of institutions may be seen, for example, in the complementarity of the white Protestant home, the white Protestant church, and the white Protestant common school in the nineteenth century. As Cremin notes:

> What we have traditionally thought of as the extraordinary influence of the nineteenth-century common school . . . derived not so much from the common school per se as from a configuration of education of which the common school was only one element. It was a configuration in which the values and pedagogies of the several component institutions happened to be mutually supportive.[7]

In contrast, an example of dissonance in contemporary life is the conflicting teaching about sexual practices by religious leaders, school personnel, and many families on the one hand, and the media (including advertising, films, videos, and much popular music) on the other. Clearly, what one may learn from one institution is not the same as what one may learn from the other. Understanding that various institutions in a community may complement or conflict with one another, of course, does not mean that teachers must necessarily seek out in detail *all* the ramifications of *all* the institutional messages which are available. It does, however, mean that teachers must be sensitive to the complexity of the educational enterprises in which their students participate. Too often, educators tend to ignore the fact that students "have a life" outside school and that in that life, they acquire knowledge, attitudes, and values—in short, an identity. Students today, for example, interact with and around popular culture to a degree never seen before. Giroux and Simon write that educators neglect that reality at the peril of both their students and themselves:

> By ignoring the cultural and social forms that are authorized by youth and simultaneously empower and disempower them, educators risk complicity silencing and negating their students. This is unwittingly accomplished by refusing to recognise the importance of those sites and social practices outside of the schools that actively shape student experiences and through which students often define and construct their sense of identity, politics, and culture.[8]

An important aspect of the institutional component of the educational field is the actual organizations through which it is realized. In daily life, as Bierstedt has noted, all institutions are supported by organizations and groups through which their social functions are realized. The institution of the family is realized in *particular* families; the institution of religion is realized in *particular* churches, synagogues, and mosques; the institution of the economy is realized in *particular* businesses, governments, and agencies. And, as we have seen, particular families, churches, and businesses vary widely in their nature, habits, attitudes, values, knowledge, and customs. Thus, it is the *particular* organizations and groups in Grover's Corners, and their relation to one another, that determine the nature of the education available to people in that community—and the *educational* messages they receive and internalize. The educational field in the community also has a bearing on how successful efforts to institute change in schooling might be.

Let's say, for example, that Grover's Corners is in upstate New York and is a largely Protestant town with a large proportion of its families regularly attending church. We will say, further, that it is a largely white, lower-middle-class and middle-class town, with a small percentage of African-American families (also largely Protestant and church-going) who have been residents of the town for nearly fifty years. Most of the African-American families migrated here from the deep south after World War II to work in the town's relatively small factories, factories which produce such items as light bulbs, firefighting foam, and appliances. Let's further suppose that industries are suffering from severe competition from other sources, both domestic and foreign. Business is not good. Educators in Grover's Corners, attempting to participate in a national movement toward less competitive and more cooperative learning environments, seem to be running into a great deal of criticism for their innovations from the public, most of whom went to school in Grover's Corners themselves, at a time when students routinely heard the exhortations "Keep your eyes on your own paper" and "Don't talk to your neighbor." The criticism does not, however, stem entirely from tradition or habit. Rather, one can argue that the educational messages of Protestantism (one stands in a one-to-one relationship with God; one achieves salvation through one's own works), white, middle-class values (individual effort, consistently applied, will conquer whatever problems one encounters), and a highly competitive economic climate in which people vie for a limited number of jobs all contribute to an institutional environment in which school personnel are expected to do their part in socializing children to the realities of a "dog eat dog" world. Parents, employers, and other community members think, with some justification, that children must be taught to be competitive and to win in competitive situations; it is survival that seems to be at stake.

Teachers who are sensitive to the subtle and not so subtle messages of local institutions will understand that altering one of the very pillars of school life—competition—will not be easy. Moreover, they will be cognizant of the reasons for criticism when they meet it and will act in ways that show sympathy for the real concerns of the public. This does not mean they need simply comply with public opinion. Rather, they will attempt to find other aspects of the institutional configuration which will reinforce their aims. One thinks, for example, of the Christian sense of sharing, the white, middle-class value of helping one's neighbor, and the economic incentive to welcome better-educated and more productive workers.

A second component of the educational field in Grover's Corners is made up of the actual instructional efforts in individual settings there. In order to begin to see the variety of educative settings in a community, we must first understand the enormous increase in the need for educational services in the United States in recent years and then ask the question "Just where is deliberate instruction and learning going on?"

In recent years, the demand for new (as well as old) educational services from new (as well as traditional) populations has mushroomed. Several factors help to account for this. First, technology is changing almost faster than we can keep up with it. The computerization of the workplace—in all industries and businesses—is a new fact of life. Similarly, computer-driven processes of production, new systems of managing human resources, and new attitudes toward the relationship between management and labor all provide the impetus for a massive educational effort. Thus, one of the major providers of educational services is business, which offers, and sometimes requires, training and development coursework for both management and bargaining-unit employees. Businesses are also offering basic education in math and literacy to those who lack such skills and require instruction.

Second, major changes are taking place in the family. An increase in the number of educational programs in day care centers (indeed, the provision of day care services at all), for example, is directly related to the increase in the number of middle-class women who have entered the work force. Poor women and men have always worked outside the home and have always needed appropriate care for their children, but until the middle-class woman entered the labor market, child care did not become a major social issue. The middle class has both the desire and the political influence to demand child care, and also to demand that such care be not just custodial but also educational. In addition, working parents need activities for children that occupy them after school and during the summer; this need has produced a tremendous increase in recreational and learning efforts aimed at the school-age child and teenager.

A third reason for the increasing demand for educational services has been that many people have more time available for learning. As the age of the population has increased,

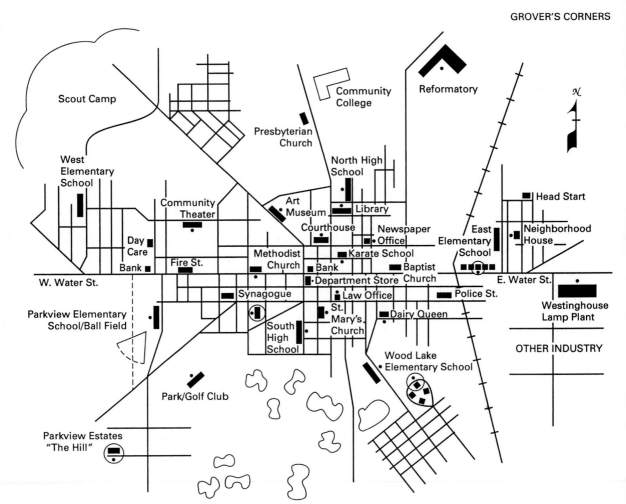

**FIGURE 11.1**    A map of Grover's Corners.

large numbers of retired people have leisure time to pursue new kinds of learning, just for fun and self-fulfillment. As the number of hours in the work week has decreased, more time has become available to working adults for additional study.

A fourth factor in increasing educational demands is the contemporary emphasis on health and the prevention of disease. Indeed, health education—in schools, but also in hospitals, clinics, health museums, malls, sports facilities, and doctors' offices—now constitutes one of the largest sets of educational services offered in the United States.

There are, of course, other factors at work, but perhaps you get the idea that deliberate, systematic educational activities are available in many kinds of settings. The question then becomes, just what *kind* of educational resources are available in any particular community? What's going on in Grover's Corners? If we drew a map of Grover's Corners, where might the educational activities be located, and what could we learn from knowing where they are?[9] Figure 11.1 shows such a map.

Now that we know something about where the educational settings are located, we have a better idea of what kinds of educational resources exist in Grover's Corners, and that knowledge is useful in at least four ways (maybe you can think of more). First, it can help us discover where there is education that is complementary to schooling and also where there is education that is, at least potentially, antagonistic to schooling. Second, it can help us discover existing resources for schooling—people who might come into the school on a voluntary basis, for example—or places where we could refer students for instruction that we cannot provide. Third, it can help us discover where people in schools already have useful linkages (for example, with the museum, which provides interesting field trips for students, or the library, which stocks certain books and materials linked to recurring assignments), and where linkages may not exist but should (for example, between teachers in day care centers and teachers of kindergarten and first grade). And finally, it can help us understand where and how our students are getting the attitudes, values, skills, habits, and knowledge they bring with them to school. For this, however, we need to examine the educational community of Grover's Corners as it has an impact on and is used by individual students and teachers. In order to do this, we need to examine the personal educational networks through which individuals move.

### Personal Educational Networks in Grover's Corners: Or, How Are People Using Available Educational Resources?

Educational institutions and activities define the educational field—all the available educational recourses—but the actual education that individuals receive or obtain depends on the access they have to various parts of the educational community and on their motivation and purposes in utilizing the resources. Thus, the educational community can also be perceived as a set of overlapping personal educational networks of people moving around and through the town. When talking about such networks, one must ask the following kinds of questions: Where does the person live and what educational resources are available to her or him by virtue of the neighborhood(s) in which he or she grows up? What is the ethnic, religious, social class, and occupational character of the person's family and what educational messages is she or he likely to receive because of membership in these groups? How old is the person and how varied are the settings in which she or he participates? Are there special characteristics of the person that might place him or her in particular settings? For example, does the person have a chronic health problem that might lead her or him to have special knowledge of medicine, physical therapy, or the like? Has the person had contact with the juvenile or adult justice system for some reason? Does the person have a special talent or interest (music, art, science, computers, stamp collecting) that might have resulted in participation in related activities or instruction? In other words, what educational resources have been or are readily available to this person? Are any resources in the community closed to him or her?

Let's play with the map of Grover's Corners and trace the educational networks of two male and two female high school students who live there.

*Richard Williams* is a 16-year-old African-American. He has lived his entire life with his grandmother and grandfather (retired and at home), his mother (an assembly line worker at the light bulb factory), his aunt (a cleaning woman at the museum), two brothers, and a sister, in a house near the factory on East Water Street. He doesn't know who or where his father is. His older brother is in the local reformatory for drug-related crimes. As a child, Richard played basketball at the neighborhood house near his home and continues to help out there with younger children. He attends North High School and is in the college prep academic program. He is a member of the high school golf team, which practices at the local golf course; is on the school newspaper staff, which is advised by an editor of the Grover's Corners newspaper; and works after school and weekends at the golf course.

*Tom Peterson* is also 16, is white, and lives in a large and comfortable house on The Hill with his parents and a younger sister. His father is a lawyer and his mother, an artist, is in charge of the adult volunteers (called Docents) at the museum, where Tom sometimes works for special exhibits. Tom also attends North High School, and is in the college prep academic program and on the golf team. In addition, he is a member of Thearts, the high school drama club, which is coached by a member of the local community theater. As a child, Tom played Little League baseball, belonged to the Boy Scouts, and traveled in the United States and in Europe with his family. Tom takes karate lessons every week, and participates in formal demonstrations of the martial arts.

*Toni Catalano* lives in a pleasant ranch house on a cul-de-sac near Wood Lake Elementary School on the south side of town. She is the youngest of a large, extended Italian Catholic family. She is also 16, and is majoring in business subjects at South High School, planning to become a secretary in one of the factories in town—perhaps at the lamp plant, where her father works—or in the office of one of the banks. Her family has always been very involved with the church, and she gained a considerable amount of attention and praise by becoming the first altar girl at St. Mary's. Two of her aunts are nuns; one of them, Sister Rita, is a missionary sister in El Salvador. One of her uncles is a priest in a church in the next town and disapproves heartily of her aunt's being in Central America. Nevertheless, her family keeps in close contact with Sister Rita, and Toni corresponds with her frequently. In school, Toni receives reasonably good grades, is on the cheerleading squad, and is a scorekeeper for the wrestling team. She dates a number of boys, mostly athletes, and works on weekends at a nearby Dairy Queen.

*Jennifer Collins* also lives on the south side of town and attends South High School, where she is in the gifted education program and, so far, has a straight A average. Her mother and father are divorced. She lives with her mother, who works as a bookkeeper for a local department store, and sees her father, who lives in another state, only several times a year. She has an older brother who is stationed on a nuclear submarine in Virginia. As a child, Jennifer was a Girl Scout for a while, but dropped out. She has gone to Sunday School at the Methodist church all her life. After school and on Saturday, Jennifer works at the main branch of the public library downtown, saving most of the money she makes for college. She does not have either the time or the inclination to date much, but she does find time to go to all the exhibitions at the museum and to all the local community theater productions. Once, she even had a small part in a play. Since she and her mother are alone, they spend as much time together as possible. Her mother has taught her to sew and she makes almost all of her own clothes. She worries about leaving her mother alone when she goes to college, and is trying to decide whether or not to attend the local community college for two years before actually leaving home. Because she takes advanced placement courses in high school, she will be eligible for courses at the college in her senior year and will probably become a student there.

Figures 11.2 through 11.5 show the personal educational networks of these four students. What do you notice about them—their size, shape? What educational influences are a part of each of these students' lives? Where, if at all, do the networks overlap? How likely are these students to come into contact with one another? Where? How many

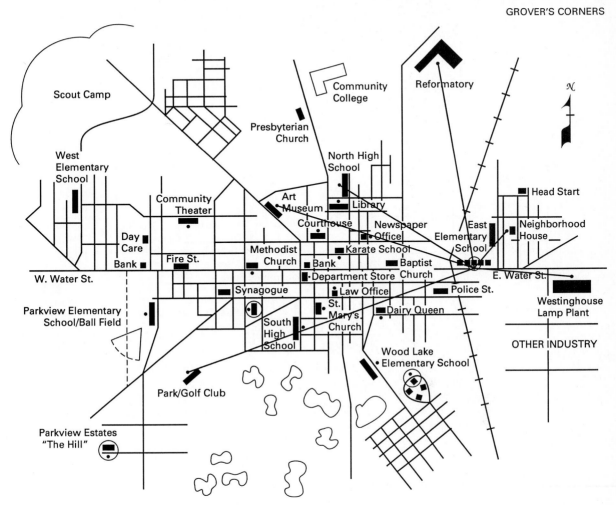

GROVER'S CORNERS

**FIGURE 11.2**   Personal educational network: Richard Williams.

of the educative settings in which these students find themselves result from imposed participation and how many from choice?

## WHEN INTERORGANIZATIONAL AND PERSONAL NETWORKS MEET: THE EDUCATIONAL COMMUNITY AND THE SCHOOL

In order to understand how differences in the nature and content of both personal educational networks and the educational field of a community can have an important effect on schooling in that community, let's leave Grover's Corners and look at an example provided by Seymour Sarason in a discussion of social change.[10] Implicit in Sarason's argument is the idea that the educational dimension of a community—of which schools

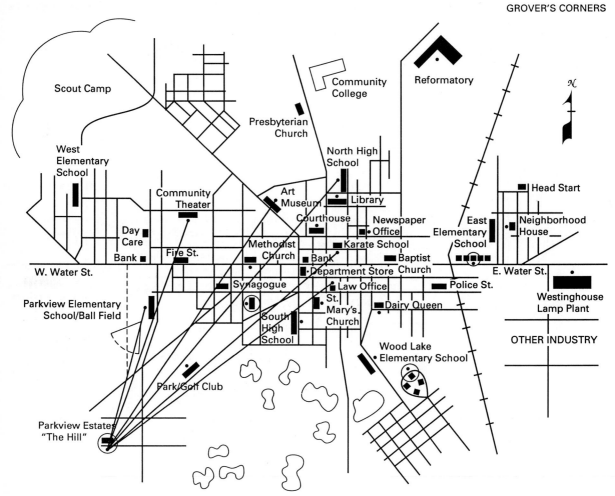

**FIGURE 11.3**    Personal educational networks: Tom Peterson.

are a part—can at one and the same time place constraints on schooling and provide important resources for schools.

## The Educational Community as a Constraining Factor

Sarason, the Director of the Yale Psycho-Educational Clinic, was responsible for providing school psychological services for a number of communities in Connecticut and its surrounding areas. At one point, he was involved in the provision of these services to schools in two communities which he calls Town A and Town B. The towns had similar demographic characteristics in terms of size and economic factors, and were located adjacent to one another. However, after working in the schools of these towns

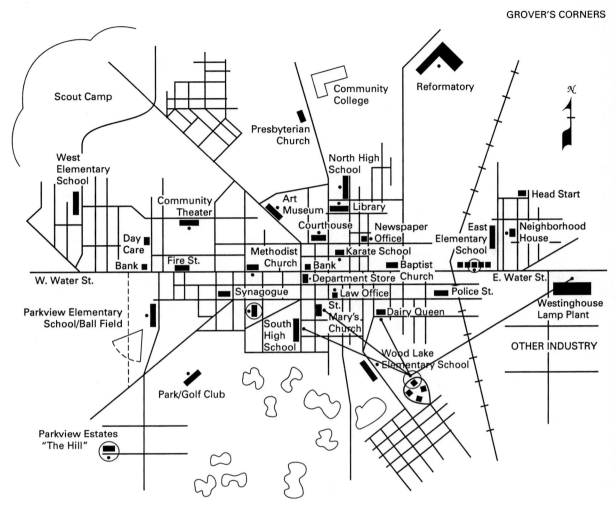

FIGURE 11.4    Personal educational network: Toni Catalano.

for a while, Sarason and his colleagues became aware of some subtle and not so subtle differences.

In Town A the high school was akin to a military establishment with scores of published rules about dress, conduct, and general comportment; and these rules were enforced by a principal who was no less than a petty tyrant. The high school in Town B was much looser and anarchic, with numerous problem students and generally poor morale among teachers and students. The differences between the two high schools were marked in the extreme and in no way compatible with our guiding assumption that we were dealing with highly similar towns. If these two towns were as similar, as we and everyone else believed, how did we account for the extreme differences? If our assumption was correct that characteristics were directly and indirectly reflected in its schools, we had to conclude that the two towns were not all that similar, external appearances and popular belief to the contrary notwithstanding.[11]

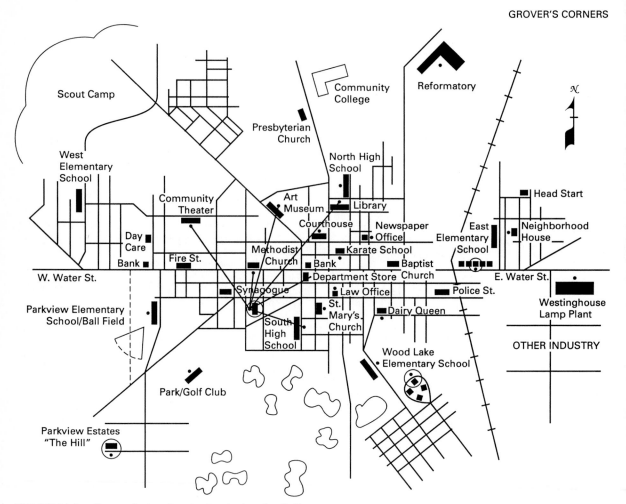

**FIGURE 11.5**   Personal educational network: Jennifer Collins.

After some investigation, they found that Town A was a predominantly white, Italian community, in which more than 90 percent of the students and teachers were Catholic. About 70 percent of all school personnel were born and brought up in the town. Half the teachers were trained in a local teachers' college, and about 40 percent were trained in one of three Catholic colleges. The parents of Town A decidedly approved the militaristic organization of the high school, and supported the principal with enthusiasm. The new superintendent in Town A had been a student of this principal. Perhaps as a result of the cohesiveness of the people in Town A and their support of the schools, a school levy had never been turned down in that community.

Town B, on the other hand, was a much more heterogeneous community, with a variety of religious groups and a growing black population. There appeared to be little or no connection between the schools and the community, and Town B had voted down two school referenda. Later, Town B also suffered a major teacher strike and a series of subsequent hostile contract negotiations.

An examination of the personal and interorganizational educational networks in the two towns can help to explain differences in the relations between the schools and their communities, and may also help us understand the dynamics of the two situations. In Town A, common educative experiences characterized many of the schools' teachers and administrators, as well as those of the parents. Most of the teachers and many of the parents had grown up in the town, had gone to the same schools and attended the same churches. The learning they had acquired—particularly the attitudes and values of the Catholic Church—was congruent and shared. This was clearly part of the reason for support for the schools, and one can also assume that it accounted for the support of a military style principal, one whose methods others might find distasteful, if not unsound. On the other hand, it is likely that the religious and racial diversity of the people in Town B meant that their educational networks differed widely, that as a whole they did not share common learnings, and that the educational field of the community was less congruent. While such diversity can provide a certain freedom from community constraint, it may also lessen the chances that the schools can depend on community support, and, indeed, that seemed to be the case.

It is, of course, too simplistic to say that religion, by itself, made the difference. It was clearly important, however, that attention to differences in the religious composition of the two towns is important in understanding how schools in communities that on the outside looked so similar could be so different. Sarason writes:

> The obvious point I wish to make is that institutionalized religion is a major characteristic of a community, an organizing and ramifying force, a force not only significant in the lives of many of its individuals but also significant for other community institutions and forces. To understand individual students and teachers in Town A requires far more than attending to their religion; but, similarly, in order to understand the culture of their school, to comprehend what they absorb and how they absorb it, we cannot ignore the role of religion in their community. One can, of course, ignore it because ordinarily one cannot *see,* and by law one is not *supposed* to see, religion in public schools. But the controversy about prayers in the schools, and about celebrations of religious holidays, reveals that in schools and their communities religion is both an organizing and a divisive factor. And if one follows the modern history of the issues surrounding the use of public monies to support parochial schools, it is impossible to deny that religion is an ubiquitous factor in our communities, and one that interrelates with other factors basic to an understanding of a community.[12]

## The Educational Community as a Set of Resources for Schools

While the educational community of a town can, and usually does, place constraints on school personnel, it also can be a source of irreplaceable resources for teachers. Much has been written of late about the necessity for partnerships between people in community organizations and people in schools, with particular attention to creating working relationships between businesses and schools. Central to this proposition is the belief that because businesses are the future workplaces of students (and a lingering if unfortunate belief that school personnel do not run their organizations as well as businesses do), school personnel can profit from the expertise of businesspeople. In fact, a number of businesses have created relationships with schools, particularly in urban areas, and these partnerships have made a variety of human, material, and financial resources available to individual "adopted" schools.

While the official or contractual association of particular businesses with particular schools is one example of the ways in which the educational field in a community can provide resources for schools, it is not the only one, and indeed, it may be somewhat limited. Another example follows.

## Central Elementary School and Project Open Door

In 1971, Central Elementary School was one of six elementary schools in the Bedford, Ohio, City School District, a district serving four towns in northeastern Ohio. Central Elementary is located in the city of Bedford, a suburb of Cleveland with about 18,000 people. In 1971, its student population was overwhelmingly white. A majority of its 400 to 500 children walked to school. The socioeconomic status of the school population was changing; lower-income families were moving into the school's service area, and the school had become a Chapter I school, which meant that more than 10 percent of its students were eligible for free lunches and other welfare services, including a special reading program. From 1968 to 1980, the average IQ of Central's students, as measured by tests given in the fourth and sixth grades, declined by about 15 points. Now, presumably the two best predictors of school achievement are IQ and socioeconomic status. Yet in that same period, the achievement of Central's students was maintained at above-average levels or went up.

An important part of the reason was Project Open Door, a volunteer program organized and operated by parents and other community residents that deliberately opened the doors of the school to the community and took advantage of local and regional educational resources. In effect, the POD Program, as it was called, identified existing personal and organizational educational networks and created new ones where none existed before.

Beginning with an after-school program that enlisted volunteers to create interest groups for children, the POD Program at its zenith had nine different elements:

1 An after-school program that centered around multiple student interests;

2 The provision of adult aides for teachers;

3 The provision of adult tutors for individual students;

4 The provision of 5-week minicourses taught by community residents and professors from a nearby community college;

5 The provision of one-time talks, exhibits, and conversations with local community residents who had something of interest to bring to the school (e.g., collectors, artisans, or travelers);

6 An evening adult education program, both credit and noncredit, administered in connection with the community college;

7 A paid program coordinator originally funded by a foundation grant but subsequently funded by the school board and a parent advisory council;

8 A cross-age tutoring program involving high school students and elementary students;

9 The provision of people to take care of the preschool children of other people who volunteered in the POD Program.

Like many such programs, Project Open Door began in a fairly small way and grew as opportunities and ideas presented themselves. Key to the process was the principal, Paul Patton, who began the process by starting a study group with parents, where they read and discussed a number of books about schooling that were popular at the time. He and about fourteen parents met on a weekly basis during the 1971–1972 school year. Out of that group grew the realization that it was possible for parents to participate in the school in a meaningful way, possible for parents to find growth experiences in the context of the school, and possible for parents and community members to really *do* something that made a difference. Without the initial guidance and continued support of Paul Patton, it is doubtful that the program would have progressed. Clearly it would not have grown to the extent that it did.

At its height, Central School had 300 adults in the school on an annual basis, a majority of whom were there at least several times a year and many who were there on a regular weekly basis. A number of special projects evolved because of the program. For example, one year NASA's Lewis Space Center, which is located near Cleveland, adopted the school and provided staff and materials for a curricular focus on energy (there was also a visit from an astronaut who arrived in a helicopter). In that year, parents and community residents helped to build an operating windmill on the roof of the school, and constructed a hydroponic garden in an unused building space. Another special project involved sixth-grade students who took books to elderly local residents every two weeks, also stopping to visit with them. All teachers had at least one aide, and many had two or three. Partly as a result of available adult help, the music teacher and a colleague were able to start a children's musical theater group which has since become a separate regional children's theater.

Community residents were able to open many doors for the children at Central School over a period of more than ten years, and additional benefits accrued to the school and the school district. In addition to maintaining or increasing student achievement, the school broadened its constituency. Local residents who were not parents of school-age children became deeply involved in and committed to the school, and that support extended to voting for school levies for the district. Local people knew what was going on at the school because they were a part of it—during the day as volunteers, in the evening as students, as neighbors of people who were active in the program, and as the recipients of other school services like the book program. Contacts were made with local and regional agencies of various kinds which increased the access of school personnel and students to assistance not otherwise ordinarily available.

Project Open Door is not unique, but there are not many programs like it. Indeed, other elementary schools in the district did not adopt such programs, largely because most principals did not want to bother with so many community members in their schools. It was messy; it was sometimes chaotic; children and adults were always in the halls doing something or other—reading to one another, writing, demonstrating lasers (the second-graders had a unique opportunity to work with lasers). Sometimes, people who were scheduled to come couldn't make it. But it was a school that helped the community love its children in very concrete ways and it was a school truly loved by its community.

In Hawaii, a similar effort—in this case, a coordinated, statewide program—has involved community elders of Hawaiian ancestry, called Kupuna, who regularly come into the schools to help bring Hawaiian culture to children. This program bridges generations while bringing a slowly fading culture to life for all the children of Hawaii in an affective, involving manner.

## THE EDUCATIONAL COMMUNITY AND THE FUTURE

There are perhaps more obstacles in 1991 than there were in 1971 to the initiation of such programs. More mothers are working, many children are poorer, differences between people seem more acute, intergroup hostility appears to be rising, and real dangers lurk in the streets outside many schools. In an era when schools are locking their doors for security reasons, when police are patrolling the halls, and when students are encumbered by increasing numbers of rules, it seems hard to think of a school that, figuratively at least, leaves its doors wide open to the community and, in some sense, turns its children loose. But the principle has not changed and the need is greater. Teachers and other school personnel can enlist enormous amounts of aid from the communities in which they live, and such aid can come from the poorest neighbor as well as the wealthiest corporation. What is required is the awareness of possibilities and the willingness to ask questions and to ask for help. The educational community is there, and if it becomes visible, it can be mobilized for everyone's benefit. In the final chapter of this section, we will be talking about schools that are doing just that—schools in poor neighborhoods, schools in small towns and schools in large cities—schools of the future that take seriously the notion that education is a community responsibility and not simply the function of schooling.

## ACTIVITIES

1 Draw a map of the community you grew up in. What was your educational network like? What people and institutions in the community contributed to your educational experiences? In what places did you come into contact with others who did not share most of your experiences? What were these interactions like for you? In what places did you have little experience? What implications does this fact have for you today?
2 Draw a map of a community to which you have ready access. Interview a few students from this community and draw the educational network in which they regularly participate. What implications does this have for their present experiences? How might this information be useful to a teacher?

## REFERENCES

1 Thornton Wilder, *Our Town* (New York: Avon, 1957).
2 For a description of other views of personal networks, see Richard D. Alba and Charles Kadushin, ''The Intersection of Social Circles: A New Measure of Social Proximity in Networks,'' *Sociological Methods and Research,* vol. 5, no. 13, Aug. 1976, pp. 77–102; T. Caplow, ''The Definition and Measurement of Ambiences,'' *Social Forces,* vol. 34, no. 1–4, October 1955, pp. 28–31; and Jules Henry, ''The Personal Community and Its Invariant Properties,'' *American Anthropologist,* vol. 60, no. 5, Oct. 1958, pp. 827–831.
3 For different interpretations of the idea of interorganizational networks, see Michael Aiken and Jerald Hage, ''Interdependence and Intraorganizational Structure,'' in Merlin B. Brinkerhoff

and Phillip R. Kunz (eds.), *Complex Organizations and Their Environments* (Dubuque, IO: Wm. C. Brown, 1972), pp. 367–394; Herman Turk, ''Interorganizational Networks in Urban Society: Initial Perspectives and Comparative Research,'' *American Sociological Review,* vol. 35, no. 1, February 1970, pp. 1–19; and Roland L. Warren, ''The Interorganizational Field as a Focus for Investigation,'' *Administrative Science Quarterly,* vol. 12, no. 3, December 1967, pp. 396–419.

**4** Robert Bierstedt, *The Social Order* (New York: McGraw-Hill, 1974), pp. 329–332.

**5** R. B. Webb and R. R. Sherman, *Schooling and Society,* (New York: Macmillan, 1989), 2d ed., pp. 95–96.

**6** Lawrence A. Cremin, *Public Education* (New York: Basic Books, 1976), pp. 30–31.

**7** Ibid., p. 36.

**8** Henry Giroux and Roger Simon, *Popular Culture: Schooling and Everyday Life* (Granby, MA: Bergin and Garvey, 1989), p. 3.

**9** This map of our imaginary town is designed to exhibit some of the features characteristic of communities in the United States. For example, in most American communities there is either a natural divider (a river, for instance, or a hill) or a structural one (often a railroad track) that separates residential sections by social class. Wealthier families tend to live in the western section of town, poorer ones in the eastern section. Industry is usually located either in the center of town or on its edges. Poorer families and ethnic families tend to live near factories or other job centers, in part because transportation costs to work are lower and because housing is often cheaper. Commercial sections tend to be centralized (the typical downtown—although this is changing with the advent of malls).

**10** Seymour B. Sarason, *The Psychological Sense of Community: Prospects for a Community Psychology* (San Francisco: Jossey-Bass, 1977).

**11** Ibid., pp. 133–134.

**12** Ibid., p. 135.

# CHAPTER 12

# THE TRANSFORMATION
# OF CURRICULUM

*It is through necessity that the means of perception are developed. Therefore, oh man, increase your necessity.*

Jalaludin Rumi

\*    \*    \*

### A Parable

Once there were three men who had never seen oranges. They had heard many wonderful things about the fruit, and wanted very much to have some. The first man set out full of excitement. He traveled for many days, and began to worry that he would get lost. The farther he went, the more he worried. Finally he sat under a tree, deep in thought. "No silly fruit is this important," he decided. He got up and turned toward home.

The second man was a very bold fellow. He rushed off, dreaming about oranges as he traveled, and ended up at the same tree. Round orange fruits were all over the ground and in the branches. Thrilled, he grabbed one of the fruits off the ground and bit into it. It was rotten and bitter. "Ugh! What a stupid fruit," he said, and returned home empty-handed.

The third man did research before he left home. He also asked questions of people he met as he traveled. Lo and behold, he found the same tree full of oranges. He examined many oranges, and chose one that was not too hard or too soft. It was juicy and delicious. He took some seeds home, planted them, and eventually became a famous grower of fruit.

\*    \*    \*

It is the rare person who sometime in life does not seek out a dream, a treasured prize, a better way of life. Like the seekers of the orange tree, we all wish to find those things held out to us as great and wonderful. Today, the orange tree may very well be a more peaceful world in which all people can flourish in safety and freedom. The world we live in is far from such an ideal, almost inconceivably far from a world without hunger, without hatred, without war. Yet many Americans, from the very beginnings of their history, have dreamed the dream to which Martin Luther King, Jr., gave such eloquent expression and have placed their faith in schooling as a principal mechanism of altering their society toward these ends.

There are a number of areas in which this attention to change can be seen: in the nineteenth-century insistence on a common school, in the diversification of programs of study to include not only classical studies but also modern humanities and the sciences, in the seemingly inexorable expansion of who could and should be educated. One of the many themes that run through the history of American schooling is a progressively broader inclusion—of people, of ideas, and of ways of looking at the world. Indeed, it is our national conviction that inclusiveness is a key element of democracy that often gets us into trouble, for to include the "other" is always difficult. For some, like the first traveler to the orange tree, the journey is too wearying and frightening. For others, initial experiences with that which is other, leave a bitter taste in the mouth, and they go away in frustration, and sometimes in anger. But for a few, who persevere, the taste of even small success is sweet, and seeds are planted to grow again another day. For those people, like the third traveler in the tale, a central element in the success of their enterprise seems to be a willingness to acquire new knowledge, an ability to ask questions, and an interest in taking the time to select what look like the ''juiciest'' ideas.

This chapter will focus on one of the most important areas of schooling, the curriculum. We will emphasize ways in which the present standard curriculum can be changed—*transformed* is the word we use—in the time-honored, peculiarly American direction of inclusion. Some of them may already be familiar to you, since many schools today are experimenting with curriculum change. Some will perhaps strike you as very different, perhaps odd or unnecessary. We do not claim that all these ideas and strategies are equally valid for every situation; certainly they will not all be easy to institute. What we ask you to do is think seriously about them; discuss them; play with them. And select the juiciest.

## CURRICULUM: WHAT ARE WE TALKING ABOUT?

When we use the word *curriculum,* we expect that you will have some idea of what we are talking about. However, the word *curriculum* has been used in a variety of ways, and perhaps you will be thinking about something that we are not. Let us therefore look at some of the definitions of *curriculum* and agree, for our purposes here, to share a particular meaning.

Understanding that conceptions of curriculum vary in breadth and depth, the theorist Robert Zais has outlined at least six different perspectives:[1]

**1 *Curriculum as the Course of Study***   Some people, when asked about the curriculum of a school or school district, will oblige by providing a list of course offerings available and/or required. This is a somewhat narrow definition of curriculum, and even a vague one, since titles seldom indicate much about the actual content of a course. Titles may indicate a general area or theme, but they don't usually convey the intentions or purpose of the program and how the course meets that agenda.

**2 *Curriculum as Course Content***   *Curriculum* can also refer to the actual content of a course, which may be set forth in a syllabus, outline of units, or the like. Used in this way, *curriculum* means only the specific information covered in a course and does not include other important elements such as the environment in which students come into contact with the material or the activities planned by the teacher.

**3 *Curriculum as Planned Learning Experiences***   A broader definition, and one commonly used today, conceives of *curriculum* as ''all the experiences which are offered to learners under the auspices of the school.''[2] Used this way, *curriculum* means the total set of learning experiences officially sanctioned by the school, including in-class and extracurricular activities and other school services, as a part of an overall program of education. Closely related to this meaning is the term *manifest curriculum,* meaning a set of publicly stated goals for education usually drafted by school boards and subscribed to by administrators, teachers, counselors, and other school personnel.

**4** *Curriculum as Experiences "Had" Under the Auspices of the School*   Planned content and learning activities do not constitute the sum total of what students learn in school. Indeed, the very nature of the planned curriculum often entails unplanned or unintended outcomes. These are often referred to as the *hidden,* or *latent, curriculum,* meaning that portion of learning that students acquire as either a result of the form in which material, learning activities, and other school services (counseling, for example) are presented or, in some cases, as a result of particular content. Placement in lower reading groups, for instance, often teaches children that they cannot (rather than do not at the moment) read as well as some of their peers. The organization of subject matter into disciplines often has the result of teaching students that knowledge is segmented, that one discipline has no relation to another (e.g., history is divorced from art and literature), and that life in schools is not representative of life in the "real world." The actual subject matter presented may itself have unintended consequences. For example, girls and members of many ethnic groups often learn that they have not contributed much to human knowledge because their actual contributions are so often absent from curricular materials. Both planning and evaluation of an existing curriculum, defined in this way, may be enhanced by attention to the selection of content, activities, and services in terms of unintended outcomes.

**5** *Curriculum as a Structured Series of Intended Learning Outcomes*   For some people, curriculum is conceived not as a particular set of contents and learning activities planned in advance, but rather as a set of learning outcomes. For these people, the curriculum begins with what you want to see coming out—what you want to be the end results of instruction. Under this definition, *curriculum* and *instruction* are separated: curriculum is a guide for instruction based on learning outcomes but does not specify the means by which the outcomes are to be produced. The program of studies, the course content, the planned learning experiences, and even all the actual experiences "had" by students are seen as a part of instruction—guided by the curriculum, which is based not on activities but on outcomes.

This view of curriculum has some difficulties, perhaps the chief one being that, in theory or in practice, it is not really possible to separate outcomes from the means used to achieve them. *How* something is taught has real and immediate implications for what is learned. For instance, we have all experienced the difference in our own learning from a dry, dull lecture full of allusions and analogies that we don't understand, and a fast-paced, exciting lecture which touches our immediate experiences and concerns. The same material can be presented in both ways: it is the *how* of it that seems to make the difference.

Nevertheless, at some level, the notion that curriculum and instruction may be thought of not as one thing, but together, has some significance. For one thing, it allows us to think about each separately (remembering always that they are related). What are our intended goals? How are we going to design instruction to fulfill those goals?

**6** *A Compromise Concept of the Curriculum*   One answer to these questions lies in thinking about the curriculum as a continuum, with the ultimate goals at one end and the immediate and specific means (or limited goals) at the other.[3] This kind of definition has the virtue of being able to encompass course content (syllabi, programs of studies), learning activities, latent functions, and unintended outcomes at some point on the continuum. Further, it allows us to move back and forth along a continuum of actual process fairly easily. Zais describes some consequences of this kind of definition:

> Put in a more general way, we might say that the curriculum provides direction for classroom instruction, but it does not consist of a series of lesson plans. It is the teacher's prerogative and responsibility to interpret and translate the curriculum in terms of her own and her students' experience.[4]

Let's agree, then, that for our purposes curriculum and instruction are part of the same whole and that whole consists of what we want students to learn, including information, skills, attitudes, and values. Throughout all the discussions in this book, the learning of what we might call traditional school content is assumed. That is, we want children to learn to read, to manipulate numbers, to know about and understand history, social studies, grammar and literature, foreign languages, and the sciences. We also want them to be able to participate in the democratic processes of our society with diligence and creativity, and to have some sense of ethical issues and how to go about resolving them, as well as to be able to solve new problems that neither they nor we can as yet imagine. Beyond these goals, however, we have at least two others. First, we want *all* students to achieve them, not just some students. This involves issues of access and equity that we have been talking about all along. Second, we want all students to be able to interact effectively, and if possible pleasurably, with people who may not share their backgrounds, beliefs, values, linguistic constructions, or ways of looking at and acting in the world. This involves issues of inclusion—the expansion of curricular materials, of learning activities, of methods of evaluation, and of pedagogical methods to include items heretofore not included.

It is our belief that a fundamental interest in inclusion as a guiding principle, or fulfilling one's need to belong as recognized by the culture-general framework, can begin the process of transformation needed to achieve our goals. We regard transformation as a process analogous to the process by which a caterpillar becomes a butterfly; it involves change, certainly, but not just any kind of change. The curriculum and instruction we envisage for the coming years have all or most of the ingredients familiar to us, but they are transformed—rearranged, evolved, given new purposes and new shapes—until they not only look different, but eventuate in some new and different outcomes.

## TRANSFORMING LEARNING OUTCOMES: THE CASE OF PREJUDICE

Since we cannot outline here every single way that every single desirable learning outcome might be transformed, we will look at one particularly desirable outcome in detail and examine how curricular alterations might be used to effect it. We have chosen the reduction of prejudice, in part because that is one of the most common barriers to the kind of knowledge and skill outcomes we wish to promote (and you will recall that it, too, is one of the eighteen culture-general themes addressed earlier). We will assume that in your own personal reflection as well as in classroom discussions and other kinds of learning activities you will expand on the suggestions here and relate them to other instances of potential curricular and instructional use.

## Three Components of Prejudice

Categorization, stereotyping, and prejudice were discussed in detail in Chapter 3. Suffice it to say here that if prejudice served no useful function, it would disappear from human behavior.[5] Obviously, it has not gone away! Nevertheless, to benefit from the potential that all have to offer requires learning to see beyond narrow perspectives. In this chapter we will present curricular strategies intended to help develop a broader perspective and reduce the occurrence of prejudice, while simultaneously attending to academic achievement.

Prejudice has three components: cognitive, affective, and behavioral. The cognitive component, generally referred to as *stereotyping,* is a cultural universal. People the world over engage in the process of categorizing their environment in order to reduce the cognitive demands that they face. Stereotypes are merely categories of people that we can learn to modify or alter. The same can be said of the behavioral and affective components of prejudice—what people do about and how they respond emotionally to the categories they create. Educational efforts designed to reduce the negative impact of prejudice can have good results. We make the assumption that it is in the best interest of individuals, our schools, the community and world to apply our efforts in these areas.

## Prejudice Formation

Children are aware of differences in others from a very early age. It is in the early childhood and elementary school years that children's attitudes toward other groups are being formed and crystallized. It has been suggested that it is a critical role of the elementary school to provide experiences which cause children to rethink their beliefs about group differences.[6] In general, children are unlikely to do this on their own.

Byrnes summarizes the literature on prejudice formation in children and identifies four basic ways that children may learn to be prejudiced:[7]

**1** Children learn prejudice by observing the behavior of others, particularly respected elders. If those who surround a child hold biased beliefs about a particular group (e.g., the disabled, members of a certain religion, the physically unattractive), children may follow suit. While children learn much from the subtle messages given by others, some learn prejudice as a result of more blatant efforts of parents and community.[8] Some children, for instance, are from a very early age actively prepared for adult roles in such organizations as the Ku Klux Klan or the Irish Republican Army.

**2** Children, like other individuals, need to feel that they belong to a group. If excluding or devaluing certain ''others'' is considered the proper thing to do by one's group, not doing so can entail serious consequences. Thus, children may learn prejudice simply as a survival technique.

**3** Children may learn prejudice through their exposure to the media. While the media may not actively teach prejudice, it may reinforce stereotypes or in some cases introduce stereotypes where they may not already exist. Cowboy and Indian films, for instance, have been shown to have a significant impact on children's views of Native Americans.[9] Children's stories in both electronic and print media often equate beauty with goodness and ugliness with evil. The symbolic association with evil of physical disabilities such as hunchbacks, peg legs, eye patches, and hooked arms may encourage children to associate such disabilities with the cause of personal ill fortune or more widespread disaster.[10]

**4** The more orthodox or fundamental one's religious beliefs are, the greater the prejudice toward other religious and cultural groups is likely to be.[11] Strict adherence to certain religious practices may actively encourage the belief that all other doctrines are at best ''wrong'' and at worst dangerous—as are the individuals who believe in them.

Now, what can be done in schools to help reduce the occurrence of prejudice?

## Prejudice Reduction in Children

We are fortunate that the educational research literature supports the possibility of prejudice reduction. Indeed, there is some indication that we may even be able to decrease the likelihood that prejudiced attitudes will develop.[12] Reviewing the literature, Byrnes finds that educational strategies with demonstrated ability to reduce prejudice generally fall into four basic categories: (1) improving social contact and intergroup relations, (2) increasing cognitive sophistication, (3) improving self-esteem, and, (4) increasing empathy with and understanding of other groups.[13] All of these have curricular implications. We will next look at each in some detail.

## Improving Intergroup Interaction

From a programmatic standpoint, the most promising of all change efforts stems from the work of those interested in intergroup interaction. Gordon Allport, in proposing the contact hypothesis, suggests that one way to reduce prejudice is to bring representatives of different groups into close contact with one another.[14] While sometimes this proves helpful, that is not always the case; occasionally prejudice is reinforced, or even formed where it did not previously exist.[15] A different hypothesis suggests that it is the *conditions* under which groups came together that are critical. To assure positive outcomes, the contact situation should have certain characteristics. Efforts under many different circumstances (bilingual classrooms, integrated housing and schools, summer camp programs) have led to recommendations concerning the best conditions for social contact. They include the following:

**1 *Equal Status Contact*** Amir, working in integrated school settings in Israel, found that if individuals coming together perceive that they have equal status, or equal access to any rewards available, conditions are set for improved relations.[16] In Switzerland, for instance, French, German, and Italian are all recognized as official languages of the country. Official documents and media presentations are made available in all three languages. Speakers of all these languages, therefore, are all appreciated, well-informed, and encouraged to participate in the society at large. (Note the current movement under way in many states in the United States to make English the official language, even though the United States boasts the fourth largest Spanish-speaking population in the world!)

In the school context, equal access to rewards can mean equal access to such things as knowledge, grades, and extracurricular offerings. For all students to have equal access to knowledge and grades, culturally appropriate curricula and instructional strategies may need to be employed. Equally at issue is the necessity to encourage all students to participate in extracurricular offerings. In the ''natural'' course of events this may not always occur. As discussed in Chapter 5, social class status has significant impact on the kinds of school experiences a child has. Children from lower socioeconomic groups tend to participate in fewer after-school activities than their middle-class counterparts, thus not reaping the potential benefits of participation, for example the development of skills related to group and team thinking and action that have been shown to be associated with managerial or other higher-level employment. Recent legislation regarding equal rights for disabled persons (of whom there are more than 43 million in the United States) is also intended to bring about equal access of children with disabilities to these kinds of activities.

**2** *Superordinate Goal or Common Task*   Having equal status is not sufficient. Individuals who come together and work toward achieving some superordinate goal or common task that requires the participation of all involved are more likely to learn to get along. This concept stems from the work of Sherif, who, though able to create hostility and aggression rather easily between two groups of boys at summer camp, found it quite difficult to bring them back together as one larger, cooperative group.[17] Finally, after much trial and error, he was able to bring both groups together after staging an incident in which a bus got stuck in the mud while on the way to a camp outing. In order for the bus to continue on its way, all the campers had to work together to push it back onto the road. This superordinate goal, which could not have been achieved without everyone's participation, motivated all the boys to work together.

In the school context, superordinate goals are readily available in the form of team sports, drama productions, and music performances, as well as through cooperative learning activities that can be easily integrated in the classroom setting (see Chapter 13 for more on cooperative learning). When students with disabilities participate in the mainstream of school life, including extracurricular activities as well as more academic classroom experiences, such coparticipation with nondisabled peers in pursuit of common goals is possible. Similarly, students who have opportunities to work with others across racial and ethnic boundaries in activities like these tend to develop more positive attitudes toward one another during and after such encounters. In schools with more homogeneous populations, it is often necessary to plan activities deliberately to involve those from different groups. Such attempts may involve learning to ''see'' invisible differences, such as differences in learning style, differences in religious attitudes, or differences in knowledge and perceptions related to sex role. They might also involve cooperative efforts with other communities and schools, an effort to institute international exchange student programs, the encouragement of integrated activities between individuals with and without handicaps, or across traditional age barriers, say between high school and elementary school students or between older people in the community and students of all ages.

**3** *Appropriate Social Norms*   The social norms of the institution must encourage intergroup interaction and the reduction of prejudice. In order to be effective, efforts to reduce prejudice must be seen as important at all levels of the school. Such efforts cannot be seen entirely as the whim or ''cause'' of a particular teacher or particular group.

Teachers and school administrators (and as many other adults as possible, including parents and other residents in the community) must actively encourage and show support for such efforts. Do not mistake this caveat, however, for a statement that the individual teacher cannot make a considerable difference by initiating such changes. As innumerable teachers acting independently or with a small group of colleagues have demonstrated, the initial efforts of a single individual can have broad effects. Especially in curricular selections and decisions about types of learning activities, teachers often feel more constrained than they actually are. Although the school system often controls much of one's ability to make significant and permanent change—partly by how it controls available resources—it by no means controls everything. Indeed, many if not most school systems today are eager to support a teacher who is trying something new in the way of curricular revision. Careful documentation of the process and the results of such revisions by the teacher is often one of the best ways to begin to institutionalize the changes that are effective, and is invaluable in assessing and refining the teacher's initial work.

The need to continue using new methods over an extended period of time, with revisions as necessary, cannot be overestimated and is very much in line with current thinking about the relationship between attitude and behavior change. Social psychologists have had a difficult time demonstrating that significant, long-lasting behavior change follows from short-term attitude change efforts. While it may be possible to demonstrate a change in attitude as a result of a short-term intervention (during a summer camp session, for instance), there is little evidence either that the attitude change persists or that it leads to a subsequent long-term change in behavior. The converse may in fact be true. Research on attitudes toward people with disabilities is instructive in this regard. An individual who has had little contact with persons with disabilities may react initially with discomfort and/or pity, being acutely aware of the disability. For example, in one study teachers participating in an intensive 5-week summer training institute focusing on teaching young children with disabilities actually demonstrated a negative change in attitude, as measured by the *Attitudes toward Disabled Persons* scale.[18] Positive attitudes as defined by this scale, however, are those that consider a disabled person as essentially like everyone else, not someone "special." For many of the teachers in this study, this was a first exposure, both to extensive content concerning disabilities and to working with children with disabilities. They were acutely aware of the difficulties, very sympathetic, and eager to help. Later follow-up interviews confirmed this and revealed subsequent shifts toward more "normalized" attitudes over time.

Studies of the effects of classroom integration of handicapped children generally have shown that mere exposure does not necessarily result in the formation of friendships. Teachers need to actively promote social interaction, model an attitude of accepting and valuing all children, and design activities that enable handicapped and nonhandicapped children to work together.[19] The experience may initially be disappointing, but often insufficient *time* has been allowed before sociometric measures have been used. For example, in one study involving preschool children, nonhandicapped children seldom selected handicapped peers in play situations initially, but repeated observations several weeks later showed significant change.[20]

If we can get people to the point where they are behaving in new and different ways for an extended period of time, then perhaps their attitude about themselves and others may follow suit. If, for instance, organizational structure can be modified so as to encourage or require significant intergroup interaction over an extended period of time, people may begin to see themselves and others as tolerant, understanding, and easy to get along with. Federal legislation in certain cases mandates changes in structure on a national level. Official support and status of bilingualism in Canada, for instance, seems to be a promising example. Never believe, however, that mandates alone will do the job. What is required is committed and persistent face-to-face activity—and a good deal of trial and error!

**4** *High Acquaintance Potential*   The contact situation must have a high acquaintance potential, encouraging rather intimate contact. In other words, people must have the opportunity to get to know the ''other'' in ways that render the stereotypic image clearly inappropriate. It is very difficult, for instance, to believe that all people on welfare are lazy when one knows firsthand that Susan and her mother are both working as much as they are allowed to within the welfare rules, and that if Susan's mother took an available job that paid a decent wage but did not include health benefits, she would lose the health card that is the only thing standing between Susan and continual health problems with chronic asthma.

In addition to the suggestions above, students can be placed in different heterogeneous groups for a variety of purposes, and can be encouraged or required to participate in mixed team sports—any scheme that will give them ample opportunity to get to know each other better. There should also be time for informal activity, perhaps even structured into the day or on weekends.

## Increasing Cognitive Sophistication

A second set of strategies that have been shown to have a positive impact on prejudice reduction are those designed to increase cognitive sophistication. A considerable amount of research points to the fact that individuals who think in narrow terms are more likely to be very prejudiced. Strategies designed to help individuals avoid stereotypes and overgeneralizations as well as to become aware of the biases in their thinking and behavior do help people become less prejudiced.

Strategies for increasing cognitive sophistication focus on improving students' critical thinking skills. Thinking in a critical manner, as Walsh says, is antithetical to prejudicial thinking.[21] Rather than acting quickly, from emotion, people must search for and examine the reasons or motivations behind their thoughts and actions. When one thinks critically, one questions, analyzes, closely examines, and suspends judgment until all available information is perceived and understood. Ten essential criteria in the development of critical thought are identified by D'Angelo.[22] These include *intellectual curiosity; objectivity*—relying on evidence, not emotions, in making one's argument; *open-mindedness,* or a willingness to consider a wide range of possibilities; *flexibility in one's thinking,* or an ability to change one's method of inquiry; *intellectual skepticism,* or evaluating considerable evidence before accepting a hypothesis; *intellectual honesty*—a willingness to accept evidence even if it conflicts with a previously held belief; *being systematic,* or consistent in one's line of reasoning; *being persistent; being decisive*—making conclusions when enough supporting evidence is available; *having respect for other points of view* and responding in an appropriate way to what others are saying.

Teachers should work hard to create the kind of classroom environment that encourages critical thought. Included in such a classroom are the following characteristics:[23]

**1** The classroom and school climate must be one where students feel respected and have a certain degree of trust, again, satisfying one's need to belong. As explained in Chapter 3, students will not function at higher cognitive levels when their anxiety level is high. Feelings of safety and trust are thus a corollary of student risk taking.

**2** The classroom must become, as Lipman states, a "community of inquiry."[24] Such an environment is characterized as much by a balance between asking the right question and providing the right answer as it is by asking questions that have more than one "right" answer. Indeed, some feel that even a modest interest in exigencies in the world outside the school requires that teachers' questions be designed to stimulate students to consider a number of aspects of a problem, a process which may produce conflicting answers.

**3** Teachers must strike a balance between teacher talk and student talk. Students must believe that their ideas are important and that what they have to say is critical. It is through discussion with others, and the sharing of ideas and problems, that critical thinking develops.

**4** Students should meet with success in the classroom, thus increasing their self-esteem—so critical to prejudice reduction, as we will see in the following section.

**5** Students should be taught to think about their thinking, and should be able to justify their reasoning with evidence. *Metacognition,* or becoming aware of how one has come to a decision, should be emphasized.

We will discuss the goal of developing critical thinking further in Chapter 13. Here we would like to stress what should be obvious: that to think critically means to think broadly, to take a number of aspects of a problem into account, to weigh the evidence—in short, to avoid simplistic approaches. Students often are encouraged to "learn what is in the book," which frequently means to avoid thinking altogether. Teachers who strive to create an environment which encourages risk taking, where cooperative problem solving is stressed, and where mistakes are not perceived as sins or personal faults are more likely to help students achieve.[25] An emphasis on thinking skills should not be seen as an "addition" to an already overcrowded schedule. It does not require a special course or time of day. Rather, it is a goal which requires a style of presentation that should be integrated into every lesson, and into all contacts with students.

## Improving Self-Confidence and Self-Acceptance

Pettigrew established a clear inverse relationship between the degree of prejudice a person harbors and that person's sense of self-worth.[26] That is, the more confident one is of his or her own identity, competence, and place in the universe, the lower their degree of prejudice, and vice-versa. While the relationship is not necessarily a cause and effect one, there are strong indications that self-acceptance is critical to mental, physical, and emotional health. Classroom activities designed to increase self-confidence and self-esteem also tend to bring about a decrease in levels of prejudice. Children can develop confidence in themselves when they are in educational environments where they feel secure and accepted, where their participation is valued, and where they know the boundaries or limits.[27] Creating such environments should be of prime concern to educators.

### Increasing Empathy for and Understanding of Others

Effective learning about others must have an affective component. Students cannot simply be told what it is we wish them to know and do. When long-term transfer of information to behavior change is desired, educational experiences which actively engage the emotions are much more effective.

Activities designed to help students see the world from another's perspective are useful empathy builders. Classroom simulations are an excellent tool for helping children become sensitive to others who act or look different. Shaver and Curtis, for example, offer a simulation to help children understand what it is like for those with speech difficulties.[28] They suggest students put something in their mouths (such as a small, clean rubber ball or dental cotton—large enough that it won't be swallowed) and then make a telephone call to a store and ask for information. Students can then discuss how it feels to be unable to communicate effectively.

The classic cross-cultural simulation BAFA BAFA, or the children's version RAFA RAFA, is excellent for helping students understand what it is like to move into another cultural group.[29] In this experience, individuals learn ''proper'' behavior associated with the creation of two distinct cultural groups. After some time, members of each group have the opportunity to interact with one another. They very quickly experience feelings of anxiety, rejection, apprehension, and confusion—those feelings often referred to collectively as *culture shock,* encountered by most individuals who have moved from one country or culture to another. This simulation provides a foundation of experience from which students (and teachers or parents) can explore the feelings and experiences of immigrant, migrant, or refugee students; international exchange students; students in newly desegregated schools; newly mainstreamed children with disabilities; or just about anybody cast in the role of ''new kid on the block.''

Students may also write stories or act out plays and dramatizations of situations in which acts of prejudice and discrimination take place. Students can take the role of a person who has suffered discrimination, and they may get a much better idea what that is like.

### TRANSFORMING LEARNING OUTCOMES: THE INTERNATIONAL DIMENSION

As we have said repeatedly, teachers today need to prepare students for a world quite different from any that has existed in the past. In the United States, four-fifths of new jobs created are the result of foreign trade. Political boundaries are rapidly changing, creating opportunities and challenges not imagined in recent decades. More and more, day-to-day activities bring people into closer contact with others different from themselves. How can curricula address issues necessary to prepare citizens of the twenty-first century? What concepts and skills are necessary to function effectively in an interdependent world? What exactly do we mean by a global or international perspective?

## A Model of Intercultural Education

It is useful to contrast individual cognitive demands with the changing needs of society. Hoopes used such an approach when he presented a rationale and model of intercultural education.[30] Hoopes distinguished three levels of society and identified some basic cognitive requirements at each. At one level, the *local-traditional level,* people are able to satisfy their daily needs within their rather small, closed group. Little interaction between groups is necessary in order to satisfy ordinary requirements. When interaction does occur, it is usually fraught with conflict, disagreement, apprehension, and fear. There is little need, or desire, to understand the perspective of the other group. In the historical past, these characteristics were associated with tribal groups, large extended families or clans living in close proximity, and perhaps very small rural towns and villages.

At the next level, the *national-modern level,* group needs are such that everything people require cannot be obtained in one's own surroundings. Services, goods, and knowledge that others have access to may be desired and needed. Thus, methods of barter, trade, or other means of negotiation can be established between individuals and groups. Money as a medium of exchange becomes very important, and communication increases. These characteristics can be associated with most western societies at least from the latter part of the seventeenth century onward. At this level, people and societies are interdependent, but only to a small degree. For the most part, nation-states can remain relatively autonomous; towns and cities may develop and maintain themselves with only the help of surrounding areas; individuals may not have to go very far to obtain and trade, buy or sell the things they need or want.

A third level, one which many societies and nations of the world are entering today, Hoopes called the *global-postmodern level.* Here, people and nations are so inextricably bound that they cannot satisfy their needs without significant relations with numerous others. These characteristics are also associated with the daily lives of most individuals who live in those societies. People obtain their food, not from their own or neighboring farms, but from a supermarket that carries foodstuffs from around the world. Their clothing comes, not from their own or their neighbors' fields, spinning wheels, looms, and needles, but from stores that manufacture, buy, and sell internationally. People do not build their own or their neighbors' houses without materials from around the planet, nor do most build their own machinery at all. If there is an oil spill in the Bering Sea, it is likely to affect the lives of people in the Gulf of Mexico. If there are food shortages in the Soviet Union, it is likely to affect the lives of people in the United States. If a large international company in the United States is bought out by a large international company in Germany, it is likely to affect the jobs of people in Taiwan, Singapore, or China. When something happens in Tanzania or Venezuela or Saudi Arabia, people in Alaska, Sweden, Australia, and South Africa know it within minutes or hours. When there is war, it affects everyone. Indeed, the survival of the planet may now depend on the smooth, interdependent functioning of many governments, economies, technologies, communications systems, and the people who make those institutions come alive. It is such a level that we refer to when we speak of a global society or a global economy. To the extent that these characteristics apply, people live in what has been referred to as a *global village.*

Most would agree that in order to develop satisfactory relationships, to understand others' motivations and needs, as well as to interact effectively with people who are different, a certain degree of empathy is necessary. Hoopes suggests that further development of empathy, or the ability to project oneself into the mind of others, and to feel what they are feeling, is critical to the move from the local-traditional level to the national-modern level.[31] Empathy becomes much more necessary for some (but not all) at the national-modern level when people must understand others in order to consummate bilateral trade agreements. It is indispensible at the postmodern-global level, for everyone.

The postmodern-global world has numerous players. Each of these participants has a different perspective, distinct wants and needs, and different ways of thinking, interacting, and expressing themselves. A well-functioning global society demands that individuals be able to think, perceive, communicate, and behave in new and different ways. The preparation of individuals for these kinds of interactions is the goal of *global* or *international education*.

### Education for a Global Perspective

The National Council for the Social Studies defines a *global perspective* as developing "the knowledge, skills, and attitudes needed to live effectively in a world possessing limited natural resources and characterized by ethnic diversity, cultural pluralism, and increasing interdependence."[32] Teaching toward a global perspective emphasizes that (1) human experience is an increasingly global phenomenon, and people are constantly being influenced by transnational, cross-cultural, and multicultural interaction; (2) there is a wide variety of actors on the world stage, including states, multinational corporations, numerous voluntary nongovernmental organizations, as well as individuals; (3) the fate of humankind cannot be separated from the state of the global environment; (4) there are linkages between present social, political, and ecological realities and alternative futures; and (5) citizen participation is critical at both local and international levels.[33] Education for a global perspective integrates learning which enhances students' ability to comprehend their condition in the community and the world and their ability to make good judgments. It includes the study of nations, cultures, and civilizations, including our own pluralistic society and the societies of other peoples, with a focus on understanding how these are all interconnected and how they change, and on the individual's responsibility in this process. It provides the individual with a realistic perspective on world issues, problems, and prospects, and an awareness of the relationships between an individual's enlightened self-interest and the concerns of people elsewhere in the world. The catchphrase "Think globally; act locally" has served the growing field of global education well.

Making these somewhat abstract concerns concrete, immediate, and meaningful is important, especially with younger children. Of all the disciplines typically taught in school social studies has been, almost by definition, in the best position to appreciate and to integrate a global perspective. However, if education from a global perspective is perceived as an add-on to an already overcrowded curriculum, it will meet with much resistance and have little impact. Rather, we must learn to integrate a global perspective throughout the disciplines. Nevertheless, we can learn a good deal from our colleagues in the social studies, who have paved the way for the rest of us.

Most discussion of global education refers to Robert Hanvey's paper "An Attainable Global Perspective."[34] In this work, Hanvey defines some elements of a global perspective which might help us lay a foundation for development of important skills and sensitivities. The dimensions Hanvey discusses cut across many disciplines and can be applied across the grade levels. Sensitive and able teachers can find numerous ways to integrate them into their teaching.

## Five Elements of a Global Perspective

Hanvey discusses five elements which contribute to the formation of a global perspective. The first, *perspective consciousness,* addresses the recognition or awareness of the individual that she or he has a view of the world that is not universally shared, that this view has been and continues to be shaped by influences that often escape conscious detection, and that others have views of the world that are profoundly different from her or his own.[35]

This dimension differentiates opinion from perspective. *Opinion* refers to the surface layer of one's innermost thoughts. It is the tip of the iceberg, so to speak, only showing a small portion of itself. Underneath the surface lie the generally hidden, unexamined assumptions and judgments people make about life, about others, about right and wrong—many of those subjective elements of culture which are so difficult to grasp. The assumption that human dominance over nature is both attainable and desirable is an example of a perspective that lies deep in many western minds. It was not until this traditionally unexamined assumption surfaced that many philosophical choices that previously escaped our attention were raised. As a result, debate on our relationship with the environment began. The feminist movement raised the consciousness of women and men regarding the role of women in society. In the process, deep layers of chauvinism inherent in much of our thinking about male and female roles was revealed. And concerned parents, addressing the unmet needs of their exceptional children, pointed out how the educational system, and society in general, discriminated against a large segment of society.

Hanvey's second element is *state of the planet awareness.* This is an awareness of the prevailing world conditions and developments, including emergent conditions and trends such as population growth and migration; economic conditions; resources and the physical environment; political developments; advances in science and technology, law, and health; and internation and intranation conflicts.[36] Most people, even from highly mobile societies like the United States, spend the majority of their time in their local area. However, developments in communication technology have brought the world, if not into most people's homes, certainly within most people's reach. Extensive global coverage via television news is now making its impact felt at the diplomatic table as well. The liberal weekly *Die Zeit* of Hamburg, Germany, relates two incidents which reveal the extent of the impact of the aggressive CNN news broadcasting team:

> In the summer of 1989, when the U.S. government was searching for a response to threats that hostages in Lebanon would be killed, a White House advisor was asked where President George Bush was spending the day. "He is in his office, watching CNN," the advisor said. "CNN is interviewing Middle East experts; maybe one of them will have an idea that the president can use." And when the Americans marched into Panama in December, 1989, Soviet leader Mikhail Gorbachev made use of the medium. CNN's Moscow correspondent was called to the Kremlin in the middle of the night. There, a press aide read a condemnation of the invasion for the

camera. The official note to the U.S. ambassador was not delivered until hours later. The Kremlin's excuse was that it was counting on Washington's getting the Kremlin's reaction immediately via CNN.[37]

Then, in the winter of 1991, the world was drawn together in a kind of awful fascination by television coverage of the war in the Middle East. It is necessary, however, to learn to "read between the lines," and understand the purpose of the news media, the conditions under which it works, as well as its limitations. For the most part, the news media focuses on extraordinary events, such as the war. There are a number of problems here, one being that if we are not careful, it is very easy to come to believe that the real world consists only of televised images—the world according to CNN so to speak. Another problem is that television and print news is selective. For example, an outbreak of the measles (as has happened in recent years in various parts of the United States) or a famine in Ethiopia is newsworthy, while chronic hunger (as affects millions of Americans and others around the world) is not. Also, not all parts of the world receive the same news. One of the authors of this book traveled to Australia during December 1989 and January 1990. On arriving he was warned to keep his family protected from the hazardous rays of the sun, especially since the hole in the ozone layer had, in recent years, moved from Antarctica to reach the southern parts of Australia. In fact, conditions were such that Australia now had the world's highest rate of skin cancer! Major efforts were under way throughout the country to warn people against unprotected exposure to the sun. Parents went to all extremes to make certain their children's skin was covered while they played outside. Everyone wore hats. Even adolescents, who typically might go to any length to show off a suntan, were making efforts to protect themselves. Attempts were also being made to make high-SPF sunscreens prescriptive medications so people could deduct their cost from their income tax, thereby encouraging their use. However, the American public was somehow, and for some reason, prevented from knowing about the extent of the hole in the ozone and the severe impact it was having on people's lives. The information never hit the American news wires. This is an example of selective news coverage.

General public awareness of the state of the planet, as well as the nation, must become a priority, and is attainable. Children must be encouraged to reflect and to ask questions which go beyond the obvious. Do we know that 43 million Americans are considered disabled or handicapped? Do we know that 35,000 children around the world die each day of hunger-related causes? How many people go hungry or are homeless in our own nation? How many children are being born addicted to cocaine or infected with the AIDS virus? Students must be actively encouraged to expand their knowledge base, to review international news sources, and to inquire into the knowledge and perspective of international visitors. This, incidentally, will help to develop the first dimension of global education, perspective consciousness.

Hanvey's third dimension, *cross-cultural awareness,* includes an awareness of the diversity of ideas and practices found in human societies around the world, of how such ideas and practices compare, and at least a beginning awareness of how the ideas and ways of one's own society might be viewed from other vantage points.[38] Hanvey suggests that this dimension may be the most difficult of all to attain, since people typically do not have or take the time to truly know the motivations and reasons which determine why human beings act as they do. We now know that understanding of others does not necessarily follow from simple contact. Rather lengthy, intimate contact which enables one to "get into the heads" of those in another culture is often required for significant culture learning.

How can schooling best develop this perspective in young people? To define goals, and assess what can be accomplished given available resources, it may be helpful to consider four levels of cross-cultural awareness posited by Hanvey.

• *Level 1—Awareness of superficial or extremely visible cultural traits:* From this surface awareness stereotypes often emerge. Much of this information is obtained through textbooks, television, and tourism. At this level, the individual outside a given culture typically interprets observed actions of others as exotic, or worse, bizarre.

• *Level 2—Awareness of significant and subtle cultural traits that contrast markedly with one's own:* Such information is gained as a result of culture conflict situations, and also is interpreted as unbelievable. The reaction here, however, is more on an emotional level. Interactions are considered frustrating, irrational, and against "common sense."

• *Level 3—Intellectual analysis:* Level 3 also includes an awareness of significant and subtle cultural traits that contrast markedly with one's own. However, this level *is characterized by more intellectual emphasis and analysis.* Others' behavior is then interpreted as believable because it can be understood.

• *Level 4—Awareness of how another culture feels from the perspective of an insider:* People attain this perspective through cultural immersion; that is, from living the culture. Information is perceived as believable, not simply because it is understood at the cognitive level, but because one is familiar at the subjective, or affective level. This might be likened to reaching the state called "home" on the U-curve of cross-cultural adjustment described in Chapter 2.

Effective culture learning is more an affective and behavioral process than a cognitive process. One truly learns about another culture by living it, not by being told about it. Development of intercultural competence may be, as Hanvey and others have noted, the most difficult, yet most critical, of the five dimensions to achieve.[39]

However, strategies do exist which can assist one on their way to becoming interculturally competent. The culture-general framework introduced in Chapter 3 has been demonstrated to have a significant impact on cognition, affect, and behavior in cross-cultural settings. It is a cognitive tool which engages the emotions, and may be just the tool for the school context.

Hanvey's fourth dimension is *knowledge of global dynamics.* Attaining this requires a modest comprehension of key traits and mechanisms of the world system, with an emphasis on theories and concepts that may increase intelligent consciousness of global change.[40] A systems analysis is utilized, stressing the interconnectedness of things, and asking people to consider the impact one decision or action will have on another. Consider this example of the interconnectedness of elements in an ecological system. In southeastern Australia, fluctuation of various fish populations in area river basins was recently found to be caused by an increase in estrogen in the water. But how did this estrogen find its way into rivers and streams? It was determined that the hormone found its way into area waterways after being flushed out in toilet wastewater. Women using birth control pills eliminated higher than usual levels of estrogen in their urine. This directly affected the behavior of fish downstream! This is a good example of an unanticipated outcome. Now consider an example of the vulnerability of ecological systems to changes in distant parts of the world. The recent increase in mosquito populations across the United States can be directly tied to our tremendous appetite for inexpensive fast-food hamburgers. An increasing proportion of the meat in our diet comes from cattle raised on land that was once rainforest in Central and South America. These rainforests provided the winter nesting sites for many of the northern hemisphere's migrating bird populations. As an increasing percentage of the rainforest is destroyed, so too are the winter nesting sites for these birds, which are dying. The decline in bird population has resulted in fewer songbirds returning north, and the population of mosquitoes, which form a major part of their diet, is increasing. This is a vivid example of the impact individual choice can have. "Think globally; act locally" again becomes paramount.

A critical principle of change is the implication, ramification, and "spin-off" of events. When a new element is introduced into any system it has unanticipated effects. Hanvey suggests that there are no "side effects," only surprise effects. When we intervene in any system, we should be prepared for some surprising consequences. We confront numerous other examples of this principle in action almost every day. Depletion of the ozone layer, the greenhouse effect, the poisoning of groundwater, and the weakening of the eagle's egg as a result of DDT moving up the food chain are all examples of these surprise consequences, which we are now trying to correct. We must learn, as Hanvey suggests, to look for the "concealed wiring," the hidden functions of elements in a system.

Hanvey's fifth dimension, *awareness of human choices,* is perhaps the most critical. The problems of choice which confront individuals, nations, and the human species as a whole as consciousness and knowledge of the global system expand are addressed here.[41] Until rather recently, people were generally unaware of the unanticipated outcomes and long-term consequences of their actions, how they might impact upon others, and the links between events, as well as societies. This is no longer the case. A global consciousness or cognition is emerging. People now need to consider the implications of our expanded knowledge and communication base. Negligence, or even making an unwise choice out of ignorance, may set the stage for countless problems at some future time.

Fortunately, we know a great deal more than we used to, and choices do exist. Consider the growing problem of chlorofluorocarbons (CFCs) and the growing problem of ozone depletion. We have two choices: we can continue to use CFCs because at the present time they make refrigeration and propellants possible, or we can stop using them because of their effect on the environment while actively seeking other ways of providing the benefits they used to provide. The simple substitution of pump spray mechanisms for propellant sprays on a variety of products is a good example of a successful alternative. It is awareness of the problem, however, that often makes the difference in the success of alternatives.

Children can make remarkable strides toward realizing their power to make change. In the 1970s, Israeli elementary schoolchildren went on a campaign to protect some of their nation's threatened wildflower population. They raised the awareness of adults to such an extent that the adults stopped indiscriminately picking the flowers. Many of the threatened flowers have since been removed from the endangered species lists. During the early 1980s, one of the authors of this text initiated a classroom writing project and school exchange between fifth- and sixth-grade children in northeast Ohio and school-children in the Yucatan in Mexico, and in Belize. Seventeen children went on the first trip from Ohio to Belize. One gesture of appreciation they made to their host community was to present the village school with a world atlas signed by everyone at the visitors' school. This gift seemed to be the first book the school actually owned. This made such an impression on the students from Ohio that on their return home they decided to do something about the situation. All the fifth- and sixth-grade students in the school became involved in operating an after-school snack bar, collecting usable books from the community, and packaging them for shipment overseas. With the proceeds from their snack bar and their organizational efforts, students were able to send more than 500 books to their peers in this small village in Belize. Needless to say, they felt tremendous pride, realizing that they, personally, could have such an impact on individuals so far away. This is a lesson no textbook could teach them and that they will not forget.

## Framework for a Social Studies Curriculum

Experience must be linked to a cognitive dimension if it is to have long-term value. Kniep has presented a framework for a social studies curriculum reflecting a global perspective; it develops four essential elements.[42]

**1** *The study of systems* includes study of economic, political, ecological, and technological systems.
**2** *The study of human values* looks at both cultural universals and culture-specific values.
**3** *The study of persistent issues and problems* looks at such issues as peace and security, development issues, environmental issues, and human rights.
**4** *The study of global history* focuses on the historical development of global systems and the historical roots of today's global issues.

Conceptual themes, or big ideas which form mental structures or language used in thinking about the world, are an important dimension of Kniep's proposed plan. These powerful concepts act as organizers in the development of a global perspective. Such concepts include interdependence, change, culture, scarcity, and conflict, and can act as central foci around which other concepts can cluster.

Persistent problems associated with modern life are also addressed by Kniep's global curriculum. Such problems vividly illustrate the interdependence of people and places while encouraging students to identify how they themselves are a part of the solution or the problem. Most problems fall into the following four categories: *peace and security,* including the arms race, east-west relations, terrorism, colonialism, and democracy versus tyranny; *national and international development,* including such issues as hunger and poverty, overpopulation, north-south relations, appropriate technology, and the international debt crisis; *environmental problems,* such as acid rain, pollution of streams, depletion of rainforests, nuclear waste disposal, and maintenance of the world's fisheries; *human rights,* including apartheid, indigenous homelands, political imprisonment, religious persecution, and refugee issues.

Such a curriculum strives to help students recognize the importance of their individual efforts to address collective problems. Kniep says: ''For a number of our most pressing environmental and social problems—contamination of the environment, warming of the atmosphere, world hunger, international terrorism, the nuclear threat—there will be international solutions or no solutions at all.[43]

## Adding an International Dimension Across the Curriculum

Development of a global perspective should be integrated throughout the curricular domains, not restricted to the social studies. Large-scale infusion is possible.[44] But even without any large-scale change, an international perspective can be integrated into the curriculum by individual teachers through international focus courses, by internationalizing instructional methods and materials, and by internationalizing the disciplines.[45]

*International focus courses* exist in such areas as anthropology, regional history, geography and global or world studies, foreign language study, art and music, world religions, ethnic group studies, and international business. Such courses seem most appropriate at the secondary level and quite readily emerge from the disciplines themselves.

*Internationalizing instructional methods and materials* might mean promoting intercultural interaction in the classroom, utilizing the experiences of immigrant and international students as resources. Teachers should employ culturally appropriate instructional and assessment strategies. Textbooks should be reviewed for balance. Partnership programs with other schools and countries can be developed. One very fruitful partnership project initiated by Parents and Teachers for Social Responsibility in Moretown, Vermont, links American students with peers overseas in collaboration on a joint writing project. The Partnership Stories, as they have come to be called, are started by children in one country and completed by children in another.[46] The first story, *The Monkey's Dilemma,* a fairy tale cowritten and coillustrated by American and Soviet children, was printed in both Russian and English (see Figure 12.1).[47]

Another approach to adding an international dimension to educational materials is through international cooperation in curriculum development. Such projects as Legacy International's *My Future—My World: The Crisis of the Environment* and the Pacific Circle Consortium's *The Ocean Project* bring together educators from many countries to create a common product to be used in schools of the nations involved.

*Internationalizing the disciplines* means incorporating key elements of a global perspective into all courses already being taught. There are numerous ways this can be accomplished at all levels and in all content areas. For instance, in reading and language arts, students might study various forms of the world's use of English. Works of non-American and non-British writers can be used. World literature courses should strive to include numerous non-Western works. Children's literature and trade books can be used to present concepts of interest in international education. Classic Dr. Seuss books, such as *The Lorax* and *The Butter Battle Book,* can be used in a study of the environment and the nuclear arms race, respectively. Students might also analyze the portrayal of minorities and internationals in basal textbooks.

In science education students might propose solutions to global environmental problems, an exercise which will require knowledge of intergroup relations and cross-cultural skills. While technology may be universal, its application is quite specific. The study of appropriate technology and its transfer demands sensitivity to a number of elements such as local environment, culture, history, and language. The topic of unplanned change can

The monkey was bored.

She went to the house of her friend the ghost. There was some good-smelling soup simmering on the stove.

She couldn't help herself — she took a sip...and then another...and then another. It tasted so good and felt so warm.

Before she knew it, the pot was empty. She had eaten the whole meal.

Обезьянке было скучно.

Она пошла в гости к своему другу Привидению. В его доме вкусно пахло — В печке кипел суп.

Обезьянка не могла удержаться и отхлебнула чуть-чуть... Но было так вкусно, что она отхлебнула еще немного...И еще...и еще... Суп был необыкновенно вкусным, а в животике у нее было так тепло... Обезьянка не заметила, как съела все. Кастрюлька была пуста.

FIGURE 12.1    A page from *The Monkey's Dilemma*.

be introduced through the study of biology and evolution. Inequities of energy consumption across the planet can be explored. Finally, the global nature of such systems as the water cycle, the mineral cycle, and the energy cycle can be studied.

In foreign language education, cultural studies can be expanded beyond the mother country to include colonized people as well as immigrant and refugee populations. The role of translators in world diplomacy can be studied. Foreign languages can be taught through folk songs, and English as a second language can be introduced to foreign language teachers and students.

Mathematics education should stress the metric system. Math concepts can be illustrated by using problems that simultaneously teach about world trends and global issues.

Traditional numeration systems from other cultures can be studied. The mathematics and possible computer application of Islamic art can be analyzed. The impact of women on the development of mathematics can be introduced.

Finally, history and social studies courses should stress alternate perspectives. The American Revolution, for instance, certainly looked different through British eyes. Studying other nation's textbooks or discussing current events with international students can go far in developing perspective consciousness. Issues of population growth, personal family migration, history, and cultural diffusion can become the focus of historical inquiry, as can the interaction between geography, culture, and the environment.

## THE PROCESS OF CURRICULUM TRANSFORMATION

The foregoing discussion may make it appear that the process of transforming curriculum and instruction is relatively simple and requires only an exercise of will. Unfortunately, although deciding that such transformations *should* occur is necessary, it is usually not sufficient. We are all creatures of our own cultures. We tend to raise our children as we were raised, and school our children as we were schooled, even when we would like to redirect our efforts. Continual monitoring of our plans and actions is therefore necessary. Second, because an important function of schooling is, as we have said before, the preservation of society, there are always conservative forces in the school which act as countervailing forces to change; not the least of these is the notion that the teacher is the expert and should be in charge. Third, students themselves—particularly older students—are often resistant to change. The very students who might stand to benefit the most from the changes we have been advocating often create their own structures within the school that operate to preserve their status as outsiders and nonachievers.[48] Also, many students of every background become uncomfortable with and resist change when it appears to threaten the stability of the classrooms they know and understand. High-achieving students, for instance, often do not want to work cooperatively, because they are afraid either that some members of their group may not do their fair share or that group grading may lower their grade-point averages. Moreover, students who have become accustomed to, and have internalized, the ''Keep your eyes on your own paper, and don't talk to your neighbor'' dictum of past years often suspect that group work somehow involves cheating.

Do not underestimate the power of habit and belief in you or in your students. Understand that neither you nor your students are passive recipients of learning but actively, although sometimes in very subtle ways, seek to control the classroom environment. Changing traditional ways of thinking and acting is not easy. Nevertheless, it is quite possible, and often an exciting undertaking.

A number of educators have developed schemas for a more inclusive curriculum. Much of this work comes out of the new scholarship on women; it focuses on expanding the curriculum to include the perspective and experiences of women, and is the result of several years of experience in transforming curricula for both children in schools and young adults in college. Such examples can help us as we think about broadening the curriculum. While the process is ongoing, these schemas have some of the benefits of hindsight and they carry a certain authority of experience. Often referred to as *phase theories,* they are useful in providing an outline of the process of curriculum transformation from the point of view of the teacher and help to illuminate some of the ways in which our own thinking undergoes the transformation necessary to change what and how we teach. It is important to note that the phases we will describe are not discrete stages that we go through. We do not finish one stage and go on to the next; rather, we move continuously back and forth between them,[49] depending on the sophistication of our thinking, on our opportunities, on our discipline, and on who our students are. Phase theories are not prescriptions for change but are descriptions of the process of making curricular thinking more inclusive.

Most of these theories set forth five phases of curriculum transformation. The various authors name them differently, but we will attempt to summarize them in the following way:[50]

**Phase 1—The Absence of the "Other."**   In the beginning, we are unaware that anything is amiss. Subject matter "knowledge" exists, *out there,* apart from the experience of teachers, learners, and—more important—the ordinary people who created it and lived with its implications. The curriculum is highly formalized: history is the study of kings, governments, economics, and war; mathematics is the study of facts, computation, and theorems; science is the study of discoveries, formulas, and principles; language is the study of grammar, syntax, and vocabulary; literature is the study of forms, style, and symbolism. Furthermore, selection of the examples that we traditionally study in the disciplines is a given. In general, *first-phase knowledge* is rooted in western civilization, not in the civilizations of other parts of the world. In history and literature, for example, the work of white, upper- or middle-class, European and American men is emphasized. Knowledge of either the problems or the contributions of white women or men and women with other cultural or class backgrounds is seldom offered. The situation is the same in mathematics and science, and in addition mathematical and scientific "knowledge" is most often completely separated from the people who actually discovered, developed, and refined it; we do not study the problems they wrestled with, or the circumstances of their lives and the times they lived in. Furthermore, nontraditional forms and types of literature, mathematics, and science are usually ignored.

**Phase 2—The Addition of Significant "Others."**   Recognition that there are other possible "worlds," that the experiences, beliefs, and activities of women and men who have been excluded from the curriculum might possibly contribute to our understanding of disciplinary knowledge, often results in a kind of add-on approach to the curriculum. In *second-phase thinking,* members of excluded groups and an occasional alternative idea are added to the material already covered. However, the world view is very much the same; the "exceptional" woman, or the "exceptional" Hispanic, or the "exceptional" person with a disability is lumped together with examples of other "significant" people as if either the characteristics that had excluded them before didn't make a difference, or they were able to "rise above" such difficulties. Here we learn, perhaps, that Susan B. Anthony was a "hero" of the nineteenth-century women's rights movement, or that Albert Einstein (usually included in any study of physics anyway) was probably learning-disabled but managed to be a genius in spite of it. Second-phase thinking may be a step beyond first-phase, but it implies that members of excluded groups and alternative ideas are only valuable insofar as they meet traditional standards of inclusion.

McIntosh refers to this phase as a kind of "affirmative action program" for the disciplines and asserts that "institutions are model places which need only to help a few of the 'inferior' others to have the opportunity to climb onto [the heights] with their "superiors."[51] She writes:

> Phase 2 curricular policies, like most affirmative action programs, assume that our disciplines are functioning well, and that all that women or blacks or Chicanos could need or want is to be put into higher slots on the reading list. In other words, the World Civilization course just needs a little attention to Africa, as a disadvantaged culture, giving Africa the time of day but from a position of "noblesse oblige."[52]

Phase 2 thinking does not incorporate the notion that the dominant group has much to learn from the "other." It also "never recognizes 'ordinary' life, unpaid labor, or 'unproductive' phenomena like human friendship."[53]

**Phase 3—The "Other" as a Problem.**    When enough heretofore excluded knowledge comes to light—usually through the concerted scholarship of dedicated people committed to reexamining the traditional knowledge base of the disciplines—ideas that differ from, and often conflict with what has always been studied become viewed as a problem or an anomaly. In this phase, teachers and curriculum planners begin to ask questions that emerge from this new knowledge, chief among them being, "Why has this knowledge been excluded from the curriculum?" *Phase 3 thinking* often involves anger at both the fact of omission and the notion that when the "other" is included it is often perceived as deficient in some way. Speaking about the experience of many women in this phase, McIntosh also speaks for members of other excluded groups when she says:

> Disillusionment is also a feature of Phase 3 realizations, for many teachers. It is traumatically shocking to white women teachers in particular to realize that we were not only trained but were as teachers unwittingly training others to overlook, reject, exploit, disregard, or be at war with most people of the world. One feels hoodwinked and also sick at heart at having been such a vehicle for racism, misogyny, upper class power and militarism.[54]

Other questions asked in phase 3 might be "Who defined greatness in [my] discipline?" "Who do such definitions serve?" "What are the consequences of exclusion for [my] discipline?" "What is it we don't know, and what does our ignorance mean for us?" It is in phase 3 that members of excluded groups and ideas that run counter to tradition begin to gain a recognizable "voice," but that voice is primarily the voice of an oppressed group and has yet to gain status in the mainstream.

**Phase 4—The "Other" as a Primary Focus.**    In Phase 4, the desire and determination to make that voice heard, to listen to it, and to understand its implications gains great impetus. In *phase 4 thinking,* there is a kind of love affair with the other. New curricula are designed focusing on the omitted knowledge on its own terms. Such curricula are often aimed at target populations—women or blacks or other excluded groups, and they often have *therapeutic* aims. It is assumed that women, minorities, and advocates of various "new" approaches to social problems will "feel better about themselves" if they study a curriculum designed to explore "their worlds." In fact, there is much merit in this view. It is not difficult to understand, for example, that African-American children might be very interested to learn that many ideas that they meet in traditional classes found initial or concurrent expression in African civilizations. It can be extremely comforting to realize that the "Black Savage" image of the "Native African" is far from reality; that African cultures had exactly the same human problems to deal with as European ones, and that they, too, came up with ingenious (and mistaken) solutions. However, when such curricula are seen *only* as therapeutic, there is a danger that their content will be regarded not as important knowledge deserving of rigorous attention, analysis, and evaluation but rather as something that will make "those folks" feel better and remain quiet. As critical as phase 4 thinking is to the raising of new questions and the development of new knowledge, there is a point at which it loses some of its effectiveness if it does not begin to alter or transform traditional knowledge.

Thus, in phase 4 thinking, the view that difference is not deficit and that differences should be considered not only on their own terms but in terms of what they have to offer to dominant ideas and ways of thinking, feeling, and behaving is critical. In phase 4 thinking, the Native American belief that human beings are one with nature could be considered for its implications not only for preserving the natural systems of the planet but also for the development of research programs in geology, anthropology, and other sciences. Women's experience as mothers can be examined not only for what it might offer to nations at war with one another but also in terms of its implications for the ways in which we understand history and read literature. The cooperative mode in which African-American children are frequently taught to work at home can be discussed not only in terms of its divergence from traditional classroom practices but also in terms of its value for classroom learning of all kinds.

Concrete examples of phase 4 curriculum work have been given by McIntosh in terms of attention to women; however, they seem broadly applicable:

> Curriculum work in Phase 4 . . . breaks all the rules of ordinary research or teaching. One studies American literature in the 19th century not by asking, "Did the women write anything good?" but by asking "What did the women write?" One asks not "What great work by a woman can I include in my reading list?" but "How have women used the written word?" In Phase 4 one asks, "How have [people] of color in many cultures told their stories?" not "Is there any good third world literature?" Phase 4 looks not at [medieval heroes] but at that [peasant] who didn't have any "pure" theology or even understand the heresies, but who rather had an overlay of platitudes and "Old Wives' Tales" and riddles and superstitions and theological scraps from here and there. . . . In Phase 4, one looks at the mix of life, and instead of being scared by the impurity of the mix, notices that the impurities reflect the fact that we have been terribly diverse in our lives. Biology taught from a Phase 4 perspective does not define life in terms of the smallest possible units that may be isolated and then examined in isolation. When you are doing Phase 4 Biology, it seems to me you particularly teach reverence for the organism, identification with it, and you see in terms of large, interlocking and relational systems which need to be acknowledged and preserved or whose balance needs to be observed and appreciated.[55]

In phase 4, teaching materials tend to be nontraditional because the teacher is creating them from new scholarship. Moreover, boundaries between the disciplines begin to break down. One cannot approach any accurate understanding of a historical period or a piece of writing or a sociological process—or even a mathematical one—without also understanding something about the art, the music, the economy, the politics, and the social organization in which that event or novel or discovery is embedded. Other boundaries begin to dissolve as well: the boundary between teacher and learner (all are teaching and learning together), between the subject studied and the person studying it (''knowledge'' exists in part in terms of the student's perception of it), and the degree to which the student's own experience connects with it. When done well, phase 4 thinking in curriculum development recognizes both differences and commonalities, and seeks to understand how they are related and how they can be enhanced.

**Phase 5—The Redefinition of Knowledge.**  *Phase 5 thinking* in curriculum has hardly been conceptualized, let alone clearly defined. Lerner talks about it in terms of understanding our past and future through a serious consideration of new questions and through new scholarship.[56] Tetreault, calling this phase *multifocal scholarship,* adds the notion of a redefinition of knowledge in terms of serious attention to human perspectives associated with gender, race, and class.[57] McIntosh adds the idea that the *purpose* of such a redefinition of knowledge is important, that it should serve to enhance our understanding of ourselves as related to one another and to our physical, economic, and social environments.[58]

Central to each of these views is the recognition that knowledge is created by human beings, that the creation of certain kinds of knowledge has concrete consequences which need to be examined, and that the process of examination itself contributes new knowledge to our store. Clearly, no one yet knows what phase 5 thinking will produce. What seems certain, however, is that phase 5 knowledge will be as different from phase 1 knowledge as the caterpillar is from the butterfly. At this point, it appears that trying to discern what possible forms such knowledge might take is the best we can do. We are out looking for that orange tree; how shall we find it?

## WHERE TO BEGIN

Curriculum transformation requires attention to issues of process as well as content. One must determine which knowledge, skills, and attitudes already exist, and which must be developed. Below is a list of considerations and strategies for teachers attempting to modify an existing curriculum or school program. It should not be viewed as a blueprint, nor will you find many experienced teachers following such a format. Once you become adept at asking the appropriate questions, expanding the materials you have available, and providing children with a varied range of experiences, this task will become second nature.

**1** Strive to achieve multiple perspectives by emphasizing many different groups in many different ways, not just the experiences of one group. As well as providing an expanded knowledge base, this helps to reduce the tendency people have to form and use stereotypes.

How might this be accomplished? In the content areas, students should know of the contributions that women and members of various ethnic and national groups have made to the field. Other perspectives and viewpoints should be presented as often as possible; not just the exotic or bizarre differences of others, but the similarities between people should be stressed. The impact of racist and sexist attitudes and practices on the knowledge base generally available should also be explored.

Becoming knowledgeable about other groups is not an easy task, but it is a challenge that professional educators must face. Bennett provides a series of suggestions which teachers and students can follow as they strive to become better acquainted with the experiences and perspectives of others.[59]

**a** Start small, and select one or two groups or nations which have special meaning to you or your students.

**b** Become informed about this particular groups' perspectives on current events as well as your subject area.

**c** Become familiar with various community resources which can provide the needed knowledge, as well as resource people you can use.

**d** Examine the textbooks and materials you use for bias as well as exclusion.

**e** Develop and maintain a current resource file of relevant primary sources and teaching strategies.

**f** Identify one or more areas of your educational program which have been overlooked. Integrate the various perspectives where appropriate.

**2** The curriculum should be interdisciplinary. That is, efforts to address issues of diversity should not be restricted to the social studies, language arts, or the performing arts. Attention to diversity is necessary in all areas, including mathematics, the sciences, and physical education.

**3** If the curriculum is to help students make broad connections, it must develop cognitive, affective, and behavioral skills. Especially in the area of culture learning significant active participation of the student is necessary.

**4** To bring people from different backgrounds into closer contact and thus to improve understanding while broadening one's experience base, local populations should be emphasized whenever possible. Individuals from the community who are able to share their lives and their special knowledge and talents should be utilized.

The path ahead will not be an easy one for you or most of your students. Nevertheless, it must be traveled. Viewing yourself as a professional educator places considerable control in your hands. With sufficient practice and attention to curriculum transformation, your classroom can become a significant locus of the change so badly needed in schools today. The perspectives and skills you bring to your teaching will make your students better able to adapt in many different contexts in today's rapidly changing world.

## ACTIVITIES

**1** Consider the use of instructional material related to one content area (e.g., reading, social studies, science). Select two commonly used textbooks from different publishers (or other material) and survey them for inclusion of traditionally excluded groups. In what kinds of situations are various individuals depicted? What are they doing? Is there balance of representation of various groups? Are stereotypic images or presentations maintained or broken? Which textbook or material would you recommend for use and why? What modifications, if any, would you recommend, and why?

**2** Interview some teachers, parents, and students in integrated schools. How do they evaluate the school's efforts to deal with problems of prejudice? What efforts or characteristics of people seem to work well within the school? What suggestions would they have for improving intergroup relations between the various sectors of the school and community? Compare their suggestions with those presented in the chapter.

**3** Interview a teacher, administrator, parent, or student about the problems between various groups in their school. Propose a plan to improve intergroup relations in the school. In your proposal, consider the various findings from the research on prejudice reduction. What efforts would you suggest? How do they fit with the findings and suggestions from the literature?

**4** Increased attention is being given to the importance of adding an international dimension to the experiences of students in schools. Select two textbooks for the same content area and grade level which are in common use. In what ways are the five dimensions of a global perspective proposed by Hanvey developed in these materials? Which of the materials best develops an international dimension? If Hanvey's dimensions are not clearly addressed in the materials you have, in what ways might they be addressed without detracting from the overall objectives?

**5** Consider the content area in which you expect to teach, or consider the various content areas if you are elementary or early childhood oriented. In what ways might an international perspective be developed? In what ways might the contributions of excluded groups be integrated? What key contributions have been made by women? By minorities? By foreign nationals?

**6** Read a news article of international or intercultural relevance. What have you learned about that culture, nation, or group? Next, read about that particular group; about their culture, behavior, language, perspective, and so forth. Reread the news article and consider your level of comprehension and appreciation after the first and then the second reading. How did your knowledge of the culture help you to better understand the article? What implications might this have for your teaching?[60]

# REFERENCES

**1** Robert S. Zais, *Curriculum: Principles and Foundations* (New York: Harper & Row, 1976), pp. 6–12.

**2** Ibid., p. 8.

**3** Ibid., p. 12.

**4** Ibid., p. 13.

**5** Brislin, *Cross-Cultural Encounters: Face to Face Interaction.* (New York: Pergamon Press, 1981).

**6** P. A. Katz, "Developmental Foundations of Gender and Racial Attitudes," in R. H. Leahy (ed.), *The Child's Construction of Social Inequality* (New York: Academic Press, 1983), pp. 41–78.

**7** Deborah A. Byrnes, "Children and Prejudice," *Social Education,* vol. 52, no. 4, April–May 1988, pp. 267–271.

**8** R. M. Dennis, "Socialization and Racism: The White Experience," in B. P. Bowser and R. G. Hunt (eds.), *Impacts of Racism on White Americans* (Beverly Hills, CA: Sage Publications, 1981).

**9** Deborah A. Byrnes, *Teacher, They Called me a _____!: Prejudice and Discrimination in the Classroom* (New York: Anti-Defamation League of B'Nai B'rith, 1987).

**10** D. Bicklin and L. Bailey (eds.), *Rudely Stamp'd: Imaginal Disability and Prejudice* (Washington, DC: University Press of America, 1981).

**11** D. A. Byrnes and G. Kiger, "Religious Prejudice and Democracy: Conflict in the Classroom," *Issues in Education,* vol. 4, no. 2, 1986, pp. 167–176.

**12** G. Pate, "What Does Research Tell Us about the Reduction of Prejudice?" Presented at the 1987 Anti-Defamation League Conference, American Citizenship in the Twenty-First Century: Education for a Pluralistic, Democratic America.

**13** Byrnes, op. cit. (ref. 7).

**14** Gordon Allport, *The Nature of Prejudice* (New York: Doubleday, 1958).

**15** Yehuda Amir, "Contact Hypothesis in Ethnic Relations," *Psychological Bulletin,* vol. 71, no. 5, May 1969, pp. 319–343.

**16** Ibid.

**17** M. Sherif, ''Superordinate Goals in the Reduction of Intergroup Tension,'' *American Journal of Sociology,* vol. 63, no. 4, 1958, pp. 349–356.

**18** J. Stahlman, P. Safford, S. Pisarchick, C. Miller, and D. Dyer, ''Crossing the Boundaries of Early Childhood Special Education Personnel Preparation: Creating a Path for Retraining,'' *Teacher Education and Special Education,* vol. 12, no. 1, Jan. 1989, pp. 5–12.

**19** P. Safford, *Integrated Teaching in Early Childhood.* (White Plains, NY: Longman, 1989).

**20** K. Dunlop, Z. Stoneman, and M. Cantrell, ''Social Interaction of Exceptional and Other Children in a Mainstreamed Preschool Classroom,'' *Exceptional Children,* vol. 47, no. 2, Oct. 1980, pp. 132–141.

**21** Debbie Walsh, ''Critical Thinking to Reduce Prejudice,'' *Social Education,* vol. 52, no. 4, April–May 1988, pp. 280–282.

**22** Edward D'Angelo, *The Teaching of Critical Thinking* (Amsterdam: B. R. Gruner, 1971).

**23** Walsh, op. cit.

**24** Matthew Lipman, *Philosophy in the Classroom* (Philadelphia: Temple University Press, 1980).

**25** Walsh, op. cit.

**26** T. F. Pettigrew, ''The Mental Health Impact,'' in B. P. Bowser and R. G. Hunt (eds.), *Impacts of Racism on White Americans* (Beverly Hills, CA: Sage Publications, 1981) pp. 97–118.

**27** S. C. Samuels, *Enhancing Self-Concept in Early Childhood* (New York: Human Sciences Press, 1977).

**28** J. P. Shaver and C. K. Curtis, *Handicapism and Equal Opportunity: Teaching about the Disabled in Social Studies* (Reston, VA: Council for Exceptional Children, 1981).

**29** R. Gary Shirts, *BAFA BAFA, A Cross Cultural Simulation* (Del Mar, CA: SIMILE II, 1977).

**30** David Hoopes, *Intercultural Education.* Phi Delta Kappa Fastback no. 144 (Bloomington, IN: Phi Delta Kappa Educational Foundation, 1980).

**31** Ibid.

**32** National Council for the Social Studies, *Position Statement on Global Education,* Washington DC, 1982.

**33** Ibid.

**34** Robert Hanvey, *An Attainable Global Perspective* (New York: Center for Global Perspectives, 1978).

**35** Ibid.

**36** Ibid.

**37** In ''CNN: Television for The Global Village,'' *World Press Review,* vol. 37, no. 12, December 1990, p. 34.

**38** Hanvey, op. cit.

**39** Kenneth Cushner and Gregory Trifonovitch, ''Understanding Misunderstanding: Barriers to Dealing with Diversity.'' *Social Education* vol. 53, no. 5, Sept. 1989, pp. 318–322.

**40** Hanvey, op. cit.

**41** Hanvey, op. cit.

**42** W. Kniep, ''Social Studies within a Global Education,'' *Social Education,* vol. 53, no. 6, Oct. 1989, pp. 399–403.

**43** Ibid., p. 399.

**44** Ibid.; A. DeKock and C. Paul, ''One District's Commitment to Global Education,'' *Educational Leadership,* vol. 47, no. 1, Sept. 1989, pp. 46–49; A. Crabbe, ''The Future Problem-Solving Program,'' *Educational Leadership,* vol. 47, no. 1, Sept. 1989, pp. 27–29.

**45** K. Cushner, ''Adding an International Dimension to the Curriculum,'' *The Social Studies,* vol. 81, no. 4, July/Aug 1990, pp. 166–170; Gail Hughes-Wiener, ''An Overview of International Education in the Schools, *Education and Urban Society,* vol. 20, no. 2, February 1988, pp. 139–158.

**46** K. Cushner, ''Creating Cross-Cultural Understanding through Internationally Cooperative Story Writing,'' *Social Education,* in press.

**47** Reprinted with permission from *The Monkey's Dilemma: A Fairytale of the Twentieth Century,* written jointly by American and Soviet Children (Moretown, UT: Parents and Teachers for Social Responsibility, 1990).

**48** Lois Weis (ed.), *Class, Race, & Gender in American Education* (Albany, NY: State University of New York Press, 1988).

**49** Peggy McIntosh, ''Interactive Phases of Curricular Re-Vision: A Feminist Perspective,'' Working Papers Series, no. 124 (Wellesley, MA: Wellesley College Center for Research on Women, 1983).

**50** This typology is based on the work of the following, all of whom are instructive in different ways and worth consulting: Gerda Lerner, ''The Rise of Feminist Consciousness,'' in Eleanor Bender, Bobbie Burk, and Nancy Walker (eds.), *All of Us Are Present* (Columbia, MO: James Madison Wood Research Institute, 1984); Marilyn Schuster and Susan Van Dyne, ''Placing Women in the Liberal Arts: Stages of Curriculum Revision,'' *Harvard Educational Review,* vol. 54, no. 4, November 1984, pp. 413–428; Mary Kay Thompson Tetreault, ''Feminist Phase Theory,'' *Journal of Higher Education,* vol. 56, no. 4, July–August 1985, pp. 363–384; Margaret L. Anderson, ''Changing the Curriculum in Higher Education,'' in Elizabeth Minnich, Jean O'Barr, and Rachel Rosenfeld (eds.), *Reconstructing the Academy: Women's Education and Women's Studies* (Chicago: University of Chicago Press, 1988), pp. 36–68.

**51** McIntosh, op. cit., p. 8.

**52** Ibid.

**53** Ibid., p. 9.

**54** Ibid., p. 10.

**55** Ibid., pp. 17–18.

**56** Lerner, op. cit. (ref. 44).

**57** Tetreault, op. cit. (ref. 44).

**58** McIntosh, op. cit.

**59** The following activities first appeared in Bennett, *Comprehensive Multicultural Education: Theory and Practice,* 2d edition, (Boston: Allyn and Bacon, 1990).

**60** Larry Samover, Richard Porter, and Nemi Jain, *Understanding Intercultural Communication* (Belmont, CA: Wadsworth, 1981).

# **13**

# THE TRANSFORMATION
# OF PEDAGOGY

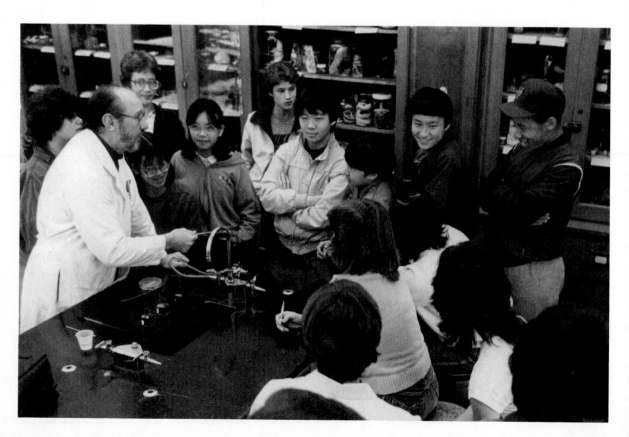

*Teaching is not telling.*

Jean Piaget

In this chapter, we will present a variety of approaches to instruction and classroom organization which have been shown to have significant impact on the life in classrooms and schools; on achievement; and on development of attitudes, knowledge, and behavior that are congruent with an intercultural perspective. We will not present lists of specific activities except to illustrate a point, since many such lists are available elsewhere. Here, we will introduce you to some basic ways of thinking, considerations, and strategies. Most of these are not subject-, age-, or grade-specific, but rather are broadly applicable and can serve as tools for you to modify and integrate as needed. You, the teacher, ultimately control much of what and how you teach children. The choices you make with regard to creating and selecting teaching options will be based not only on what options are available to you, but also on the degree to which you understand and can articulate the reasons for your choices. It is therefore important that you begin now to think through the implications of all we have been talking about in this book for your actual practice.

## THE MEANING OF PEDAGOGY

The term *pedagogy* derives from the Latin *paidagogos,* the teacher or leader of boys in ancient Greece. Often, the *paidagogos* was a slave, whose job it was literally to take or accompany the boys to school and to instruct them there. Over the centuries, the word *pedagogue* has come to mean one who instructs in a dogmatic manner—a "know it all." *Pedagogy,* however, is usually understood on today's educational scene to mean "the art and science of teaching."

But the word *teaching* has many meanings and connotations. Thomas F. Green calls teaching a "vague concept," writing that, "its boundaries are not clear. However accurately we may describe the activity of teaching there will, and always must, remain certain troublesome border-line cases."[1] Green names several activities that may be associated with the idea of teaching. Among these are conditioning and training, which may be associated with the formation of behavior and conduct, and instructing and indoctrinating, which may be associated with knowledge and beliefs. He argues that each pair lies on a continuum where one can fade almost imperceptibly into the other. If, however, there is no well thought out basis for distinguishing one from another, it is possible for the teacher to move in the first case toward intimidation and physical threat, and in the second toward propagandizing and lying. In the former case one thinks of the intimidation of the grade, and of the common use of physical threat—the ruler, the switch, and the paddle—which are only now in American schools losing some of their legitimacy. At the other extreme, schools have been and are frequent sites of propaganda

("American," of course) and, in some cases, of lying (it is not the case that the contribution of women and minorities to American history and life are negligible when compared to the contributions of white men).

Green notes that the two concepts closest to that of teaching are training and instruction, and that in some cases *teaching* and *training* may be used interchangeably because teaching is often thought of, in part, as the formation of habits and training is one way habits are introduced and shaped. But he argues that while one may *teach* a dog to perform specific activities, this activity is not, or should not be, the same thing as *teaching* a child—it is more like training. The difference lies in the intelligence of the creature who is learning.

> Dogs do not ask "Why?" They do not ask for reasons for a certain rule or order. They do not require explanation or justification. It is this limitation of intelligence which we express by speaking of training rather than teaching in such circumstances.[2]

The need to justify, to submit evidence, seems to be at the heart of the concept of instruction, which Green asserts "involves a kind of conversation"[3] between teacher and learner. This seems to be more closely associated with *teaching* as we would like to think of it, and yet *teaching* and *instructing* are not necessarily the same thing. Remember the dog, who has been "taught" to fetch? Central to all this discussion is this point of Green's:

> The concept of teaching, as we normally use it, includes within its limits a whole family of activities, and we can recognize that some of these are more centrally related to teaching than others. We have no difficulty, for example, in agreeing that instructing and certain kinds of training are activities which belong to teaching. We may have more difficulty, and some persons more than others, in deciding whether conditioning and indoctrinating legitimately belong to teaching. There is, in short, a region on this continuum at which we may legitimately disagree, because there will be many contexts in which the criteria which tend to distinguish teaching and conditioning or teaching and indoctrination will not be clearly exemplified. Thus, there is an area of uncertainty on this continuum, an area of vagueness neither to be overcome nor ignored, but respected and preserved.[4]

We believe that the foregoing analysis is important in the consideration of teaching generally, but perhaps especially important when thinking about teaching with human diversity in mind. What was the role, for example, of indoctrination and conditioning in the pedagogy of the assimilationist? To what extent can it be justified in terms of having to create a "unified" society? Similarly, to what extent are we required to give reasons for an emphasis on a multicultural curriculum and its related methods of instruction? Is teaching really a conversation between teacher and learner?

Bernier puts an interesting slant on this issue when he refers to schools as "contact points" at which people with diverse physical and psychosocial characteristics meet.[5] Differences, he writes, must be neither ignored nor reified, but rather inquired into and *negotiated*. Implied in his discussion, as in Green's, is the notion that inquiry, investigation, discussion, and communication are important teaching and learning skills which must be incorporated not only into the education of teachers but also into the normal life of the classroom.

## SOME EXEMPLARS OF TEACHING METHOD

We are not concerned here with describing all available pedagogical methods; we are concerned with helping you understand the role of teaching in a diverse society. However, it is assumed here that the teacher's choice of pedagogical method has a direct relationship to the success of students in personal and social as well as cognitive development. And unfortunately, much recent research has revealed that while a variety of methods of instruction are available to teachers, most teachers avail themselves of only two or three.[6] For that reason, we will look at a number of possible teaching methods, understanding that some may be more useful than others for our purposes here.

One of the more interesting ways to learn about teaching methods is to study famous teachers. Harry Broudy has identified several challenges to education and examined the pedagogical responses of a number of famous teachers or historical schools to these challenges.[7] A brief summary follows:

### The Sophists and the Need for Eloquence

Much teaching has always revolved around language acquisition and use, including reading, and synthesizing what has been heard and read. In early Greece and Rome, when only those destined for public life were schooled to any great extent, language training was geared to the education of young men to take their places as citizens of democratic Athens and republican Rome. For these students, effective oratory—capable of persuading the listener through argument or moving him (the listeners were almost all males) emotionally—was paramount. Broudy observes that in order to produce effective oratory, one had to have "1) access to the evidence, 2) skill in argument, 3) a facility with the evocative or nonreferential use of language, and 4) a practical command of social psychology."[8] The sophists, who were a class of teachers who contracted to teach young men for a considerable sum of money, developed a system of instruction that would not look too strange in modern classrooms. First, through analysis of instances of good writing and speaking, they developed rules for effective speaking and writing. This included the classification of words by type and function (nouns, verbs, etc.) as well as rules for effective phrases and clauses. The sophists also analyzed rules of logic, debate, and argument—for example, the tactic of taking an opponent's conceded point and using it to begin a further argument.[9] Students were required to do a number of exercises based on practice in writing and speaking, as well as the following:

> retelling fables, plausible fictions, and stories from history; delivering narrations dealing with persons; amplifying proverbs into a moral essay; refuting an argument; taking a set of facts typical of a class of situations and applying them to a particular case; praising or dispraising a thing or person; making comparisons; composing imaginary speeches that might have been given by some historical or mythological figure; describing objects and events vividly; arguing on set questions (e.g., Should a man marry?); and speaking for or against a piece of legislation.[10]

Broudy notes that while this type of pedagogy has been rightly criticized as artificial and formalistic, it has certain merits. Among these are definite expectations, reliance on habit formation, flexibility of choice of models, and—because students were required to follow a practicing orator about, learning to imitate him—recognition of the importance of learning through apprenticeship. Think about these methods and activities in terms of your own schooling. While we certainly do not emphasize public speaking in general schooling as the early Greeks and Romans did, we have all done our share of comparing and contrasting, of writing themes or essays based on a motto, proverb, or quotation, of refuting an argument, describing a person or event, and reciting historical "truths." Indeed, this set of methods is a staple in most English classes, and in history and social studies classes as well.

## Socratic Dialectic and the Question of Value

Teaching students to compose and deliver effective speeches might be considered a form of training, although a complex and sometimes creative one. And because it is based on *form,* such teaching does not require teachers to be particularly brilliant in the art itself. Nor do they always have to know or understand the *substance* of the speech, but only how to give it the proper and effective form. While the methods of rhetoric can be used with creative sensitivity, they often are not; rather, they become ends in themselves.

Here arises the problem of incorporating value into the educational process. We would like to think that instruction involves more than mechanics, that it involves making students aware of the issues raised by the argument, leading students to examine their own thinking on the subject, helping them to discipline and refine their thinking so as to include the values at the heart of the matter, and teaching them the processes necessary to adjudicate disagreement or come to a deeper understanding of the topic. Socrates developed the art of *dialectic,* a process through which students come to be *converted*— that is, through the exploration and redefinition of accepted "truth," they are literally "turned around" in their thinking on the issue. Dialectic is primarily an interactive process between teacher and student and requires great skill on the teacher's part, as she or he keeps prodding the student to further thought on the subject. The socratic teacher focuses on the abilities of the student to explore new dimensions of an issue and to reason them through.

## Scholasticism and the Education of Teachers

By the Middle Ages, knowledge was increasing at a rapid rate, fueled in large measure by the rediscovery of classical philosophy and the nascent scientific mentality that wished to understand the world in an empirical way. The challenge, according to Broudy, was to prepare "teachers who could conceptualize all realms of life so as to synthesize Christian theology, ancient philosophy, and science."[11] If there was, and is, a great debate between "teaching how" and "teaching that," scholasticism in the person of Peter Abelard provided some sort of compromise. Not often discussed in undergraduate education, Abelard is a figure who should be known. Broudy writes:

> Abelard deserves a place in the history of teaching for a number of reasons. He was a teacher and a teacher of teachers. All his glory and most of his professional difficulties were related to his teaching activity. Second, his teaching employed a method of structuring and presenting materials that helped to set the style for the age of Scholastic education. Third, his personal charm made him one of that fortunate tribe of teachers who need no special devices to motivate

their classes. He drew throngs wherever he taught. He exemplified in his teaching a life style that fascinated the would-be scholars of his time. Fourth, Abelard was a prime example, as were Socrates and other great teachers, of how current controversies can dominate the strategy of teaching. Finally, he represented an emphasis on the use and evaluation of knowledge and skill presumably acquired at an earlier period in the student's schooling.''[12]

Very simply stated, Abelard's pedagogy placed the logic of the rhetor at the disposal of religious questioning in a way that bore much resemblance to socratic dialogue. In the process, he set up teaching devices to impel students to investigation; in other words, he set forth the material in a way that compelled students to action. For example, in one presentation of questions about fundamental current beliefs of orthodox Christianity, he listed one column of affirmative answers and another column of negative answers, making no move to resolve the issues so created.[13] If we might take some liberties with a classic, it was like asking the question ''Can a particular group of students achieve well in school?'' and then listing both positive and negative answers of ''experts'' with no commentary. Seeing them in stark contrast, students might be incited to further inquiry.

However, to pursue such an inquiry, students would need several skills: the ability to ''do scholarship,'' that is to seek out other views on the subject; the ability to analyze, compare and contrast, and critique the answers; the ability to make judgments on the relative merits of the answers; and the ability to discover and interpret the context in which the passage had been written, and the intent of the author. If none of these strategies provided a resolution to the problem, then one of two conclusions could be reached: (1) this is a mystery, or a problem that cannot be solved but has to be accepted, at least for the time being; (2) a new theory or way of looking at the problem is required. All these skills are to be modeled by the teacher in the form of a lecture, at which form Abelard was an unquestioned artist, and practiced by both teachers and students in debates or disputations. While this process presents a number of difficulties—including that of avoiding a preconceived ''correct'' answer—it is a method designed to intrigue both teachers and students and to engage them in active investigation and argument. Like dialectic, it is a transactional method whereby students are involved and involve themselves in inquiry. As used in colleges of education, it provides a form of practice teaching that we often call *clinical experience,* in which students are required to present their material in lectures, argue their beliefs, and demonstrate their methods to their classmates.

## The Jesuits and School Organization

A fourth challenge identified by Broudy occurred during the Renaissance, and once again had to do with a problem that repeats itself today: How are teachers to prepare increasingly diverse students to succeed and contribute in a world of increasing knowledge, increasing interest in human values, and increasing conflict? Such was the condition of society in the Renaissance; such it is today.

The advent of what we know as *humanistic education* during the Renaissance expanded both the curriculum and the student population of educating agencies. Education—in a form that would produce a ''cultured gentleman,'' or a person at home in public life and able to converse intelligently about a variety of subjects, including history, art, literature, and commerce—became available not just to the wealthy or titled sons of

Europe, but also to the sons of an emerging middle class of merchants and artisans and—in some small measure and normally in the privacy of the home—to the daughters of those classes. At the same time, new knowledge: the synthesized work of medieval scholars, the more recently rediscovered work of Greek and Roman philosophy, and scientific knowledge, was growing apace.

Broudy selects the Jesuit schools that flourished in this period,

> not because of their originality in content, form, or even spirit, but because they illustrate how schooling can be organized and systematized to make materials, methods of instruction, and teachers uniformly effective over broad regions of space and time.[14]

Systematizing all areas of schooling, the Jesuits created schools in which the most knowledge could be taught to the most people in the most efficient manner. Jesuit evaluation of student work required that all aspects of the work—its creation, implementation, and delivery—be scrutinized and evaluated in terms of the depth and breadth of ideas and examples. It was education for intellectuals par excellence, intended to produce leaders of ability and finesse. Broudy notes that the problems of teaching method became themselves the object of serious study to the Jesuits, who thus contributed to the development of teaching as a profession.[15]

Humanist education centered on the study of ancient civilizations and is therefore something of a curiosity to us, who are often skeptical of the value of knowing anything that happened more than ten years ago. But when a society is fascinated by a particular style of life, young people often want to emulate that style and will work exceedingly hard to learn how to do it. The Jesuits captured that enthusiasm and developed a number of teaching strategies to take advantage of it. One of these was individual and group competition between teams, "armies," and the like. Another form of competition involved assigning each student an "opposite number," whose duty it was to catch and correct every mistake that was made. Debates between classes, with suitable rewards bestowed, and public displays of student abilities were commonplace. But the most important reward of all was praise from the teacher.

Broudy notes that a certain amount of psychological "savvy" was apparent in Jesuit pedagogy. While methods of punishment for misdeeds were available, it was felt that a teacher would often do well to ignore or "not see" some inappropriate behavior. Another rule of the Jesuits—that corporal or other forms of severe punishment never be administered by the teacher, but rather by a specified official—has come down to us today in the person of the "Assistant Principal" to be found in most high schools.

Homework also was a regular feature of Jesuit schools, and assignments were corrected by the teacher, by other students in an exchange of papers, and sometimes by the student who did the work, using a model provided by the teacher. Student monitors were also utilized by the teacher, sometimes to report wrongdoing. It is interesting to note that this pedagogical model, while as fresh in our memories as perhaps last year, is nearly 600 years old. The problem with this model and models which have evolved from it is that they focus almost entirely on language, on print, on classical themes, and on the production of "gentlemen" able to conduct the discourse of public life. They were, however, and can be, markedly successful in that regard, and remain a staple in higher education today.

## Comenius and the "Natural" Child

Often cited as a forerunner of the kind of democratic common school education adopted by Americans in the nineteenth century, the seventeenth-century educator John Amos Comenius published the first school picture book in 1658; advocated the teaching of foreign languages, including Latin, through translations into one's native language; and both wrote and recommended text material that focused on everyday experiences as opposed to the traditional focus on Greek and Latin heroes. While some of his methods were not entirely new, Comenius is credited with pulling the old methods together, and adding many of his own, in a system of universal education based on what he perceived to be principles of natural human development.[16] He believed, for example, that young children see the whole before the parts, and that, pedagogically speaking, that meant that subject matter should be presented first in terms of basic ideas or "first principles," and later exemplified in greater and greater detail. Drawing many of his ideas from the new natural sciences, including biology, Comenius's prescriptions for pedagogy have drawn a number of criticisms. Basing one's ideas on analogies from plant and animal life, for example, presupposes that human life is quite similar, which it is not. "Universals" drawn from nature have the peculiar property of being interpreted differently by various human cultures and thus losing their universal status.

Comenius can be credited with the notion that understanding is more important than rote learning, and material learned through demonstration is more readily absorbed than material acquired from external expert sources. He also believed that learning was best done through teaching, and therefore promoted the idea that students should give lessons to their classmates—always, however, imitating the teacher. Likening the function of the school to the process of gardening, Comenius thought that the behavior of students was not entirely the teacher's responsibility, but was the product of various factors including the behavior of parents, civil and other authorities, the environment of the school, and the nature of the curriculum and pedagogy employed in the classroom. All these affected learning outcomes. Although the pedagogical recommendations of Comenius sound very much as if they were aimed at revolutionizing educational practice, his justification for them was that they would enhance traditional learning outcomes.

According to Broudy, the challenge faced by Comenius was incorporation of the new science and the new emphasis on sense perception into traditional school practices. Today we face the same kind of challenge, but we are faced with some new problems, particularly the difficulty of reconciling science and technology with human ethical considerations, and the need to provide students of many backgrounds with the ability to make decisions about issues we cannot even conceive. Part of the solution to these problems lies in accurately naming and classifying objects around us, a skill that Johann Pestalozzi promoted in the eighteenth and nineteenth centuries. Like Comenius, Pestalozzi believed that education was like gardening—a process of helping living things grow. Unlike Comenius, he thought that it was more "natural" to learn by moving from the particular to the general—to name and classify things before the more general characteristics of those things were apprehended. He was an advocate of the concrete, the immediate, and the familiar—a proponent of experience and, to some extent, guided discovery. Believing that the concrete was easier to learn than the abstract, and that simple things were easier to learn than complex ones, Pestalozzi recommended *object lessons,* the study of a real object, including the understanding of progressively more complex rules that governed the object. He also pioneered the use of slates and pencils, alphabet "flash cards," and whole-class instruction.[17] Indeed, Comenius and Pestalozzi resembled those teachers today who love teaching devices—they would, perhaps, have had a good time imagining creative uses for computers.

Of course, there have been other great teachers, and other schools that exemplified pedagogical principles still useful today. Our aim, however, is to entice you, to suggest that other ideas about pedagogy await your questions and your investigation. It is also to suggest that although there may be little that is new under the sun, much has been forgotten, or is underutilized or underrepresented in today's classroom. Pedagogical resources abound that can be used to enhance traditional classroom work and design new kinds of work. We believe that part of your responsibility as teachers will be to discover and expand them.

## THE TRANSCENDENT GOALS OF TEACHING

Implicit in our selection of pedagogical approaches and our discussion of them is the idea that teaching is an activity that principally involves teachers and learners in interaction with one another and with subject matter. Hopefully you realize that you will not be solely a teacher of content once you find yourself in the classroom. Whatever your field, the actual content or discipline you teach will be secondary to the fact that you will be a teacher of students. Unfortunately, many teachers, especially those in secondary education, lose sight of this fact and pride themselves on the amount of knowledge they have attained and can attempt to transfer to their students. One might call this the "injection theory" of education: the purpose of teaching is to inject as much knowledge as possible into the heads of the students in your class.

Underlying all good teaching, however, are certain goals and objectives that transcend specific disciplines. Often more process-oriented than content-oriented, many of them are directly relevant to developing a classroom environment which promotes effective interaction and learning. Many of the strategies introduced in this section have multiple goals. Among them are to help young people develop the following characteristics and to create classrooms in which the following environments are nurtured:

**1 Students Need to Develop a Positive Self-image** *Self-concept* or *self-image* can be defined as "a complex set of beliefs that an individual holds true about himself or herself."[18] This self-image may be broad, that is, reflecting a view about the total self; or it may be quite specific, that is, reflecting beliefs about one's academic ability, physical attractiveness, or ability to get along with others.

Research reveals that the relationship between self-image and school success is somewhat unbalanced. That is, while individuals with low self-esteem rarely achieve well in school, a good self-image does not necessarily guarantee that a student will perform well academically.

A low self-image can have an overpowering effect in the classroom. Bennett writes:

When a student with low-self-esteem enters a classroom, self-concept becomes one of the most challenging individual differences in how he or she will learn. Because students with a negative self-image are not fully able to learn, school becomes an arena for failure that prevents them from achieving the success needed for high self-esteem. A vicious cycle develops whereby the school itself, by providing experiences of failure, helps keep the student's self-image deflated."[19]

Methods for nurturing positive self-image, however, are the subject of much debate. In a recent commentary in *Time* magazine, for example, Charles Krauthammer argues strongly against "the newly fashionable self-esteem curriculum wherein kids are taught to feel good about themselves."[20] Asserting that emphasis on self-esteem has led American education to the place where our students cannot compete with students in other countries, he asserts that "the pursuit of good feeling in education is a dead end. The way to true self-esteem is through real achievement and real learning."[21]

Of course, the definition of real achievement and real learning are open to debate. Presumably, Krauthammer would define effective teaching as that which placed primary emphasis on the acquisition of subject matter knowledge. However, as we have seen, everyone in school does not have access to the same curriculum, nor does everyone have ample time in which to master material which, for any reason, may be difficult for them. Tracking, for example, which begins in reading and math groups in the elementary grades, may lead almost inexorably to entirely different curricula and teaching methods in the higher grades and in high school. If different curricula were viewed as equally valuable, this might not be such a problem. Goodlad illustrates this point by comparing the likely consequences for children in the early grades who exhibit different strengths in learning style:

> One of the myths [of schooling] is that there are two kinds of people. Those of one group—perhaps our academically oriented group of early elementary students—learn to use their heads and should go on to work with their heads. Those of another—maybe those who preferred painting—learn to use their hands and should go on to work with their hands. School is where one cultivates the head. Consequently, "headedness" more than "handedness" is needed for and valued in school—especially in the "grammar" or "grade school."[22]

Arguing that schools and teachers promote certain values in students, Goodlad notes that:

> Research shows also that children performing in the bottom group, whether or not regularly promoted to the next grade, show up less well on indices of both personal and social adjustment. They are the students most likely to perceive themselves as not doing well in school or having high expectation of further failure, and most likely to want to quit. . . . Students' self-esteem in the academic area appears to be rather closely tied to their perception of which side of the separation [between head and hand] they perceive themselves to be on. . . . Students sometimes come to perceive that "if you don't want to go to college, this school doesn't think you're very important."[23]

Nurturance of self-esteem in the classroom *is* possible, and does not require either a relaxation of "standards" or inattention to subject matter. Indeed, it should be one of the overriding goals of good teaching. Environments which invite student participation and where involvement is highly encouraged send the message that students and their concrete experiences are respected and valued and that their contributions are important. Providing students with the means and the time to fail is also important, when "failure" is perceived as only one step on the road to achieving success and not as a final destination. Pedagogical methods that generate a sense of community in the classroom and convey the sense that everyone in the class will succeed can go a long way toward building self-esteem *in the context* of learning information, concepts, and skills. Further, remember that teachers and students bring internalized ideas of value based on race, class, gender, and disability with them into the classroom. Addressing issues of individual self-esteem also helps to reduce prejudice (see Chapter 12), thereby helping to create a classroom environment that is free of destructive competition, discrimination, and conflict.

**2 Personal Identity** Closely related to issues of self-esteem are issues of personal identity. A healthy classroom climate helps students *develop a sense of identity,* related to the need to belong which was discussed in Chapter 3. Most children come to school having developed a sense of who they are within the context of the home or neighborhood. Once in school, they are faced with the need to find their sense of place and define who they are in this new and different environment. This is often not an easy thing to do. Recall the culture-general framework, which recognized that all people need to feel that they belong and to reduce their anxiety if they are to function well. Teachers do not know children's names (or, perhaps more important, their nicknames), their strengths and weaknesses, their likes or dislikes. The rules which operate in this new culture must also be determined. New criteria are established for what it means to be "good" and "bad." As Tiedt and Tiedt state, echoing Goodlad, "In many classrooms only students who do well on multiple-choice standardized tests are labeled 'good students'; the others are 'bad students' by default. This 'bad student' label often hides students whose accomplishments and abilities simply are not recognized by the schools."[24]

There are many strengths, interests, and abilities that may not "naturally" emerge in the course of the regular school day. To judge a student based on the rather narrow display of behaviors typically expected in school is unfair at best. A teacher's responsibility becomes one of encouraging students to "bring themselves into the classroom," of creating an atmosphere which recognizes individuals and rewards their contributions to the school environment.

**3 Sense of Pride** At the same time as teachers are striving to help students develop a sense of personal identity, they can also create an environment which helps children *develop a sense of pride in their own particular group(s).* This is a complicated issue, because as we have noted, most people belong to many different groups. When confronted with a situation in which one of their groups is not recognized as a viable entity, or worse, is discriminated against, many people tend to feel excluded, and to become withdrawn, perhaps even hostile. We have learned about the absence or distortion of material on the larger minority groups and on women in the curriculum. What we need to learn more about now is how such absence or distortion can be mediated by the teacher. The use of personal histories, conversations with people who have witnessed critical events, the taking of oral histories from older people, and the design of classroom activities that put the student in someone else's shoes are all strategies that broaden the experience and understanding of all students.

When the contributions of a particular group to the economic, political, and social life of the United States are recognized and valued in the classroom and the school, self-esteem improves and a healthy individual and group identity is more likely to develop. When students learn about the contributions of their ethnic or religious groups, they are likely to develop pride in their membership in those groups and identify with them. This does *not* mean, however, that more traditional knowledge about "mainstream" contributions is ignored. What is required (see Chapter 12) is a more inclusive curriculum and a greater emphasis on discussion and debate about the actual roles of various groups. As Cottrol notes:

> In an honest, serious multicultural education, one in which students encounter the rich diversity of the American heritage, our students should learn about the greatness of Thomas Jefferson's ideas *and* that, as a slaveholder, he betrayed America's ideals. Our students should learn about the great achievement that was the opening of the American West *and* about the tremendous price America's indigenous populations paid in the process.
>
> The fact is that American history—like any history—offers no simple, pure truths. Our history is neither great nor terrible, but a complicated mix of both, with good growing from evil, and evil growing from good. It is this complexity that makes history interesting and challenging. We shouldn't deny students of any color the richness of this American dilemma.[25]

**4 Sense of Connectedness** Creating an effective pedagogy that attends to and appreciates human diversity means also that a teacher must help students to *develop a sense of connectedness* with one another rather than perpetuate the individualism and competitiveness that is traditional in many classrooms. This may be a particularly difficult task, because not only are most teachers reared themselves to espouse the American value of individualism, but schools are frequently organized to reward only individual effort. Therefore, teachers must be creative in developing the notion that "we're all in this together." Students can be encouraged to discover the ways in which their classroom "community" is autonomous, and the ways in which it is related to the whole school, to its town or city, to the state and the nation, and to the whole world. Using the classroom as a base, students can be led to begin to explore the various ways in which each of them are similar, yet different; how their behavior affects others and is affected by others; how their destinies are intertwined; and how their efforts can contribute to a greater whole. An emphasis on developing good interpersonal relationships and intergroup interaction skills is useful, as is tracing the nature and content of personal linkages with people in other schools, cities, states, and parts of the world. Unfortunately, this is usually done only when some part of the country faces a disaster, such as an earthquake or a flood, or when the country is at war. Then much discussion and debate swirls around the connections between students, teachers, and people experiencing these events. At those times, we would argue, a good deal of learning occurs, learning that stays with the student, perhaps for the rest of his or her life. We would argue that this making of connections is, for both students and teachers, the heart of the pedagogical process.

**5 Sense of Confidence** Understanding an issue or a problem or the flow of certain events is, however, insufficient for an effective pedagogy. Students must also *develop a sense of confidence in their ability to act,* especially when confronted by prejudice, injustice, or discrimination. One of the overall goals of schooling is citizenship education—developing citizens who are knowledgeable and are also reflective decision makers who can act in their community, their nation, and the world. If this goal is to be attained, students must have the opportunity to experience, to practice, to act with the knowledge and skills they gain in class. If we want individuals to be able to take action, they must have opportunities within the safety of the school to practice the democratic process. Classroom environments which create opportunities for students to establish rules and procedures and which invite all to participate in this process can foster development of citizen action skills.

## SOME MODELS OF INSTRUCTIONAL ORGANIZATION

As you have undoubtedly discerned, no discussion of pedagogy can take place without reference to issues of curriculum, classroom organization, and methods of learning. Pedagogy is complex and discussion of it reaches into nearly all aspects of schooling, including the culture of the school itself. In this chapter, however, we are emphasizing instructional decisions that can, to a large extent, be made by individual teachers. We have already discussed one such set of decisions, the variety of options the teacher might select from in presenting lessons. Another closely related set of choices relates to the organization of classroom instruction—or, put more broadly, the way students will participate in the activities of learning.

Although the organization of instruction occurs within the context of the curriculum adopted by a school system, and of fundamental community values as well, the teacher has a great deal of latitude to decide how instruction will be organized and will proceed. Unfortunately, they often do not take advantage of the options available. Think about your own learning experiences and the kinds of classroom environments you have been in. Chances are they have been highly teacher-directed, with the teacher talking and students listening. In most cases when interaction occurred it was between teacher and students in a whole-class question and answer session. Typically in this situation the teacher asks a question, and the students who think they know the answer raise their hand and wait for the teacher to call on them. Those who are not chosen to answer may be disappointed; those who were not prepared to answer the question are relieved of responsibility, this time. This is a structure, as Spencer Kagan says, that sets kids against each other,[26] and that may, in fact, encourage quiet or confused students to stop trying. Some students, it seems, never participate.

Certainly there are alternative organizational structures that help to facilitate interaction, to assist children in acquiring new information, and to make children more active in the learning process.

### Competitive and Individualistic Learning

Three patterns of learning can typically be found in America's classrooms. *Competitive learning,* typical of most classroom situations, rests on the assumption that when one wins, another loses. Competitive learning is characterized by *negative goal interdependence:* that is, when one student makes a mistake, others are happy. If someone has failed to answer a question correctly, others can then raise their hands, and they have another opportunity to demonstrate that they know their stuff. In a competitive learning situation, evaluation is based on ''correct'' answers, and that view is built into the strategies used to assess achievement. The bell curve, which typifies our most used evaluation processes, demands that each success must have a corresponding failure. The traditional spelling bee, which seems so harmless (after all, didn't *you* survive years of this activity?) is a typical example of this win-lose dimension in action. In most instances the game is played until there is only one person left standing. All the other players have lost and are sitting down, feeling, if not dejected, at least not successful. And, from a purely instructional standpoint, the winner is most probably the one who didn't even need the practice! The arguments for this type of instructional organization are many. First, it is long established, dating from historical periods in which most learning was rote learning, when there was not as much to learn, and when only those who needed any academic knowledge at all went to school. Second, it is based on an assumption that students have similar abilities to memorize, reason, and synthesize information. This is also a historical legacy, in this case from the eighteenth century Enlightenment, which proposed that the very essence of human beings, the thing that separated them from the rest of the animal world, was the ability to use their minds, to reason. The logic goes this way: I am human, therefore I can reason; therefore, I can learn.

Of course, we know that individuals differ with respect to cognitive abilities, and we know that there are a great many reasons for those differences, most of which have nothing at all to do with so-called "native" ability. There must be some other factors involved in the decision to organize classrooms around competitive learning. One of these has already been discussed, and has to do with the role of the school in promoting basic American values, including independence and competition. We admire the self-made person; we like winners; and we expect the schools to teach those values implicitly as well as explicitly. Another reason for a decided inclination toward competitive learning is that it is very easy to measure, and thus easy to evaluate. An answer is either right or wrong; the student either knows the answer or not; on a test, points are either given or not. It is very simple, and outcomes, in the form of numerical scores, are easy to manipulate in terms of averages, medians, and so forth. Such numbers, in a society that is very much attracted to scientific knowledge and methods, seem quite real and quite valuable. We "know" how we are doing and we have some "logical" basis for sorting students into groups for a variety of purposes—reading groups, academic and nonacademic tracks, admission to college, and finally, jobs and careers. An important consequence of competitive learning, however, is that students learn very early that "knowledge" is either "true" or "false," and that the very "maybe-ness," or "that depends on" quality of most issues in life outside school is not valued in the classroom. Competitive learning also teaches students not to think for themselves. The role of the teacher in competitive learning is most often that of exemplar—one who "knows" the information and "tells" it to the students—as well as judge—one who decides if the student is correct or not.

Another, perhaps less typical but not uncommon kind of learning going on in classrooms is *individualistic learning,* developed partly in response to the problems of human diversity and the adverse outcomes of some kinds of competitive learning. In this situation, the student is judged on criteria set forth only for her or him. The performance of other students has no effect on one's success, and learning has no relation to other people. Therefore, we say that there is *no goal interdependence.* Programmed instruction, and the individualized learning kits so common in many reading and language arts programs, utilize individualistic learning. It is also the basis of the Individualized Educational Program (IEP) mandated by law for students enrolled in special education programs, and can also be one of the strategies for improving performance in individual sports such as swimming and individual track and field events. One tries to "beat" oneself.

Arguments for individualistic learning are based on recognition of individual differences. One hears a good deal of talk about students working at their own pace, about the motivating power of competing with oneself, and—not incidentally—about the cost effectiveness of such instruction. Programmed learning kits, for example, do not require a teacher to do much more than provide the kits, show the student what is required, and evaluate the results—most of which are still codified in terms of "right" and "wrong" answers. Individualistic instruction may, however, provide a unique opportunity for the teacher to act as "coach," to encourage, and help the student complete the assigned tasks. While individualistic instruction can be effectively used, and may offer a number of possibilities for encouraging the development of individual strengths and talents, we believe it does little to reinforce the idea that the problem of teaching is the problem of making connections for the student.

## Cooperative Learning

A third kind of learning found more recently in some classrooms is *cooperative learning,* which, like other instructional strategies, encompasses a variety of instructional techniques. In general, cooperative learning environments are characterized by *positive goal interdependence:* that is, common goals for individual as well as group success are expected. Members of the group are accountable to one another. The group sinks or swims together, working in concert toward a particular instructional goal.

Discussing his interest in cooperative learning, Kagan relates some findings from his early research on children's play in Mexico.[27] One finding that nagged at him was that children from rural parts of Mexico were more cooperative with one another than were their peers in urban settings. Intrigued and somewhat bothered by this finding, he extended his work to look at cooperation and competition between children in other parts of the world. What he discovered is what appears to be a universal difference between students who live in rural and urban areas: that is, worldwide, regardless of cultural group, children in urban environments are more competitive than their rural counterparts. This finding, coupled with the fact that the world is becoming increasingly urban, raised considerable concern in Kagan's mind. Out of fear that the social character of the nation and world would become increasingly competitive, Kagan began exploring ways to help reverse the tendency children had to become more competitive with age. He found that using cooperative teams in the classroom, often referred to as *cooperative learning,* worked quite well.

Kagan provides the following example of a cooperative group strategy; it is called Numbered Heads Together, and can be used as an alternative to the whole-class question and answer strategy.[28] Students typically work in heterogeneous groups or teams consisting of one high-, two middle-, and one low-achieving student. Each student is assigned a number from 1 to 4. As usual, the teacher asks a question. However, rather than search the room for one student to call on, everyone is asked to put their heads together to make sure that everyone in each group knows the answer to the question. After students have had ample opportunity to make sure everyone knows the answer, the teacher calls a number. Only those students whose number has been called are asked to give the answer. In such a situation, all students are involved in discussing the question and therefore benefit by direct involvement with the content. However, no one feels bad if they weren't called on, as one of their group usually knows the answer. The Numbered Heads approach integrates positive goal interdependence—that is, if any student knows the answer, the likelihood of each student's success is increased. Likewise, individual accountability is also required, since once a number is called the individual is on his or her own to respond. Such an approach leads to cooperative interaction between students. And like many such strategies, it can be applied at any grade level and to any subject matter.

Another popular cooperative learning strategy, known as Student Teams—Achievement Division (STAD), is described by Slavin.[29] As usual, the teacher first presents a lesson to the class. As with other cooperative strategies, students work in mixed-ability groups to master the material. Students may have worksheets, workbooks, or other classroom material, might drill one another on math facts or spelling lists, or might work math problems and then compare answers. No matter what the subject matter, students are urged to work together, discuss problems, and explain their ideas to each other. After the study period, which can be as short as a class period or as long as several days, all students take a test or quiz on which they cannot help one another. Teachers may then tally test results of individual members to arrive at a group score—thus providing additional incentive for each group member to help others learn the material. Alternatively, the teacher may graph individual improvement and assign points accordingly. An approach such as this does not require much change in classroom organization, yet can have a profound effect on student learning.

It is important to emphasize that cooperative learning does not imply either devaluation of individual contributions or lack of individual accountability. And when individuals of diverse backgrounds and differing physical, linguistic, or other characteristics have the opportunity to work together in pursuit of a common goal, the barriers of stereotype that prevent people from knowing each other as individuals are likely to be broken down. Friendships are more likely to form. Individual accountability is explicitly addressed in cooperative learning strategies in the following ways: task specialization, or determination of group scores for team assignments, or both.[30]

*Task specialization,* or assignment of a specific subtask to each member of a team or group, is particularly effective in ensuring that students with disabilities, for example, contribute significantly to the group effort. Sometimes a student with a disability may be uniquely able to carry out a certain task, because students with physical, academic-cognitive, or emotional-behavioral differences are also people with *abilities.* Thus, not only can the self-image and identity of students with disabilities be enhanced, but all students can, through firsthand experience, realize this fundamental reality.

By far the greatest number of students identified as handicapped, based on definitions of P.L. 94–142, can be described as academically handicapped. That is, they experience difficulty with some (specific learning disability) or most (mental retardation) areas of academic learning. Clearly, traditional classroom organization contributes to negative peer attitudes toward low-performing students. While research does not support segregation in special classes on this account, the mere presence of these students in the regular classroom cannot in itself realize the potential of mainstreaming. In Slavin's words,

> If mainstreaming is to fulfill its potential to socially integrate handicapped children, something more than the usual instructional methods is needed. If the classroom is changed so that cooperation rather than competition is emphasized and so that academically handicapped students can make a meaningful contribution to the success of a cooperative group, acceptance of such students seems likely to increase.[31]

In addition to those just discussed, other well-known cooperative learning strategies include Jigsaw[32] and Group Investigation.[33] We cannot provide detailed summaries of all the possible cooperative learning strategies here. Rather, we hope you will consider learning more about this approach and will seek out the resources you need to become familiar with the various techniques.

Considerable research has been done over the years that has shown that cooperative learning strategies make a significant difference in student achievement.[34] Because success is desired by all in the group and academic achievement becomes a valued activity, hard workers tend not to be labeled ''teacher's pet'' or ''nerd.'' Cooperative learning also encourages students to help one another learn.[35] Students who explain, as most experienced teachers would agree, learn much in the process themselves. Students are also encouraged to provide individual assistance to one another—something usually discouraged in the typical classroom. In this way, learning does not become equated with a competitive sport where for one to win, one must lose. All should achieve and thus maintain a higher self-esteem. This group orientation, incidentally, is much more congruent with many ethnic groups' preferred learning style.

Cooperative learning also affects areas other than achievement. Considerable evidence suggests that cooperative learning improves intergroup relations in the classroom and school.[36] When students of diverse backgrounds work together to achieve a common goal, they begin to understand one another better and respect one another more. Cooperative learning has also improved relations between handicapped and nonhandicapped students.[37]

Johnson and Johnson point out the positive relationship between cooperative learning strategies and the criteria for improving intergroup relations already identified when they state:

> Cooperative learning experiences promote greater acceptance of differences and interpersonal attraction among students from different ethnic backgrounds and among handicapped and non-handicapped students. Putting students in cooperative contact who might not ordinarily seek such interactions and having them work cooperatively moves students beyond initial prejudices toward other students to multidimensional views of one another. Furthermore, such experiences allow them to deal with each other as fellow students rather than as stereotypes.[38]

Research also suggests that cooperative learning has other positive outcomes: student self-esteem improves, attendance is better, time on task is greater, and liking for school and subject matter increases.

Slavin identified two factors which seem to account for most of the effects of cooperative learning.[39] First, cooperative groups must work to achieve a group goal: they must work together to make certain that all have mastered the content and have earned grades or other forms of recognition. Remember that enlisting cooperation of all members to accomplish a goal is one way to create positive relations between group members (see Chapter 12). Second, each individual in the group is still held accountable. That is, the group's success depends on each individual learning the required material. Such group success might be reflected in the sum of the individual members' test scores or the presentation of a group report. In other words, each individual in the group must have differentiated tasks.

Kagan's research shows that up to 85 percent of college undergraduates have never worked in a cooperative situation in the classroom. Certainly a tremendous discrepancy exists between the stated goals of many schools (to develop citizens who work well with others) and the reality of student experience. Adoption of cooperative learning techniques is one way to translate this goal into action.

## SOME ADDITIONAL PEDAGOGICAL MODELS

No discussion of pedagogy for diverse classrooms would be complete without attention to several pedagogical models that focus on the development of critical thinking skills, encourage students to be active rather than passive learners, and pursue educational goals related to social reconstruction. Three such models will be discussed here: inquiry teaching, liberation pedagogy; and feminist pedagogy, or gender-based models of education.

### Inquiry Teaching

Frances Maher notes that, in social studies at least, critical thinking goals for instruction are at least as old as John Dewey.[40] Students today must be taught how to think critically in *all* areas of study so as to be able to make judgments and decisions in rapidly changing situations. One approach to this goal is *inquiry teaching.* Similar in some ways to Abelard's pedagogy, inquiry teaching seeks to bring systematic, rational inquiry to bear on both intellectual and practical problems by leading students through a series of steps based on the scientific method. This method is deemed to be nearly universal in its applicability, in both public and private life. Inquiry teaching differs from most kinds of teaching in that it is aimed at a wider sphere of influence than just the public world.

After first defining the problem, students are encouraged to hypothesize about possible answers or solutions. Then evidence is collected, evaluated for usefulness and accuracy, and used to test the hypothesis. Last, a conclusion emerges, which is then retested against further problems of the same kind to check its validity. Proponents argue that inquiry teaching leads to "objectivity, respect for other people's viewpoints, tolerance of ambiguity, and respect above all for reason and evidence."[41] In inquiry teaching, personal feelings, biases, and prejudice are acknowledged as limitations to the process, and compensations for these "emotional" responses studiously made. The goal is to be as objective as possible, and to find the best possible answer or solution to the problem, and the role of the teacher is to facilitate that choice.

### An Example of Inquiry Teaching: The Touchstones Project

The Touchstones Project was originated by faculty at St. John's College in Annapolis, Maryland, and first instituted in public schools in Maryland in 1984. This project attempted to develop a discussion class for middle and high school students that would not only introduce them to a body of knowledge but also encourage them to take an active part in their own learning and to learn to respect differences among themselves.[42] A stated purpose was to develop curriculum materials and teaching methods that would enable students of varying ability to work together. Believing that discussion is a valuable teaching format, they also thought that these classes should not be a "one-shot" deal in a particular grade, but should continue throughout the high school years. They therefore developed a series of materials, called *Touchstones I, II (Part 1 and Part 2), and III,* for classes of different ages and different degrees of experience with the project. The following "typical" incident from a Touchtones session illustrates what might happen in such a class. The subject is Euclidian geometry:

> "Luke" is the star 7th grade student in an inner-city Hartford school. "Tom" is failing and hasn't participated in any class for over four months. On this day, a regular class period is being used for a session of Touchstones. The seats are arranged in a circle instead of in rows. The format is not lecture or recitation but a discussion of a short list of definitions from Euclid's *Elements,* a reading in *Touchstones, Vol. I.* The teacher-leader asks what a straight line is, and Luke, as he always does, addresses his answer to the teacher: "A straight line is an infinite set of points with direction." A silence of almost 15 seconds greets his response.
>
> Finally, Tom's voice enters the space the silence has opened. "Those aren't your words," he says, and after waiting a moment, asks his classmates what Euclid's definition of a straight line as *breathless length* could mean. Luke, taken aback, remains quiet; other students enter the discussion. Eventually, Tom and Luke begin speaking with each other about whether one could ever see geometrical straight lines or only think about them.[43]

While Touchstones classes are organized around the text materials, many of which are short excerpts from classic works, the text often plays a subordinate role. The teacher-leader's task is, in part, to guide the students closer to or farther away from the text depending on the students' needs. For example, more academically proficient students are often "bound" to the text, dependent on teacher approval of text-related proficiencies, and less able to utilize their own experiences in reference to text materials. In addition, while they are inclined to listen to the teacher, they are less likely to really listen to other students. For these students, experience in discussion groups where they are required to work cooperatively with other students and where the teacher is not the font of all wisdom broadens both social and reflective abilities. On the other hand, students who are less academically proficient have less difficulty relating "problems" to their own lives and are better at listening to and identifying with other students' experiences, but often have much difficulty identifying their own lives with text materials. The creators of the Touchstones Project note that:

> In Touchstones discussions, high-performing students learn to be more reflective and less dependent on teacher approval. For the students, the result of discussing texts such as these is an increased thoughtfulness about and understanding of what they have previously taken for granted. Less skilled students, by experiencing the recognition of their classmates and teachers, gain confidence in their ability to contribute to and learn from academic activities.[44]

A number of pedagogical themes run through the Touchstones Project. The classes are deliberately inclusive; they focus on cooperative effort while attending to individual skill development; they are designed to empower students by placing them in the center of activity as active learners; they employ text materials of a rigorous nature; they enhance a sense of connectedness, both with other students and with text material; they emphasize the need to inquire into the material from a variety of perspectives; they use student strengths to foster improvement in needed skills. In short, the Touchstones Project is a good example of transformative inquiry teaching and learning.

## Critical or Liberation Models of Pedagogy

*Liberation pedagogy,* also often called *critical pedagogy,* like inquiry teaching, seeks to place the student at the center of the educational process. Unlike inquiry teaching, however, liberation models do not seek objectivity, but rather are based on the premise, espoused by Paulo Freire[45] and others, that most students represent oppressed groups and should be empowered by education to alter the social constructions that oppress them. They are thus primarily models of teaching aimed at the public world, although, in the case of women, they may also analyze power relations in the family and other private sphere situations. Liberation pedagogy is especially conscious of issues of power and powerlessness, in the classroom and outside it. Maher writes:

> According to theorists of liberation pedagogy, students who are not white elite males are seen through heavily ideological lenses in traditional educational institutions. They are deemed to share certain natural qualities which are considered severe handicaps for becoming educated at all. They are considered intellectually inferior, particularly in abstract and scientific reasoning, the highest form of knowledge. They are also considered generally emotional, instinctual, and best handled by being subdued by the superior powers of reason (or by the offices of white elite men). Finally, all these groups are seen as sharing common coping and passive-resistance mechanisms: silence, accommodation, ingratiation, evasiveness, and manipulation.[46]

Liberation pedagogy consists of a careful process of naming, describing, and analyzing important aspects of the world students live in. It is directed toward students who belong to minority groups, including women, who although they are a numerical majority, are often categorized as a minority group on the basis of relative powerlessness. Proponents consider the process of naming and analysis crucial to the development of a consciousness that the way things are is not necessarily the way they have to be. When one understands the means of oppression, and grasps the idea that society is a construction, not an immutable reality, one can act to alter the constructions. By acting, one learns more about the complexities of social life and about oneself.[47] The role of the teacher in liberation pedagogies is that of coach, strategist, and iconoclast. To teach is to help students break through walls of ignorance, poverty, and isolation. Thus, in all liberation teaching strategies, the concept of *voice* is important: one's personal experiences come to represent the voice of oppressed peoples, a voice that has been neither heard nor understood by oppressing groups. Education, in school and outside it, is intended to be a profoundly liberating process, but it is not the same kind of liberation as espoused by proponents of a classical liberal education. Indeed, the Euro-centered curriculum and classical pedagogy of the white elite is the very antithesis of liberation pedagogies. Like inquiry teaching, liberation pedagogies may arrive at a ''best'' solution to a problem—however, it will be based on the requirements of social justice.

## An Example of Liberation Pedagogy: Radical Math

Marilyn Frankenstein describes a course she calls Radical Math, in which arithmetic skills are learned in the process of analyzing social issues such as hunger, the use of nuclear power, and welfare. It is a college course, taught to adults who need basic math skills, but could be adapted for high school students with relative ease. The course presents arithmetic concepts and skills in the context of an advocacy of empowerment for students. Frankenstein writes:

> The content of this course teaches arithmetic while simultaneously raising political conscious-ness. Its methods try to break down traditional authoritarian teacher-student relationships by giving students meaningful control over their learning process. The aim of the course is to educate people to want radical social change while giving them both the math literacy tools necessary to challenge ruling ideas and the cooperative learning experiences necessary to create and live in a new society.[48]

Involving students deeply in both the content and the process of the class is a central objective. Students begin "teaching" one another from the very beginning:

> At the beginning of the term, I have students explain problems at the board and then, after discussing the difference between explaining and teaching, I gradually train them to teach. As various students practice teaching, they begin to involve many other students and to ask them to justify their answers. I remain quiet; the class checks itself and rarely lets a mistake go by. The students get very involved, arguing constructively and thinking creatively about solutions to the problems.[49]

Frankenstein suggests that, in addition to raising consciousness and teaching math skills, the course offers several other benefits. First, using math to analyze complex adult issues enhances the intellectual self-image of students and both adds to their general background knowledge and utilizes knowledge they already have from the outside world. Second, by encouraging students to develop their own math problems, practice in re-searching data, formulating questions, and developing a slow, careful manner of thinking a topic through are all enhanced. Third, since students are developing some of their own problems, they are likely to raise issues that require information the teacher does not have. Frankenstein notes that

> This provides students with an important experience; realizing that the teacher is not an "ex-pert" with all the answers. It encourages students to become skilled at searching for information to answer their own questions. Thus, students become what Freire calls "critical co-investigators in dialogue with the teacher.[50]

Finally, by utilizing math concepts and skills in a social context, the course begins to challenge traditional views of math (and, indeed, any subject matter) as divorced from the basic concerns of human beings.

As in all liberation pedagogy, efforts to alter both the student and the society are paramount. Such methods entail certain risks, including falling into the trap of having only one "right" answer to a social problem, or of giving credence only to views that are "politically correct" according to a single advocacy group. But the idea of involving students deeply in their own instruction and learning, of relating academic subjects to human concerns, and of enhancing the problem-solving skills of students are valuable ones in the context of a democratic society.

## Feminist Pedagogy

Like liberation models, *feminist pedagogy* is concerned with the concept of voice and also focuses on various forms of oppression, particularly those used against women. Like inquiry teaching and liberation pedagogies, it seeks to place the student in the forefront of the educational enterprise, encouraging both females and males to take charge of their own lives. Unlike inquiry teaching, however, both liberation and feminist models stress the personal, the subjective experiences of students as opposed to the ''objective'' and ''rational.'' Unlike both inquiry teaching and many liberation pedagogies, feminist pedagogy does not seek the one best answer to a question or a problem; rather, feminist pedagogy recognizes and at least theoretically appreciates multiple solutions which can be compared but not ranked hierarchically.

Feminist pedagogy is based on the observation that all human experience is *gendered,* or shaped by social constructions of gender. What it means to be male or female in society is deemed central to the meaning and form of all social encounters, including education. Taking its direction from perceived female qualities of nurturance, caring, and an inclination toward connectedness, feminist pedagogy rests on the assumption that knowledge is neither static nor ''given'' outside of the real experiences of human beings; that the claim of objectivity is inherently suspect and, in any case, not very useful because it denies individual perspectives; and that the traditional dichotomies—reason and emotion, thinking and feeling, public and private—are not truly dichotomies at all but rather aspects of reality and equally valid in understanding the world.[51] Consequently, feminist teaching stresses the use of personal history documents, journals and letters written by individuals in the process of living history, the formation of multiple hypotheses about the meaning of events, and the understanding that complex events mean different things to different people. For the feminist teacher, there is no one ''right'' answer, although there may be some questions and some solutions that are more effective than others. Critical thinking for the feminist teacher means ''examining relationships among choices, constraints, and consequences''[52] rather than coming up with a ''correct'' solution to a problem. Like inquiry teaching, feminist pedagogy stresses the role of the teacher as a democratic facilitator; however, the central element in teaching and learning is not the reach for objectivity but rather the proposal of a certain authoritative but limited perspective.[53] Feminist teaching includes the reconstruction of society among its aims; unlike liberation pedagogies, however, feminist pedagogy does not necessarily see women as oppressed. Rather, feminist teachers look to female experiences, especially as mothers and especially in the private sphere, as sources of knowledge and value for all society.

## An Example of Feminist Pedagogy: The HAFFI Cards

One feminist teaching tool that also aims to help students ''walk in the shoes of another,'' and also to encourage participatory learning was developed by Andrea Makler in the context of an eleventh-grade American History course.[54] Wanting to present the material in a way that would help students understand the different experiences of America's people, she worked with three colleagues to develop a set of *Historically Accurate Fictional Family Identity* (HAFFI) cards. Providing a structure for historical inquiry, each of these cards contained ''historically plausible life 'scripts' for members of 35 different families representing the major racial, ethnic, and religious groups in the United States.''[55] Each card contains the following information: the year in which the character is living; the character's name, age, marital status, race, religion, occupation, and place of residence. Students are asked to construct the details of their character's life in terms of a given time period and particular events also given on the card. In a unit covering the period from 1590 to 1789, for instance, all students are given the following instructions:

> Create a family history for yourself back to the year 1590. You must indicate a migration to North America some time before 1788. Indicate the places your ancestors lived and how they were affected by the events and dates listed below.
>
> > 1590—The Roanoke Colony
> > 1630; 1692; 1731; 1789
> > The French and Indian War
> > The Battle of Trenton
> > Intolerable Acts
> > 2nd Constitutional Convention
> > Proclamation of 1763.[56]

Students are also given specific instructions on each card. For example, one character is Missy, a 15-year-old black Christian house slave, unmarried with an infant daughter, living in South Carolina in 1789. The student who is Missy is asked to:

- Give your owner's name and explain how you came to be his property.
- Explain the circumstances of your daughter's birth, her name, and age.
- Describe a typical day and then explain what keeps you going when life seems really grim.[57]

Another character is Lydia Jewett, a 40-year-old caucasian Protestant midwife, married and living in Salem, Massachusetts, also in 1789. In addition to the general instructions, the student who is Lydia Jewett has the following special notes:

- Your family was in the first group of Puritans who settled in the Plymouth area. Why and when did they come to America?
- Produce the pages from your great, great grandmother's diary that discuss the trials in Salem in 1692.
- How did you get into your line of work and what are your major concerns about it?[58]

New HAFFI cards are assigned with each unit so that students "become" different people in different time periods. Makler writes:

> As the units progress, some pupils find themselves in uncomfortable roles, asked to express the perspectives of people whose race, religion, or political credos are very different from their own: a slave-trader, an American Tory, a fundamentalist lay preacher, an unwed mother, a bootlegger's widow, a radical union organizer, a wealthy politician, a member of the Ku Klux Klan, a pacifist, and so forth. Since each HAFFI card presents a person at a different stage of life, students must consider issues of age, gender, race, and geography.[59]

Curricular approaches such as this have a number of advantages. They do not require new texts or materials; they require students to do considerable research, to organize a large body of data coherently, and to discuss historical events and issues from the perspective of their "character"; they involve sharing information with others; and they help make historical information real, concrete, and alive. Moreover, a biographical approach such as this could be adapted to many subjects, allowing students to study literature, math, science, geography, and foreign languages in terms of people (both fictional and real) who developed the ideas and had to live with their consequences. This approach becomes a time machine in which students can, with some degree of freedom, inhabit both the past and the future.

## CREATING THE DEMOCRATIC CLASSROOM: PEDAGOGY FOR THE NEW COMMON SCHOOL

The United States is a democracy, one of the first experiments in such a process of government. The American common school originated as a way of enabling young people to learn to participate in a democratic polity; today, that polity has global implications and a new form of ''common school'' seems to be required.

We have repeatedly stressed that knowledge alone is rarely sufficient to bring about significant change in behavior. The educational philosopher John Dewey knew this when he insisted that children learn by experience as well as from instruction. We cannot transmit the democratic ideals of our nation, then, merely by giving students information. Students *must* have concrete experiences which enable them to develop the necessary skills and outlooks needed to fulfill the goals of our nation's charter.

The school and classroom are the perfect place to put into practice the ideals and behavior we hope our students will one day express and exhibit as adults—those of participatory, reflective, and informed decision makers who act within their community, their nation, and in their world. The school, then, can be envisioned as a minisociety where appropriate classroom management and disciplinary strategies can create a climate conducive to democratic practice and achievement of the transcendent goals of teaching outlined above. In a democratic classroom and school, all students participate or have a say in establishing rules which consider the needs of everyone. Such an environment encourages the development of self-regulating behavior. That is, discipline should be perceived not as punishment but as a process that evolves within the individual. Such a classroom promotes critical thinking, group problem solving, and decision making; encourages a sense of belonging, and the development of a positive self-esteem.

A democratic classroom is a complex environment which considers the individual as well as the range of abilities, experiences, knowledge, attitudes, and values she or he brings to the classroom. Remember that this applies to teachers as well as to students! As you think about appropriate instructional approaches, the following may be helpful:[60]

**1** True democracy requires flexibility. Plan a variety of activities and vary instructional methods often. Learning should be engaging and fun, not boring.

**2** Democracy is not just for some, it is for everyone, and everyone will learn, and learn to participate, at a somewhat different rate. Know where each of your students is academically, and consider encouraging students to help one another.

**3** When possible, in consultation with any student who appears to be in real trouble, with their parents, their counselors, and, quite possibly, their friends, explore likely reasons for the difficulties. Consider such differences as language, learning style, communication barriers, and sense of belonging, any of which might affect student learning.

**4** Select the most critical instructional goals and objectives for each student and set these as your targets.

**5** Demonstrate that teaching and learning is a dynamic process. Remembering that teaching is an *interactive* process, work *with* the student, thereby encouraging participation and a sense of belonging while helping to develop decision-making skills. Provide a choice of activities, and select one or more learning activities to supplement your traditional instructional format. Be certain to consider alternative and varied forms of responses (alternate oral and visual activities with written ones, for instance). Consider shorter assignments and abbreviated tasks to help build confidence. Consider the use of learning contracts with students to gain their interest while clarifying their (and your) responsibilities. Check the readability levels of texts, and match with the student's progress. Consider supplementary materials with content that matches students' interests. Provide first-language materials for limited-English-proficient students when possible.

**6** Employ one strategy at a time, fully evaluating its effectiveness, and modify as necessary. Whenever it is the least bit possible, involve students in the process, modeling the democratic process at a personal level.

**7** Establish clearly defined academic and behavioral expectations. Communicate what is expected, and provide clear, unambiguous instructions to all students.

**8** Consider what students are to do when they have completed the task at hand. Providing interesting and relevant activities helps to establish an atmosphere conducive to learning.

**9** You may also wish to work with other teachers during this process, recognizing that most change is slow and requires continuous feedback and encouragement from others.

## SUMMARY

Just as a transformation of curriculum seems to be required for effective education in contemporary American society, so too is a concomitant transformation of pedagogy. This does not mean a wholesale disposal of everything that has gone before. As the Touchstones Project illustrates, a commitment to knowing and understanding old ideas is compatible with the redesign of practice in new and creative forms. And even a casual perusal of some of the newer pedagogical models reveals roots in ancient ideas and practices. There is nothing inherently right or wrong with most pedagogical methods. What is important is the spirit in which they are used and the purposes to which they are put. Freed of the baggage of old social norms and educational aims that have lost their relevance, teaching methods from ancient Greece to modern Mexico and Japan are available for scrutiny, for development, and for transformation. And we believe this task should be a cooperative one—between teachers and students, between schools and communities, and between nations. Cooperation is a value not only for schools, but for society. If we are to survive as human beings and transform a world of inequality, international conflict, and potential nuclear disaster, young people must develop cooperative skills and values more fully than their elders have. Since we live in an increasingly interdependent society, we are ethically bound to both teach and model collaborative learning and cooperative activity, for with it comes the possibility of survival, justice and peace.[61] Cooperation may be the linchpin on which our transformations depend.

## ACTIVITIES

**1** Consider some of the following differences between typical American versus non-American (sometimes called *contrast-American*) ways of thinking and interacting.

a *Thinking patterns:* The thinking patterns favored by the culture determine, to a great extent, the way people in that culture learn and teach. What are the consequences for students of the differences listed below? For educators? What modifications in instruction might facilitate learning? Consider, for example, pacing, experiential versus didactic presentations, and assessment and motivational strategies.

| American cognitive pattern | Contrast-American pattern |
| --- | --- |
| Operates with facts and data | Operates with ideas |
| Concerned with immediate results | Concerned more with the process |
| Highly analytical | Holistic or relational |

b *Role relationships:* People orient themselves relative to society and family in different ways. This affects interaction patterns between student and teacher as well as parent/community and teacher. Consider the two lists below. What are the consequences for students? For educators? What modifications in instruction might accommodate such differences?

| American structure | Contrast-American structure |
| --- | --- |
| Little emphasis on hierarchies among people (a relatively "classless" society) | Great emphasis on hierarchies among people |
| High need for individual achievement and recognition | High need for belonging |
| Independence | Dependence |

2 Interview some teachers regarding their perception of cooperative education in the classroom. What do they perceive to be overall objectives and outcomes of such efforts? Have they applied cooperative learning strategies? In what ways? With what results?

3 Consider a typical lesson or series of lessons you might find in a textbook from your proposed area of teaching. How might you apply cooperative learning strategies to it? Beyond the immediate objective of the lesson, what outcomes would you expect to achieve?

4 Observe a classroom in action. In what ways do you see democracy being put into action? In what ways do you see contradictions between what is preached (i.e., democratic ideals and practice are a desired outcome of schooling) and what is practiced? What modifications would you recommend in this classroom? (Always write up your reports in an objective manner without identifying the teacher(s) you observed.)

# REFERENCES

1 Thomas F. Green, "A Topology of the Teaching Concept," in Joe Park (ed.), *Selected Readings in the Philosophy of Education* (New York: Macmillan, 1974), p. 56.

2 Ibid., p. 57.

3 Ibid., p. 59.

4 Ibid., pp. 61–62.

5 N. R. Bernier, "Beyond Instructional Context Identification," in Judith L. Green and Cynthia Wallar (eds.), *Ethnography and Language* (Norwood, NJ: Ablex, 1981), p. 302.

6 See, for example, John A. Goodlad, *A Place Called School: Prospects for the Future* (New York: McGraw-Hill, 1984).

7 Harry S. Broudy, "Historic Exemplars of Teaching Method, in Nat Gage (ed.), *Research on Teaching* (Chicago: Rand McNally, 1963), pp. 1–43.

8 Ibid., p. 5.

9 Ibid., p. 6.

10 Ibid., p. 8.

11 Ibid., p. 4.

12 Ibid., p. 16.

13 Ibid., p. 17, referring to Peter Abelard's *Sic et Non.*

14 Broudy, op. cit., p. 22.

15 Ibid., p. 23.

16 Ibid., p. 26.

17 Ibid., p. 32.

18 C. I. Bennett, *Comprehensive Multicultural Education; Theory and Practice,* 2d. ed. (Boston: Allyn and Bacon, 1990) p. 182.

19 Ibid.

20 Charles Krauthammer, "Education: Doing Bad and Feeling Good," *Time,* February 5, 1990, p. 78.

21 Ibid.

22 Reprinted with permission by McGraw-Hill, Inc. Goodlad, op. cit., p. 142.

23 Ibid.

24 Tiedt and Tiedt, *Multicultural Teaching: A Handbook of Activities, Information, and Resources,* 3rd ed. (Boston: Allyn and Bacon, 1990), p. 51.

25 Robert J. Cottrol, (1990) "America the Multicultural," *American Educator,* Wtr., p. 20. Reprinted with permission from the winter 1990 issue of the *American Educator,* the quarterly journal of the American Federation of Teachers.

26 Spencer Kagan, "The Structural Approach to Cooperative Learning," *Educational Leadership,* vol. 47, no. 4, Dec. 1989/Jan. 1990, pp. 12–15.

27 Ibid.

28 Ibid.

29 R. E. Slavin, "Cooperative Learning and the Cooperative School," *Educational Leadership,* vol. 45, no. 3, Nov. 1987, pp. 7–13.

30 ———, *Cooperative Learning: Theory, Research, and Practice* (Englewood Cliffs, NJ: Prentice-Hall, 1990), p. 12.

31 Ibid., p. 39.

32 E. Aronson, N. Blaney, C. Stephan, J. Sikes, and M. Snapp, *The Jigsaw Classroom* (Beverly Hills, CA: Sage Publications, 1978).

33 S. Sharan, R. Hertz-Lazarowitz, and Z. Ackerman, "Academic Achievement of Elementary School Children in Small-Group versus Whole Class Instruction," *Journal of Experimental Education,* vol. 48, no. 1, fall 1980, pp. 125–129.

34 Robert Slavin, "Research on Cooperative Learning: Consensus and Controversy," *Educational Leadership,* vol. 47, no. 4, Dec. 1989–Jan. 1990, pp. 52–54.

35 Ibid.

36 ———, "Cooperative Learning: Applying Contact Theory in Desegregated Schools," *Journal of Social Issues,* vol. 41, no. 3, 1985, pp. 45–62.

37 N. A. Madden and R. E. Slavin, "Mainstreaming Students with Mild Academic Handicaps: Academic and Social Outcomes," *Review of Educational Research,* vol. 53, no. 4, winter 1983, pp. 519–569.

**38** David Johnson and Roger Johnson, "Student-Student Interaction: Ignored but Powerful," *Journal of Teacher Education,* vol. 36, no. 4, July–August 1985, p. 23.

**39** Robert Slavin, op. cit. (ref. 37), pp. 52–54.

**40** Frances A. Maher, "Inquiry Teaching and Feminist Pedagogy," *Social Education,* vol. 51, no. 3, March 1987, pp. 186–192.

**41** Ibid., p. 186.

**42** Geoffrey Comber, Howard Zeiderman, and Nicholas Maistrellis, "The Touchstones Project: Discussion Classes for Students of All Abilities," *Educational Leadership,* vol. 46, no. 6, March 1989, pp. 39–42. Reprinted with permission of the Association for Supervision and Curriculum Development. Copyright 1989 by ASCD. All rights reserved.

**43** Ibid., p. 39.

**44** Ibid., p. 41.

**45** Paulo Freire, *Pedagogy of the Oppressed* (New York: Herder and Herder, 1970); *The Politics of Education: Culture, Power and Liberation* (South Hadley, MA: Bergin & Garvey, 1985).

**46** Frances A. Maher, "Toward a Richer Theory of Feminist Pedagogy: A Comparison of 'Liberation' and 'Gender' Models for Teaching and Learning," *Journal of Education,* vol. 169, no. 3, fall 1987, p. 93.

**47** For a more detailed explanation of liberation pedagogy, see Henry Giroux, "Radical Pedagogy and the Politics of Student Voice," *Interchange,* vol. 17, no. 1, 1986, pp. 48–69.

**48** Marilyn Frankenstein, "A Different Third R: Radical Math," in Susan Gushee O'Malley, Robert C. Rosen, and Leonard Vogt (eds.), *Politics of Education: Essays from Radical Teacher* (Albany, NY: State University of New York Press, 1990), p. 220.

**49** Ibid.

**50** Ibid., p. 222.

**51** Maher, op. cit. (ref. 44), p. 188.

**52** Ibid., p. 190.

**53** Ibid.

**54** Andrea Makler, "Recounting the Narrative," *Social Education,* vol. 51, no. 3, March 1987, pp. 180–185.

**55** Ibid., p. 180.

**56** Ibid., p. 182.

**57** Ibid.

**58** Ibid.

**59** Ibid.

**60** Adapted from J. J. Hoover and C. Collier, *Classroom Management through Curricular Adaptations* (Lindale, TX: Hamilton Publications, 1986; H. Hernandez, *Multicultural Education: A Teacher's Guide to Content and Process* (Columbus, OH: Charles E. Merrill, 1989); and Bennett, op. cit. (ref. 18).

**61** Nancy Schniedewind and Ellen Davidson, *Cooperative Learning, Cooperative Lives: A Sourcebook of Learning Activities for Building a Peaceful World* (Dubuque, IA: William C. Brown, 1987).

# 14

# THE TRANSFORMATION
# OF SCHOOL CULTURE

*For every complicated problem, there is an answer that is short, simple, and wrong.*

H. L. Mencken

## A CALL FOR REFORM

For the time being, at least, everyone is talking about schools. The decade of the 1980s saw more than thirty study commissions and reports aimed at identifying problems in and at improving the American educational system. Among the major reports were:

• *A Nation at Risk: The Imperative for Educational Reform:*[1] Perhaps the most widely cited of all the reports (thanks in part to its media-made tag line, "the rising tide of mediocrity"), this one was initiated by Secretary of Education T. H. Bell, and based its findings on papers commissioned from experts and testimony from educators, students, parents, professional groups, and public officials. The report asserts that American schools are falling behind those of other countries in their ability to produce citizens with a shared base of knowledge and skills and that, as a result, American workers will be increasingly unable to compete with workers of other nations.

• *The Paideia Proposal: An Educational Manifesto:*[2] Written by Mortimer Adler for the Paideia Group, this document conceptualizes an American schooling system based on the acquisition of knowledge of the liberal arts for all children and dedicated to preserving America's commitment to democracy.

• *A Place Called School:*[3] The result of an eight-year study of American schools at all levels conducted by John Goodlad and his associates, this report attempts to "get inside" the school and look at the various contexts in which teachers, students, administrators, and parents struggle to maintain schooling in the face of a changing society.

• *High School:*[4] Emerging from a three-year study directed by Ernest Boyer, this report profiles the successes and problems of the American public secondary school, and includes recommendations for reform.

• *Barriers to Excellence:*[5] This report surveys and evaluates educational trends in the United States with particular attention to poor and minority students, and also critiques many of the other reports and their recommendations.

All of these reports have some characteristics in common. Far from being "objective," they are written by national leaders who are interested parties in the educational process in the United States. And although they appear to be factual, they represent particular constituencies. Webb and Sherman note that:

**1.** They are written to verify the public suspicion that the quality of American education has declined.

**2.** They are written by nationally known, well-respected leaders from business, politics, education, and the general public. The varied affiliations and collective prominence of the commissioners lend an air of objectivity to the documents they produce.

**3.** All make policy recommendations for improving public education. These suggestions generally serve the interests of each commission's funding sources and/or sponsoring organizations.

**4.** All are designed to galvanize public opinion behind an effort to improve the nation's schools. The reports are written in a passionate and streamlined style. Grim statistics are followed by lists of straightforward, nonradical recommendations. Clear writing, quotable quotes, shocking facts, and manageable recommendations ensure that the reports get maximum media attention.[6]

Underlying all of these reports are five assumptions about American education.[7]

**1** *Education is correlated with economic and social development:* It is assumed that the economic and social well-being of the individual and the nation depend on improved educational outcomes.

**2** *Quality education as a lifelong process is a universal right:* That is, quality schooling through high school is the right of all people, but only the beginning of an education. Public schools should teach not only content but how to learn, so that individuals are better equipped to continue with postsecondary educational opportunities.

**3** *Public schools will continue as a mainstay of our society:* While all the reports are rather pessimistic about the present state of our public schools, none of them gives any serious consideration to major alternatives to the public school model.

**4** *Quality teachers and teaching underlie improved learning:* Substantial improvement in schools is directly dependent on quality teachers and teaching. Without a heavy investment in human capital, all improvement efforts will fail.

**5** *Accountability and leadership must increase:* While earlier critiques of schools tended to identify a particular weak link, these suggest that all sectors of society have a major role to play in school improvement. Increased accountability and leadership in the public sector at the federal, state, and local level, and also from the private sector, are needed if school reform is to succeed.

In 1990, President George Bush and the nation's governors put forth six national goals for public education designed to establish a set of standards and incentives to guide reform efforts during the coming decade.[8] These goals include:

*Goal 1:* By the year 2000, all children in America will start school ready to learn.
*Goal 2:* By the year 2000, the high school graduation rate will increase to at least 90%.
*Goal 3:* By the year 2000, American students will leave grades 4, 8, and 12 having demonstrated competency in challenging subject matter, including English, mathematics, science, history, and geography; and every school in America will ensure that all students learn to use their minds well, so that they may be prepared for responsible citizenship, further learning, and productive employment in our modern economy.
*Goal 4:* By the year 2000, U.S. students will be first in the world in mathematics and science achievement.
*Goal 5:* By the year 2000, every adult American will be literate and will possess the skills necessary to compete in a global economy and to exercise the rights and responsibilities of citizenship.
*Goal 6:* By the year 2000, every school in America will be free of drugs and violence and will offer a disciplined environment conducive to learning.

While the recommendations of the commissions and the goals put forward by the Governors' Conference are clear enough, how they will all be achieved is a matter of considerable—and often acrimonious—debate. Webb and Sherman offer an interesting typology of commission reports that indicates the nature of the problem.[9] All the major commission reports, they say, fit into one of four categories: (1) reports that emphasize economic and technical excellence, (2) reports that focus on academic excellence, (3) reports that envision institutional excellence, and (4) reports that emphasize excellence and equity.[10]

Central to *economic and technical excellence reports*—*A Nation at Risk* is a primary example—is the belief that American schools are failing to produce people who can compete in the global economy. They are business-oriented, and emphasize the ways in which curricula should represent an effective entry into the job market, with particular emphasis on mathematics, science, and computers. These reports recommend closer relations between schools and businesses in terms of setting and achieving school goals. They assert that there is no conflict between equity and excellence and strongly recommend that *all* students receive an equal education. If there should be conflict between these ideals, however, they come down on the side of excellence. Authors of these reports emphasize a top-down administration, generally do not see teachers as effective change agents (indeed, some believe teachers are part of the problem), and emphasize competition, high standards of academic achievement, and the role of schooling in identifying the "best and the brightest" students.[11]

The *academic excellence reports* focus not on the workplace per se, but on the role of general knowledge in maintaining and advancing American democracy. Mortimer Adler, a professor of philosophy and one of the founders of the University of Chicago Great Books program, wrote the most famous of these, *The Paideia Proposal*. He believes that the two greatest contributions of the United States to western culture are compulsory public education and universal suffrage. He thinks that our greatest challenge now is to make sure that all students are provided with an academic education of high standards; he is thus vehemently against tracking for any purpose. This education should be based in the liberal arts, which in his view give the best preparation for citizenship, for work, and for life. While *The Paideia Proposal* acknowledges that some students are more academically talented and will, in the end, probably learn more than others, it asserts that it is the nature of all human beings to be able to reason, to observe, to ask questions, to learn, to think, and to communicate. No child should be deprived of the opportunity to develop those innate skills. Because some children come to school less ready to learn what the schools have to teach, *The Paideia Proposal* also recommends early childhood instruction for those most likely to be unprepared.[12] In one of the most controversial sentences in this report, Adler asserts that it is the responsibility of the state to guarantee readiness for schooling by providing one to three years of early childhood instruction designed, in effect, to alter the socialization of children in families that are regarded as unable to provide socialization patterns congruent with schooling: "The sooner a democratic society intervenes to remedy the cultural inequality of homes and environments, the sooner it will succeed in fulfilling the democratic mandate of equal educational opportunity for all."[13]

Authors of what Webb and Sherman call *institutional excellence reports* shift the focus somewhat and concentrate on the nature of the school as a whole. Written by educators closely concerned with the preparation of teachers and with the educational establishment in higher education, these reports look at how all the elements of schooling—teaching, learning, administration, parent and community linkages—add up to an environment for learning. Perhaps the most readable, as well as the most visionary, of these is John

Goodlad's *A Place Called School.* Goodlad and others assert that there is a marked difference between elementary schools and high schools. Most elementary schools, and their teachers, focus on children and their needs, thereby creating a place where a certain flexibility and humane outlook enhances the ability of children to learn and to like learning. In contrast, these authors see American high schools as "routinized, generally quiet, needlessly unproductive, and intellectually dull."[14] Of prime concern to Goodlad is the notion that schools are being asked to do too much in a society in which there are multiple institutions and organizations that educate. An important task ahead, therefore, is for educators and other interested people in the community to decide just what schools *can* do best, and set about organizing the school to do just that. The two central features of schooling which for Goodlad appear to hold the most promise are (1) academic instruction and (2) the promotion of citizenship, or civic education, understood as the development of decency and civility.[15] The lives of teachers in schools are another major emphasis of *A Place Called School,* with particular attention to the ways in which the culture of the school can be altered to provide working conditions for teachers that will enable them to do what they do best. Without such alterations, teaching will not improve and the recommendations of all other reports have little chance of success.[16]

Finally, there are several reports which focus on *excellence in terms of equity,* addressing the equity needs of poor and minority students as a prerequisite to talking about academic achievement. That is, they emphasize discriminatory practices in schools that prevent some students from receiving the same education as their more economically fortunate classmates, even when basic ability may be the same. Thus, for example, overcrowded and underfunded schools, inexperienced teachers, and lower expectations create an environment in which these students are less likely to learn what they need to know.[17] Equal educational opportunity may be viewed as either an equal chance or an equal share. An equal chance assumes that all students are allowed to come to school but that some will "naturally" fail and that the school cannot help the fact that some students will achieve more. An equal share assumes that prior commitment to ensuring equal education for all children is necessary, and that the school should assist "at risk" students in whatever ways are necessary to accomplish that goal. For the authors of excellence and equity reports, equal educational opportunity means an equal share.

## THE RECURRING PROBLEM OF EQUITY AND EXCELLENCE

As we have discussed, education in America has historically struggled with the reality of diversity in a nation of immigrants. In colonial times, formal education was essentially a male prerogative—and one reserved for the politically and economically privileged— yet the Latin schools operated in Philadelphia under the Quakers enrolled girls as well as boys. Daniel and Laurel Tanner note that "throughout the eighteenth century a theme of Quaker humanitarianism was that women, blacks, and Indians should be educated on a equal level with whites and males."[18] This view, however, was highly unusual.

Although schools increasingly served females after the Revolution, the disparity between rich and poor continued. For many years private academies served the former and charity schools the latter, especially in larger cities. There was also growing concern about the social problems of delinquency and idleness among urban youth, which no doubt inspired a variety of philanthropic educational efforts. Further fragmentation occurred with the establishment of separate native language schools for diverse northern European groups.

The common school concept represented the belief that such class and group distinctions were counter to the democratic spirit. Horace Mann was convinced that through education the children of the poor could, and must, participate as equal members of an informed and competent electorate, and that a two-tiered class structure was inimical to the ideals of democracy.

Beginning in the latter half of the nineteenth century, massive waves of immigration made the issue of diversity even more urgent. Many educational leaders believed that the increasing presence of immigrant children from southern and eastern Europe challenged the schools to create "Americans" from this "wretched refuse"; the concept was clearly to change the child to fit the school.

As is not surprising in a pluralistic society where schooling is a political as well as an educational enterprise, the reform of schooling has been a priority (some might even say obsession) of Americans at least since the rise of the common school. Diane Ravitch describes what she calls the "pendulum swing" of the past half-century:

> In the 1940s and early 1950s, a "good school" used progressive methods based on student interests and activity projects. After the Soviets put Sputnik into orbit in 1957, a "good school" was defined as one with high academic standards and special programs for gifted students, especially in subjects such as science, foreign languages, and mathematics. By the late 1960s, the once-high standards started to fall, and the "good school" was one where student participation and choice were emphasized. Since the mid-1970s, the educational pendulum has swung back toward "basics," "standards," and a coherent curriculum, and away from the free-wheeling experimentation of the 60s and 70s.[19]

The current set of reform recommendations and national goals tend to fall very much in the "high standards" column. Most prescribe more academics—for example, they may suggest that minimum numbers of certain courses be required for graduation; longer instructional periods, achieved either by lengthening the school day, increasing the number of days spent in school per year, or making more efficient use of class time; and "stricter" standards, such as requiring the use of standardized tests for promotion to the next grade.[20] More disturbing is the fact that while the majority of the reports give lip service to both equity and excellence in education, exactly what this means in terms of educational practice and how the necessary changes in our educational system can be achieved are not fully addressed. A quality curriculum and sufficient instructional time are essential for most students, but especially for the "underachieving students, who are highly susceptible to boredom, intolerant of conformity, vulnerable to uncaring teachers, and who are dropping out of school."[21]

What is meant by *equity, excellence,* and *quality* in education? *Equity* does not necessarily mean equal or identical; rather, the term should suggest comparable in terms of outcome. Implementation of the first of the national goals put forth by President Bush, readiness to learn on entering school, should manifest equity in three ways.[22] *Equity of access* demands that, due to such factors as cultural bias in assessment strategies and conflict between cultural norms in the home and cultural norms in the school, chronological age be the only criterion for deciding time of entry into school. As Kagan has stated,

This position rejects the idea of holding children out of school until they are 'ready for school' and assumes that it is the school's responsibility to be 'ready for the youngster.' Therefore, measures of readiness should rate not a child's performance, but an institution's.[23]

*Equity of assessment* is a second important issue. The fact that young American children have so often been overtested has long been an issue in the professional literature. For many reasons, assessment strategies for young children have resulted in inaccurate judgments, misdiagnosis, and poor self-image. Many have gone so far as to suggest that formal testing be forbidden until the sixth grade. Rather, educators should continue to strive to develop alternative assessment strategies.

Finally, *equity of standards and support* must be the rule. Common standards for kindergarten facilities, equitable salaries for preschool teachers who have training and experience comparable to elementary and secondary teachers, and access to quality in-service education for all who work closely with young children should be instituted.

A quality education certainly means more than completion of the prescribed number of pages in a text or workbook. Quality education includes the acquisition of knowledge, the development of problem-solving and inquiry skills, the development of an appreciation for the arts, the maintenance of self-respect and respect for others, and the achievement of a certain degree of personal and social responsibility.[24] It thus becomes the responsibility of the teacher and the school to deliver instruction in such a manner that it reaches all students—not just some, who by virtue of their socialization have an easier time succeeding in the existing culture of the school.

It is far from clear that simply raising standards will result in a comparable improvement in achievement. For many students, raising standards without providing subsequent opportunities in the form of appropriate materials, alternative instructional approaches, and modified motivational strategies may in fact raise the level of frustration and increase the likelihood that they will drop out of school. This is another case in which *equitable* does not mean *identical.* Gay discusses equity and excellence as the challenge we face to provide *all* with the opportunity to learn to their highest possible level of ability, regardless of where they live, their family structure, their gender, economic background, ethnic identity, home-based cultural orientation, or condition of health.[25] Such an effort requires providing a quality of facilities, resources, and instruction comparable to that which those who typically succeed in school receive.

We should also stress that *comparable* does not necessarily mean *equal;* it can also mean equivalent in terms of instructional outcome. Our efforts must be directed at the outcome of education; that is, the attainment of knowledge, skills, and attitudes deemed appropriate. Comparable education demands that teachers provide the experiences necessary to enable a child to learn. Materials, for instance, might be congruent with the abilities of some, but might demand modification so that an individual with some kind of handicap is able to achieve. Comparable does not have to mean more homework for the child who is struggling and who may already feel that the work he or she is doing is overwhelming; it may mean searching out an alternative approach which enables that child to achieve as well as other children. Nor does comparable mean an indiscriminate substitution of culture-specific materials: as Gay argues, comparable curriculum does not mean that a teacher can equate the poetry of Robert Frost for caucasian children with the rap music of M. C. Hammer for African-American children. Rather, material written by Maya Angelou or Langston Hughes more appropriately serves as an alternative.[26] Comparable does not mean that a teacher should give more tests to the child who does not take tests well; it might mean that the teacher should seek out appropriate alternative means to assess student achievement. Paper-and-pencil tests are certainly not the only way to tell if a child has learned something. Perhaps most important, student diversity should not mean that educators lower their expectations or their standards of achievement for any child. The responsibility for change should be in the hands of teachers and schools as they search for appropriate means to reach their students. The eye must be on outcomes. As the old proverb says, ''there's more than one way to skin a cat.'' Appropriate strategies for delivering an education to diverse learners can be developed and applied with creativity and sensitivity.

## EFFECTIVE SCHOOL CULTURES: THE GOOD NEWS

An examination of the way schools respond to issues of equity and excellence as they attempt to interpret and implement current reform recommendations is central to any discussion of the subject of effective schools. It was not until the 1960s that educators began to seek out the criteria that might set ''effective'' schools apart from less effective ones. In this section, we will look at findings from the research on effective schools, and how they can be applied in a variety of settings.

Before we do that, however, let's spend a little time discussing what we mean when we say ''the culture of the school.'' To begin with, schools are both a part of and separate from the wider community and society. Thus, life in schools reflects both similarities to and differences from life outside them. To illustrate this point, consider that the norm (and law) against personal violence against another person applies to both life in schools and life outside them; and so do the values of waiting your turn, letting the other person ''have a say,'' and making room for everyone. There are ways, however, in which values or practices operative outside schools may not be encountered inside them. The concept of majority rule, so close to the heart of a democratic state, for instance, has little resonance in schools. It is, of course, ''taught,'' but not practiced, for the ''majority'' in all schools are children. Similarly, the sharing of knowledge which, outside of school, is widely valued and practiced, is often anathema in schools. At home, in the neighborhood, in the community at large, the inclination to share knowledge is everywhere; we speak to the heart of that value when we say that everyone teaches something to someone all the time. Knowledge is mostly free for the asking in the community; ask any librarian, any museum curator, nearly any person on the street. Ride a bus sometime, and listen to information being shared, explained, interpreted. In schools, however, knowledge is considered private property—first of the teacher (and the people who wrote the books), and then of those students who have ''worked'' to obtain it. To share knowledge in school is often ''to give someone the answer,'' and that is usually frowned on. Indeed, to share knowledge with a classmate is often considered cheating, and both the giver and the receiver are punished for the offense.

In its simplest sense, the culture of the school consists of the norms, rules, conditions, social structure, values, beliefs, habits, and experiences of life in schools. One can get a sense of this meaning by thinking about what it takes to become a ''native'' in the school environment—a person who understands, without paying much attention to the fact that she or he understands, exactly how to behave in what situations with what particular people at what particular time. Cultural elements of schools vary, of course, but it has been truly said that a person from Maine can walk into a school in Georgia, Texas, California, or Michigan, and pretty much know where things are, what roles various people play, and what the rules are. Indeed, it has been asserted that someone who went to school in the 1840s might very well feel reasonably sure of how to behave in a school in the 1990s!

So when we speak of "effective" schools we will not just be talking about schools whose students achieve certain outcomes; we will be speaking of what it is like to "live" in schools—as students, teachers, secretaries, custodians, counselors, nurses, administrators, parents, and sometimes members of the community. The question is: How do these natives understand their environment?

The majority of the comprehensive studies of school effectiveness have been undertaken in large, inner city schools, which of course skews the findings somewhat. Nevertheless, findings from these studies are valuable. *Effectiveness* has typically been defined by their authors as academic achievement greater than that in most schools with similar "poverty" conditions and similar students. However, definitions of effective schools do vary. Some educators speak of effective schools as those that are self-renewing—that is, schools in which teachers, administrators, students, and parents are able to identify problems and then devise strategies to resolve them. Others speak of effective schools as those that promote personal growth of students as well as independent study skills or a love of learning.[27] Still others include in their definition an attention to goals which involve multicultural education and cultural pluralism.[28] Clearly, the definition of effectiveness changes depending on the purposes of those doing the defining.

Elements which define effective schools go far beyond simple routines, coverage of material, and time on task. As you might expect, for us effective schools are the ones where those in charge understand that providing good education for a democratic society *means* addressing issues of diversity, intercultural competence, and teacher expectations, as well as social relationships in the classroom and school. In such schools, parental support and involvement extends beyond mere endorsement of the school's activities and includes their presence on site and their participation in instruction and other activities.

A plethora of studies done during the 1980s attempted to identify common characteristics of schools where achievement levels are high regardless of socioeconomic or cultural background. One of the earliest of these was conducted by the late Ronald Edmonds.[29] Edmonds defined effective schools as ones where working-class children achieve as well as middle-class children on a series of standardized achievement tests. He and his colleagues analyzed a large number of data on a variety of variables, from such things as the amount of homework given and the degree to which parents were involved in ongoing communication to the amount of dirt and dust found in hallways and the length of time it took maintenance personnel to repair broken windows and desks. Other researchers have made similar analyses of teacher, student, and parental behavior in the hope of identifying practices common to effective schools.[30]

A summary of the studies undertaken in what has been called the *effective schools movement* suggests that schools that are helping their students achieve do have certain identifiable characteristics.

First, students and teachers in these schools carry out their daily tasks in a *safe, predictable, and orderly environment* which emphasizes discipline as training in self control rather than punishment and therefore is conducive to teaching and learning. Such an environment is humane, not oppressive, enabling a relatively high degree of trust to develop among both teachers and students. The emotional needs of individuals in a complex environment are recognized and actively addressed. People have a sense that they belong, that they have a niche, and because people know what is expected of them, there is little ambiguity and a corresponding low degree of anxiety. Both roles of individuals and expectations of all are well defined and established.

Second, there is a *clearly stated and communicated school mission,* which emphasizes a shared commitment to instructional priorities, goals, and objectives, and to accountability. Again, there is little ambiguity and uncertainty on this point. All teachers, students, and community members know and are generally in agreement with the mission statement. Moreover, the mission and goals are the same for *all* students, and all interested parties work together to help students achieve them.

Third, teachers communicate the message that they have *high expectations and requirements of all students.* Students are not categorized as those who can succeed and those who cannot. The belief that all can and will master basic skills and more is communicated and strived for in all cases. Assuming that mastery of the curriculum is possible for all, greater and more intense curricular change often occurs, designed to assure that a comparable curriculum is delivered to all. Efforts are consistently made to adapt both curriculum and instruction to a variety of learning and communication styles. Such strategies as reteaching and curriculum alignment are employed as needed.

Fourth, resolute attempt is made to *focus instruction on basic skills and academic achievement.* Good schools focus their efforts on learning. Time on task is high, meaning that, as much as possible, students are engaged in activities designed to master basic skills or objectives. All activities in the school, including both formal and compensatory education programs, are united under one umbrella. School routines discourage disorder and keep classroom disruptions to a minimum. Schools which have strong athletic programs do not place these above academic success. Even public sports ceremonies recognize and honor high academic achievement.

Fifth, there is *vigorous leadership by a principal who stresses instructional effectiveness* and makes clear, consistent, and fair decisions. This principal is highly visible, spending a good part of the day out in the building, interacting with teachers and students, and participating in individual classrooms. Such a principal encourages teachers to continually develop as professionals and thinks of all adults in the school as active learners. In addition, such principals have the latitude and ability to integrate needed and mandated reforms. Effective principals are proactive in their programmatic decisions and care intensely about instruction.

Effective principals establish a climate which adequately represents the student body. Understanding that a poor self-image develops if the culture of the home is ignored, effective principals—and teachers—make it their business to learn about the various cultures represented in their schools, visit homes, participate in various community organizations, go back to school themselves, and may even work to learn a second language. Principals can also control the physical environment of their building by displaying student work in art and creative writing, encouraging students to display family photographs as well as family histories, and may even encourage the painting of murals on school walls. The importance of the principal in effective schools cannot be overestimated; if we know anything at all, it is that the role of the principal as instructional leader is key to much that happens in a school.

Sixth, there is *frequent monitoring of student progress,* with results communicated in a variety of ways, including but not limited to standard report cards, interim reports, parent-teacher conferences, letters, notes, and phone calls. Moreover, the results of student evaluation are not used simply to assess individual and school performance; rather, they become the starting point for understanding problems and creating solutions that will improve the school's instructional program.

## Key Factors in Successful Innovation

Analysis of schools that are successful with diverse populations and/or actively address issues of diversity in a changing society confirms the effective schools research in many ways. There is, however, no way in which a formula for effective schools can be developed and applied to any particular school. Successful innovation is more likely to occur when school personnel make the effort to adapt what is known about effective schools to their own situations. In addition, often the school is not the sole initiator or actor in such a process. Rather, some partnership or collaboration with others outside the school has proved to be an essential element in a successful change process. In many cases, an important change may not seem very dramatic. For instance, the teaching of Italian in a traditional manner from a traditional textbook is not particularly innovative in and of itself. But simply offering Italian as a foreign language option in a school that has a large Italian population might be enough to help bring about a desired climate just because the needs and identity of a certain set of students and their families are recognized and appreciated. Sweeping, dramatic changes are not often necessary; indeed, they are very often doomed from the start. Nor is additional money necessarily a key element. Often the most effective innovations are small, shared, relatively unobtrusive, and closely monitored for their results and implications. We can look at successful innovation in terms of four key elements: (1) the inclusion of representative groups within the school environment, with accompanying genuine attention to their needs and interests; (2) the expansion and modification of curriculum; (3) the modification of pedagogy and/or instruction; (4) attention to assessment strategies. Each of these contributes to that sense of belonging, identity, and community, development of self-esteem, attainment of the knowledge and goals deemed critical by the school and community, and attention to and readiness for civic participation at the local, national, and international levels.

## Sociocultural Inclusion

Building a sense of community from within the school as well as from without helps to remove barriers of access to knowledge, to the mainstream society and culture, as well as to one's own identity. By accepting and integrating various cultures, languages, and experiences, all may begin to learn to negotiate life in a society characterized by multiple layers of identity and affiliation. This can be realized in many different ways and at numerous levels. In successful schools, there is often an attempt to transform the physical surroundings—to make the school look less "institutional." Photographs of children, of families, of the local community may hang in the hallways. The school thus begins to look like a place where real people live and work together, people who can be identified, recognized, and admired as participants and role models. The family may be woven into the fabric of the child's experience in school. Parents may become tutors, classroom aides, and/or decision makers in the school community. This often helps children to see the ethnic (or other) makeup of adults as more congruent with those of their local community. Remember that until a greater diversity of people enters the teaching force, most teachers will be members of the dominant culture. Children may thus come into contact with few role models similar to themselves. Relevant connections can be made to the real world in other ways—for example, by offering community internship experiences.

Equally important here is a dialogue that can develop between a community and its schools, particularly with regard to negotiating between the purposes of the school and community expectations. Culturally appropriate means to introduce the community to the school are critical. The frequent complaints of Vietnamese parents, for instance, that the school does not value respect for age or authority, and that children waste time in school without significant teacher-directed instruction suggest that distinctly different values exist. A variety of approaches are possible in this situation; however, one can be more 'right' in a given context if care is taken in advance to think about the approach from the point of view of the listener. Prudence, as well as good sense and a sense of justice, might suggest that the learning styles inculcated by the socialization practices of particular populations be accommodated at the outset. Later on, as has been demonstrated by the KEEP program in Hawaii, individuals can be taught other styles which then allow for successful entry into the larger society.

In addition, a sense of community can be developed within the ranks of teachers and administrators as well as within the student population and between teachers and students. In successful schools teachers share ideas, materials, and feedback. They perceive themselves as helpers to their colleagues. Parents are often included in school activities and learn ways of keeping their child's learning alive before and after the school day and especially during the summer months when many gains made during the school year are lost. The establishment of a sense of order is also vitally important. For many children, life at home and in the neighborhood is chaotic and hazardous: relatively high degrees of anxiety, ambiguity, and uncertainty are facts of life for them. In order for children to feel safe, secure, and loved, the school must strive to be an orderly, predictable environment. Children, too, can work to create a sense of community in the school environment. Pairing younger and older children within a school, between schools, or even across district lines can go a long way toward helping individuals reach out and participate in the lives of those around them. Successful ''reading buddy'' programs that bring early readers and older students together over a significant period of time help to develop bonds such that children begin to look out for one another. All of these efforts act to include individuals in the activities of the school, recognize and encourage their contributions, and enable diverse individuals to find their niche. Thus a sense of belonging and personal identity develops, and anxiety and ambiguity are reduced.

## Curriculum Expansion

Curriculum inclusion and expansion is the second key element of successful innovation. One must continually ask if a standard, universal curriculum is best for all students and teachers or if diversification is more effective. The former choice rests on the assumption that teachers and students are more alike than they are different. For many who adopt this view (Mortimer Adler, for example), a universal curriculum compliments all learners by assuming that all *can* learn what is taught. The latter choice is based on the assumption that differences between people are closely tied to learning, and that a rich, expanded, and diverse curriculum encourages plurality and facilitates not only subject matter learning but also the development of respect for and understanding of difference.

We of course tend toward the latter view, endorsing a curriculum presented in such a way that it not only takes diverse student preferences and pacing into account but also seeks to expand their abilities to deal with many kinds of materials. In reading, for instance, children can be encouraged to read silently, in small groups, or in large discussion groups with a teacher. As much as possible, children can be allowed to control the speed of their learning. Is it more important that children ''get it'' on a particular day, or that they ''get it'' at all? Such an approach puts the responsibility for student success on the teacher and the school as much as on the student. With the assumption that all can learn some particular content (shared, incidentally, by those who advocate a relatively limited curriculum), it becomes the teacher's responsibility to provide ample time and to search for innovative and appropriate approaches to enable and empower a student. Students can and should be exposed to a variety of languages as early as possible. A fundamental understanding that there are many legitimate perspectives, and that such a thing as subjective culture exists, is important.

Inclusive curricula focus on all students. Unlike earlier efforts in multicultural education which introduced specialized content aimed only at minority students, educational objectives which emphasize pluralism in an increasingly interdependent society seek lifelong learning for everyone in a world characterized by change; diversity of ideas, values, and behaviors; and rapid technological development. An emphasis on flexibility, creativity, human rights, and shared values becomes the core of such efforts.

## Modification of Pedagogy

Successful teaching reflects both the living hand of cultural tradition, including culture-specific learning styles, and the social, linguistic, and cognitive requirements of the future in a rapidly changing industrial society. Teachers and other school personnel must meet the student wherever he or she is, must adapt learning activities to the student's current needs and abilities, and must work from that point toward assisting all to become better able to function effectively in diverse settings. Teaching from this perspective does *not* mean throwing out knowledge and understanding necessary for success in the dominant society. So long as we live in a society where individuals are punished—economically, socially, and sometimes physically—for their inability to participate in the dominant society, it is the responsibility of the teacher to see that children acquire that knowledge and those skills. However—and this is a big ''however''—it is not at all necessary to do so by negating, ignoring, and not taking advantage of the knowledge and skills children bring with them to school. Indeed, one could easily argue that the dominant culture in the United States has not done well in terms of its relations with the rest of its citizenry and with its international co-citizenry. Clearly, members of the dominant culture have a great deal to learn from those who live ''other'' lives. Viewed from this perspective, teaching and learning among diverse individuals becomes a transactional experience, and all individuals become increasingly bicultural, multicultural, or pluralistic. It is not a process of loss, but a process of gain.

### Attention to Assessment Strategies

Methods of assessment which consider the complex interrelationships of race, class, ethnicity, religion, gender, and disability in students are characteristic of effective schools, although specific methods vary. Assessment is used in determining student achievement of instructional objectives, in decisions on advancement from one grade to another, in diagnosing individual student needs, and also to gain insight into the appropriateness of a given curriculum or instructional intervention. Test reliability studies have repeatedly indicated that considerable bias (cultural, gender, linguistic, experiential, etc.) may exist, such that a given test administered to an individual may produce results which are significantly determined by factors other than actual achievement or ability. Based on such testing, students are often excluded a priori from some of the curricular and instructional choices available in a school. For example, a student with inferior skills in the majority language who performs poorly on a certain test early in their educational career may find his or her subsequent educational experiences restricted.

Students and parents need accurate assessment of their work. Behavior described in terms of individual performance and development, often taking advantage of parent participation in the process, frequently provides a more accurate and sensitive measure of achievement than paper-and-pencil tests. Assessment strategies which consider cultural and other differences provide students and parents with better indicators of student performance. Assessment strategies which measure individual achievement relative to a particular starting point provide a clearer picture of an individual's growth in a given area.

Clearly, there is considerable good news about the transformation of schooling in the United States. It is good news that the nation is paying attention to its schools; it is good news that increasing numbers of educators and others are beginning to develop new ways of examining schools and new understandings of what life in schools is all about; it is good news that researchers are looking at schools that make a difference in the lives of students and teachers, with an eye to describing commonalities for others to adapt to their own environments. Slowly but surely, we are becoming a bit more sophisticated in our understanding and in our approaches to the teaching-learning process. If we as educators can maintain this momentum, if we are allowed the time to think carefully about practice, to observe, to experiment, to share our findings with others, then perhaps schools can become more livable, exciting places to be. But there are factors acting to constrain the process of exploration and experimentation, and those factors should not be underestimated. The traditional culture of the school is not without its ability to resist any changes that threaten its autonomy, its traditions, and its power.

## EFFECTIVE SCHOOL CULTURES: THE BAD NEWS

As we have said, schooling in the United States has two principal functions: to preserve the society and to change it. Historically, these two functions have been viewed as at odds with one another: either schooling acts to preserve or to alter the society, but it doesn't do both at the same time. In a heterogeneous society, it frequently seems that the primary role of schooling is to bind us together. Indeed, one of the fundamental notions at the heart of the common school movement was that a common educational experience would provide a kind of "glue" to hold the society together. This belief is a powerful factor in resistance to attempts to alter schooling; there is a sense in which such alteration can be perceived to threaten our democratic experiment.

Apart from the degree to which transforming schooling is perceived to be a disservice to the nation, there are other difficulties inherent in the nature of the school as a social organization. Seymour Sarason is one of the few people writing today who has attempted to look at the problems inherent in changing organizations, including the school.[31] In his work, Sarason has developed several propositions about organizational change that are worth considering.

First, "real" or fundamental change, as opposed to cosmetic or surface change, requires changing one's way of thinking. This is extraordinarily difficult for people to do, particularly when they are caught up in day-to-day activities embedded in traditional ways of thinking and acting. Some evidence for this proposition can be found in the knowledge that schools seem always to be "changing": curriculum content changes; new activities are introduced; the issues people talk about change. But life in schools goes on pretty much as it did before.

Second, altering thinking about schools requires questioning of what Sarason calls "existing regularities," or structures that have become "givens" in schools. And that requires that some alternative perspectives exist, if only for purposes of contrast. In other words, people must be aware of other possibilities in order to seriously question what exists. Sarason's regularities are so much a part of our way of thinking about schools that it is hard to distance oneself from them long enough to imagine something different. Ask yourself, for example, the question that Sarason asked a number of school personnel: Why is it that math is taught every day? Sarason writes:

> The naive person might ask several questions: Would academic and intellectual development be adversely affected if the exposure was for four days a week instead of five? Or three instead of five? What would happen if the exposure began in the second or third grade? What if the exposure was in alternative years? Obviously, one can generate many more questions, each of which suggests an alternative to the existing programmatic regularity. From this universe of alternatives how does one justify the existing regularity?[32]

The responses—many of them emotional—that Sarason received to this question reveal a good deal about the difficulty inherent in thinking differently about our givens. The first response, he relates, was usually laughter: the listener assumed he was making a joke. In order to keep the discussion going, he often opined that no one, with the exception of those whose work entailed the use of mathematical concepts, used any but the simplest computation skills in adult life, and that the legitimacy of twelve years of mathematics every day was thus at least open to question.

> And now the fur begins to fly. Among the more charitable accusations is the one that I am anti-intellectual. Among the least charitable reactions (for me) is simply an unwillingness to pursue the matter further. (On one occasion some individuals left the meeting in obvious disgust.) One can always count on some individuals asserting that mathematics "trains or disciplines the mind" and the more the better, much like Latin used to be justified as essential to the curriculum.[33]

Clearly, the consideration of alternatives to existing regularities is profoundly difficult. Moreover, the asking of questions about existing structure often connotes on the part of the listener a feeling of threat to the establishment, and on the part of the questioner a feeling of being alone and somehow weird. Neither of these feelings fosters an environment in which asking fundamental questions is encouraged.

A third problem, too often unconsidered by those who wish to see significant change, is that not everybody in the school can be counted on to share that wish. As Sarason notes:

> There are those among the "change agents" whose ways of thinking are uncluttered by the possibility that others see the world differently than they do. In my experience, the number of these individuals is far exceeded by those, in and out of school systems, who know that their plans and intended changes will not be viewed with glee but who seem to assume that either by prayer, magic, sheer display of authority, or benevolence, the letter and the spirit of the changes will not be isolated from each other. Far more often than not, of course, letter and spirit are unrelated in practice if for no other reason than that in the thinking of planners the relation between means and ends was glossed over, if it was considered at all.[34]

None of this implies that attempts to fundamentally alter schooling should not be made. We do suggest that the processes of fundamental change are difficult, fraught with distractions and unconsidered problems, and probably will not occur in the lifetime of one set of transformers. What this means in practical terms is that one has to know that success will not be immediate, nor even perhaps come in the foreseeable future; nevertheless, one must act as if it were just around the corner.

A final difficulty that we wish to consider here (and there are, of course, more that we will not even discuss), is that those who wish to undertake new ways of thinking about and doing things in schools are often ignorant of the history of education and thus are simply unaware of possible alternatives that have already been conceived and attempted. This problem is not, of course, unique to educators. Most professions and skilled crafts today exist in a kind of time warp in which past and future are lost to one another. Because we don't know much about our own history, we are inclined to think that what is has always been; at the same time, we are deprived of examples of potentially useful alternatives. Thus, educators have been criticized for either moving too slowly, or worse, retaining models and strategies deemed effective in the past which are not effective now. The words of June Edwards echo the concerns of many before her:

> Today's secondary schools are designed as though students will face the same kind of life as their grandparents did. In previous generations, children were trained for industrial work. They learned to be punctual, obedient to authority, and tolerant of repetition, boredom, and discomfort, for such was the lot of factory workers. Judgment, decision-making ability, creativity, and independence were neither taught nor desired.
>
> Industries have changed in recent years, but schools have not. Students, herded by bells, are still for the most part expected to be obedient, dependent, and accepting of discomfort and boredom. Though some outstanding instructors encourage creativity and critical thinking, the majority of secondary classrooms are teacher-centered, focused on isolated facts, and constrained by standardized curricula and tests.[35]

Edwards follows this statement with a review of an educational model designed by Helen Parkhurst in 1921 and known as the Dalton Plan, a model she suggests would serve our needs well today.[36] In examining this plan, think about the ways in which it required a way of thinking about schools that is significantly different from our current one.

Under the Dalton Plan, the entire school day was restructured into subject labs, with students determining their own individual schedules. Traditional classrooms were dismantled, and bells were eliminated. The Dalton Plan was student-centered, self-paced, and individualized by means of monthly contracts. Teacher-designed contracts stressed academic learning as well as independent thinking and creativity. Homework was not assigned, but students could complete work at home if desired. Students moved to the next grade when they completed their contracts for a year's work, and as in colleges today, students graduated when they completed the requisite number of courses. Edwards suggests that this model is quite appropriate for contemporary postindustrial society:

> As we move into the postindustrial age—with corporations splintering into minicenters, with work being done on home computers at all hours of the day and night, and with diversity rather than standardization fast becoming the norm—the single-skilled employees who are punctual and can follow orders are no longer in great demand. Instead, the need is for employees who are self-disciplined, creative, capable of carrying out a variety of tasks, and able to work well alone or with others.[37]

The Dalton Plan could benefit students in many ways. Students might learn responsibility and self-discipline; might work slowly and learn thoroughly or quickly and advance rapidly if desired; might feel freer to take risks and fail without penalty; might actively be involved at all times; might work in a nonthreatening, noncompetitive environment; might be able to request individual help as needed; might develop and enjoy long-term relationships with peers and teachers; might be able to miss school for days if needed without falling behind; and might have the freedom to vary their school hours. Teachers might benefit by spending all their time on educational matters; having the opportunity to be friend and counselor, as well as teacher to students; working in a room free from disruptions; working with students who are interested, motivated, and self-reliant; and being able to specialize as well as working cooperatively with colleagues as needed. School districts, too, might benefit by reducing complex scheduling; being able to accommodate midyear and other transient students more readily; enabling limited-English-proficient students to join English immersion groups as needed; more easily integrating students and first-year teachers to the professional ranks; and having the flexibility to reassess the organization of the school day to include early morning, evening, and holiday hours.

Notice that we have said that students, teachers, and school organizations *might* benefit from this kind of plan. The point is not that this is a model for imitation; the point is that it is an actual plan that was carried out at one time that seems to have some potential for today's school life. What is required at this point is questioning, discussion, and thought. Would such a plan really resolve some of the issues we face? How? What would be its constraints? What constraints are there to its adoption? Are there any portions of the plan that seem more applicable than others? Why? And so on.

Despite the obvious difficulties in instituting change in schools, numerous projects have been carried out around the United States, and in other countries, to increase school effectiveness. Successful practices from the effective schools research are being applied in many inner city school districts and are being explored by many state departments of education.

In some instances, significant achievement gains have been recorded. In Milwaukee, Wisconsin, a school improvement effort known as Project RISE (Rising to Individual Scholastic Excellence) has demonstrated a continual improvement in test scores in reading and mathematics.[38] Similar results have been recorded in numerous schools which have applied various findings from the effective schools research.

However, there have also been many projects which have not resulted in improvement. Kritek suggests that a distinct culture is at work in those schools that have been able to move toward effectiveness.[39] In more successful schools, for instance, staff appear to have accepted responsibility for school improvement and are active in the pursuit of excellence.[40]

While we have been suggesting all along that significant change must occur with the individual teacher in the classroom, we are not blind to the fact that a teacher's responsibilities, especially the new teacher's, are such that it is extremely difficult to attend to behavioral and curriculum modification while accomplishing the day-to-day tasks of teaching. Such change takes time. It also requires an awareness of the processes by which change occurs.

## THE PROCESS OF CHANGE: FROM SELF TO OTHER

Recall the story of the Wheat Religion and the Grainers in Chapter 1, and the resistance people have to change that which is familiar to them. Change at the individual level is critical. Combs stressed the importance to the change process of individual beliefs and behavior patterns:

> [Changing] must concern itself with the inner life. Simple exposure to subject matter (or new information or ways of doing things) is not enough. The maturation of an effective professional worker requires changes . . . in perceptions—his feelings, attitudes, and beliefs and his understanding of himself and his world. This is no easy matter, for what lies inside the individual is not open to direct manipulation and control. It is unlikely to change except with the active involvement of the . . . [person] in the process.[41]

Change cannot occur on a large scale until those involved are able to alter their perceptions and see themselves as active participants in the process. Change is also facilitated when the process is a welcome and sought after one. We have looked closely at the adjustment process and have recognized that there will be predictable stages that individuals pass through as they internalize any new situation. People must also perceive themselves from a new perspective in order to fully internalize and actualize their new situation. Only then can one become a role model for change. Again, we stress that significant change cannot come about simply as a result of new information. Active participation is required.

Teachers, like everyone else, experience a myriad of emotional reactions and obstacles when they confront change. Six stages that teachers move through as they face any innovation have been identified in the literature.[42]

• *Level 0—Awareness:* Although the teacher may be aware of the problem, there is little concern or involvement on the teacher's part in the innovation.

• *Level 1—Informational:* The individual has a general awareness of the possible change and is beginning to show some interest in learning more.

• *Level 2—Personal:* The individual is beginning to question his or her own adequacy as well as what will be demanded of him or her in order to make the intended change.

• *Level 3—Management:* The individual is focusing on the ''nuts and bolts'' of seeing the change through and is beginning to identify the various tasks required to make the change happen.

• *Level 4—Consequence:* The teacher is focusing on the potential impact the innovation will have on students in his or her immediate sphere of influence.

• *Level 5—Collaboration:* The teacher is beginning to think beyond him or herself by cooperating with others in carrying out the innovation.

• *Level 6—Refocusing:* The individual is focusing on universal benefits of the innovation and what alternatives or modifications may be in order.

Restructuring schools so that they become more inclusive and so that individuals become empowered toward equity and excellence on all fronts *does* require teachers to become mavericks. This idea may go against the image people have of teachers. Teaching tends to be a rather conservative activity, with most teachers acting so that the status quo is maintained. In fact, some innovative teachers may rightly perceive themselves to be punished by the system in which they work when they do take a stand and encourage change. Yet change must occur if schools and society are to become more equitable and inclusive.

Cherrie Banks identifies five responsibilities of the potential leader who wants to implement change toward diversity in an educational context.[43] She calls them challenging the process, inspiring a shared vision, enabling others to act, modeling the way, and encouraging the heart.

*Challenging the process* is an active effort initiated by the individual who wants change. The individual at this time must be a risk-taker and must be willing to confront the status quo. She or he must be willing to experiment, to make mistakes, and keep aware of new ideas.

*Inspiring a shared vision* refers to the recognition of the need, and the potential, for change. A major responsibility here is to voice issues and enlist the assistance of others. Strong interpersonal and communication skills are required to reach out and affect others. Teachers, for instance, must strive to communicate that all can learn, improve, and meet with success.

*Enabling others to act* is necessary because it is very difficult to encourage and make change by oneself. Collaboration must be fostered, thus enlisting others in the project at hand. In doing so, one must make every effort to strengthen others so that they perceive that they also benefit by the effort. A collective orientation, or ''we'' identification, should be a goal.

*Modeling the way* requires you, the teacher, to set an example. Plan small so that you can demonstrate successes rather than failures, and reward yourself for your gains. Your actions alone will do much to demonstrate your commitment and your concern, as well as showing others what is possible.

When you *encourage the heart,* you recognize the contributions of others and celebrate their accomplishments. Successes should be measured in inches rather than miles. Teaching for diversity is an ongoing process which requires constant attention.

## IN CONCLUSION

Throughout this book we have been striving to better prepare today's teachers to achieve their goals of delivering an effective education to diverse students who are living in a complex, interdependent world. The approach we have chosen begins by recognizing the kinds of experiences many, but not all, individuals who become teachers bring with them. We believe that it is teachers, in concert with their peers and community, who can make effective education possible. Most education students are from the majority culture and have limited experience with people of diversity. For that reason we attend to such issues as people's emotional responses and other kinds of experiences people have when they encounter difference or diversity. Understanding the socialization process in terms of cultural development and the obstacles to culture learning helps us gain insight into the reasons for typical responses and facilitates the processes necessary to transcend one's conditioning. Understanding how many of the various processes such as communication and learning style impact upon interaction and learning is also critical to effective teaching. We then looked at how society and education have responded to cultural diversity, exceptionality, and gender as discrete elements. The fact that each of the diversities addressed in this book mediates the others and that they do not act in isolation, thus further complicating our task but nonetheless critical to our understanding of classroom interaction, was addressed before looking at specific strategies which can be employed by schools and teachers.

Our nation has been addressing issues related to diversity only relatively recently. In a few short decades, theory in related fields has tended to move from an assimilationist perspective to one of recognizing the value of pluralism in a diverse, democratic society. Schools, as well as individuals who have been successful at addressing such issues, *have been working on these issues for a long time*. Innovations in individual perspective and behavior as well as in curriculum and instructional modification cannot show immediate results. Such efforts require a long-range commitment on the part of many actors— teachers, administrators, students, parents, community, and developers of curriculum materials—before any of the hoped for changes can be realized. Removing the various barriers and modifying conditioned behavior takes time. Accordingly, we must be willing to act and work over the long haul, and must not be discouraged in the short run. Successes, when they do come, are incremental. Therefore, efforts must begin in the early stages of education, for both children and adults, and must continue throughout. Such efforts are not ones that can be effectively addressed in one short course, in one class, or in a short period of time. Continuous efforts must be made at many different levels in the educational process. We hope for you that this is just one step on a personal and professional path of continual growth, development, and interaction.

## REFERENCES

**1** The National Commission on Excellence in Education, *A National at Risk: The Imperative for Educational Reform,* (Washington, DC: U.S. Department of Education, 1983).

**2** Mortimer J. Adler and the Paideia Group, *The Paideia Proposal: An Educational Manifesto,* (New York: Macmillan, 1982).

**3** John Goodlad, *A Place Called School: Prospects for the Future* (New York: McGraw-Hill, 1983).

**4** Ernest L. Boyer, *High School: A Report on Secondary Education in America* (New York: Harper & Row, 1983).

**5** Board of Inquiry, National Coalition of Advocates for Students, *Barriers to Excellence* (Boston: National Coalition of Advocates for Students, 1985).

**6** Webb and Sherman, *Schooling and Society,* 2d ed., (New York: Macmillan, 1989), pp. 559–560.

**7** "The National Reports on Education: A Comparative Analysis," in B. Gross and R. Gross (eds.), *The Great School Debate: Which Way for American Education?* (New York: Touchstone Books, 1985), pp. 50–71.

**8** See *Phi Delta Kappan,* December, vol. 72, no. 4, 1990 issue, with articles by L. Cuban, S. L. Kagan, N. L. Gage, L. Darling-Hammond, I. C. Rothberg, L. Mikulecky, and R. A. Hawley, all addressing national goals.

**9** Webb and Sherman, op. cit., pp. 564–583.

**10** Ibid., p. 564.

**11** Ibid., p. 566.

**12** Ibid., pp. 568–569.

**13** Adler op. cit., p. 39.

**14** Webb and Sherman, op. cit., p. 576.

**15** Ibid., p. 577.

**16** Ibid.

**17** Ibid., p. 581.

**18** D. Tanner and L. Tanner, *History of the School Curriculum* (New York: Macmillan, 1990), p. 35.

**19** Diane Ravitch, "The Educational Pendulum," *Psychology Today,* vol. 16, no. 10, October 1983, pp. 63–71.

**20** A. R. Contreras, "Use of Educational Reform to Create Effective Schools, *Education and Urban Society,* vol. 20, no. 4, Aug. 1988, pp. 399–413.

**21** Ibid., p. 402.

**22** S. L. Kagan, "Readiness 2000: Rethinking Rhetoric and Responsibility," *Phi Delta Kappan,* vol. 72, no. 4, Dec 1990, pp. 272–279.

**23** Ibid., p. 276.

**24** Contreras, op. cit.

**25** G. Gay, "Designing Relevant Curricula for Diverse Learners," *Education and Urban Society,* vol. 20, no. 4, Aug. 1988, pp. 327–340.

**26** Ibid.

**27** A. C. Ornstein and D. U. Levine, *Foundations of Education,* 4th ed. (Boston: Houghton Mifflin, 1989).

**28** L. Stedman, "The Effective Schools Formula Still Needs Changing," *Phi Delta Kappan,* vol. 69, no. 6, February 1988, pp. 439–442.

**29** R. Edmonds, "Programs of School Improvement: An Overview," *Educational Leadership,* vol. 40, no. 3, December 1982, pp. 4–11.

**30** See Ornstein and Levine, op. cit.; also, *What Works: Research about Teaching and Learning* (Washington, DC: U.S. Department of Education, 1986).

**31** Seymour B. Sarason, *The Culture of the School and the Problem of Change* (Boston: Allyn & Bacon, 1971).

**32** Ibid., p. 69.

**33** Ibid., p. 70.

**34** Ibid., pp. 8–9.

**35** J. Edwards, ''To Teach Responsibility, Bring Back the Dalton Plan,'' *Phi Delta Kappan,* vol. 72, no. 5, January 1991, p. 399.

**36** Ibid.

**37** Ibid., p. 400.

**38** W. J. Kritek, ''School Culture and School Improvement,'' paper presented at the 67th annual meeting of the American Educational Research Association, San Francisco, CA, April 1986.

**39** Ibid.

**40** D. U. Levine, ''Creating Effective Schools: Findings and Implications from Research and Practice,'' *Phi Delta Kappan,* vol. 72, no. 5, Jan. 1990, pp. 389–393.

**41** A. W. Combs, *The Professional Education of Teachers* (Boston: Allyn & Bacon, 1965), p. 14.

**42** G. E. Hall, A. C. Wallace, and W. A. Dossett, *A Developmental Conceptualization of the Adoption Process within Educational Institutions* (Austin: Texas Research and Development Center for Teacher Education, University of Texas, 1973).

**43** Cherrie Banks, remarks made in presentation at National Council for the Social Studies Annual Convention, Anaheim, CA, November 1989.

# INDEX

# AUTHOR INDEX

# SUBJECT INDEX

Adjustment:
    cross-cultural, 18, 28–30, 44, 90
    as a function of prejudice, 56
    of immigrants, 30, 49
    U-curve hypothesis, 28–30, 44, 274
        Figure 2.1, 29
Adolescent culture, 21
Africa, 39, 84
Ambiguity, 30, 48–51, 62, 160, 227,
    325, 327
    in culture-general framework, 41
    tolerance for, 90
Americans with Disabilities Act (1992),
    141
Analytic learners, 110–111
Anglo conformity, 133–134
Anthropology, 25–26
Anxiety, 25, 29, 30, 44, 46–49, 58, 62,
    80, 86, 87, 120, 160, 268, 269,
    298, 325, 327
    in culture-general framework, 41
    in test-taking, 48
Appearance, 80–81
Architectural Barriers Act (1968), 137
Arizona, 5
Asia, 81, 84

Assimilation:
    ideology of, 133–134, 147, 153, 157,
        165, 216–217
    related to gender, 208
    role of schools in, 100, 152
Attitudes toward Disabled Persons scale,
    266
Attribution:
    in culture-general framework, 43
    fundamental error in, 32–33, 61
    isomorphic, 34, 62
    process of, 18, 23, 31–34, 50, 60–62,
        80–81, 84
Australia, 273

*Barriers to Excellence,* 317
Behavior:
    changes in, 10, 333–334
    difficulty of change in, 5
    gender expectation of, 196–197
    social patterns of, 19, 23, 25
Belize, 276
Belonging, 44, 58–60, 134, 160, 262,
    268, 298–299, 311–312, 325–327
    in culture-general framework, 41

349